The Good, the Bad
and the Ancient

ALSO EDITED BY SUE MATHESON
AND FROM McFARLAND

*A Fistful of Icons: Essays on Frontier Fixtures
of the American Western* (2017)

The Good, the Bad and the Ancient

Essays on the Greco-Roman Influence in Westerns

Edited by SUE MATHESON

McFarland & Company, Inc., Publishers
Jefferson, North Carolina

This book has undergone peer review.

Library of Congress Cataloguing-in-Publication Data

Names: Matheson, Sue, editor.
Title: The good, the bad and the ancient : essays on the Greco-Roman influence in westerns / edited by Sue Matheson.
Description: Jefferson, North Carolina : McFarland & Company, Inc., Publishers, 2022 | Includes bibliographical references and index.
Identifiers: LCCN 2022036930 | ISBN 9781476667645 (paperback : acid free paper) ∞
ISBN 9781476646107 (ebook)
Subjects: LCSH: Western films—United States—History and criticism. | Civilization, Greco-Roman—Influence.
Classification: LCC PN1995.9.W4 G625 2022 | DDC 791.43/65878—dc23/eng/20220912
LC record available at https://lccn.loc.gov/2022036930

British Library cataloguing data are available
**ISBN (print) 978-1-4766-6764-5
ISBN (ebook) 978-1-4766-4610-7**

© 2022 Sue Matheson. All rights reserved

No part of this book may be reproduced or transmitted in any form or by any means, electronic or mechanical, including photocopying or recording, or by any information storage and retrieval system, without permission in writing from the publisher.

Front cover: The three stars of the 1948 film
3 Godfathers (left to right) Pedro Armendáriz,
John Wayne and Harry Carey, Jr. (MGM/Photofest)

Printed in the United States of America

*McFarland & Company, Inc., Publishers
Box 611, Jefferson, North Carolina 28640
www.mcfarlandpub.com*

In honor of Judith P. Flynn, *optimis magistris*

Acknowledgments

I would like to thank Ray Merlock, Kathy Merlock Jackson, Kim Laycock, Harvey Briggs, and Dan Smith for their encouragement and outstanding support of this project. I must especially thank Layla Milholen, my editor, for her patience and her guidance while I was working on this manuscript during the pandemic. I am particularly grateful to all the contributors whose enthusiasm, dedication, and hard work brought this collection to life. Most important, I would like to thank Stuart and Rebecca Matheson who herded the sheep and patiently bottle-fed our foster puppies while this collection was being completed.

Table of Contents

Acknowledgments	vi
Introduction: America and Antiquity: Force and Thumos in the Western SUE MATHESON	1

Prologos — 15

West of "Them": Classical Allusions in Western Film
 KIRSTEN DAY — 17

Aristotle and the Wild West: The Western as a Rhetorical Device
 CHRIS YOGERST — 37

Tragic Trails in Indian Country — 51

Chorei, Satyr-Drama, and the Birth of Tragedy in John Ford's *Cheyenne Autumn* (1964)
 SUE MATHESON — 53

Peckinpah and the Problem of Catharsis; or: How Well Does *The Wild Bunch* Fit Aristotle's *Poetics*?
 MARTIN M. WINKLER — 66

Euripidean Sunsets: Tragedy, the Western, and Conflicts Within
 MARIA CECÍLIA DE MIRANDA N. COELHO — 83

Cowboys and Catharsis — 97

Pharmakos and the Bad Citizen *Topos* in Charles Marquis Warren's Westerns: *Trooper Hook, Tension at Table Rock* and *Charro!*
 FERNANDO GABRIEL PAGNONI BERNS — 99

"Scratched blood": The Erinyes and Anthony Mann's *The Furies*
 KELLY MACPHAIL — 111

The Splendor of Bart Allison: Antigone and the Tragic Western Hero
 CHRISTOPHER MINZ — 127

Homer on Horseback — 137

Homer's *Odyssey* and Cattle Drive Westerns
  ANDREW HOWE — 139

Lonesome Dove: Uva uvam vivendo varia fit and Tragic Elements in a Western Epic
  BENJAMIN HUFBAUER — 151

Blondie's Odyssey: The Homeric Journey and American Mythmaking in *The Good, the Bad, and the Ugly*
  CHRISTOPHER J. OLSON — 161

Writing and Rewriting History: Myth in the *Iliad* and *Heaven's Gate*
  BRIAN BREMS — 171

Catastrophe — 187

Gunsmoke's Boot Hill and the Classical Underworld
  JIM DAEMS — 189

Orpheus on the Frontier: *Slow West*
  CYNTHIA J. MILLER — 198

Influence of Classical Literature in Western Film: A Selective Bibliography
  CAMILLE MCCUTCHEON — 211

About the Contributors — 213

Index — 215

Introduction

*America and Antiquity:
Force and* Thumos *in the Western*

SUE MATHESON

America began grounded firmly in The Greats. Like the Roman general Cincinnatus, George Washington left his plow in a field and led his countrymen to victory. Then, like Cincinnatus, he resigned and returned home—an embodiment of civic virtue and republican ideals. In 1820, a writer for the *Cincinnati Western Review* observed, "[S]hould the time ever come when Latin and Greek…be banished from our universities and the study of Cicero and Demosthenes, of Homer and Virgil [be considered unnecessary], we should regard mankind…fast sinking into an absolute barbarism."[1] As Bradley J. Birzer remarks in "The Importance of Marcus Tullius Cicero," "[t]he world of the founding [of America] was a deeply classical world, a Protestant world immersed in antiquity," and its Founders "knew Cicero as intimately as they knew anyone."[2] Forrest and Ellen McDonald remark that American college students (usually 14 or 15 years old) were steeped in the Classics: to prove his fluency in Latin and Greek, a student would need to "read and translate from the original Latin into English 'the first three of [Cicero's] Select Orations and the first three books of Virgil's Aeneid, before translating the first ten chapters of the Gospel of John from Greek into Latin."[3] They also mention "Americans who had had any schooling at all had been exposed to eight- and ten-hour days of drilling, at the hands of stern taskmasters, in Latin and Greek. This was designed to build character, discipline the mind, and instill moral principles, in addition to teaching language skills. (Educated French military officers who served in the United States during the Revolution found that even 'when they knew no English and Americans knew no French, they could converse with ordinary Americans in Latin.')"[4]

According to Birzer, America's Founding was "a return—purified, reformed, Christianized, and mythologized—to antiquity,"[5] and its Founders, who staunchly embraced the works of Roman Greats like Cicero, Virgil, Livy and Tacitus, wished to create a virtuous Republic. There is, however, little evidence of such a republic existing on the new nation's western frontier. In his *Letters from an American Farmer* (1782), J. Hector St. John de Crèvecoeur observes of the West that "[t]here men appear to be no better than carnivorous animals of a superior rank. There, remote from the power of example and check of shame, many families exhibit the most hideous parts of our society … prosperity will polish some, vice and the law will drive off the rest, who uniting again with others like themselves will recede still farther"[6] A year before the conclusion of the American Revolution, Crèvecoeur deemed the frontier "barbarous country."[7] As the settlement of Indian Territory advanced to the Pacific Ocean, the area that came to be known to the Marshal's Service as "the Western District" was brutal indeed. Throughout the 19th century, there was neither Latin west of St. Louis, nor Cicero's (or the two Cato's) values west of Fort Smith. Despite attempts to maintain law and order on the frontier, disorder ruled until Isaac C. Parker began his judgeship in Fort Smith in 1875—and during the twenty-one years that followed, of the "some 13,400 cases docketed, 12,000 were criminal in nature—ranging from theft to murder. Three hundred and forty-four men stood before Parker accused of major crimes; 160 were convicted and 79 hanged. Some 65 of Parker's 200 deputy marshals were gunned down."[8] Just north of Oklahoma, frontier justice was also wild and wooly. It isn't hard to imagine Aristotle throwing up his hands after the unreasonable dismissal of Frank Loving's murder charges when the coroner proclaimed that Loving shot Levi Richardson in self-defense on April 5, 1879, in Dodge City's Long Branch Saloon.[9] By 1890, however, Frederick Jackson Turner's "New England preacher and school-teacher" in "The Significance of the Frontier in American History" (1893) had left their marks on the West. Classical curriculums beginning at the early high school level regulated the frontier intellect despite the frontier's practical demands. As Turner observes, what "the Mediterranean Sea was to the Greeks," the "ever-retreating frontier" was to Americans—being "the outer edge of the wave" of conquest and settlement, "a meeting point between civilization and savagery."[10]

With this in mind, America's Founding Fathers certainly would have disapproved of the on-going debates in the 1890s to provide frontier children with a liberal, scientific, utilitarian training instead of the classical education offered in the East.[11] Today, they would find the lack of schooling about the Greats throughout America simply shocking. They believed Americans had to understand the virtues and values of the Roman Republic in order to embrace and implement them. However, here it is important to note that although Americans are no longer required to learn Greek and Latin, America's core values have not changed. Citing Gary Wills, David Walker Howe remarks of the "many things that might interest one—law and politics, philosophy, oratory, history, lyric poetry, epic poetry, drama—there will be constant reference back to the founders of those forms in our civilization."[12] As Howe points out, this reference conveys republican values with special relevance to Americans. Such references are also found in America's popular culture, their values, those of the Western. John Ford, Raoul Walsh, Howard Hawks, Anthony Mann, and Sam Peckinpah (to name only a few outstanding directors) all have borrowed from antiquity's epics, tragedies, and comedies while defining the American Character and inventing the American Experience in the West. Celebrating, affirming, and critiquing nation-building on the frontier, Graeco-Roman values in their films (and other Westerns) have shaped our perceptions of westward expansion, the West's heroic nature, family life on the frontier, and American ideals of masculinity. Westerns like *The Searchers* (1956), *They Died with Their Boots On* (1941), *Red River* (1948), *Winchester '73* (1950), and *The Wild Bunch* (1969) owe much of their success to The Greats.

Tellingly, the Western also understands that the ancient Greeks speak to us "more profoundly than the Romans, having originated many of the intellectual institutions we increasingly value as characteristically American."[13] For example, the frontiersman's westering pursuit of happiness on screen has remained closely related to Aristotle's *eudaimonia,* which translates most directly to the English word *happiness,* carrying with it connotations of success, fulfillment, and flourishing growth.[14] As Emily Parrish in "Life, Liberty, and the Pursuit of Happiness: Aristotle in America," remarks, Aristotle would have thought that Americans historically "have sought happiness from the right sources: not from life itself, but from living, from flourishing, from finding the next thing."[15] Simone Weil, on the other hand, would argue that the true subject or center of the Western is force.[16] For those like Weil, who see force as the center of human history, the Western is driven by the same power that propelled Agamemnon and Achilles to Troy. Force in the Western compels the sodbuster, the cavalryman, the cowboy, the gambler, the Indian agent, the banker, the rancher, the businessman, and the newspaperman to seek their fortunes on the frontier. Their fighting souls (Weil would say) are conditioned by and tied to force in the West. They are at times constrained by it *and* blinded by it. In what Weil calls "its grossest and most summary form,"[17] force kills. Weil reminds us that the *Iliad* never tires of presenting this tableau:

> ...the horses
> made the swift chariots thunder along the paths of war
> in mourning for their blameless drivers. On the earth
> they lie, much dearer to the vultures than to their wives [11.159–62].

Poems of force, Westerns also are littered with dead bodies and populated with riderless and driverless horses. As Weil notes, "[n]early all of the *Iliad* takes place far from warm baths."[18] Situated in the wilderness, the Western's Last Stands and Alamos occur along the paths of war, without the pleasures offered by civilization. Far from "warm baths," George Custer (Errol Flynn) in Raoul Walsh's *They Died with Their Boots On* (1941), Fen (Coleen Gray) in Howard Hawks' *Red River* (1948), Ben Vandergroat in Anthony Mann's *The Naked Spur* (1953), the members of the Wild Bunch in Sam Peckinpah's *The Wild Bunch* (1969), John McCabe (Warren Beatty) in Robert Altman's *McCabe and Mrs. Miller* (1972), Lee Clayton (Marlon Brando) in Arthur Penn's *Missouri Breaks* (1976), Nathan D. Champion (Christopher Walken) in Michael Cimino's *Heaven's Gate* (1980), Stonesipher (David Steen) in Quentin Tarantino's *Django Unchained* (2012), and Toby Howard (Chris Pine) in David Mackenzie's *Hell or High Water* (2016) are just a handful of those swept away, subjected to force, reduced to starting over. Exercised to its limit, force in the Western turns man into what Weil says in the *Iliad* is a thing in the most literal sense, making "a corpse out of him."[19]

According to Turner, the harshness of frontier life that produced rugged Americans remarkable for their self-reliance, individualism, inventiveness, restless energy, mobility, materialism, and optimism also created "intellectual traits of profound importance."[20] The American's exceptional character is generally considered the subject of the Western. Ancient Greeks would identify the drive underpinning this exceptionalism as *thumos*. Arguably, *thumos* is the heart of the Western. Key to the psychology of the hero in Homer's works, *thumos* is defined as essential to *andreia*, "manliness," or the essence of being a man. Offered in heroic action, in heroic thought, and even in heroic discourse as an instrument of force, *thumos* lies in "our will to fight, our need to rebel against that which is intolerable ... is what makes us stand up and declare 'I will not be silenced!.' It is what makes us dive headlong against the devastation of this world; what compels us to courageously fight the good fight. And if we are to fail, *thumos* is the thing within the human spirit that requires us to go down swinging, cursing our oppressors all the while."[21] As Andrew and Judith Kleinfeld point out in *WSJ Opinion*, cowboys, America's Homeric heroes, are marked by *thumos*. Their son, Joshua, a Yale philosophy major, goes so far as to say, "America is [*thumos*]."[22] Because of their *thumos*, Crockett and Bowie became icons at the Alamo and Custer, a hero at Little Big Horn; ironically, the James brothers achieved celebrity status by robbing banks, trains, and stagecoaches; Wyatt Earp and Doc Holliday became famous lawmen. Driven by *thumos*, Wild Bill Hickok, Buffalo Bill, Annie Oakley, and Calamity Jane became superstars in Wild West shows, and then legends of the silver screen.

In Plato's *Republic*, Socrates divides the soul into three parts: the rational, the spirited (*thumos*), and the appetites. In Plato's *Phaedrus*, Socrates offers the allegory of the chariot to explain the workings of the tripartite soul. Socrates affirms the charioteer represents Reason; the dark horse, man's appetites; and the white horse, *thumos*.[23] As Brett and Kate McKay remark, "[t]he masterful charioteer does not ignore his own motivations, nor the desires of [*thumos*] and appetite, but neither does he let his two horses run wild. He lets Reason rule, takes stock of all his desires, identifies his best and truest ones—those that lead to virtue and truth—and guides his horses towards them. He does not ignore or indulge them—he *harnesses* them. Each horse has its strengths and weaknesses, and the white horse can lead a man into the wrong path just as the dark horse can, but when properly trained, thumos becomes the ally of the charioteer. Together, reason and [*thumos*] work to pull the appetites into sync."[24] Westerns offer their viewers a similar, if more prosaic, conceit. Chuckwagons, stagecoaches, and buckboards, familiar means of transportation, are not as romantic as antiquity's two-wheeled chariot, used for fighting and racing, but the same skills are required by their drivers. To be successful, the driver and his team must work in concert. *Thumos* can be a creative force. Plato says that balancing *thumos* with reason creates "'harmony' in the soul, because *thumos* is tamed by the reason and reason is aroused and sustained by *thumos*." These principles of human nature, "one the spirited and the other the philosophical," Plato explains, must "(like the strings of an instrument) be relaxed or drawn tighter until they are duly harmonized… [he who] best tempers them to the soul, may be rightly called the true musician and harmonist in a far higher sense than the tuner of the strings…[a]nd such a presiding genius will be always required in our State if the government is to last."[25]

In John Ford's *Rio Grande*, a fine display of Roman riding reminds its viewer of the importance of such self control (and Socrates' allegory). Trooper Travis Tyree (Ben Johnson), Trooper Jefferson "Jeff" Yorke (Claude Jarman, Jr.), and Trooper Daniel "Sandy" Boone (Harry Carey, Jr.) are trained to be ideal citizens. Standing atop a pair of galloping horses with one foot on each horse, each man demonstrates himself capable of harmonizing and binding Reason, *thumos*, and appetite into one unit. Later, rescuing the Fort's children, Tyree, Yorke, and Boone all display Plato's spirited sense of *thumos* and the desire to combat injustice, while embodying the qualities of Plato's ideal citizen by retaining "under all circumstances a rhythmical and harmonious nature, such as will be most serviceable to the individual and to the State…[to] preserve [the State] against foreign enemies and maintain peace among [its] citizens at home."[26] In George Stevens' *Shane* (1953), the American cowboy embodies *thumos*. Shane's *thumos* also becomes an instrument of force. Hired by a homesteader, Joe Starrett (Van Heflin), when Shane (Alan Ladd) learns that Rufus Ryker (Emile Meyer), a cattle baron, is intimidating settlers, who have claimed their land legally under the Homestead Acts, and compelling them to leave the Valley, *thumos* impels him to start a range war. Marian Starrett (Jean Arthur) and her young son are fascinated by Shane's drive to right social injustice. Young Joey (Brandon De Wilde), in particular, admires Shane, even following him on foot to witness him kill Ryker and his gang of murderers. The action of John Ford's *Wagon Master*

(1950) too is informed by its heroes' willingness to do the right thing. When a Mormon wagon train travelling through the Utah Territory is run out of Crystal City, horse traders Travis Blue (Ben Johnson) and Sandy Owens (Harry Carey, Jr.) take the settlers under their protection, creating and maintaining safe passage to the San Juan Valley. In the Western, troopers, marshals, cowboys, settlers, and good badmen are all remarkable for their ability to balance reason with *thumos*. Moderating passion with reason leads to virtue, wisdom, and truth in John Ford's *3 Godfathers* (1948). In *3 Godfathers*, *thumos* drives three outlaws on the run to risk their lives in the desert to return a newborn baby to civilization. Their efforts save the baby's life, and Robert Marmaduke Sangster Hightower (John Wayne), the surviving good badman, finds a better way to live and is welcomed back into society.

In part, the Western's *thumos* is responsible for the genre's remarkable appeal. In 1939, as individuals braced themselves for the war in Europe, *thumos* reunited the Western with Hollywood's A-list audiences. Synchronizing *thumos*, reason, and force, the heroes of these Western blockbusters courageously fought "the good fight," restoring social harmony. In John Ford's *Stagecoach* (1939), the Ringo Kid (John Wayne) breaks out of jail to right the wrong of his father's and brother's murders. In George Marshall's *Destry Rides Again* (1939), Tom Destry (James Stewart) stops Bottleneck's saloon owner, Kent (Brian Donlevy), from stripping homesteaders of their land. *Thumos* also drives Frenchy (Marlene Dietrich), a jaded saloon girl, to sacrifice herself to ensure law and order prevail. Michael Curtiz's *Dodge City* (1939) features Wade Hatton (Errol Flynn), a Texas cattle agent, and Abbie Irving, a spirited journalist (Olivia de Havilland), who fight for justice and social order. United by *thumos*, they then travel on to tame another lawless Western town. Henry King's *Jesse James* (1939) follows the fortunes of Jesse James (Tyrone Power) and Frank James (Henry Fonda) who become bandits to avenge their family's eviction from their farm by railroad agents.

In later Westerns, the demands of the *thumos* are complicated. Swept up in events beyond their control, Marshal Will Kane (Gary Cooper) in Fred Zinnemann's *High Noon* (1952) and John McCabe (Warren Beatty) in Robert Altman's *McCabe and Mrs. Miller* (1971) discover *thumos* alienates them from others. Kane survives his showdown with Frank Miller (Ian McDonald) and Jack Colby (Lee Van Cleef), because his wife, a pacifist Quaker, submits to force to protect her husband and shoots Jim Peirce (Robert J. Wilke). Friendless, McCabe is out-numbered and outgunned by Butler (Hugh Millais), the Kid (Manfred Schulz), and the Breed (Jace Van Der Veen). Subject to force in the end, he becomes a "thing"—a frozen corpse in a snowbank outside his hotel.

Thumos also refers to the rage, grief, horror, or sorrow of any individual who is faced with atrocities. In John Ford's *Cheyenne Autumn* (1964), *thumos* inspires the starving Northern Cheyenne to defy the United States government, jump their reservation, and return to their homelands. Walter Hill's *Geronimo: An American Legend* (1993) depends on Geronimo's (Wes Studi) *thumos* which ignites and sustains the Apaches' armed resistance to the U.S. government. In *Devil's Doorway* (1950), a highly decorated Shosone veteran, Lance Poole (Robert Taylor) cannot ignore his *thumos*. He attempts to save his family's ranch in spite of anti–Indian legislation and bigotry. The dark, conflicted heroes of revenge Westerns also act according to the demands of *thumos*. Ethan Edwards in John Ford's *The Searchers* (1956) is driven to avenge the murder of his brother's family and find his kidnapped niece. In Henry Hathaway's *The Sons of Katie Elder* (1965), John (John Wayne), Tom (Dean Martin), Bud (Michael Anderson, Jr.), and Matt

(Earl Holliman) Elder make right the murder of their father and the swindling of their mother. In Clint Eastwood's *Unforgiven* (1992), a prostitute with a scarred face and her co-workers hire William Munny (Clint Eastwood), "the meanest goddam son-of-a-bitch alive," to find the men responsible for her disfigurement and deliver frontier justice. When Munny's partner, Ned Logan, is murdered after the cowboys are shot, *thumos* also drives Munny to right that wrong by killing "Skinny" Dubois (Anthony James) and "Little Bill" Daggett (Gene Hackman).

The abuse of force is an important subject in the Western, for the tragedy of human misery (subject to changing fortunes and necessity) complicates and deepens the genre's *thumos*. Consider the numerous Westerns—classical, epic, psychological, professional, spaghetti, psychedelic, steampunk, feminist, and revisionist—that chart the agony produced by the Southern diaspora that swept settlers to the West in the 1870s and 1880s. In *The Searchers* (1956), the Civil War's *thumos* informs the actions of Ethan Edwards, a veteran who refuses to give up his sword; in *Fort Apache* (1948), Owen Thursday's (Henry Fonda) *thumos* fast tracks his post–Civil War career to a tragic Last Stand; in Samuel Fuller's *Run of the Arrow* (1957), O'Meara (Rod Steiger), a Confederate veteran, goes West, joins the Sioux, takes a wife, and refuses to be an American, but his *thumos* demands that he choose a side when the Sioux go to war against the U.S. Army; Rooster Cogburn (John Wayne/Jeff Bridges) and LaBoeuf's (Glen Campbell/Matt Damon) antagonistic relationship reflects the animosity of their Confederate and Union *thumoi* in Henry Hathaway's *True Grit* (1969) and Ethan and Joel Coen's 2010 remake.

Reflecting (and refracting) the workings of force, the Western is, as Weil would say, one of the most "flawless of mirrors."[27] In part, the foregrounding of force explains why the genre's popularity peaked throughout the 20th century when America was on the brink of or engaged in war. Restored to the Hollywood A-list in 1939, Westerns also garnered impressive box office returns after the Second World War—as the country entered the Cold War. In 1940, *Boom Town* earned a whopping $9.1 million at the domestic box office; in 1946, *Duel in the Sun* grossed $20.4 million domestic box office; and in 1951, *Across the Wide Missouri* earned $5.5 million domestically. Because the Western was a dependable moneymaker, John Ford directed *Fort Apache* (1948) to rescue Argosy Productions in its infancy from bankruptcy and later used the proceeds of *Rio Grande* (1950) to finance the production of *The Quiet Man* (1952). A box office hit, Fred Zinnemann's *High Noon* cumulatively grossed $8 million worldwide. Released in 1953, *Hondo* grossed $8.2 million domestically, *Shane*, $20 million. In 1954, *Apache* earned $6 million domestically and *Vera Cruz*, $9 million. Released in 1955, *River of No Return* grossed $3.8 million domestically. In 1956, *Love Me Tender* earned $9 million domestically and *Giant*, $30 million. Released in 1958, *The Bravados* grossed $4.4 million domestically and *The Big Country*, $10 million. In 1959, *Rio Bravo* earned $5.8 million domestically; in 1960, *The Alamo* grossed $7.9 million domestically; in 1963, *McLintock!* grossed $14.5 million and *How the West Was Won*, $46.5 million.[28]

During America's involvement in the Vietnam War, the number of Western hits, fuelled by *thumos*, actually increased at the box office in the United States. Released in 1965, *The Sons of Katie Elder* grossed $13.3 million and *Shenandoah*, $17.2 million. In 1966, *The Professionals* earned $19.5 million; released in 1967, *Per un pugno di dollari* grossed $3.5 million, *Per qualche dollaro in più*, $4.3 million, *El Dorado*, $6 million, *The War Wagon*, $6 million, and *Il buono, il brutto, il cattivo*, $6.1 million. In 1968, *Shalako* earned $2.6 million, *Hang 'Em High*, $6.8 million, and *Bandolero*, $12 million. In 1969,

Once Upon a Time in the West grossed $5.3 million, *The Undefeated*, $8 million, *True Grit*, $31.1 million, and *Butch Cassidy and the Sundance Kid*, $102.3 million. Released in 1970, *Chisum* earned $6 million; released in 1971, *Big Jake* grossed $7.5 million, *McCabe and Mrs. Miller*, $8.2 million, *Little Big Man*, $31.5 million, and *Billy Jack*, $98 million. In 1972, *Joe Kidd* grossed $6.3 million and *The Life and Times of Judge Roy Bean*, $16.5 million; in 1973, *Pat Garrett and Billy the Kid* earned $8 million and *High Plains Drifter*, $15.7 million; in 1974, *The Life and Times of Grizzly Adams* grossed $45.4 million. Released in 1975, *Rooster Cogburn* earned $8 million and *Bite the Bullet*, $11 million.[29]

Interest in the Western waned in the United States after the fall of Saigon on the 30th of April 1975. In 1976, *Across the Great Divide* did earn $18.8 million domestically and *The Outlaw Josey Wales*, $20 million[30]—but as Plato points out in *The Republic*, *thumos* is rejected when it proves itself to be ineffective. The appeal of the Western's *thumos* declined sharply as America's film viewers turned from oaters (and their tales of conquest) to crime dramas. A Western blockbuster occurred in 1980 when *Urban Cowboy* grossed $46.9 million, and then, throughout that decade, there were only four Western hits: in 1984, *The Legend of the Lone Ranger* grossed $13.4 million domestically; in 1985, *Pale Rider* earned $41.4 million and *Silverado*, $33.2 million; in 1988, *Young Guns* grossed $44.7 million.[31]

Remarkably, after America entered the First Gulf War in 1990, domestic box office grosses indicate that the Western (and its *thumos*) began to rally despite the popular belief that the genre had exhausted itself. Although fewer Westerns have been made throughout the 1990s and the early part of the 21st century than throughout the 1950s and 1960s, the genre has re-established itself at the domestic box office and on the Hollywood A-list. In 1990, *Quigley Down Under* earned $21.4 million, *Young Guns II*, $44.1 million, and *Dances with Wolves*, $184.2 million. After the First Gulf War, *Unforgiven* grossed $101.1 million in 1992. In 1993, *Wagons East* earned $4.3 million; *Geronimo: An American Legend*, $18.2 million; and *Tombstone*, $56.5 million. In 1994, *Bad Girls* earned $15.1 million; *Lightning Jack*, $16.8 million; *Wyatt Earp*, $25 million; *City Slickers II: The Legend of Curly's Gold*, $43.4 million; *Legends of the Fall*, $66.5 million; and *Maverick*, $101.6 million. In 1995, *Wild Bill* grossed $2.1 million and *The Quick and the Dead*, $18.5 million. In 2000, *All the Pretty Horses* earned $15.5 million and *Shanghai Noon*, $56.9 million. In 2001, *American Outlaws* grossed $13.2 million.[32]

During the War on Terror, high-grossing Westerns also displayed the genre's resurgence. In 2003, *The Missing* earned $26.9 million domestically, *Open Range*, $58.3 million, and *Shanghai Knights*, $60.4 million. In 2004, *The Alamo* grossed $22.4 million domestically, *Hidalgo*, $67.2 million. At the domestic box office in 2007, *The Assassination of Jesse James by the Coward Robert Ford* earned $3.9 million and *3:10 to Yuma*, $53.6 million. In 2008, *Appaloosa* grossed $20.2 million domestically. Then, in 2010, *True Grit* earned a whopping $171.2 million at the domestic box office; in 2012, *Django Unchained* grossed $162.8 million domestically; in 2013, *The Lone Ranger*, $89.3 million. In 2014, *A Million Ways to Die in the West* grossed $42.7 million domestically; in 2015, *The Hateful Eight*, $54.1 million; in 2016, *Hell or High Water*, $27 million, and *The Magnificent Seven*, $93.4 million. In 2017, *The Beguiled* earned $10.5 million domestically, *Hostiles*, $29.8 million, and *The Dark Tower*, $50.7 million.[33]

An abbreviated overview of television Westerns also discloses the genre's hardiness. As poems of force, Westerns thrived on the small screen from 1949 to the late 1960s. During this period, over 100 Western series aired on the television networks.

8 Introduction

NBC edited a backlog of Hopalong Cassidy feature films to broadcast length for children, making *Hopalong Cassidy* the first network television series to air on June 24, 1949. *The Lone Ranger* (ABC, 1949–57) quickly followed. Six years later, *The Life and Legend of Wyatt Earp* (ABC, 1955–61) was the first Western television series written for adults, quickly joined by serial oaters like *Gunsmoke* (CBS, 1955–75), *Cheyenne* (ABC, 1955–62), *The Rifleman* (ABC, 1958–63). The Western dominated prime time TV serials. Aptly, *Gunsmoke* which aired for an astounding 20 seasons from 1955 to 1975, offering 635 episodes, ended the same year as the Vietnam War. At the end of its run, *Los Angeles Times* columnist Cecil Smith remarked: "*Gunsmoke* was the dramatization of the American epic legend of the west. Our own *Iliad* and *Odyssey*, created from standard elements of the dime novel and the pulp Western as romanticized by [Ned] Buntline, [Bret] Harte, and [Mark] Twain. It was ever the stuff of legend."[34]

Gainsaying the demise of the Western (and its *thumos*) throughout the latter half of the 1970s, Western series and miniseries continued to appear on television. The ever-popular *Little House on the Prairie* (NBC, 1974–1983) was joined by *Barbary Coast* (ABC, 1974–76), *The Oregon Trail* (NBC 1976–77), *How the West Was Won* (ABC, 1976–79), *Young Maverick* (CBS, 1979), and *The Chisholms* (CBS, 1979–80) in the 1970s. Throughout the 1980s, *Best of the West* (ABC, 1981–82), *Bret Maverick* (NBC, 1981–82), *Father Murphy* (NBC, 1981–83), *Gun Shy* (CBS 1983), *Wild Side* (ABC, 1985), *Red Serge* (CBC, 1986–87), *Outlaws* (CBS, 1986–87), *Bordertown* (CTV, 1989–91), *Paradise* (BBC One, 1988–90), and *The Young Riders* (ABC, 1989–92) also aired briefly. Then CBS released *Lonesome Dove* on February 5, 1989. The mini-series proved to be so successful that it created spinoffs: *Return to Lonesome Dove* (CBS, mini-series, 1993) *Larry McMurtry's Streets of Laredo* (CBS, mini-series, 1995), *Dead Man's Walk* (ABC, mini-series, 1996), and *Comanche Moon* (CBS, mini-series, 2008). Throughout the 1990s, Western television series generally continued to have short lives, evidenced by *Zorro* (The Family Channel, 1990–93), *The Adventures of Brisco County, Jr.* (1993–94), *Dr. Quinn, Medicine Woman* (1993–98), *Hawkeye* (1994–95), *Lonesome Dove: The Outlaw Years* (Syndication, 1995–96), *Dead Man's Gun* (Showtime, 1997–99), *The Magnificent Seven* (CBS, 1998–2000), and *Nothing Too Good for a Cowboy* (CBC 1998–2000). Western television series at the start of the 21st century also seemed to be following this trend with *Ponderosa* (PAX TV, 2001–02) and *Peacemakers* (USA Network, 2003); however, the series *Deadwood* (HBO, 2004–06) and *Heartland* (CBC, 2007–present) provided evidence of the genre's continuing popularity. The successes of neo-Western series, *Walker, Texas Ranger* (CBS 1993–2001), *Breaking Bad* (AMC, 2008–13), and *Sons of Anarchy* (2008–2014), resting on the Western's *thumos*, paved the way for hit series like *Justified* (FX, series, 2010–15), *Hell on Wheels* (AMC, series, 2011–16), *Longmire* (A&E, series, 2012–14; Netflix, series, 2015–17), *Westworld* (HBO, series, 2016–present), *Godless* (Netflix, mini-series, 2017), and *The Mandalorian* (Disney, series, 2019–present).

To date, some excellent pioneering studies regarding Graeco-Roman reception in the Western have been published. Among these, one finds Martin M. Winkler's "John Ford, America's Virgil," and "Tragic Features in John Ford's *The Searchers*," Kostas Myrsiades' "Reading *The Gunfighter* as Homeric Epic," and Kirsten Day's *Cowboy Classics* (Edinburgh University Press, 2018).[35] No collection of Western scholarship, however, has been devoted to the genre's association with antiquity despite many of its films' intimate relations with The Greats. Consisting of fourteen essays and a selected bibliography, this volume offers a variety of approaches by Western scholars and classicists from

North and South America on selected topics about the Western's connexions with the Graeco-Roman world.

Tipping its Stetson to Euripides, *The Good, the Bad and the Ancient* begins by offering its reader an explanatory *prologos*, in which two essays outline the territory to be travelled. Examining classical allusions in the Western, Kirsten Day's "West of 'Them': Classical Allusions in Western Film" begins this volume's *prologos*. Day's examination is not only concerned with the ways in which the genre promotes the view of classical antiquity as America's cultural progenitor; it also examines how the Western bolsters the problematic notion of Western civilization as a white European cultural inheritance while working to complicate this perception. Chris Yogerst's "Aristotle and the Wild West: The Western as a Rhetorical Device" follows. Yogerst shows how Westerns adopt elements of Aristotelean reasoning to fashion a rhetoric of their own, making theirs a genre that Aristotle would recognize as a "public art for resolving practical issues."[36]

Drawing on the works of Homer, Aristotle, Aeschylus, Sophocles, Euripides, and Homer, the essays which follow investigate the impact that Graeco-Roman myths, legends, pre-tragedies, comedies, tragedies, and epics have had on the Western. These essays are presented in three sections. Observing Aristotle's dictum that tragedy is the highest form, "Tragic Trails in Indian Country," which houses considerations of tragic action in individual Westerns, and "Cowboys and Catharsis," containing conversations about the importance of the Western's tragic characterizations, follow the *prologos*. For those whose tastes run to the epic, "Homer on Horseback" then offers essays concerned with how the epic informs our understanding of individual Westerns.

Presenting the impact of classical tragedy on individual Westerns, "Tragic Trails in Indian Country" begins with Sue Matheson's investigation of John Ford's presentation of the Northern Cheyenne Exodus as a pre-tragedy and their return H-O-M-E as the birth of tragedy in the West. In "*Chorei*, Satyr-Drama, and the Birth of Tragedy in John Ford's *Cheyenne Autumn* (1964)," Matheson traces the film's action, governed by its competing choruses and the insertion of an irreverent satyr-drama (dubbed "The Dodge City War") which concludes with the creation and immediate exile of its tragic hero. Martin M. Winkler's "Peckinpah and the Problem of Catharsis; or: How Well Does *The Wild Bunch* Fit Aristotle's *Poetics*?" follows. Linking Sam Peckinpah's treatment of ecstasy to the action of Euripides' *The Bacchae*, Winkler demonstrates how the tragic and epic elements of *The Wild Bunch* underpin and direct the emotional power of the film's infamous violence. Maria Cecília de Miranda N. Coelho's examination of the influence of Euripides that marks four psychological Westerns completes this section. In "Euripidean Sunsets: Tragedy, the Western, and Conflicts Within," Coelho considers parallels between the Western and Euripides' tragedies to understand (and appreciate) how personal dilemmas in *The Gunfighter* (1950), *Track of the Cat* (1954), *The Lonely Man* (1957), and *Decision at Sundown* (1957) link our modern world with the Graeco-Roman.

Then, "Cowboys and Catharsis" offers essays that consider the impacts that scapegoating, antiquity's chthonic forces, and the action of *até* (Homer's and Aeschylus' spirit of Ruin) have on heroes in psychological Westerns. In "*Pharmakos* and the Bad Citizen *Topos* in Charles Marquis Warren's Westerns: *Trooper Hook*, *Tension at Table Rock* and *Charro!*" Fernando Gabriel Pagnoni Berns argues the connected leitmotif of scapegoats (and scapegoating) in the films of Charles Marquis Warren, made during Hollywood's black listing and ideological persecution, evokes the ancient, yearly ritual of *pharmakos*. According to Berns, *pharmakos* underpins and enables Warren's critique of hypocrisy, silence, and the attitude of "look the other way" that these films strongly transmit. Then, next in "'Scratched blood': The Erinyes and Anthony Mann's *The Furies*," Kelly MacPhail finds Anthony Mann uses the leitmotif of the Furies to reconsider the nature of frontier justice. According to MacPhail, Mann's classical references that accompany the broken oaths, familial betrayal, and personal vengeance in *The Furies* insist that a future is possible only after the Erinyes' revenge has been served. Following, Christopher Minz uses Lacan's interpretation of the Antigone tragedy to examine the relationship of Boetticher's film with Sophocles' *Antigone*. He concludes that like Antigone, Bart Allison makes a choice with radical implications involving *até* which is not to be envied or emulated.

Next, "Homer on Horseback" contains conversations about the Western's enduring relationship with Homer's works and America's frontier epic. Andrew Howe's "Homer's *Odyssey* and Cattle Drive Westerns" finds trail driving films are frontier epics which particularly resonate with classical themes in the *Odyssey*. Drawing on the genre's penchant for bricolage, Howe identifies a dangerous journey (with many digressions), tests of skill between those on the journey, omens and fate, and a search for home as specific points of contact between *Red River* (1948), *Lonesome Dove* (1989), and the *Odyssey*. As Aristotle points out, tragedy and the epic are not exclusive forms.[37] Benjamin Hufbauer's "*Lonesome Dove: Uva uvam vivendo varia fit* and Tragic Elements in a Western Epic" next offers a reading of an epic narrative via its tragic elements. Charting Larry McMurtry's characterization of *Lonesome Dove's* cowboys, who proclaim their associations with the ancient world by literally carving them into wood and rock, Hufbauer concludes that McMurtry's understanding of *catharsis*—with its emotional release—is the key to his epic's success, both as a novel and a miniseries. Christopher J. Olson's "Blondie's Odyssey: The Homeric Journey and American Mythmaking in *The Good, the Bad, and the Ugly*" follows. In this essay, Olson examines how Leone's masterpiece borrows from the general "journey" structure from Homer to deconstruct the Western's frontier myth and destabilize the values, ideologies, and national identity of traditional Westerns. Olson's reading of *The Good, the Bad, and the Ugly* concludes that "[s]torytelling media may have changed since Homer's time, but the impulse of mythmaking practiced in the ancient epics continues to thrive—posing contemporary challenges to our dominant narratives and idealized views of a nation's past, present, and future."[38] Then, in "Writing and Rewriting History: Myth in the *Iliad* and *Heaven's Gate*," Brian Brems argues that *Heaven's Gate* is a Western epic that attempts to re-mythologize the American West by sharing themes of catastrophe and failure with the *Iliad*. According to Brems, Cimino uses the story of Troy to depict a wild (but purposeful) exaggeration of the struggle of poverty-stricken immigrants, cattle farmers, and small business owners that is a chaotic, triumphant, brutal, and glorious struggle like that found in the *Iliad* even as their individual efforts are rendered pointless.

With apologies to Aeschylus, *The Good, the Bad and the Ancient*'s "Catastrophe"[39] brings its conversation to an end, offering papers which broach the matter of resolution in two very different Westerns. Jim Daems' "*Gunsmoke*'s Boot Hill and the Classical Underworld" investigates Matt Dillon's (James Arness) Boot Hill monologues. Daems concludes that Dillon's journeys to Boot Hill not only provide insights similar to those of Odysseus and Aeneas after they visit the Underworld; they also provide a "temporal, interpretive" lens as well as a moralizing introduction to the individual episodes of *Gunsmoke* in which they occur, critiquing and justifying social and political resolutions required by westward expansion. Cynthia J. Miller's "Orpheus on the Frontier: *Slow West*" draws from another important classical tradition, exploring the confluence of myths of antiquity and the Orphic figure with the myth of the frontier in *Slow West* (2015), John McClean's flawed New Zealand Western. Miller proposes McClean's classical disruption of the typical frontier narrative hinges on the disappointment of Jay Cavendish (Kodi Smit-McPhee), an Orphic hero who travels West to recover the woman he loved and lost. According to Miller, Cavendish's necessary failure supports this revisionist Western's rejection of the romantic hero and support of the good badman as it attempts to fuse irreconcilable opposites and bridge the gap between what is possible and what is forbidden.

The Good, the Bad and the Ancient does not claim to be a comprehensive work about the reception of Graeco-Roman thought in the Western genre and how deeply rooted American culture and the American Character was (and, arguably, still is) in antiquity. Critical work that remains to be done in this area could easily fill volume after collected volume. Essays dealing with tragic portrayals of other characters in Anthony Mann's and Budd Boetticher's psychological canons, for example, could not be housed here. There is not space for the Western's adaptations of stories gleaned from Ovid's *Metamorphoses*. Epic tales of action and settlement in Westerns re-enacting stories from Virgil's *Aeneid* also call for critical attention and offer new frontiers for researchers. Considerations of Cavalry films and professional Westerns, replete with references to the *Iliad* and *The Odyssey*, too require the attention of Western scholars and classicists. Encouraging interest in these (and other) areas, Camille McCutcheon's "Influence of Classical Literature in Western Film: A Selective Bibliography" concludes *The Good, the Bad and the Ancient*, listing books, book chapters, and journal articles already written about the influence of classical literature in Western film. These materials range from texts devoted to classical subjects to those which examine classical allusions in Western films. It is hoped that these excellent resources will encourage further viewing of Westerns, inspire more reading about Western films, and produce more scholarship about the relationship that the Western has with the Classics and the Graeco-Roman world.

Because Westerns, in film and on television, have been and continue to be important markers of the American Experience, it is my hope that readers, interested in the intellectual cornerstones of American culture, will appreciate how popular receptions of the works of Plato, Aristotle, Herodotus, Thucydides, Homer, Virgil, and the Athenian and Roman playwrights have formed our characters and influenced our lives. I look forward to the conversations that *The Good, the Bad and the Ancient* will generate and anticipate that opportunities for further study of this subject will continue as long as Westerns continue to be made. That being said, the open range of this volume's *prologos* beckons its readers to go West… (re)discover America's relationship with antiquity … and grow old with the country.[40]

Notes

1. Cited in Bradley J. Birzer's "The Importance of Marcus Tullius Cicero," in *The Imaginative Conservative*, February 25, 2013, https://theimaginativeconservative.org/2013/02/the-importance-of-marcus-tullius-cicero.html.

2. Bradley J. Birzer, "The Importance of Marcus Tullius Cicero," in *The Imaginative Conservative*, February 25, 2013, https://theimaginativeconservative.org/2013/02/the-importance-of-marcus-tullius-cicero.html.

12   Introduction

3. Forrest MacDonald and Ellen MacDonald, *Requiem: Variations on Eighteenth Century Themes* (University Press of Kansas, 1988), 1–2.

4. *Ibid.*, 5.

5. Birzer, "The Importance of Marcus Tullius Cicero," https://theimaginativeconservative.org/2013/02/the-importance-of-marcus-tullius-cicero.html.

6. J. Hector St. John de Crèvecoeur, *Letters from an American Farmer*, in *Project Gutenberg*, http://www.gutenberg.org/cache/epub/4666/pg4666.html.

7. *Ibid.*

8. See "Fort Smith: National Historic Site Arkansas," in *Founders and Frontiersmen, Survey of Historic Sites and Buildings*, updated August 29, 2005, https://www.nps.gov/parkhistory/online_books/founders/sitea3.htmFounders.

9. In The Long Branch Saloon on April 5, 1879, Frank Loving accused Levi Richardson of disrespecting his wife. The two men got into an argument that turned into a gunfight across a table. Loving was grazed on the hand by one bullet; Richardson was shot three times and died. Town Marshal Bassett arrested Loving, but on April 7, the coroner's inquest ruled that Loving had acted in self-defense; he was released without charges.

10. Frederick Jackson Turner, "The Significance of the Frontier in American History," *The Project Gutenberg eBook, The Frontier in American History, by Frederick Jackson Turner*, https://www.gutenberg.org/files/22994/22994-h/22994-h.htm.

11. For more information, see Allen Oscar Hansen's discussion of the influential Western Literary Society and College of Teachers proposal for and development of a utilitarian education for frontier students in *Early Educational Leadership in the Ohio Valley*.

12. David Walker Howe, "Classical References in America," *The Wilson Quarterly* (Spring 2011), https://www.wilsonquarterly.com/quarterly/spring-2011-the-city-bounces-back-four-portraits/classical-education-in-america/.

13. *Ibid.*

14. Emily Parrish, "Life Liberty and the Pursuit of Happiness: Aristotle in America," *Bear Market: Economics, Politics, and Ethics for the Ursuline Girl*, https://bearmarketreview.wordpress.com/2015/05/01/life-liberty-and-the-pursuit-of-happiness-aristotle-in-america/.

15. *Ibid.*

16. Simone Weil begins "*The Iliad* or the Poem of Force" by stating that "[t]he true hero, the true subject matter, the center of the *Iliad* is force. The force that men wield, the force that subdues men, in the face of which human flesh shrinks back. The human soul seems ever conditioned by its ties with force, swept away, blinded by the force it believes it can control, bowed under the constraint of the force it submits to. Those who have supposed that force, thanks to progress, now belongs to the past, have seen a record of that in Homer's poem; those wise enough to discern the force at the center of all human history, today as in the past, find in the *Iliad* the most beautiful and flawless of mirrors" (322).

17. Weil, "The *Iliad* or, The Poem of Force," *politics* (November 1945): 322. Available online at http://marx.libcom.org/files/politics%20(November%201945).pdf.

18. *Ibid.*, 322.

19. Weil, "The *Iliad* or, The Poem of Force," 321.

20. Turner, "The Significance of the Frontier in American History."

21. A Tradition of Thumos," *Classical Wisdom*, June 23, 3014, https://classicalwisdom.com/culture/traditions/tradition-thumos/.

22. Andrew Kleinfeld and Judith Kleinfeld, "Go Ahead, Call Us Cowboys," *WSJ Opinion*, July 19, 2004, https://www.wsj.com/articles/SB122704519961438615.

23. In the *Phaedrus*, Socrates observes, "The right-hand horse [*thumos*] is upright and cleanly made; he has a lofty neck and an aquiline nose, his color is white, and his eyes dark; he is a lover of honour and modesty and temperance, and the follower of true glory; he needs no touch of the whip, but is guided by word and admonition only. The other [representing the appetites] is a crooked lumbering animal, put together anyhow; he has a short thick neck; he is flat-faced and of a dark colour, with grey eyes and blood-red complexion; the mater of insolence and pride, shag-eared and dear, hardly yielding to whip and spur."

24. Brett and Kate McKay, "What Is A Man? The Allegory of the Chariot." *In A Man's Life Featured, On Manhood, On Virtue, Personal Development, Philosophy*, March 4, 2013, last updated September 25, 2020, https://www.artofmanliness.com/articles/what-is-a-man-the-allegory-of-the-chariot/.

25. Plato, *The Republic* at *Project Gutenberg*, https://www.gutenberg.org/files/1497/1497-h/1497-h.htm.

26. Plato, *The Republic*, https://www.gutenberg.org/files/1497/1497-h/1497-h.htm.

27. Weil, "The *Iliad* or, The Poem of Force," 321.

28. These domestic box office grosses, not adjusted for inflation, are found at "All Time Worldwide Box Office for Western Movies," *The Numbers; Where Data and the Movie Business Meet*, https://www.the-numbers.com/box-office-records/worldwide/all-movies/genres/western. Their cumulative worldwide box office grosses are as follows: released in 1953, *Hondo* grossed $8.2 million cumulatively worldwide, and *Shane*, $20 million; released in 1954, *Apache*, $6 million and *Vera Cruz*, $9.2 million; released in 1955, *River*

of No Return, $3.8 million; released in 1956, *Love Me Tender*, $9 million and *Giant*, $30 million; released in 1958, *The Bravados*, $4.4 million and *The Big Country*, $10 million; released in 1959, *Rio Bravo*, $5.8 million; released in 1960, *The Alamo*, $7.9 million; released in 1963, *McLintock!*, $14.5 million and *How The West Was Won*, $46.5 million.

29. These domestic box office grosses, not adjusted for inflation, are found at "All Time Worldwide Box Office for Western Movies," *The Numbers; Where Data and the Movie Business Meet*, https://www.the-numbers.com/box-office-records/worldwide/all-movies/genres/western. Their cumulative worldwide box office grosses are as follows: released in 1965, *The Sons of Katie Elder* grossed $13.3 million cumulatively worldwide and *Shenandoah*, $17.2 million; released in 1966, *The Professionals*, $19.5 million; released in 1967, *Per un pugno di dollari*, $3.5 million, *Per qualche dollaro in più*, $4.3 million, *El Dorado*, $6 million, *The War Wagon*, $6 million, and *Il buono, il brutto, il cattivo*, $6.1 million; released in 1968, *Shalako*, $2.6 million, *Hang 'Em High*, $6.8 million, and *Bandolero*, $12 million; released in 1969, *Once Upon a Time in the West*, $5.3 million, *The Undefeated*, $8 million, *True Grit*, $31.1 million, and *Butch Cassidy and the Sundance Kid*, $102.3 million; released in 1970, *Chisum*, $6 million; released in 1971, *Big Jake*, $7.5 million, *McCabe and Mrs. Miller*, $8.2 million, *Little Big Man*, $31.5 million, and *Billy Jack*, $98 million; released in 1972, *Joe Kidd*, $6.3 million and *The Life and Times of Judge Roy Bean*, $16.5 million; in 1973, *Pat Garrett and Billy the Kid*, $11 million and *High Plains Drifter*, $15.7 million; in 1974, *The Life and Times of Grizzly Adams*, $45.4 million: released in 1975, *Rooster Cogburn*, $8 million and *Bite the Bullet*, $11 million.

30. These domestic box office grosses, not adjusted for inflation, are found at "All Time Worldwide Box Office for Western Movies," *The Numbers; Where Data and the Movie Business Meet*, https://www.the-numbers.com/box-office-records/worldwide/all-movies/genres/western. Their cumulative worldwide box office grosses are as follows: released in 1976, *Across the Great Divide* earned $18.8 million and *The Outlaw Josey Wales*, $20 million.

31. These domestic box office grosses, not adjusted for inflation, are found at "All Time Worldwide Box Office for Western Movies," *The Numbers; Where Data and the Movie Business Meet*, https://www.the-numbers.com/box-office-records/worldwide/all-movies/genres/western. Their cumulative worldwide box office grosses are as follows: released in 1980, *Urban Cowboy*, grossed $46.9 million; released in 1984, *The Legend of the Lone Ranger* grossed $13.4 million; released in 1985, *Pale Rider*, $41.4 million and *Silverado*, $33.2 million; released in 1988, *Young Guns* $44.7 million.

32. These domestic box office grosses, not adjusted for inflation, are found at "All Time Worldwide Box Office for Western Movies," *The Numbers; Where Data and the Movie Business Meet*, https://www.the-numbers.com/box-office-records/worldwide/all-movies/genres/western. Their cumulative worldwide box office grosses are as follows: in 1990, *Quigley Down Under* earned $21.4 million cumulatively worldwide, *Young Guns II*, $44.1 million, and *Dances with Wolves*, $424.2 million; in 1992, *Unforgiven*, $159.1 million; in 1993, *Wagons East* earned $4.3 million, *Geronimo: An American Legend*, $18.2 million, and *Tombstone*, $56.5 million; in 1994, *Bad Girls* earned $15.1 million, *Lightning Jack*, $16.8 million, *Wyatt Earp*, $25 million, *City Slickers II: The Legend of Curly's Gold*, $43.4 million, *Legends of the Fall*, $160.5 million, and *Maverick*, $183 million; in 1995, *Wild Bill* earned $2.3 million and *The Quick and the Dead*, $18.5 million; in 2000, *All the Pretty Horses*, $18.1 million and *Shanghai Noon*, $71.1 million; in 2001, *American Outlaws* earned $13.6 million.

33. These domestic box office grosses, not adjusted for inflation, are found at "All Time Worldwide Box Office for Western Movies," *The Numbers; Where Data and the Movie Business Meet*, https://www.the-numbers.com/box-office-records/worldwide/all-movies/genres/western. Their cumulative worldwide box office grosses are as follows: in 2003, *The Missing* earned $38.2 million cumulatively worldwide, *Open Range*, $68.6 million, and *Shanghai Knights*, $88.3 million; in 2004, *The Alamo*, $23.9 million; in 2004, *Hidalgo*, $108 million; in 2006, *Bandidas*, $ 19.2 million; in 2007, *The Assassination of Jesse James by the Coward Robert Ford*, $15.3 million and *3:10 to Yuma*, $71.1 million; in 2008, *Appaloosa*, $27.9 million; in 2010, *True Grit*, $252.2 million; in 2012, *Django Unchained*, $449.8 million; in 2013, *The Lone Ranger*, $260 million; in 2014, *A Million Ways to Die in the West*, $86.7 million; in 2015, *The Hateful Eight*, $152.6 million; in 2016, *Hell or High Water*, $37.5 million and *The Magnificent Seven*, $162.1 million; in 2017, *The Beguiled*, $28 million, *Hostiles*, $36.9 million, and *The Dark Tower*, $113.4 million.

34. Cecil Smith, "A Legend Goes Down the Tubes," *Los Angeles Times*, "View Part IV," September 1, 1975: 1, 13.

35. See "John Ford, America's Virgil" in Martin M. Winkler's *Classical Literature On Screen: Affinities of the Imagination*, 214–46 (Cambridge: Cambridge University Press, 2017); "Tragic Features in John Ford's *The Searchers*," in Martin M. Winkler, ed. *Classical Myth and Culture in the Cinema*, 118–47 (New York: Oxford University Press, 2001); Kostas Myrsiades' "Reading *The Gunfighter* as Homeric Epic," *College Literature*, Vol. 34, No. 2 (Spring 2007): 279–300; Paul Seydor's "*The Wild Bunch* as Epic," in Michael Bliss, ed. *Doing It Right: The Best Criticism on Sam Peckinpah's* The Wild Bunch, 113–57 (Southern Illinois UP, 1994); Kristen Day's *Cowboy Classics* (Edinburgh: Edinburgh University Press, 2016).

36. Chris Yogerst, "Aristotle and the Wild West: The Western as Rhetorical Device," in Sue Matheson, ed. *The Good, the Bad and the Ancient* (Jefferson, NC: McFarland, 2022), 37.

37. In *Poetics* XXIV, Aristotle finds that the epic like tragedy "must be simple, or complex, or 'ethical,'

or 'pathetic.' The parts also, with the exception of song and spectacle, are the same; for it requires Reversals of the Situation, Recognitions, and Scenes of Suffering." According to Aristotle, the epic differs from tragedy only "in the scale on which it is constructed, and in its meter." He also remarks that unlike tragedy, in the epic "many events simultaneously transacted can be presented; and these...add mass and dignity," creating "grandeur of effect to diverting the mind of the hearer, and relieving the story with varying episodes." For more information, see S.H. Butcher, trans. *Poetics*, in *Internet Classics Archive*, http://classics.mit.edu/Aristotle/poetics.3.3.html.

38. Christopher J. Olson, "Blondie's Odyssey: The Homeric Journey and American Mythmaking in *The Good, the Bad, and the Ugly*," in Sue Matheson, ed. *The Good, the Bad and the Ancient* (Jefferson, NC: McFarland, 2022), 167.

39. In the Greek tragedies of antiquity, the *catastrophe* is the final resolution, unraveling intrigue and bringing closure.

40. "GO WEST, YOUNG MAN, GO WEST" was an expression first used by John Babsone Lane Soule in the *Terre Haute Express* in 1851. Newspaperman Horace Greeley misrepresented Soule's expression in an editorial in the *New York Tribune* on 13 July 1865: "Go West, young man, and grow up with the country." When the phrase gained popularity, Greeley printed Soule's article to show the source of his inspiration. The phrase captured the imaginations of young men who moved West to homestead after the Civil War. In *The Man Who Shot Liberty Valance*, editor Dutton Peabody (Edmond O'Brien) engages in more Western rhetoric misrepresenting Greeley's misrepresentation of Soule: "As for you, Horace Greeley, go West, old man and grow young with the country."

Works Cited

Aristotle. "XXIV." In *Poetics*, trans. S.H. Butcher. *Internet Classics Archive*. At http://classics.mit.edu/Aristotle/poetics.3.3.html.

Birzer, Bradley J. "The Importance of Marcus Tullius Cicero." In *The Imaginative Conservative*, February 25, 2013. At https://theimaginativeconservative.org/2013/02/the-importance-of-marcus-tullius-cicero.html.

de Crèvecoeur, J. Hector St. John. *Letters from an American Farmer*. In *Project Gutenberg*. At http://www.gutenberg.org/cache/epub/4666/pg4666.html.

Day, Kirsten. *Cowboy Classics: The Roots of the American Western in the Epic Tradition*. Edinburgh: Edinburgh University Press, 2016.

"Fort Smith: National Historic Site Arkansas." In *Founders and Frontiersmen, Survey of Historic Sites and Buildings*. Updated August 29, 2005, https://www.nps.gov/parkhistory/online_books/founders/sitea3.htmFounders.

Hansen, Allen Oscar. *Early Educational Leadership in the Ohio Valley*. Bloomington, IL: Public School Publishing Company, 1923.

Howe, David Walker. "Classical References in America." *The Wilson Quarterly* (Spring 2011). At https://www.wilsonquarterly.com/quarterly/spring-2011-the-city-bounces-back-four-portraits/classical-education-in-america/.

Kleinfeld, Andrew, and Judith Kleinfeld, "Go Ahead, Call Us Cowboys," *WSJ Opinion*, July 19, 2004, https://www.wsj.com/articles/SB122704519961438615.

MacDonald, Forrest, and Ellen MacDonald. *Requiem: Variations on Eighteenth Century Themes*. Lawrence: University Press of Kansas, 1988.

Parrish, Emily. "Life, Liberty, and the Pursuit of Happiness: Aristotle in America." *Bear Market: Economics, Politics, and Ethics for the Ursuline Girl*. At https://bearmarketreview.wordpress.com/2015/05/01/life-liberty-and-the-pursuit-of-happiness-aristotle-in-america/.

Plato. "Phaedrus," trans. Benjamin Jowett. *Internet Classics Archive*. At http://classics.mit.edu/Plato/phaedrus.html.

Winkler, Martin M. "John Ford, America's Virgil." In *Classical Literature on Screen: Affinities of the Imagination*, 214–46. Cambridge: Cambridge University Press, 2017.

_____. "Tragic Features in John Ford's *The Searchers*." In Martin M. Winkler, ed. *Classical Myth and Culture in the Cinema*, 118–47. New York: Oxford University Press, 2001.

Yogerst, Chris. "Aristotle and the Wild West: The Western as a Rhetorical Device." In Sue Matheson, ed. *Westerns and the Classical World*. Jefferson, NC: McFarland, 2021.

Prologos

LaBoeuf: As I understand it, Chaney ... or Chelmsford, as he called himself in Texas ... shot the senator's dog. When the senator remonstrated, Chelmsford shot him as well. You could argue that the shooting of the dog was merely an instance of *malum prohibitum*, but the shooting of a senator is indubitably an instance of *malum in se*.
Rooster Cogburn: Malla-men what?
Mattie Ross: *Malum in se*. The distinction is between an act that is wrong in itself, and an act that is wrong only according to our laws and mores. It is Latin.

—*True Grit* (Joel and Ethan Coen, 2010)

West of "Them"

Classical Allusions in Western Film

Kirsten Day

In recent decades, scholars of Classics and Westerns, as well as those from other disciplines, have begun to acknowledge an important relationship between Western film and Greco-Roman mythology, tragedy, and most commonly, epic, both through examinations of individual films and through broader generic studies.[1] These connections are often based on recognition of how similar values and ideologies emerge in the mythic-historic tales of heroic men who worked to build the foundations of what was destined to become a great and powerful nation. In addition to these larger thematic parallels, however, from its earliest days, Western film has made its particular interest in Greek and Roman antiquity evident through a steady stream of classical allusions. These more explicit attempts to associate the heroes—and villains—of the Old West with the classical past suggest that in addition to broader parallels that might apply equally well to other heroic foundational myth systems, something more specific, intentional, and political is going on here: that is, the association of the Old West and classical antiquity works to pinpoint ancient Greece and Rome as America's direct cultural ancestors, both as a perhaps somewhat benign means of deepening and strengthening the roots of our very young nation, but also as a vehicle for associating white American settlers with what is often considered the pinnacle of European civilization as a means of intensifying the us/them binary needed to justify the violent actions on which our civilization was built.[2] Yet while the genre at first glance seems to unreflectively promote this vision of a glorious classical heritage, a closer look reveals points where it works to challenge this view, prodding the audience to scrutinize the propagandistic notions which underlie our national self-image instead of passively accepting them.

Foundational Parallels

One strategy that Westerns use for asserting classical antiquity as a cultural and ideological ancestor of the United States is to frame narratives of foundation and progress from the classical past as a close parallel to or model for U.S. development and westward expansion even from its earliest days. This connection is subtly implied, for instance, in Victor Fleming's 1929 *The Virginian* when a baby is mistakenly christened "Charles Augustus" rather than "Leonidas" after the titular hero (Gary Cooper) and his buddy Steve (Richard Arlen) mischievously switch the two children.³ Though humorous in tone, this scene from one of the first large-scale studio-produced Westerns of the sound era is an early indication of the important association between Greco-Roman antiquity and narratives of the West. By assigning these babies the names of two men who played central roles in shaping the destinies of Greece and Rome—the Spartan king who fought to the death at the Battle of Thermopylae and the first Roman emperor—Fleming effectively links the development of our nation's future to what is implied is our ancestral past, while also neatly symbolizing the Roman usurpation of Greek culture.

Another early example is found in the 1944 Republic film serial *Zorro's Black Whip*, which focuses on the struggle between corrupt politicians who would prevent statehood in Idaho and progressive, civilizing forces championed by the mysterious "Black Whip"—Linda Stirling's Barbara Meredith. In the fifth installment, an undisguised Meredith is captured and forced to call the newspaper to present the villains' threats against her life if the Black Whip does not present himself. In doing so, she directs the editor to print the ultimatum in "octavum verbum" ("eighth word") font⁴—a clue that she is using an encryption technique akin to a "Caesar's shift," named after its first recorded use by Julius Caesar.⁵ By associating the protagonist, who works for statehood, with both the Latin language and with a cipher used by the Roman conqueror, this serial too makes a significant, if subtle, connection between the progress and development of our young nation and empire-building in classical antiquity.

We find an example from the genre's Golden Age in John Ford's 1962 *The Man Who Shot Liberty Valance* when newspaper editor and affable town drunk Dutton Peabody (Edmond O'Brien), surprised in the middle of a grandiose, drunken monologue by a menacing Liberty Valance (Lee Marvin) and his gang, adapts *Henry V*⁶ to the occasion, barely missing a beat: "…when the blast … of war blows in our ears, then we summon up—Liberty Valance … and his Myrmidons." In addition to positioning him as a man of learning, Peabody's reference casts Valance as an Achilles figure; but in the scene that follows, Valance viciously beats Peabody and leaves him for dead, highlighting his *furor* (impassioned fury) and aligning him more properly with Turnus, Aeneas' Rutulian foe in Virgil's *Aeneid*, who himself was cast as a negative version of Achilles. By extension, then, the film's tragic hero Tom Doniphon (John Wayne) is paralleled with Aeneas, the heroic warrior who, like Doniphon, sacrifices his personal desires in the interest of building a nation destined for greatness. Thus, Peabody's reference subtly implies an equivalence between the foundations of Rome and the settling of the American frontier⁷ and casts Peabody himself as an ally of the divinely sanctioned civilizing project.

The positioning of classical antiquity as America's cultural and ideological ancestor continues in post–Golden Age Westerns. In Tom Gries' 1967 *Will Penny*, this relationship is again suggested through allusive names. The film's plot hinges on a dust-up over rights to an elk between Penny (Charlton Heston) and his companions and the Quint family, in the course of which one of the sons—Romulus (Matt Clark)—is killed. As a Latin root meaning "fifth," the name Quint seems aptly chosen for a family which, when they first appear in the narrative, contains five members, while name Romulus recalls Rome's founder and namesake, who killed his own brother Remus in a similar dispute over ownership. In addition, the two remaining Quint brothers, Rufus and Rafe, are meaningfully named as well, "rufus" being the Latin word for "ruddy," and Rafe being a name of Old Norse origin meaning "wise wolf"—perhaps in reference to Romulus and Remus' famous suckling by a she-wolf, an image of which came to represent the city of

Rome itself. As such, through carefully chosen names, the Quints are clearly connected with Rome's foundational mythology, as is appropriate to their identity as rawhiders, one of the first wave of settlers in the Old West. This association takes on added significance when Penny settles in with a widow and her son Horace (Jon Francis), representing the homesteaders who replaced the first-wave frontiersmen. As the historical Horace was both the leading lyric poet in Rome during the Golden Age of Latin literature and an urbane and erudite man who advocated for adherence to the Golden Mean, the name in this context seems purposefully chosen for a boy who represents progress in civilizing the West and the nation's future. Thus, here again, a connection between Rome's founding and development and the process of "civilizing" the American West is subtly suggested through carefully chosen appellatives.

Augustus McCrae's sign ends with its Latin "motto." *Lonesome Dove* (Motown Productions, 1989).

The 1989 miniseries *Lonesome Dove*, too, uses character names to associate the heroes of the West with classical antiquity, but reinforces this correlation with the inclusion of Latin. Robert Duvall's Augustus McCrae is not only the namesake of Rome's first emperor, but he reveres antiquity and the education that provides access to it to the extent that he paints the phrase *UVA UVAM VIVENDO VARIA FIT* on a sign advertising his Hat Creek Cattle Company & Livery Emporium. Although he has no idea what the Latin means, McCrae holds this sign so dear that he carries it with him on his Odyssean journey, and in the end, his friend Captain Call (Tommy Lee Jones) places it in tribute on his grave.[8] This "motto," as he calls it, is in fact a corruption of a phrase found in a scholia to Juvenal's *Satires*,[9] which originally says, "*Uva uvam videndo varia fit*"—"The grape ripens seeing another grape"—again implying the benefits of modeling the U.S.'s growing organizational structures on those of ancient Rome and reinforcing the association suggested by the hero's name.

Westerns of the new millennium continue to demonstrate resonances between nation-building in classical antiquity and the settling of the West, often by recognizing parallels between Roman history and western expansion. David Milch's critically acclaimed 2004–2006 series *Deadwood*, for instance, was initially pitched as a show about city cops in Neronian-era Rome, but since HBO already had the *Rome* series in the works, they asked if he could "engage the same themes in a different venue," with *Deadwood* as the result,[10] suggesting a production-level recognition of a fundamental similarity between the organizing principles of the Roman world and those required to advance the project of settling the West. Monica Cyrino, moreover, has observed of the series that classical allusions "occur most frequently ... when the characters are discussing the growing political organization of the camp, especially its transition from frontier outpost to livable town, or simply trying to make the camp a better place to live,"[11] once again creating a link between the development of our nation and an implied Greco-Roman heritage.

AMC's 2011–2016 series *Hell on Wheels* makes a similar association between political development in Rome and the "taming" of the West. In a telling scene, Lily Bell (Dominique McElligott), who has championed the transcontinental railroad project after her surveyor husband's death, talks with Union Pacific President Thomas Durant (Colm Meaney). As they observe from a distance a fight between the show's hero Cullen Bohannon (Anson Mount) and his comrade/rival Elam Ferguson (Common), Bell comments, "*Panem et circenses*," to which Durant responds with a puzzled look, "I'm afraid my Latin is a little undernourished." "Bread and circuses," she explains. "You engineered this fight as a distraction until you could get payroll, just like the Romans did with unruly crowds—give them food and spectacle."[12] While Durant, it seems, does not draw on these ancient tactics intentionally, Bell's observation again implies a parallel between strategies for furthering the transcontinental railroad project and those used by Roman elites for political gain.

In these examples, U.S. progress is compared implicitly or explicitly to Roman foundational myths or strategies for development with varying degrees of subtlety. Stanley Donan's 1954 *Seven Brides for Seven Brothers*, however, dispenses with subtlety entirely, focusing on a narrative whose plot takes a page directly from the 1st-century-CE Greek biographer Plutarch's tale of the rape of the Sabine women. Plutarch recounts the story in his *Life of Romulus*, where he explains that the early Romans, a ragtag collection of foreigners and men of humble origins, had difficulty obtaining wives from the neighboring peoples. Romulus, who, as noted above, was Rome's founder and first king, thus created as a pretense a great religious event, inviting all those from the surrounding communities. In the midst of the festivities, the Romans drew their swords at a given signal and abducted the young women of the Sabine tribe. After the Sabines' unsuccessful attempts to retrieve their daughters and sisters through diplomacy, war broke out, but hostilities were brought to a halt when the ravished women themselves rushed between the two armies and pleaded with their natal families to let them remain with their husbands and the children they had borne them in the interim.[13]

In Donan's film, newly married homesteader Adam Pontipee (Howard Keel) is inspired by Plutarch's story to help his six brothers—who have been frustrated in their own attempts to wed because the townsfolk scorn them as rough and rowdy backwoodsmen—obtain their own brides by capture. After Adam recounts Plutarch's tale of the "Sobbin' Women" in song, he and his brothers rush to town and kidnap the six girls they've had their eyes on, avoiding pursuit by triggering an avalanche to block the passage to their homestead. By the time the spring thaw allows their families to make the trip to retrieve them, the women have fallen for their abductors. To prevent being "rescued," each woman claims the legitimate baby of Adam and his wife Milly (Jane Powell)

The Pontipee brothers take a cue from Plutarch's story of the "Sobbin' Women." From left to right: Tommy Rall as Frank[incense]; Matt Mattox as Caleb; Jeff Richards as Benjamin; Jacques d'Amboise as Ephraim (facing back); Howard Keel as Adam; Marc Platt as Daniel; and Russ Tamblyn as Gideon. *Seven Brides for Seven Brothers* (Metro-Goldwyn-Meyer, 1954).

as her own, prompting a sextuple shotgun wedding and a comically happy ending.[14] In this way, the film's protagonists draw directly on a classical exemplum to obtain the wives needed to produce progeny and secure the nation's future. Like their Roman predecessors, the Pontipees are cast as bold pioneers laying the groundwork for the great nation to come, and extreme measures are framed as the necessary means to a noble end.

Donan's film was a box-office hit, garnering five Academy Award nominations, including Best Picture,[15] and a slew of other nominations and awards besides. And while the comical presentation of marriage-by-capture as a focal narrative thread, the portrayal of women as "plunder" and "loot" (as Johnny Mercer's lyrics put it), and the framing of Stockholm Syndrome as a happy outcome will strike many viewers today as problematic, the film was honored with placement in the National Film registry in 2004, and enjoys continuing popularity (indeed, the stage version finished its run at our local dinner playhouse while this essay was taking shape[16]). Christopher McDonough has demonstrated that the gendered framework of this film can be read against both its narrative setting and the time of its production in the 1950s, when American women were being encouraged to resume their domestic roles after the end of World War II, while he relates the film's Roman content to the popularity at that time of sword-and-sandal films and of romances set in modern day Rome.[17] But by making early Rome a direct model for foundational strategies in frontier narratives, Donan's film also unreflectively positions Greco-Roman antiquity as an ideological ancestor of the U.S., making explicit the implications found in earlier Westerns.

Classical Antiquity as the Bedrock for the U.S.'s Core Institutions

As these examples demonstrate, references sprinkled throughout the history of the Western genre, from its earliest days to the present, frame narratives of foundation and progress from classical antiquity, and from Rome in particular, as a close parallel to, and even a model for, U.S. development as the nation expanded westward. In a related trend, classical antiquity is also positioned in the Western genre as the bedrock of America's most important institutions—those which undergird our national identity and are often seen as hallmarks of civilization itself: our military, our medical practices, and our legal structures.

In John Ford's 1950 *Rio Grande*, for example, Sargent Major Quincannon (Victor McLaglen) tries to impress new arrivals by asking his seasoned cavalrymen to ride "the way the Romans used to ride. The *ancient* Romans. Standing up." Two new arrivals, Travis (Ben Johnson) and Sandy (Harry Carey, Jr.), impress him right back by jumping at his challenge to do so themselves, incorporating a jump over a six-foot fence to boot. In this film, then, Roman military techniques are positioned as an explicit model for the U.S. Cavalry, who, like the Romans, are working to clear a path for expansion and empire.

Another example is found in John Farrow's 1953 *Hondo*: when the young Lt. McKay (Tom Irish), fresh out of the academy, characterizes Vittorio (Michael Pate), the fierce Apache leader he's pursuing, as a coward, John Wayne's titular hero recounts an Indian story about "a hunter who chased a wildcat 'til he caught it; then it was the other way around." McKay responds, "The story goes back further than the Indians. It's originally attributed to the first Roman army to enter Tartary. The soldier caught a Tarter and yelled out, and the officer called back for him to come in with his prisoner, and he replied, 'The Tartar won't let me.'" McKay goes on to reminisce that the story was a favorite of one of his teachers at "the Point." Although the effect of the interchange is to cast McKay as bookish and inexperienced in frontier realities in contrast to "real men" like Hondo and his friend Buffalo Baker (Ward Bond), McKay's anecdote nonetheless gives primacy to the Roman version and points to classical learning as the basis of our military education institutions.[18]

Mattie Ross (Hailee Steinfeld), the heroine of the 2010 Coen brothers' *True Grit*, reminds the viewer that our legal structures, too, have their roots in classical antiquity when she explains the difference between an offense that is *malum prohibitum* and one that is *malum in se* for a baffled Rooster Cogburn (Jeff Bridges), further clarifying, "It is Latin."[19] Despite Cogburn's scornful disinterest, the exchange emphasizes the integration of the language of the ancient Romans into our legal system and associates the heroine with classical learning. A scene in the A&E/Netflix series *Longmire* (2012–2017) does something similar: when his reference to the writ of *habeas corpus* evinces blank stares and a confused query from his companions, the titular hero Walt Longmire (Robert Taylor) quickly explains, "It's Latin, for 'Produce the body.'"[20]

A scene in *Deadwood*, in addition, makes the American medical profession's roots in classical antiquity clear when the sympathetic Doc Cochran (Brad Dourif) discusses the Greek notion of the humors before segueing into more Greek wisdom, taking care to note that he learned it in Latin: "*primum non nocere* ... that means, 'first, do no harm.'"[21] Not only does this scene anchor the theoretical basis of our modern medical system to practices and standards first established in ancient Greece, Cochran's clarification that he learned it in Latin helps to emphasize heritage issues by reminding us that much of what the U.S. educational system got from the Romans, they got from the Greeks, implying a direct and uninterrupted line of transmission. A scene in *Longmire*, again, also hints at the anchoring of our body of medical knowledge in antiquity when a coroner's report lists the contents of a corpse's stomach in Latin.[22] That Longmire, who is in many ways a prototypical Westerner, translates it effortlessly as turkey, duck, and chicken—turducken—once again brings the notion of "the West" into close kinship with classical antiquity.

While classical references certainly do not appear in every Western, as these examples suggest, throughout the genre's history, a steady stream of allusions serves not only to foreground Greco-Roman antiquity as a model and parallel for the U.S. in its own development as a nation, but to emphasize its position as an ideological ancestor as well. In most cases, foundational parallels are drawn with Rome, an association in line with America's founders' view of "the young republic they were nurturing as in some ways a rebirth of principles first implemented in the Roman Republic."[23] By emphasizing the intimate relationship between classical antiquity and America from its infancy, the Western works to strengthen the roots of our young nation, while positioning itself as a rightful heir to the cultural and intellectual achievements of Greece and Rome.

Rome also provides a convenient model because the expansionist policies governed by the principles of Manifest Destiny are closely aligned with the Roman view of their own nation's founding and development: in much the same way as Virgil's *Aeneid* frames Aeneas' quest to establish the basis for what would become Rome as a divinely-sanctioned and pre-destined imperative, the doctrine of Manifest Destiny likewise positioned expansion throughout the continent as fated in accordance with a divine plan, so that its accomplishment was seen as a heroic duty.[24] In both cases, the effect of this strategy is to render the subjugation and oppression of native peoples as a noble rather than immoral act. The Western genre's attempt to assert a classical heritage helps to further this dynamic by subtly reinforcing our claim to what is often viewed as a white European identity as a contrast to the distinctly non–European Native Americans who must be pushed aside in order to fulfill the tenets of Manifest Destiny. Thus, underneath its somewhat benign appearance, the connection with classical antiquity that the Western stakes out not only taps into the ancient strategy of validating the indefensible by framing it as a divine and predestined heroic duty, but it also works to render the eradication of native peoples required by the nation-building process less problematic by emphasizing cultural and racial difference.

But while the above examples seem to suggest the Western genre's investment in unproblematically establishing the classical past as America's glorious and rightful heritage, a closer look demonstrates that the genre can also work to challenge this view. For instance, a classical allusion in Fred Zinnemann's 1952 *High Noon* demonstrates the genre's occasional discomfort with claiming the classical past as an inheritance. In this film, protagonist Will Kane (Gary Cooper) seeks the support of Judge Percy Mettrick (Otto Kruger) when trouble threatens, but is dismayed to find him packing his things to leave town instead. Mettrick justifies his cowardly exit by recounting an episode from 5th-century-BCE Athens, where the citizens first welcomed back a ruthless tyrant they had earlier expelled, and then did nothing while he executed the members of the former government. Mettrick then notes that a similar thing happened "about eight years ago" in the town of Indian Falls.[25] By choosing for his cautionary tale an anecdote he places in what is regarded as the Golden Age of Greece[26] and linking it to the example of a Western frontier town, Mettrick plants the notion of a significant kinship between the two; but at the same time, the parallel he asserts is a negative one used to justify his cowardly abandonment of the heroic enterprise, inverting our expectations and undercutting the notion of our classical heritage as something to be celebrated.

The 2010–2015 neo-Western FX series *Justified* provides us with a more recent example, taking us back to Roman foundational mythologies once again, but positioning classical antiquity as a problematic model for development. When his cousin Johnny (David Meunier) comments sarcastically upon seeing his ramshackle camp of outlaws in the woods that he likes what anti-hero Boyd Crowder (Walton Goggins) has done with the place, Crowder responds, "You know what Rome looked like before it became Rome, don't you? Some huts on the side of a hill, a little stream runnin' through it. What it became—well as they say, it didn't happen in a day."[27] Crowder here attempts to cast himself as the instigator of a grand and important project—he's currently training spiritually reformed criminals to "clean up" Harlan County by blowing up meth labs—much like the Romulus of Roman legend. Although he draws on a Roman exemplum in an attempt to frame his project as destined for greatness, his misguided use of this model is signaled by Johnny's wry response: "So you're building Rome? Well, I don't think this property is zoned for that." By offering up an example of distorted logic in the use of classical models, the series challenges us to scrutinize these uses more generally.

Classical Allusions and the Shaping of Character

In addition to looking to classical antiquity as a parallel to or model for our own nation's development, the Western genre also taps into the view of classical wisdom as a marker of what makes man "civilized" as a means of staking a claim to classical heritage. For much of America's short past, a grounding in classical literature, language, and history was considered the cornerstone of a full and complete education. Indeed, our nation's founders saw it as essential, in that it promoted reason and virtue while offering up the lessons of history.[28]

As such, classical allusions are often used in Westerns to suggest the quality of one's character, particularly as it relates to the nation-building project. In the majority of the examples laid out above, association with classical learning positions these characters as allies to the project of civilizing the West. This is also evident in John Ford's 1939 *Stagecoach*, where the good-natured drunkard Doc Boone (Thomas Mitchell) addresses the hotel proprietress who has unceremoniously kicked him out with, "Is this the face that wrecked a thousand ships and burned the towerless tops of Ilium? … Farewell, fair Helen!" Despite his generally inebriated state and initial ignominious expulsion from the town of Tonto, Doc's allusion to Helen of Troy via a misquote of Marlowe's *Dr. Faustus*[29] signals his later role as a staunch ally to John Wayne's Ringo Kid and thus a valuable supporter of the Western cause: in the end, he risks his life to prevent Luke Plummer (Tom Tyler) from bringing a shotgun to a showdown with Ringo, and helps facilitate Ringo's escape in the film's conclusion.

But as we saw with Judge Mettrick and Boyd Crowder, association with classical learning is not limited to heroic characters who work for the nation's betterment: it can also mark out those who threaten to obstruct the nation's progress by hindering the heroic project, so that here again, the genre sometimes suggests a more complicated relationship with classical antiquity. In Henry Hathaway's 1969 version of *True Grit*, for instance, the greedy stable owner Col. Stonehill (Strother Martin) who tries to take advantage of heroine Mattie Ross (Kim Darby), assuming the young girl to be both naïve and incompetent in business matters, responds to her demand for payment for her father's stolen horse with, "I wouldn't pay that for winged Pegasus!"[30] His classical reference here serves to intensify his patronizing demeanor along with the selfish, parsimonious attitude which threatens to derail the heroine's quest. A more menacing example is found in the 2017 Netflix mini-series *Godless*: when the ruthless villain Frank Griffin (Jeff Daniels) teaches his protégé to tame a horse using the wisdom of Xenophon,[31] the effect is to sharpen his vicious, calculating nature, reinforcing his characterization as a threat to civilization rather than a champion of it. Likewise, in the fourth episode of the USA Network's short-lived 2017–2018 (Mid-) Western series *Damnation*, strikebreaker Connie Nunn (Melinda Page Hamilton) poses as a perfume saleswoman to befriend the wife of a strike leader she's targeting, encouraging the woman to please her husband with a product called "Pandora's Delight." This reference to the mythological first woman of Greece again works to delineate her character: like Pandora,[32] Connie is a *kalon kakon*—a beautiful bad thing, attractive in appearance, but inside, a dangerous "bitch" who is tracking down the show's heroic protagonist, bent on murder, and using this reference to Pandora, appropriately, to further her deception.[33]

Furthermore, classical allusions are sometimes associated with both heroic and obstructionist or villainous characters within the same work, as was the case in *Will Penny* with the menacing Quint family and the promising young Horace. Alongside the above-mentioned foundational connections, opposing associations with the classical past are also found in *The Man Who Shot Liberty Valance* with the inclusion of two names that evoke Roman historical figures: Pompey and Cassius. The former recalls Gnaeus Pompeius Magnus, or Pompey the Great, the Roman conqueror who was first allied with and later defeated by Julius Caesar, and who, though his reputation can be varied, is largely remembered as a tragic hero of the Republic; and the latter brings to mind the Roman senator Gaius Cassius Longinus, one of the instigators of the plot to assassinate Caesar. While like Pompey, Cassius might be remembered as a defender of the Republic, his portrayal in later literature—such as Dante's *Inferno*[34] and Shakespeare's *Julius Caesar*—has associated him instead with betrayal, ambition, and greed. In Ford's film, the Pompey character, played by Woody Strode, is manservant to Doniphon. As Abigail Horne has shown, though often overlooked in this film, Pompey "consistently exemplifies the courage and competence of John Wayne's Tom and the civility and chivalry of James Stewart's Ranse."[35] In this way, he maintains a quiet but vital supporting role in civilizing the West, while his association with the historical Pompey lends him a tragic-heroic dignity. Cassius Starbuckle (John Carradine), on the other hand, is a slick-tongued orator who uses his gifts disingenuously to promote the interests of the cattlemen against those of the homesteaders, shopkeepers, and "builders of cities," as Peabody puts it in the nomination speech which launches Ranse's political career. As with Pompey, the associations of his Roman name subtly attach to him, but here, accentuate his pomposity, insincerity, and obstructionist position regarding the cause of progress.[36] In addition, both of these historical figures are associated with Rome's transition from Republic to Empire, as is appropriate to a film that works to question the framing of the civilizing of the West as an unquestionable good, so that much like with the classical name references in *The Virginian*, a subtle but important connection is made between national development in classical antiquity and in the early U.S.

We see a similar bifurcation in *Deadwood*: while Doc Cochran's classical knowledge marks him out as a man of "deep thought and broad education," as Monica Cyrino puts it, in others it reflects serious moral shortcomings. When an angry mob descends on Hugo Jarry (Stephen Tobolowsky), the corrupt county commissioner from Yankton, he warns them that if they inflict violence upon him, their actions will "seal [their] fate as irrevocably as the tyrant crossing the Rubicon,"[37] a reference that highlights Jarry's lack of self-awareness and emphasizes his distance from the concerns of the common man, whose claims are threatened by his efforts to impose state control over the territory. Later, Jarry attempts to kiss up to ruthless mining magnate George Hearst (Gerald McRaney) by positioning himself as Alcibiades to Hearst's Socrates. "Are you saying you want to fuck me?" Hearst responds angrily, to which a flustered Jarry hastily explains, "I forgot that part of the story!"[38] Just as Hearst is more conversant in Greek history than Jarry, in equal measure, Hearst is more dangerous, and more despicable. Most disturbingly, Hearst's chief geologist, the violent deviant Francis Wolcott (Garret Dillahunt), contextualizes his sexual proclivities with a reference to women prostituting themselves in service to Aphrodite on the island of Cyprus,[39] but his reference to the sacrifice of "women's generative instrument" on the altar also foreshadows his later sadistic, bloody murder of prostitutes and their madam.[40] Far from serving as a model of progress and enlightenment, here classical antiquity is drawn upon as an inspiration for murderous depravity, posing a pointed challenge to the view of our classical heritage as noble and glorious.

Likewise, a chilling scene from an episode of *Hell on Wheels* works as a scathing indictment of the use of classical learning to bolster notions of white supremacy. Here, the once again classically-named Doctor Major Augustus Bendix (Leon Ingulsrud) returns to camp bearing the heads of Native Americans on pikes despite orders to kill them having been rescinded. After our hero Bohannon condemns his ruthlessness, Bendix justifies his violent actions by positioning the native as subhuman based on phrenological analyses before offering an arrogant challenge: "Show me the savage Plato and I will read him."[41] By staking out a classical heritage in arguing for the inferiority of the natives, Bendix taps into a long history of the nefarious use of classics for white supremacist purposes in the U.S. and elsewhere. But at the same time, this scene undercuts this dynamic by attributing such reasoning to a despicable character who is set in opposition to the honorable Bohannon. Here again, we see Westerns pointedly working to problematize assertions of an illustrious classical heritage.

Classical Allusions in Alter Ego Figures

The competing uses of classical allusions in the Western genre, either as a means of glorifying our national project or as a means of challenging these strategies, is most strikingly evident in Westerns that set hero and villain up as alter egos,[42] while attaching classical associations to both. This is most clearly seen in George Pan Cosmatos's 1993 *Tombstone*, where at their first meeting, Doc Holliday (Val Kilmer) sizes up Johnny Ringo (Michael Biehn) by noting "somethin' around the eyes.... I don't know. Reminds me of ... me!," and then casually concludes, "I hate him." Wyatt Earp (Kurt Russell) excuses his friend's belligerent attitude by explaining, "He's drunk," to which Doc responds, "*In vino veritas*" ("in wine, truth").[43] The identification between the two men that Holliday has already suggested is then driven home when Ringo not only understands Holliday's Latin, but responds in kind, initiating a Latin "duel" of sorts, which ends with Doc explaining to his lady friend, "That's Latin darlin'; evidently, Mr. Ringo's an educated man. Now I really hate him."

Despite his professed disdain for education, there is a kernel of truth in Doc's characterization in this scene. The historical Doc Holliday in some ways embodied the contradictions felt in the Western's attitude towards classical learning: he was both a skilled gunfighter and a gentleman, a lawman and an outlaw, and a vagabond and a scholar, having received a healthy classical education, including rhetoric, grammar, history, Latin, and some ancient Greek, at Valdosta Institute in Georgia.[44] While it is likely, then, that Holliday would have been capable of the sort of interchange of Latin aphorisms, complete with a reference to Horace's *Satires*,[45] found in this "duel," *Tombstone*'s creators have invented Ringo's ability to match him in this arena, presumably to strengthen their pairing. By attributing competence in Latin to both hero and enemy, Cosmatos sharpens the nature of those who have access to the "wisdom" of antiquity, making Doc into a man of deep learning and Ringo, as Doc's mirror, into an even more dangerous adversary. But it also suggests the double-edged nature of classical learning: at its best, it can ennoble and enrich; at its worse, it can bolster violence and oppression.

We see something similar in *Longmire*, where, as we've seen, the titular hero's knowledge of Latin works to amplify the heroic nature which makes him uniquely qualified to promote justice and progress in the continuing project of taming the West.[46] We are explicitly prompted to relate Longmire's familiarity with classical antiquity to character when, in a voiceover that begins the fifth episode of Season 3, he reflects, "'Character is fate.' The [Greek] philosopher Heraclitus said that. I think he meant man makes his destiny through his choices and his values." And Longmire's steeping in classical learning is brought into sharper relief by the contrast with his deputy Vic (Katee Sackoff), who is at an utter loss when encountering Latin and who, in an episode involving murder by hemlock, pretends to be knowledgeable about Socrates' association with this poisonous plant, but, at a raised eyebrow from Walt, admits she "Googled it."[47]

But this seemingly straightforward ennobling of Longmire through an association with classical learning is complicated considerably near the end of Season 2 when he warns off Ed Gorski (Lee Tergesen), who has threatened Vic, with an extended Homeric exemplum drawn from the *Iliad*: "Achilles was a warrior," he says. "He had a partner, a fellow warrior. A friend. There's no greater enemy than the mortal enemy of a friend."[48] By casting himself as an Achilles figure, Walt taps into all the associations that go along with the glories of Greece and its epic literature, thus staking a claim on the side of honor, justice, and right action. Yet Gorski's pointed response—"I would not disagree with that"—serves to remind us that Gorski is acting in defense of his own friend: a law-man himself, Gorski blames Vic for his former partner's death, as his suicide was prompted when she turned him in for corruption. Their similar identities and motives, then, position them as alter egos, a relationship further signaled when Gorski's reflection appears in a mirror behind Walt. The astute viewer will notice the challenge posed to the simplistic association of classical learning with the "good guy" by noting the equivalence implied between hero and villain here, a dynamic which destabilizes the us/them binary that allows us to unreflectively glorify the foundational mythologies that underpin our national self-image, nudging us instead to recognize the problematic history on which the society we enjoy is built.

γνῶθι σεαυτόν *(Know Thyself)*[49]

The Western genre thus often takes pains to challenge the simplistic association of a classical heritage with heroic achievement, and sometimes even works to expose the racist underpinnings of motivations behind asserting this classical heritage. Several recent works, moreover, prod us to recognize that this invented classical birthright was critical to making us who we are today by associating classical learning with figures who were instrumental in our nation-building process, but who achieve this progress by morally despicable means. The association of George Hearst with classical learning in *Deadwood*, for instance, renders our classical heritage inextricable from our development as a nation: while the Hearst character in the series differs considerably from the historical figure—and in the 2019 movie ends up jailed by hero Seth Bullock (Timothy Olyphant)—the Hearst name is a prominent one in U.S. history, associated, as in *Deadwood*, with national development through mining, media, and politics.[50]

In *Hell on Wheels*, too, that an invented classical heritage enabled the progress that made the nation we live in possible is suggested by its close association with the real historical figures who spearheaded the transcontinental railroad project. Not only does Union Pacific President Thomas Durant employ a technique used by Roman elites to pacify and manipulate the "rabble" to ensure that the project moves forward smoothly, in Season 5 Central Pacific owner Collis Huntington (played here by Tim Guinee) makes clear his own steeping in classical antiquity: pleased with the progress the show's hero has made blasting rocks with the aid of a steam engine, Huntington gushes, "Oh Mr. Bohannon, you are like Hercules triumphant after his seven labors. I believe in this Colossus of yours!" When line boss James Strobridge (Reg Rogers) responds, "If you blow any more smoke up his ass, you're liable to start a fire," Huntington scoffs, "The Minotaur speaks. The sour disputatious back-looking voice of a beast locked away in a labyrinth of the past. The word is progress, Mr. Strobridge."[51]

In this context, access to classical learning helps paint Huntington as greedy and heartless, since he is unsympathetic to the fact that this machine is going to put three men out of work (although he ultimately agrees to keep them on at vastly reduced "Jakes' wages"). At the same time, however, as *Deadwood* did with Hearst and this series with Durant, *Hell on Wheels* acknowledges that ruthless businessmen like Huntington are necessary contributors to the "progress" he boasts of, the benefits of which we the audience currently enjoy. While on the one hand, this might be taken to frame claims of a classical heritage, with all its racist underpinnings, as a necessary evil, at the same time, it can be seen as a means of acknowledging the problematic strategies on which our nation was built rather than whitewashing our history in order to reconfigure our past as merely noble and heroic. In addition, Huntington's error—he references Hercules' seven labors, rather than the canonical ten or twelve—serves to further trouble the relationship between classical antiquity and foundational narratives of the Old West by implying that these claims to a classical heritage rest on flawed foundations.[52]

HBO's *Westworld* also contains an implied critique of the glorification of our classical past in the second episode, when Lee Sizemore (Simon Quarterman), head of narrative design, presents a story arc to park director Robert Ford (Anthony Hopkins) which is extravagant in its violence and depravity, calling it "Odyssey on Red River." By using a title that neatly yokes epic and Western to govern a storyline that includes "besting fearsome braves" and "seducing nubile maidens," the series suggests a link between the classical past and the oppressive systems that are enabled by claiming it as an inheritance. The scene further links this strategy to issues of identity, first when Sizemore claims that by immersing themselves in this story, park guests will "have the privilege of getting to

Lee Sizemore (Simon Quarterman) pitches a storyline called "Odyssey on Red River" in Season 1, Episode 2. *Westworld* (HBO, 2016).

know the character they are most interested in: themselves," and then when Ford rejects Sizemore's proposal, arguing that guests do not want a storyline that tells them who they are; instead, they come to Westworld because "they want a glimpse of who they could be." In effect, then, Sizemore's proposal is rejected for unmasking truths about our national identity we'd prefer to leave unacknowledged in favor of promoting a more idealized vision of who we are.

Westworld continues to intertwine issues of self-knowledge with our classical heritage in Season 2. In episode 9, for instance, when an associate at a cocktail party misquotes Plutarch, William (Ed Harris)—also known as the Man in Black—corrects him: "That's a corruption, Jack: Plutarch didn't write that. He wrote that when Alexander was told there was an infinity of worlds, he wept, for he had yet to become the lord of even one." When the man rebuffs him with "Sometimes I forget your humble roots. Only the poor kids actually read those books; the rich kids like me didn't have to," William's wife Juliet (Sela Ward) steps in: "'I would rather excel in the knowledge of what is excellent than in the extent of my power and possessions.' Plutarch: from a rich kid who read."[53] This interchange associates William with Alexander the Great, another ambitious visionary, and one whose conquests brought him the metaphorical immortality that William seeks in a literal sense.

But William's quest for immortality has already been grotesquely problematized in a prior episode where Peter Mullan park founder (and William's father-in-law) James Delos is revealed—in an episode entitled "Riddle of the Sphinx"—to be the first subject in William's experimental attempts to make human consciousness immortal—an experiment that after many tries is deemed a failure, leaving Delos to degrade into horrifying madness in his malfunctioning body. His dying speech with its enigmatic tone, reference to two fathers, and invocation of themes of vision, fate, and self-knowledge points to the Oedipal connections hinted at in the episode's title: like Oedipus, Delos ultimately faces the realization that in trying to escape his fate, he has run right into it. Likewise, William's own lack of self-knowledge is hinted at in the scene discussed above, since the misquote of Plutarch reflects William as he is seen by others—as a "successful, all-conquering Titan of industry," as Estelle Tang puts it—while the corrected version reflects how he sees himself.[54] William's arrogant attempts at playing God later contribute to his wife's suicide, and by the end of Season 2, it is made clear that his identity issues go much deeper when the finale's post-credit scene suggests that like with Delos, William's understanding both of who he is and of his own reality is utterly false.[55] Classical allusions in *Westworld* thus work as an implicit criticism of positioning our classical past as an inherited birthright by aligning classical learning with unbridled ambition, patriarchal narcissism, and a profound lack of self-awareness.[56]

Thus, while in some ways Westerns use classical allusions to bolster national identity and glorify the institutions that are seen as the bedrock of our civilization, the genre also exhibits a complicated attitude towards those who hold classical ideals dear, demonstrating that the same knowledge that aids some in the promotion of national progress can also in the wrong hands damage, degrade, and threaten to destroy the civilizing work done by more heroic counterparts. At the same time, the genre at times manages to pull aside the curtain, asking us to acknowledge the uncomfortable truth that classics' position as the "foundation of Western civilization" is a construct conceived of to bolster a nation-building project whose ends we enjoy while turning a blind eye to the violence and injustice on which it was built.

Grappling with the West

As Rebecca Futo Kennedy has observed, "In narratives of American greatness, Classics holds a special place because the ancient Greeks and Romans have served as an imaginary source of an inherited Euro-American civilization."[57] Perhaps it is unsurprising then that a genre focused on the heroes who blazed a trail westward in what has long been framed as a noble, civilizing quest to forge the foundations of what would become a great and powerful nation demonstrates a persistent interest in classical antiquity. But Kennedy's remark comes in the context of an attempt to reckon with the key place the field of Classics has had in the development of the idea of "Western civilization," while at the same time recognizing the racist and misogynistic undercurrents inherent in the unreflective veneration of what are seen as white male achievements that lies at its core.

While it may seem natural that an occasional allusion to what the nation's founders framed as the basis for both our government and our educational system would crop up in a genre concerned with nation-building and establishing foundational ideologies, as Kennedy and other scholars have shown, this sort of claim to the classical past as a cultural inheritance is not without its problems, not least in that it ignores complicated routes of transmission and presumes ownership of classical culture based primarily on flawed notions of race and religious affiliation.[58] Thus we might consider that in addition to the relatively neutral function of serving to deepen and strengthen the roots of our very young and developing nation, emphasis on the classical past has important political implications as well. In particular, the persistent association of the United States' immediate mythic-historical roots, which lie in narratives of the "Wild West," with the Greco-Roman world, which is framed as a more distant but nonetheless direct cultural ancestor, is a notion very much in line with the idea that Greek and Roman antiquity forms the basis for Western civilization more generally. And it is important to recognize that this broad division of the world into categories of "West" and "East" is consonant with the "us vs. them" mentality crucial to the foundational narratives of a nation eager to justify the extermination of native peoples and the appropriation of lands already occupied as a triumph of civilization over savagery divinely sanctioned by the tenets of Manifest Destiny.

While in many ways, the Western genre seems to promote an idealistic view of classical antiquity as America's cultural progenitor, bolstering the problematic notion of Western civilization as a white European cultural inheritance, at the same time, it works to complicate this relationship by exposing our kinship with the ancients as sometimes craven, as with Judge Mettrick's justification of cowardice using a classical exemplum; as un-self-reflective, as with Longmire's threat of Achillean vengeance against a man for threatening similarly motivated retribution; as able either to elevate, as with Doc Cochran's use of Greek wisdom in his medicine, or to corrupt, as with Francis Wolcott's violent application of ancient procreative rituals; or as sheer, self-deluded racism, as with Doctor Major Bendix's vile notions of white supremacy.

As many scholars have recognized, these films are not the simplistic white-hat vs. black-hat narratives they are often taken to be; instead, many of the better Westerns work to interrogate American mythologies through strategies such as highlighting the tendency to alter history in service to nationalistic propaganda[59] or by subtly undercutting the white pioneers' moral superiority within an ironic framework of nostalgic patriotism.[60] Along similar lines, the genre demonstrates a persistent challenge to strategies that anchor the U.S. to classical antiquity in a line of heritage as a means of distinguishing the European "us" from the savage "them," particularly in a post–World War II context, as when Hitler famously used Greek and Roman art in the propaganda of the Third Reich and justified his genocidal agenda with a distorted view of classical idealism.[61]

As today's scholars are increasingly calling into question the reduction of cultural heritage, values, and ideologies into East/West binaries and pointing out the problematic identity politics these divisions imply,[62] it is not only important to recognize where, and examine how, our popular narratives unconsciously work to establish or reinforce these long-held assumptions, but also to acknowledge how they work to question and challenge them. By doing so, we can better understand how our cultural identity is framed in the foundational narratives which help shape our national self-image as a step towards shedding the propagandistic notions that hold us back from true self-knowledge.

Notes

1. For example, see John G. Cawelti's *The Six-Gun Mystique* (Bowling Green, OH: Bowling Green University Popular Press, 1971), 55–57; George N. Fenin and William K. Everson's *The Western: From Silents to the Seventies* (New York: Grossman Publishers, 1973), 6; Nancy Warfield's "*The Man Who Shot Liberty Valance*: A Study of John Ford's Film," *The Little Film Gazette of N.D.W.* Vol. 6, No. 1 (August 1975): 15–20; Roberta Reeder's "The Mythic Mode: Archetypal Criticism and *Red River*," *Ciné-tracts* 3.2 (1980): 61–62; Rita Parks' *The Western Hero in Film and Television: Mass Media Mythology* (Ann Arbor, MI: UMI Research Press, 1982), 14–16; Gerald Mast's *Howard Hawks, Storyteller* (New York: Oxford University Press, 1982), 334–37; Martin M. Winkler's "Classical Mythology and the Western Film," *Comparative Literature Studies* 22.4 (1985): 516–40, "Homeric *kleos* and the Western Film," *Syllecta Classica* 7 (1996): 43–54; "Tragic Features in John Ford's *The Searchers*" in *Classical Myth and Culture in the Cinema*, Martin M. Winkler, ed. (Oxford: Oxford University Press, [2001]): 118–47, "Homer's *Iliad* and John Ford's *The Searchers*" in *The Searchers: Essays and Reflections on John Ford's Classic Western*, A.M. Eckstein and P. Lehman, eds. (Detroit, MI: Wayne State University Press, 2004), 145–70; Mary Whitlock Blundell and Kirk Ormand's "Western Values, or the Peoples Homer: *Unforgiven* as a Reading of the *Iliad*," *Poetics Today* 18.4 (1997): 533–69; Peter A. French's *Cowboy Metaphysics: Ethics and Death in Westerns* (Lanham, MD: Rowman & Littlefield Publishers, Inc., 1997), 80; James J. Clauss' "Descent into Hell: Mythic Paradigms

in *The Searchers*," *Journal of Popular Film and Television* 27.3 (1999): 2–17; E. Christian Kopff's *The Devil Knows Latin: Why America Needs the Classical Tradition* (Wilmington, DE: Intercollegiate Studies Institute Books, 1999); Geoffrey W. Bakewell's "Oedipus Tex: *Lone Star*, Tragedy, and Postmodernism," *Classical and Modern Literature* 22.1: (2002): 35–48; Kostas Myrsiades' "Reading *The Gunfighter* as Homeric Epic," *College Literature* 34.2 (2007): 279–300; Kirsten Day's "'What Makes a Man to Wander?': *The Searchers* as a Western *Odyssey*," *Arethusa* 41.1 (2008): 11–49, *Cowboy Classics: The Roots of the American Western in the Epic Tradition* (Edinburgh: Edinburgh University Press, 2016), and "All That Glitters…': Problematizing Golden Age Narratives in Virgil's *Aeneid* and Western film" in *Screening the Golden Ages of the Classical Tradition*, Meredith Safran, ed. (Edinburgh: Edinburgh University Press, 2020); Glenn Frankel's *The Searchers: The Making of an American Legend* (New York: Bloomsbury, 2013), 239; Judith Fletcher's "The *Catabasis* of Mattie Ross in the Coens' *True Grit*," *Classical World* 107.2 (2014): 237–54; and Carl A. Rubino's "Wounds That Will Not Heal: Heroism and Innocence in *Shane* and the *Iliad*," *Dialogue: The Interdisciplinary Journal of Popular Culture and Pedagogy* 1.1 (2014), http://journaldialogue.org/issues/issue-1/wounds-that-will-not-heal-heroism-and-innocence-in-shane-and-the-iliad/.

2. Thanks to Sue Matheson for her input on this essay. I am also grateful to co-presenters and audience members who offered feedback at the 2016 and 2018 CAMWS and 2016 and 2017 Film & History conferences.

3. There is no corresponding scene in Owen Wister's 1902 novel *The Virginian: A Horseman of the Plains*, although there is an anecdotal reference to a character named Augustus, and a more integral character named Scipio.

4. Thanks to Robert T. White for alerting me to this episode.

5. See Suetonius' *Lives of the Caesars: The Deified Julius* LVI.6.

6. From William Shakespeare's *Henry V*, III.i.6–8.

7. I previously addressed Peabody's allusion and its implications in *Cowboy Classics: The Roots of the American Western in the Epic Tradition*. See pages 172–73 and 179–80 in a chapter that looks at this film's relationship to ancient epic and drama more broadly. See also my discussion in "All That Glitters…': Problematizing Golden Age Narratives in Virgil's *Aeneid* and Western film."

8. In Larry McMurtry's original novel, this sign functions as an important marker of status and identity—and Latin an indicator of education—for many of the characters, not just McCrae, as is indicated by allusions to it throughout the narrative (see pages 35, 86–91, 100–02, 160, 188, 208, 216, 470–72, 557, 778, 785–86). In the end, however, although McCrae explicitly requests it as a grave marker, by the time it is erected, the sign has deteriorated to the extent that neither the Latin, nor McCrae's name, is preserved, and only the business title is left to be read on the crossbar (839–41).

9. Juvenal's *Satires* II.81.

10. Quoted from "The New Language of the Old West" found in the Season 1 bonus features of the full series DVD set.

11. From Monica S. Cyrino's "Ricochets off the Frontier: Classical Allusion in HBO's *Deadwood* (2004–06)," presented at the Classical Association Annual Conference, April 15 2014.

12. *Hell on Wheels*, Season 1, episode 5.

13. See Plutarch's "Romulus," Sec. 14–20.

14. The movie is based on Stephen Vincent Benét's short story "The Sobbin' Women," which has a similar premise, but there, Plutarch is not named as the specific source of this episode, which was also recounted by Dionysus of Halicarnassus, Livy, Cicero, and Ovid. In addition, in Benét's story, it is Milly who suggests, and later aids, the scheme (1937.151–52) whereas in Donan's film, she is appalled by it.

15. The film's only win was for Best Music, Scoring of a Musical Picture.

16. The play ran at Rock Island, Illinois's Circa '21 Dinner Playhouse from July 19 to September 16, 2017.

17. See Christopher McDonough, "Ancient Allusions and Modern Anxieties in *Seven Brides for Seven Brothers* (1954)," 99; 101–04.

18. *Hondo* has its roots in Louis L'Amour's short story "The Gift of Cochise," but again has been altered considerably: the short story has no Lt. McKay, no Buffalo Baker, and no reference to Rome.

19. This interchange is not found either in the 1969 Henry Hathaway film or in the Charles Portis novel on which both films were based.

20. *Longmire*, Season 3, episode 10.

21. *Deadwood*, Season 1, episode 11. While Greek wisdom is acknowledged in Westerns, Latin is generally drawn on as the *lingua franca* that acts as a bridge to antiquity, partly attributable to its familiarity, as it both has a closer connection to English vocabulary and was long the language of the Christian church, but also perhaps as an indication of transmission pathways—like Doc Cochran, we revere Greek wisdom, but understand it to have been passed down to America *via* the Romans.

22. *Longmire*, Season 2, episode 2.

23. See Daniel Walker Howe, "Classical Education in America."

24. See, for example, my discussion in "All That Glitters…': Problematizing Golden Age Narratives in Virgil's *Aeneid* and Western film."

25. This film uses John M. Cunningham's short story "The Tin Star" as a jumping off point, but with

considerable alterations (see my discussion in *Cowboy Classics: The Roots of the American Western in the Epic Tradition*, 98). In Cunningham's story, Mettrick is mayor and there is no reference to Athens.

26. The reference seems to be to Peisistratus, an Athenian tyrant of the 6th rather than 5th century BCE.
27. *Justified*, Season 1, episode 10.
28. Daniel Walker Howe, "Classical Education in America."
29. "Was this the face that launched a thousand ships/ and burnt the topless towers of Ilium?" (from Christopher Marlowe's *Dr. Faustus*, Scene XIII, 88–89).
30. Unlike Mattie's use of Latin, this reference does originate in Portis's novel.
31. *Godless*, Episode 5.
32. See Hesiod's *Theogony* 570–612 and *Works and Days* 57–105.
33. A fortune teller who goes by "Teiresias" (Bobbi Charlton) in episode 5—which features a carnival-as-katabasis, positioned at the season's midpoint in classical epic fashion—supports the interpretation of this reference as intentional. Uncoincidentally, *Damnation* was created by Tony Tost, discussed below in relation to *Longmire*. In an interview, Tost referred to his shaping of the series' pro- and antagonists in relation to models found in Homer's *Iliad* (Iblings 2018).
34. Dante's *Inferno*, Canto XXXIV.
35. Abigail Horne, "The Color of Manhood: Reconsidering Pompey in John Ford's *The Man Who Shot Liberty Valance*," 17.
36. In Dorothy M. Johnson's short story of the same name on which the film is based, the Ranse character reads Plato in the original Greek, but there is no Pompey or Cassius Starbuckle, and no reference to Myrmidons.
37. *Deadwood*, Season 2, episode 5.
38. *Deadwood*, Season 3, episode 10.
39. *Deadwood*, Season 2, episode 4.
40. *Deadwood*, Season 2, episode 6. See Monica S. Cyrino's "Ricochets off the Frontier: Classical Allusion in HBO's *Deadwood* (2004–06)."
41. *Hell On Wheels*, Episode 3.
42. For more on this dynamic in Homer and Virgil, along with an examination of its appearance in Western film, see *Cowboy Classics: The Roots of the American Western in the Epic Tradition*, 26–30.
43. A later reference to the wealth of Croesus also suggests Wyatt Earp's familiarity with classical learning.
44. Karen Holliday Tanner, *Doc Holliday: A Family Portrait*, 57.
45. See Horace's *Satires*, I.v.100–01: "credat Iudaeus Apella,/ non ego."
46. Series writer and Seasons 4 and 5 producer Tony Tost has suggested that Longmire's association with classical learning is motivated in part by the need to characterize him as a man who has "outlived his proper society. He's a figure from the idealized West who is living in the much more compromised and complicated modern West." Tost's comments in his 2015 interview suggest that creators of this series consciously use Longmire's classical references to help characterize him, perhaps somewhat counter-intuitively, as a typical Western hero—one whose heroic qualities are needed to promote justice, progress, and the taming of the West, but who at the same time is estranged from full participation in the society he protects by these same traits.
47. *Longmire*, Season 2, episodes 2 and 3 respectively. A reference to Aeschylus in Season 6 episode 1 by Walt's Cheyenne friend Henry Standing Bear (Lou Diamond Phillips) seems to complicate the function of classical allusions to strengthen the "us vs. them" division between whites and Native Americans, since of the show's characters, Henry alone shares in Walt's classical knowledge. Yet throughout the series, Henry is a loyal friend and ally to Walt, and while he serves as an intermediary between white "American" society and the native community, he does so as one who understands the inevitable trajectory of white progress.
48. *Longmire*, Season 2 episode 12.
49. This ancient Greek maxim, according to Pausanias 10.24.1, was the first of three inscribed in the forecourt of the Temple of Apollo at Delphi.
50. George Hearst was a mining magnate and U.S. Senator, both of which roles are reflected in his *Deadwood* counterpart, while his son William Randolph Hearst was a media giant who was also elected to the U.S. House of Representatives.
51. *Hell On Wheels*, Season 5 episode 3. On a related note, this episode, entitled "White Justice," highlights racial inequities in the early U.S.
52. Inaccurate references in other Westerns, too, might likewise hint at these flimsy foundations, as with Augustus McCrae's misquote, Judge Mettrick's chronological error (see FN26), or Hugo Jarry's inappropriately applied analogies.
53. The former quotation can be found in section 4 of "On Tranquility of Mind" from the *Moralia*, and the latter is recounted in a letter from Alexander to his tutor Aristotle in *Life of Alexander* (VII.7). Also notable is the presence of two Plutarch-related books (*Plutarch's Historical Methods* and *Plutarch and Rome*) among those on William's bedside table in episode 9 of Season 2.
54. See Estelle Tang's "8 Things You Missed in Tonight's Episode of Westworld." The series hints at

William's lack of self-knowledge in the earlier scene, where Ford's discussion of identity issues was intercut with scenes of the young William's first meeting with Dolores.

55. Season 3 of *Westworld* did not appear in time to take it into consideration in this article.

56. There is considerably more to say about classical allusions in *Westworld*, as is clear from the series' anchoring in Michael Crichton's 1973 film, which paired Westworld with two other parks, one of which was Romanworld; the ownership of Westworld in both productions by the Delos Corporation; and the HBO series' use of the classically-named Hector (a reference first to the Trojan hero of Homer *Iliad*) Eschaton (a Greek word meaning "utmost, extreme," but now having come to denote "the final event in a divine plan").

57. See Rebecca Futo Kennedy's "We Condone It By Our Silence: Confronting Classics' Complicity in White Supremacy."

58. See for example Kwame Anthony Appiah's "There is No Such Thing as Western Civilisation."

59. As does John Ford in works like *Fort Apache* (1948), *The Man Who Shot Liberty Valance* (1962), and *Cheyenne Autumn* (1964), and Delmer Daves in his 1950 *Broken Arrow*. See, for example, Douglas Pye's "Genre and History: *Fort Apache* and *The Man Who Shot Liberty Valance*."

60. For a discussion of this in Ford's 1956 *The Searchers* as an example, see Kirsten Day's "'What Makes a Man to Wander?': *The Searchers* as a Western *Odyssey*" (2008), 43, and *Cowboy Classics: The Roots of the American Western in the Epic Tradition* (2016), 159–160.

61. The Greco-Roman past is still, unfortunately, being drawn on by the alt-right and white nationalist groups to promote a supremacist agenda (see, for example, Donna Zuckerberg's "How to Be a Good Classicist Under a Bad Emperor," Johanna Hanink's "The American Alt-Right 'Loves the Greeks,'" and Denise Eileen McCoskey's "What Would James Baldwin Do?: Classics and the Dream of White Europe").

62. See again Kwame Anthony Appiah's "There is No Such Thing as Western Civilisation."

Filmography

Broken Arrow. Dir. Delmer Daves. 20th Century Fox Film Corporation, 1950.
Cheyenne Autumn. Dir. John Ford. Warner Bros., Ford-Smith Productions, 1964.
Damnation. Creator Tony Tost. USA, 2017.
Deadwood. Creator David Milch. HBO, 2004–2006.
Deadwood: The Movie. Dir. Daniel Minahan. HBO Films, 2019.
Fort Apache. Dir. John Ford. Argosy Pictures, 1948.
Godless. Creator Scott Frank. Netflix, 2017.
Hell on Wheels. Creators Joe Gayton, Tony Gayton. AMC, 2011–2016.
High Noon. Dir. Fred Zinnemann. Stanley Kramer Productions, 1952.
Hondo. Dir. John Farrow. Warner Bros., Wayne-Fellows Productions, Batjac Productions, 1953.
Justified. Creator Graham Yost. FX Productions, Sony Pictures Television, 2010–2015.
Lonesome Dove. Dir. Simon Wincer. Motown Productions, Pangaea, Quintex Entertainment, 1989.
Longmire. Creators Hunt Baldwin and John Coveny. A&E Television Networks, Netflix, 2012–2017.
The Man Who Shot Liberty Valance. Dir. John Ford. Paramount Pictures, 1962.
Rio Grande. Dir. John Ford. Republic Pictures (I), Argosy Pictures, 1950.
The Searchers. Dir. John Ford. C.V. Whitney Pictures, 1956.
Seven Brides for Seven Brothers. Dir. Stanley Donan. Metro-Goldwyn-Mayer, 1954.
Stagecoach. Dir. John Ford. Walter Wanger Productions, 1939.
Tombstone. Dir. George P. Cosmatos. Cinergi Pictures Entertainment, Hollywood Pictures, 1993.
True Grit. Dir. Henry Hathaway. Paramount Pictures, Hal Wallis Productions, 1969.
True Grit. Dirs. Ethan and Joel Coen. Paramount Pictures, Skydance Productions, Scott Rudin Productions, 2010.
The Virginian. Dir. Victor Fleming. Paramount Pictures, 1929.
Westworld. Dir. Michael Crichton. Metro-Goldwyn-Mayer, 1973.
Westworld. Creators Jonathan Nolan and Lisa Joy. HBO, 2016 - ongoing.
Will Penny. Dir. Tom Gries. Paramount Pictures, 1967.
Zorro's Black Whip. Dir. Spencer (Gordon) Bennet and Wallace Grissell. Republic Pictures (I), 1944.

Works Cited

Appiah, Kwame Anthony. "There is No Such Thing as Western Civilisation." *The Guardian*, November 9, 2016. At https://www.theguardian.com/world/2016/nov/09/western-civilisation-appiah-reith-lecture.
Bakewell, Geoffrey W. "Oedipus Tex: *Lone Star*, Tragedy, and Postmodernism," *Classical and Modern Literature* Vol. 22, No.1 (2002): 35–48.

Benét, Stephen Vincent. "The Sobbin' Women." In *Thirteen O'Clock: Stories of Several Worlds*, 138–61. Farrar & Rinehart: New York, 1937.
Blundell, Mary Whitlock and Kirk Ormand. "Western Values, or the Peoples Homer: *Unforgiven* as a Reading of the *Iliad*." *Poetics Today* Vol. 18, No. 4 (1997): 533–69.
Cawelti, John G. *The Six-Gun Mystique*. Bowling Green, OH: Bowling Green University Popular Press, 1971.
Clauss, James J. "Descent into Hell: Mythic Paradigms in *The Searchers*." *Journal of Popular Film and Television* Vol. 27, No. 3 (1999): 2–17.
Cunningham, John M. "The Tin Star." *Collier's* Vol. 11 (December 6, 1947): 64–73.
Cyrino, Monica S. "Ricochets off the Frontier: Classical Allusion in HBO's *Deadwood* (2004–06)." Classical Association Annual Conference: Nottingham, April 15, 2014.
Day, Kirsten. "'All That Glitters…': Problematising Golden Age Narratives in Virgil's *Aeneid* and Western Film." In Meredith Safran, ed. *Screening the Golden Ages of the Classical* Tradition, 157–74. Edinburgh: Edinburgh University Press, 2018.
_____. *Cowboy Classics: The Roots of the American Western in the Epic Tradition*. Edinburgh University Press: Edinburgh, 2016.
_____. "'What Makes a Man to Wander?': *The Searchers* as a Western *Odyssey*." *Arethusa* Vol. 41 No. 1 (2008): 11–49.
Fenin, George N., and William K. Everson. *The Western: From Silents to the Seventies*. New York: Grossman Publishers, 1973.
Fletcher, Judith. "The *Catabasis* of Mattie Ross in the Coens' *True Grit*." *Classical World* Vol. 107, No. 2 (2014): 237–54.
Frankel, Glenn. The Searchers: *The Making of an American Legend*. New York: Bloomsbury, 2013.
French, Peter A. *Cowboy Metaphysics: Ethics and Death in Westerns*. Lanham, MD: Rowman & Littlefield Publishers, Inc., 1997.
Hanink, Johanna. "The American Alt-Right 'Loves the Greeks.'" *Political Critique* July 11, 2017. At http://politicalcritique.org/world/2017/american-right-and-trump-loves-the-greeks/.
Hesiod. *Theogony, Works and Days, Testimonia*, Glenn W. Most, ed. and trans. Loeb Classical Library/Harvard University Press, 2006.
Horne, Abigail. "The Color of Manhood: Reconsidering Pompey in John Ford's *The Man Who Shot Liberty Valance*." *Black Camera* Vol. 4, No.1 (2012): 5–27.
Howe, Daniel Walker "Classical Education in America." *The Wilson Quarterly* 2011. www.wilsonquarterly.com/quarterly/spring-2011-the-city-bounces-back-four-portraits/classical-education-in-america/: accessed 9/19/2017.
Iblings, Jeff. "*Damnation* Creator Tony Tost on his Rise in Television (Interview)." In *The Tracking Board: Hollywood's Insider Information*. February 21, 2018. At http://www.tracking-board.com/damnation-creator-tony-tost-on-his-rise-in-television-interview/.
Johnson, Dorothy M. "The Man Who Shot Liberty Valance." In *The Man Who Shot Liberty Valance, and A Man Called Horse, Lost Sister, The Hanging Tree*, 25–49. Helena, MT: Riverbend Publishing, 1953.
Kennedy, Rebecca Futo. "We Condone It By Our Silence: Confronting Classics' Complicity in White Supremacy." *Eidolon* May 11, 2017. https://eidolon.pub/we-condone-it-by-our-silence-bea76fb59b21.
Kopff, E. Christian. *The Devil Knows Latin: Why America Needs the Classical Tradition*. Wilmington, DE: Intercollegiate Studies Institute Books, 1999.
L'Amour, Louis. "The Gift of Cochise." *Collier's* (July 5, 1952): 28–29, 41, 44–47.
Mast, Gerald. *Howard Hawks, Storyteller*. New York: Oxford University Press, 1982.
McCoskey, Denise Eileen. "What Would James Baldwin Do?: Classics and the Dream of White Europe." *Eidolon* August 24, 2017. At https://eidolon.pub/what-would-james-baldwin-do-a778947c04d5.
McDonough, Christopher M. "Ancient Allusions and Modern Anxieties in *Seven Brides for Seven Brothers* (1954)." In Monica S. Cyrino, ed. *Screening Love and Sex in the Ancient World*, 99–110. New York: Palgrave McMillan, 2013.
McMurtry, Larry. *Lonesome Dove*. New York: Simon & Schuster, 1985.
Myrsiades, Kostas. "Reading *The Gunfighter* as Homeric Epic." *College Literature* Vol. 34, No. 2 (2007): 279–300.
Parks, Rita. *The Western Hero in Film and Television: Mass Media Mythology*. Ann Arbor, MI: UMI Research Press, 1982.
Plutarch. "Romulus." In Jeffrey Henderson, ed.; Bernadotte Perrin, trans. *Plutarch's Lives*. Vol. 1. Loeb Classical Library/Harvard University Press, 2005 [1914].
Portis, Charles. *True Grit*. The Overlook Press: New York, 2004 [1968].
Pye, Douglas. "Genre and History: *Fort Apache* and *The Man Who Shot Liberty Valance*." In Ian Cameron and Douglas Pye, eds. *The Book of Westerns*, 111–22. New York: Continuum Publishing Company, 1996.
Reeder, Roberta. "The Mythic Mode: Archetypal Criticism and *Red River*." *Ciné-tracts* Vol. 3, No. 2 (1980): 58–67.
Rubino, Carl A. "Wounds That Will Not Heal: Heroism and Innocence in *Shane* and the *Iliad*." *Dialogue: The Interdisciplinary Journal of Popular Culture and Pedagogy* Vol. 1, No. 1 (2014). At *journaldialogue.org*.

Suetonius. "The Deified Julius." In T.E. Page, E. Capps, L.A. Post, et al, eds.; J.C. Rolfe, trans. *Lives of the Caesars*. Vol. 1. Loeb Classical Library/Harvard University Press, 1964 [1913].

Tang, Estelle. "8 Things You Missed in Tonight's Episode of Westworld," *Elle*, June 17, 2018, https://www.elle.com/culture/movies-tv/a21572917/westworld-season-2-episode-9-recap/: accessed 7 Aug. 2018.

Tanner, Karen Holliday. *Doc Holliday: A Family Portrait*. University of Oklahoma Press, Norman, 1998.

Tost, Tony. Personal interview (via email: 9/5/2015).

Warfield, Nancy. "*The Man Who Shot Liberty Valance*: A Study of John Ford's Film." *The Little Film Gazette of N.D. W.* Vol. 6, No. 1 (August 1975).

Warshow, Robert. "Movie Chronicle: The Westerner," *Partisan Review* Vol. 21, No. 2 (1954): 190–203.

Winkler, Martin M. "Classical Mythology and the Western Film." *Comparative Literature Studies* Vol. 22, No. 4 (1985): 516–40.

_____. "Homeric *kleos* and the Western Film." *Syllecta Classica* 7 (1996): 43–54.

_____. "Homer's *Iliad* and John Ford's *The Searchers*." In A.M. Eckstein and P. Lehman, eds. The Searchers: *Essays and Reflections on John Ford's Classic Western*, 145–70. Detroit: Wayne State University Press, 2004.

_____. "Tragic Features in John Ford's *The Searchers*." In Martin M. Winkler, ed. *Classical Myth and Culture in the Cinema*, 118–47. Oxford: Oxford University Press, 2001.

Wister, Owen. *The Virginian: A Horseman of the Plains*. New York: Macmillan, 1902.

Zuckerberg, Donna. "How to Be a Good Classicist Under a Bad Emperor." *Eidolon* November 21, 2016. At https://eidolon.pub/how-to-be-a-good-classicist-under-a-bad-emperor-6b848df6e54a.

Aristotle and the Wild West
The Western as a Rhetorical Device

Chris Yogerst

Westerns are often about more than just the Wild West. The frontier narrative has long served as an open canvas for critiques of historical and contemporary issues, being a perfect conduit for entertainment to channel social, political, and cultural debates. Westerns comment on the passage of time from one influential era to another as seen in *The Man Who Shot Liberty Valance* (1962) and *The Shootist* (1976). The genre has also been a playground for more divisive topics such as the Hollywood Blacklist in *High Noon* (1952). The ambiguities that the frontier, even as an allegorical setting, provide nurture political debate and encourage intellectual contemplation beyond any single film's narrative. Although Stanley Kramer, the film's uncredited producer, felt that no one recognized *High Noon* as a blacklist allegory at the time of its release,[1] today Glenn Frankel finds the film's politics "almost illegible."[2] Other films, like *The Wild Bunch* (1969), consider the philosophical nature of violence. Discussing *The Wild Bunch*, Cordell Strug evokes Plato's *Republic* to remind the reader how "the mind takes for itself the right to judge any and all forms of human activity because any and all of those forms have an effect on the general tone of human life."[3] Peckinpah's masterpiece makes it difficult to take sides with the protagonists and antagonists (are ever there any good guys?) for the purpose of considering larger themes such as the end of the Wild West, gang loyalty, aging, patriotism, and the morality of violence.

Because of their applicability, Westerns act as rhetorical devices according to the ancient spirit of Aristotle. This essay explores how the Western genre houses Aristotle's brand of reasoning seen in *The Art of Rhetoric*, a proof-centered and pertinent view of rhetoric that has been described as "both pragmatic and scientific," because it works as a "public art for resolving practical issues in the political and judicial arenas."[4] Acting as a counterpart to Plato's dialectic and hoping "to distinguish rhetoric from sophistry and groundless persuasion,"[5] Aristotle's rhetorical argumentation rests on the convincing aspects of a given issue, using commonly-held opinions as premises, since people have a natural disposition for the true.[6] As Aristotle points out, a rhetorician is always able to see what is persuasive,[7] and rhetoric is the ability to see what is possibly persuasive in every given case.[8] The possibilities of persuasive rhetoric are limitless. There are also no limits to what a storyteller can do with the Wild West—whether the story is set in the traditional frontier narrative of John Ford's *Stagecoach* (1939) or houses the futuristic wish fulfillment of Michael Crichton's *Westworld* (1973, 2016). On screen, Westerns offer their viewers rhetorical syllogisms. Their powerful, specific, deductive arguments demonstrate Aristotle's dictum about persuasion that takes place before a public audience is *not only* a matter of arguments and proofs, but also one of credibility and emotional attitudes.

Westerns and Rhetoric

Individual Westerns take on large ideas. They question the nature of heroism (*Unforgiven*, 1992), political witch-hunting (*Johnny Guitar*, 1954), gender roles on the frontier (*The Furies*, 1950), race on the frontier (*Django Unchained*, 2012), and the treatment of Native Americans (*Dead Man*, 1995). David Lusted points out that the genre combines "generic and cultural sources to organize its meaning visually."[9] Popular culture historian John Cawelti remarks that "though we need to understand the Western in terms of its expression of American myths, it was first and foremost a kind of story."[10] Cawelti observes that it is story and *mythos* that have created the Wild West. Aptly, each historical Wild West figure, from Wild Bill to Calamity Jane, that has been represented and mythologized in Western films, acts as a persuasive aspect of the genre. Indeed, there are few narratives more steeped in rhetoric and mythology than those of the Wild West, for the Western's "[m]yth expresses ideology in narrative, rather than discursive or argumentative, structure."[11] The Western's approach to storytelling certainly accords well with Aristotle's application of rhetoric. As Aristotle remarks, the function of rhetoric "is not persuasion. It is rather the detection of the persuasive aspects of each matter."[12]

In short, rhetoric is a way of testing ideas. As James A. Herrick notes, rhetoric has six functions: (1) ideas are tested, (2) advocacy is assisted, (3) power is distributed, (4) facts are discovered, (5) knowledge is shaped, and (6) communities are built.[13] Westerns test ideas as they are played out via the mythology of the Wild West on screen. In his seminal genre study *Horizons West*, Jim Kitses observes that "[t]he centrality of the Western myth, its quintessential American character, the appeal and challenge of articulating its codes, characters and settings, its popularity and commercial viability, the outdoor out-West adventure of its productions—these are the factors that made the genre so attractive to both veterans and newcomers."[14] The accessibility of Aristotelean thought in the Western can be seen in Kitses' analysis of the binary conflict between wilderness and civilization in the West.[15] These conflicts in Westerns, of the individual vs. the community, nature vs. culture, and the West vs. the East, create a never-ending dialogue within in the genre itself. For example, Kitses' understanding of the West can be seen in John Ford's *The Searchers* (1956). After Indians raid his brother's home and kill most of his family, Ethan Edwards (John Wayne) sets off to find his kidnapped niece. The conflict that occurs between Ethan, the individualist, loner/gunfighter and Martin Pawley (Jeffery Hunter), the passive collectivist, demonstrates the tension between the individual and the community. One man (Ethan) can save the community but cannot thrive within it while another man (Martin) cannot save the community but is more comfortable within its confines. Their dynamic represents the ultimate divide between wilderness and civilization. Ethan, at home in the wilderness, is effective. Martin, at home in the civilized community, is not. Because each man functions as an opposite pole in the Western's dialectic, the two characters have difficulty communicating. Their interaction, however, offers what Aristotle would recognize as being among "the strongest of rhetorical proofs ... a kind of syllogism."[16] Based on signs (*semeia*) rather than actual facts, meaning is produced by the tension created by these characters when Debbie is returned home. As sure as the turning of the earth, the film's alpha and omega coalesce: at the film's end, Martin re-enters civilization where he was introduced; Ethan remains in the wilderness from which he emerged. Those in the audience are asked to complete the film's truncated syllogism that men who wander in the West are unable to find their way home, because they simply do not belong there.

Types of Rhetorical Speech

Many Westerns feature given rhetorical situations (directly or indirectly) via Aristotle's delineations of rhetorical speech. In particular, three categories of Aristotle's rhetorical speech, deliberative, display, and litigation, are often found in the Western. These types of rhetorical speech contribute to the genre's reasoning in what Lloyd Bitzer terms a "rhetorical situation," wherein a given event calls for a specific discourse.[17]

Deliberative

According to Aristotle, deliberative rhetoric deals with advantage or harm in terms of urging something to be more advantageous or less harmful.[18] The subjects of deliberative oratory include those of revenue, war and peace, defense of the realm, imports/exports, and legislation.

For example, defense of the realm is a deliberative goal that requires "the speaker must not be unaware of how the city is defended."[19] According to Aristotle, when speaking for the defense of the realm, it is essential to be mindful of the security of the city as well as its strengths and weaknesses. Defending a way of life, which is often the goal of progress or civilization, is a central theme of the Western. Films like *The Man Who Shot Liberty Valance* (1962), *High Plains Drifter* (1973), *Unforgiven* (1991), and *Tombstone* (1993) all deal with defending a town in different ways. *The Man Who Shot Liberty Valance*, which will be discussed later in this essay, argues that necessary violence must be waged in order to solidify respect for law and order. In this film, civil behavior on the frontier is possible only after the outlaw is killed. In *High Plains Drifter*, a town hires a gunfighter to defend it against three outlaws, only to discover the gunfighter is a previous resident of that town and is seeking revenge. *Unforgiven* features bounty hunters looking for men who abuse hookers in the town of Big Whiskey, and in the process, they must kill the town's corrupt sheriff. *Tombstone* presents the legend of Wyatt Earp and Doc Holiday as the gunmen clean up a gang called The Cowboys in the town.

The goal of deliberative oratory is happiness, which is defined as "virtuous welfare or self-sufficiency in life or the pleasantest secure life or material and physical well-being accompanied by the capacity to safeguard or procure the same."[20] Many frontier narratives also share the same emphasis as Aristotle's deliberative rhetoric, such as an emphasis on the virtue of "size, beauty, strength, and competitive capacity."[21] In addition, Aristotle points to the fact that "elements of wealth are abundance of money and land" in addition to goods and security, as well as good reputation, honor, and health.[22] Families in the Wild West, be they presented on a homestead or as a group of outlaws, depend on strictures of appearance, power, and aggression. The homesteaders in *Shane* (1953), for example, want to retain their health and honor (happiness), but do not have the ability (aggressiveness) to fend off the violent ranchers. This is why the title character, Shane (Alan Ladd), is needed to protect the integrity of the Starrett family and, by proxy, the entire neighboring town. When cattle rancher Rufus Ryker (Emile Meyer) fails to buy the land he desires, Ryker hires a notorious gunfighter, Jack Wilson (Jack Palance), to intimidate the landowners and persuade them to leave their homesteads. When this strong-arm tactic does not work, Shane takes down Wilson himself. In this instance of necessary violence, the Starretts need Shane's aggressive nature to defend their right to their land during a period when lawful obedience was never assumed.

Frontier characters often represent the many layers of deliberative rhetoric that form an argument for good living. The objectives of this rhetoric used by proponents for Manifest Destiny throughout the Western canon are those espoused by Aristotle—being justice, courage, restraint, magnanimity, and splendor—all of which the philosopher describes as "virtues of the soul."[23] In *The Man Who Shot Liberty Valance,* Tom Doniphon (John Wayne) presents the benefit of strength as his salient characteristic, while Ransom Stoddard (Jimmy Stewart) embodies the benefits of security such as reputation, honor, and health. Again, violence is necessary to achieve the goals of this film's rhetoric. Stoddard needs Doniphon to set the new standard by killing the town's threat to progress, Liberty Valance (Lee Marvin). Stoddard, high-minded and self-controlled, represents half of the necessary deliberative traits to successfully argue for good living in Shinbone, while Doniphon, brave and just, embodies the other half of this conversation in the Wild West. These goals accord with the possibilities of Western rhetoric outlined in Kitses' dialectical conflict between wilderness and civilization.

As Kitses notes, "genres prevail because they create dramatic and archetypal situations peopled by diverse human character types enacted by stars who have achieved the status of legitimate fantasy figures."[24] The mythological status of many of the Wild West's real-life characters—Buffalo Bill, Billy the Kid, Wyatt Earp, and Doc Holliday—are represented on the big screen by larger than life stars who each embody a similar mythological status of their own. Aptly, as an actor, John Wayne also holds a place in the Western *mythos* that is as strong if not stronger than many of the actual people of Wild West. The iconic image of Wayne's first long zoom introducing him as the hero of *Stagecoach*, the closing shot of Wayne walking away from the homestead in *The Searchers* (1956), and his physical size and swagger transmit the rugged individual integrity associated with the frontier era.

Rugged individualism is also an important element of the Western's deliberative rhetoric, particularly throughout 1950s barring of film industry workers who had (or were perceived to have) connections with American communists. Although McCarthy did not involve himself in the Hollywood hearings (that was a house committee), the Red Scare had taken root around the country and forced many to pledge allegiance to the United States or else face the consequences of a blacklist. Some Western films focus on a town wrongly accusing an individual. In the case of *Johnny Guitar* (1954), a saloon owner, Vienna (Joan Crawford), is charged with a murder that she did not commit. In *Johnny Guitar*, the town falls victim to groupthink, forms a lynch mob, and goes after Vienna in frenzied fashion. Released during the shadow of the House Un-American Activities Committee hearings in Hollywood, *Johnny Guitar* turns "the paradigmatic Western conflict between individual and community into an anti–McCarthyist allegory."[25] *The Ox-Bow Incident* (1943) focuses on groupthink with a less political premise but also postulates its problems with courage and justice filtered through an unreliable and emotionally reactive body of people. The film, based on the novel by Walter Van Tilburg Clark, features a lynch mob that rushes to judge three men suspected of killing a local farmer. All of Aristotle's goals are tested in this film—friendships are tense, health is threatened, happiness is debated, courage is misplaced. When news of the murder of Larry Kinkaid makes its way through town, a group of townspeople hastily form a posse and set out for the killers—going against the orders of a local judge to return the men for trial. When the group finds three men sleeping near cattle assumed to have been stolen from Kinkaid, the mob swiftly acts as judge, jury, and soon-to-be executioner. Though Donald Martin (Dana Andrews) tells the group the cattle were purchased from Kinkaid who knew nothing of a murder, guilt is assumed when no bill of sale is provided.

The setting of *The Ox-Bow Incident* is that of "a wasteland of ignorance, intolerance, and hysteria that the most eloquent Western heroes cannot control."[26] This Wild West is a world in desperate need of Aristotle's rhetorical reasoning, which would help the lynch mob understand the moral implications of a death sentence without trial. After the decision to hang the men is made, debates begin about the certainty of their decision. Knowing the unjust actions would commence, Martin writes a letter to his wife to be delivered by Davies (Harry Davenport). The thoughtful reflection in Martin's last letter to his wife serves as a stark contrast to the vengeful actions and ignorant rhetoric of the posse hell-bent on frontier justice.

This type of mob mentality which was prevalent in the 1950s corresponds to Aristotle's display rhetoric, especially in terms of arguing the validity of the growing concern over the threat of communism in America. Many of the conflicts in the cinematic West express a culture clash between civilization and wilderness (as outlined in Kitses' binary) which serves as a setting for a wide range of characters and personalities embodying the opposing sides of Aristotle's views on nobility and virtue. *The Ox-Bow Incident* offers a clear clash of savagery and humanity, self-interest and social responsibility. The savage decision to hang three men without due process satisfies immediate self-interest but shows a lack of humanity and oversight of social responsibility. When the posse gets news that Kinkaid was not killed and his shooters were found, the guilt of their rushed judgment sets in.

Display

Aristotle's display rhetoric (adopted by the Western) is concerned with nobility and its virtues. Nobility, for Aristotle, is "that which is praiseworthy through being intrinsically eligible or what, being good, is also pleasant, because it is good."[27] In films like *Rio Bravo* (1959) and *True Grit* (1969), iconic Western heroes, played by John Wayne, put their lives on the line for something larger than themselves—they do what's right. Western heroes are often fundamentally good, as the "good" corresponds with progress and justice on the frontier. Indeed, the West's perspective of justice is that of Aristotle, being "the virtue through which each group of men retain their own things, in conformity with the law, injustice being the vice through which they have those of others, in defiance of the law."[28] John T. Chance (*Rio Bravo*) and Rooster Cogburn (*True Grit*) both work as lawmen who seek justice to prevent further injustice. Chance, a lawman near retirement, stays in town to protect against the intimidation of outlaws who are hoping to break one of their men out of jail. The town's sheriff, Dude (Dean Martin), is a drunk and unable to serve in any capacity. Chance, who has a history with Dude, knows that the right thing to do is to stay and help the town retain law and Dude overcome his struggle. Privileging justice over injustice, or the lack of fairness, Chance helps keep law and order in a town that may lose rightness without the suitable powers in place.

Similarly, Cogburn puts his life on the line so that young Mattie Ross (Kim Darby) can see justice for her father's killer, Ned Pepper (Robert Duvall). Without Cogburn, the murder may go without response and thus perpetuate the lawlessness of the frontier. Mattie is young but not incapable of organizing justice for her father. Hearing that Coburn is the toughest Marshal of them all, Mattie hires him and takes off after the Pepper gang. Coburn would prefer to hunt Pepper on his own but recognizes Mattie's drive to help and reluctantly allows her to tag along. Cogburn realizes that while Mattie will also need protection in the wilderness, it is more important to allow her the satisfaction of playing a role in avenging her father's murder. Both films feature central figures, each played by John Wayne, that embody nobility that is virtue in the Aristotelian sense.

On the other hand, courage and cowardice can be found throughout the Western as well. "Courage," according to Aristotle, "is the virtue by which men are productive of noble actions amid danger, as custom ordains and while obedient to the laws, cowardice being the opposite."[29] The fundamental struggle of a film like *The Searchers* (1956) is based on such a dynamic. Is it right to go after Debbie (Natalie Wood) after she is kidnapped by Indians? Once you find her, should you kill the Indians who took her? Should you kill her? This is the internal debate going on with Ethan Edwards (John Wayne) throughout the film. Ethan's drive to help his family serves as a virtuous trait; however, his hatred towards Indians proves to be a destructive vice. In this case, Edwards is the courageous hero but also has an internal struggle that represents the struggles inherent in the Western landscape. Caught between a savage nature and sympathy for humanity, Edwards not only seeks to save his surviving family members but also tries to kill the Indians responsible for the act. The two desires collide when Edwards fears that Debbie has been with the Comanche long enough to have become one of them. By the end of the film, it is unclear whether Edwards will save or kill Debbie. However, being the West's hero, he saves her and walks off into the sunset back into the wilderness where he belongs.

Productivity amongst danger is another characteristic awarded the Western hero. *High Noon* (1952), for example, features a marshal (Gary Cooper) who stands his ground without the support of his family or the town that he represents. Aptly, the production of this film took place amidst the second series of House Un-American Activities Committee hearings when *High Noon* writer Carl Foreman was subpoenaed to testify. Because of this, *High Noon* has been long regarded as a highly political Western, being written and released in the tense years of the Hollywood Blacklist. As Glenn Frankel observes, "*High Noon* has become part of the political-journalistic lexicon, a term that connotes a ritualistic confrontation between good and evil in a showdown in which good is often embodied by a solitary person."[30] In 1982, artist Tomasz Sarnecki used the iconic image of Will Kane to symbolize the anti-bureaucratic Solidarity movement in Poland. Will Kane is a useful icon that visualizes Aristotle's display rhetoric which focuses on nobility. Because the history of the film's screenplay suggests it is a liberal allegory about the Hollywood Blacklist and many have nevertheless interpreted it as a more conservative film,[31] Aristotle would surely appreciate the opportunities for debate here. Writing three years after

High Noon's release, film critic Andre Bazin argues that this type of Western is a new "super Western," a type of film "that would be ashamed to be just itself, and looks for some additional interest to justify its existence—an aesthetic, sociological, moral, psychological, political, or erotic interest, in short some quality extrinsic to the genre and which is supposed to enrich it."[32]

The last element of display rhetoric seen in the Western is found in the genre's treatments of courage and restraint. Aristotle notes that courage is "the virtue by which men are productive of noble actions amid danger, as custom ordains and while obedient to the laws" while "restraint is the virtue by which men are so disposed towards bodily pleasures as custom decrees."[33] In *The Man Who Shot Liberty Valance,* the struggle between these two poles is paramount. Ransom Stoddard shows restraint as an Easterner who leaves the comfort of a lawful land in hopes of establishing law in a lawless land. In the West, Stoddard needs Tom Doniphon, a courageous force of will, to properly implant a respect for order through violence. As an aged politician, Stoddard struggles with the fact that in order to become successful in Shinbone, he needed a murderer to position him in a place of power.

Another key element of display rhetoric for Aristotle is prudence, "the virtue of the intellect by which men are able to deliberate … with a view to achieving happiness."[34] Aristotle's definition of prudence perfectly describes Stoddard's thought process about achieving law and order (regardless of how it all actually happened). Stoddard's virtuous intellect is directed towards making a frontier town a safe community where progress can occur. Doniphon, courageous by the standards and laws of the frontier, produces this goal by sacrificing his way of life on the frontier to allow room for the next generations to prevail.

Litigation

The final piece of Aristotle's rhetoric focuses on justice and injustice as well as prosecution and defense in terms of motivations and surrounding conditions. Injustice, for Aristotle, is "voluntary illegal harm."[35] Aristotle encourages us to consider what one hopes to gain and/or avoid when setting out to do wrong, as the context will help clarify the action. Vice and lack of self-control is how Aristotle characterizes injustice, which has seven root causes: chance (cause is indefinite), nature (cause is within and ordered, same outcome either way), compulsion, habit, calculation, anger, or appetite.[36]

Aristotle's root causes of injustice can be seen in many Westerns. Take William Munny (Clint Eastwood) in *Unforgiven* (1992) for example. Munny is a retired gunfighter who performs one last bounty to help his family. The decision to take a job to kill the men who attacked hookers in Big Whiskey was based on both calculation (fueled by the needs of his family) as well as an appetite for killing. Murder is part of Munny's nature, because he can be compulsive, and his actions can be fed by anger (as in his response to the murder of his friend Ned, played by Morgan Freeman). When Munny is asked by a writer how he analyzed his order of shots before commencing fire, Munny replies, "I was lucky in the order, I've always been lucky when it comes to killin' folks." His answer leaves little room for printing a heroic legend as the character is portrayed as a reluctant killer. *Unforgiven*'s ability to engage its viewers with the history of the genre's conventions and their expectations of its protagonists is part of its power, though critics are divided on the film's implications.[37]

Motives for injustice are myriad for Aristotle. Many of them are seen in *Unforgiven*. For example, Aristotle remarks that one may act if the crime is accomplishable without getting caught or if caught there would be no punishment.[38] Munny has a long history of murder that established a reputation for being an impressive marksman and an evasive criminal. Aristotle also says that individuals may act out what are crimes if they "have a possibility of receiving an indulgence."[39] Bounty hunters, like those in *Unforgiven*, are examples of men engaged in a criminal activity for some kind of reward. Injustice may the result if someone "has many friends and if they are rich," espousing the belief that one can get away with a crime.[40] Munny takes the bounty but realizes that Little Bill (Gene Hackman), a corrupt sheriff with many friends, is allowed to act as a lawless lawman and must be taken care of as well. Thus, Little Bill's line, "I don't deserve this," before Munny's response, "Deserve's got nothing to do with it," speaks not to Munny's character as a killer but to the dialogue between justice and injustice in the Wild West.

The Western genre also corresponds directly with Aristotle's conditions regarding those who attempt crime. Aristotle argues that criminals target "those that have what they lack either in respect of necessities or of excess or enjoyment."[41] *The Wild Bunch*, for example, showcases a group of bandits who have made their careers on taking from others what they personally lack. What makes the villains in Sam Peckinpah's films intriguing is that they are presented as protagonists in a film that Paul Seydor asserts "resurrects the epic warrior in the form of the outlaw-hero."[42] Jim Kitses notes that *The Wild Bunch* opens with a scene that shows "men can be animals, that fate is inside us, that evil exists; that posture in the world, her power and menace, owes not a little to the existence of that evil."[43] As such, these Western desperadoes characterize Aristotle's definition of criminality. Juxtaposed with a scene of children setting fire to an anthill, *The Wild Bunch* begins with a bank robbery and its subsequent gunfight. While the implications of these scenes are debatable, they show a commonality between the children's disrespect for the ants' lives and the bandits' lack of respect for the lives of those whose money they are stealing.

Most Westerns accord with Aristotle's thinking regarding justice and injustice regarding the actions of "those who have been wronged by many and may not have been prosecuted," "those who have been slandered or are easy to slander," and "those who have committed many injustices or the same kind of injustice."[44] However, the philosopher's restrictions regarding "those against whom the criminal has the excuse that either their ancestors or themselves or their friends either have done ill or are so intending either to himself or to his ancestors or to those dear to him" complicate the behavior of those in the West,[45] for actions in this category are not sudden, reactionary, or recently paid for. They have a deep history that elicits response. Films like *Cheyenne Autumn* (1964), *Little Big Man* (1970), and *Ulzana's Raid* (1972) focus on the long history of oppression of Native Americans and the lasting impact of violence on the frontier. *Ulzana's Raid*, for example, is the story of a company of soldiers hunting the murderous Apache leader, Ulzana. Cultural conflicts inherent in the Wild West are apparent via the actions of the prejudiced McIntosh (Burt Lancaster) and the Apache guide Ke-Ni-Tay (Jorge Luke). As Andrew Nelson observes, this film is seemingly "out of tune with the liberal sensibilities on display in other Westerns of the period that depict Indian culture" because of its extreme depiction of hatred.[46] Nelson concludes, however, that *Ulzana's Raid* "is less a condemnation of the evils of imperialism than a commentary on the tragic futility of conflict."[47] Throughout, the history of conflict in the West is depicted with forceful imagery; such as the scene where a cavalryman shoots a woman whom he fears is about to be captured by Indians—the implication being that death is better than what is in store for her once the Indians have her. The complexity of the frontier landscape insists that such situations are neither easy to watch nor allow for simple analysis.

More recent Westerns also tackle the rhetoric of justice/injustice in the West, ranging from the television series *Justified* (FX, 2010–2015) to Quentin Tarantino's *Django Unchained* (2012). *Justified* features a morally ambivalent U.S. Marshal who thinks like a classic Westerner (justifying violence in the way Tom Doniphon would) but who lives in a contemporary world where even the "appearance of unnecessary violence is potential ammunition for punishment."[48] The ongoing struggle in the story takes place between U.S. Marshal Raylan Givens (Timothy Olyphant) and Boyd Crowder (Walton Goggins). Givens often acts as the lone law enforcement office willing to skirt the law in order to serve justice. Crowder is a smart criminal and is skilled at manipulating the strictures of law and order (which is why Givens and Crowder understand each other so well). Tarantino's Westerns present the Wild West in that director's unique, hyper violent way, while explaining frontier mythology to new audiences. *Django Unchained* considers the means of providing justice to the enslaved (in a much more literal sense than the usual gunfighter liberating a town from a violent gang) as Django (Jamie Foxx) saves his wife and seeks revenge on their slave masters. Django and his wife were sold into slavery and separated. However, the bounty hunter Dr. King Schultz (Christoph Waltz), who purchases Django, takes him on as a partner. State sanctioned injustice is corrected, as Django is given his freedom for helping Schultz.

The understanding of justice and injustice lies at the heart of every Western, just as it does Aristotle's rhetoric. Quentin Tarantino's *The Hateful Eight* (2015) features a scene that nicely summarizes the dilemma regarding justice/injustice that often occurs in the genre. Oswoldo (Tim Roth), a hangman, tells John Ruth (Kurt Russell) that when a prisoner is convicted of a crime and hung in the town square, civilized society would call the action justice. However, if the relatives of a victim find the killer and murder that person on their own, their action would be called frontier justice. Oswoldo concludes, "Dispassion is the very essence of justice. For justice delivered without dispassion is always in danger of not being justice." Like Aristotle, Oswoldo demonstrates that context is essential towards understanding why one would commit a given act. In the film, the only traditional justice being served is John Ruth (Kurt Russell) bringing fugitive Daisy Domergue (Jennifer Jason Leigh) to meet the consequences of her actions. The other instances of violence in the film, which are many, are deeds of frontier justice. General Sandy Smithers (Bruce Dern) is killed as an act of revenge, an undertaking which creates a ripple effect of vengeful or defensive killings that make up the rest of the film's narrative.

Conclusion

In sync with Aristotle's teachings, the Western is a persuasive genre that contains a setting conducive to the making of arguments and observations about our contemporary world. The genre has shown its power in its most political films. Ranging from *Johnny Guitar* to *Django Unchained*, Westerns, "far from being apolitical and nonhistorical, are myths in the sense of being saturated with ideologies and assumptions" (Durgnat and Simmon 69). Nonetheless, the genre has used its rhetoric to question authority and encourage thinking. Speaking of *The Ballad of Little Jo* (1993) and *Dead Man* (1995), Jim Kitses argues that "what we have here, finally, is an example of post-modernism's inclusiveness, the both/and rather than the either/or, two transcendental Westerns that take different trails (female and male centered), to track the spiritual odyssey of a millennial America, on the move, guided by its people of color."[49] And while early Westerns tended to stereotype Native Americans, later films show a growing trend to expand the frontier narrative and its inclusivity of "the other." In short, the Western changed, becoming more conscious about its own myths and legends of the Wild West. Subsequent decades charted the genre's turn towards the realistic in films like *Cheyenne Autumn*, *The Wild Bunch*, and *Unforgiven*. While some contemporary Westerns do not work to right the wrongs of the past (i.e., by including a previously excluded character), they do complicate the genre. *No Country for Old Men* (2007), for example, does not have a clear hero or villain, instead offering a morally ambiguous protagonist and antagonist that, one may argue, make amoral actions. Llewellyn (Josh Brolin) stumbles upon a drug deal gone wrong and takes the money. Before long Anton Chigurh (Javier Bardem) is sent to collect the cash, regardless of how many bodies pile up in the process. This film is less about a hero/villain binary and more about "the pursuit and possession of money and how [it] affects lives."[50] Drawing from Aristotle, *No Country for Old Men* presents a rhetorical situation to debate the impact of monetary pursuit. The Coen Brothers' remake of *True Grit* (2010), on the other hand, evidences nostalgia for the genre tropes that made the Western a pillar of popular culture. The character dynamics, which audiences familiar with Westerns would quickly recognize, focus on the West's familiar rhetoric. Sue Matheson argues that "throughout their adventures, distinct dialects are at work, delineating and emphasizing their speaker's social differences—Rooster's Bushwhacker patois, the Texan's dime novel rhetoric, and Mattie's use of marketplace dialects and masculine discourse."[51] This nostalgia for the past helps us contextualize the present. Drawing on the past makes for deeper engagements in contemporary frontier narratives. Each film is a means for understanding the larger tradition of the Wild West and its cultural implications.

Aristotle's teachings have been shared for many generations. As the legends and mythology of the Wild West have passed from generation to generation. Americans have found stories similar to Aristotle's told in fresh ways to engage new audiences. *Bone Tomahawk* (2015), for example, stages itself almost identically to *The Searchers*, but replaces the Comanche murder raid and kidnapping with an invasion and abduction by cannibalistic cave dwellers. Merging a classic Western story with contemporary horror tropes opens a door for the genre to continue to introduce Aristotle's modes of rhetoric to the next generation of viewers and may even lead viewers to *The Searchers* and the complexities of Ethan Edwards' heroism and prejudices as well as a deeper, complicated understanding of "the other." Westerns, Aristotle would agree, provide us with skills that are necessary to expand our understanding. Engaging viewers in multilayered interpretations of the world, Hollywood built the rhetoric of the Wild West on Aristotelean reasoning and logic, persuasion, knowledge, and command of thought. Aristotle can help us unpack the printed legend of the Wild West, so we can understand its myths for the syllogisms they are.

Notes

1. "What A Classic '50s Western Can Teach Us About The Hollywood Blacklist," *NPR* (January 30, 2018), https://www.npr.org/2018/01/30/580689793/what-a-classic-50s-western-can-teach-us-about-the-hollywood-blacklist..
2. Glen Frankel, *High Noon: The Hollywood Blacklist and the Making of an American Classic* (New York: Bloomsbury, 2017), 259.
3. Cordell Strug, "*The Wild Bunch* and the Problem of Idealist Aesthetics, or, How Long Would Peckinpah Last in Plato's Republic?" in *Doing it Right: The Best Criticism on Sam Peckinpah's The Wild Bunch.* ed. Michael Bliss (Carbondale: Southern Illinois University Press, 1994), 84.
4. James A. Herrick, *The History and Theory of Rhetoric: An Introduction* (New York: Pearson Education, 2009), 78–79.
5. Aristotle, *The Art of Rhetoric* (New York: Penguin Books, 2004), 66.
6. Herrick, 79.
7. See Aristotle in *Topics* VI.12, 149b25.
8. Aristotle, *The Art of Rhetoric*, 74.
9. David Lusted, *The Western* (Essex: Pearson Education Limited, 2003), 26.
10. John G. Cawelti, *The Six-Gun Mystique Sequel* (Bowling Green, OH: Bowling Green State University Popular Press, 1999), 3.
11. Richard Slotkin, *Gunfighter Nation: The Myth of the Frontier in Twentieth-Century America* (Norman: Oklahoma University Press, 1992), 6.
12. Aristotle. *The Art of Rhetoric*, 70.
13. Herrick, 17.
14. Jim Kitses, *Horizons West: Directing the Western from John Ford to Clint Eastwood* (London: British Film Institute, 2004), 9.
15. *Ibid.*, 12.
16. Aristotle, *The Art of Rhetoric*, 11.
17. Lloyd Bitzer, "The Rhetorical Situation," in *Readings in Rhetorical Criticism*, ed. Carl R. Burgchardt (Stage College: Strata Publishing, 2010), 47.
18. Aristotle, *The Art of Rhetoric*, 81.
19. *Ibid.*, 85.
20. *Ibid.*, 87.
21. *Ibid.*, 88.
22. *Ibid.*, 89.
23. *Ibid.*, 92.
24. Kitses, 20.
25. Peterson, Jennifer, "The Competing Tunes of *Johnny Guitar*: Liberalism, Sexuality, Masquerade," in *The Western Reader*, eds. Jim Kitses and Gregg Rickmann (New York, NY: Limelight Editions, 1998), 321.
26. Lusted, 77.
27. Aristotle, *The Art of Rhetoric*, 105.
28. *Ibid.*
29. *Ibid.*
30. Frankel, 293.
31. Douglas Brode, *Dream West: Politics and Religion in Cowboy Movies* (Austin, TX: The University of Texas Press, 2013), 165.
32. Andre Bazin, "The Evolution of the Western (1955)." In *The Western Reader*, eds. Jim Kitses and Gregg Rickman (New York: Limelight Editions, 1998), 51.
33. Aristotle, *The Art of Rhetoric*, 105.
34. *Ibid.*
35. *Ibid.*, 111.
36. *Ibid.*, 112.
37. Andrew Patrick Nelson, "Revisionism 2.0? *Unforgiven* and the Hollywood Western of the 1990s," in *Contemporary Westerns: Film and Television Since 1990*, ed. Andrew Patrick Nelson (Lanham, MD: Scarecrow Press, 2013), 23.
38. Aristotle, *The Art of Rhetoric*, 120.
39. *Ibid.*, 122.
40. *Ibid.*, 120.
41. *Ibid.*, 122.
42. Paul Seydor, *Peckinpah: The Western Films, a Reconsideration* (Urbana and Chicago: University of Illinois Press, 1997). 189.
43. Jim Kitses, "The Wild Bunch," in *Doing It Right: The Best Criticism on Sam Peckinpah's The Wild Bunch*, ed. Michael Bliss (Carbondale and Edwardsville: Southern Illinois University Press, 1994), 74–75.
44. Aristotle, *The Art of Rhetoric*, 123.

45. *Ibid.*
46. Nelson, "Revisionism 2.0? *Unforgiven* and the Hollywood Western of the 1990s," 90.
47. *Ibid.*, 92.
48. Zinder, Paul, "Osama bin Laden Ain't Here: Justified as 9/11 Western," in *Contemporary Westerns: Film and Television Since 1990*, ed. Andrew Patrick Nelson (Lanham, MD: Scarecrow Press: 2013), 121.
49. Kitses, "Introduction: Post-Modernism and the Western," 29.
50. Siska, William C., "*No Country for Men* and *There Will Be Blood*: Classic Western Values Eclipsed by Modern Capitalism," in *Contemporary Westerns: Film and Television Since 1990*, ed. Andrew Patrick Nelson (Lanham, MD: Scarecrow Press, 2013), 94.
51. Sue Matheson, "The Professional Western Revived: Southern Diaspora, Frontier Heteroglossia, and Audience Nostalgia in *True Grit* (2010)," in *Contemporary Westerns: Film and Television since 1990*, ed. Andrew Patrick Nelson (Lanham, MD: Scarecrow Press, 2013), 82–83.

Filmography

The Ballad of Little Jo. Dir. Maggie Greenwald. Fine Line Features, 1993.
Bone Tomahawk. Dir. S. Craig Zahler. RJL Entertainment, 2015.
Cheyenne Autumn. Dir. John Ford. Warner Bros., 1964.
Dead Man. Dir. Jim Jarmusch. Miramax, 1995.
Django Unchained. Dir. Quentin Tarantino. A Band Apart; Columbia Pictures, 2012.
The Furies. Dir. Anthony Mann. Hal Wallis Productions, 1950.
The Hateful Eight. Dir. Quentin Tarantino. Shiny Penny; FilmColony, 2015.
High Noon. Dir. Fred Zinnemann. Stanley Kramer Productions, 1952.
High Plains Drifter. Dir. Clint Eastwood. The Malpaso Company, 1973.
Johnny Guitar. Dir. Nicholas Ray. Republic Pictures, 1954.
Justified. Creator Graham Yost. FX Productions; Sony Pictures Television, March 16, 2010–April 14, 2015.
Little Big Man. Dir. Arthur Penn. Cinema Center Films, 1970.
The Man Who Shot Liberty Valance. Dir. John Ford. John Ford Productions, 1962.
The Ox-Bow Incident. Dir. William A. Wellman. 20th Century Fox, 1943.
No Country for Old Men. Dirs. Joel and Ethan Coen. Scott Rudin Productions; Mike Zoss Productions, 2007.
Rio Bravo. Dir. Howard Hawks. Warner Bros, 1959.
The Searchers. Dir. John Ford. C.V. Whitney Productions; Warner Bros., 1956.
Shane. Dir. George Stevens. Paramount Pictures, 1953.
The Shootist. Dir. Don Siegel. Paramount Pictures, 1976.
Stagecoach. Dir. John Ford. Walter Wanger Productions, 1939.
Tombstone. Dir. George P. Cosmatos. Hollywood Pictures; Cinergi Pictures, 1993.
True Grit. Dir. Henry Hathaway. Hal B. Wallis Productions, 1969.
True Grit. Dirs. Joel and Ethan Coen. Skydance Productions; Mike Zoss Productions, 2010.
Ulzana's Raid. Dir. Robert Aldrich. Associates and Aldrich Co; De Haven-Aldrich, 1972.
Unforgiven. Dir. Clint Eastwood. Malpaso Productions, 1992.
Westworld. Michael Crichton Metro-Goldwyn-Mayer, 1973.
Westworld. Creators HBO Entertainment; Warner Bros. Television, October 2, 2016–ongoing.
The Wild Bunch. Dir. Sam Peckinpah. Warner Bros.-Seven Arts, 1969.

Works Cited

Aristotle. *The Art of Rhetoric*. New York: Penguin Books, 2004.
_____. "Book VI." In W.A. Pickard-Cambridge, trans. *Topics. The Internet Classics Archive: Topics by Aristotle*. At http://classics.mit.edu/Aristotle/topics.6.vi.html.
Bazin, Andre. "The Evolution of the Western (1955)." In Jim Kitses and Gregg Rickman, eds. *The Western Reader*, 49–56. New York: Limelight Editions, 1998.
Bitzer, Lloyd. "The Rhetorical Situation." In Carl R. Burgchardt, ed. *Readings in Rhetorical Criticism*, 46–55. Stage College: Strata Publishing, 2010.
Brode, Douglas. *Dream West: Politics and Religion in Cowboy Movies*. Austin: The University of Texas Press, 2013.
Cawelti, John G. *The Six-Gun Mystique Sequel*. Bowling Green: Bowling Green State University Popular Press, 1999.
Durgnat, Raymond, and Scott Simmon. "Six Creeds That Won the Western." In Jim Kitses and Gregg Rickman, eds. *The Western Reader*, 69–83. New York: Limelight Editions, 1998.

Frankel, Glenn. *High Noon: The Hollywood Blacklist and the Making of an American Classic.* New York: Bloomsbury, 2017.
Herrick, James A. *The History and Theory of Rhetoric: An Introduction.* New York: Pearson Education, 2009.
Kitses, Jim. *Horizons West: Directing the Western from John Ford to Clint Eastwood.* London: British Film Institute, 2004.
_____. "Introduction: Post-Modernism and the Western." In Jim Kitses and Gregg Rickman. *The Western Reader*, 15–31. New York: Limelight Editions, 1998.
_____. "The Wild Bunch." In Michael Bliss, ed. *Doing It Right: The Best Criticism on Sam Peckinpah's* The Wild Bunch, 74–80. Carbondale and Edwardsville: Southern Illinois University Press, 1994.
Lusted, David. *The Western.* Essex: Pearson Education Limited, 2003.
Matheson, Sue. "The Professional Western Revived: Southern Diaspora, Frontier Heteroglossia, and Audience Nostalgia in *True Grit* (2010)." In Andrew Patrick Nelson, ed. *Contemporary Westerns: Film and Television since 1990*, 77–90. Lanham, MD: Scarecrow Press, 2013.
_____. *The Westerns and War Films of John Ford.* Lanham: Rowman & Littlefield, 2016.
Nelson, Andrew Patrick. "Revisionism 2.0? *Unforgiven* and the Hollywood Western of the 1990s." In Andrew Patrick Nelson, ed. *Contemporary Westerns: Film and Television Since 1990*, 15–30. Lanham, MD: Scarecrow Press, 2013.
Peterson, Jennifer. "The Competing Tunes of Johnny Guitar: Liberalism, Sexuality, Masquerade." In Jim Kitses and Gregg Rickman, eds. *The Western Reader*, 321–39. New York: Limelight Editions, 1998.
Seydor, Paul. *Peckinpah: The Western Films, a Reconsideration.* Urbana and Chicago: University of Illinois Press, 1997.
Zinder, Paul. "Osama bin Laden Ain't Here: *Justified* as 9/11 Western." In Andrew Patrick Nelson, ed. *Contemporary Westerns: Film and Television Since 1990*, 119–34. Lanham, MD: Scarecrow Press, 2013.

Tragic Trails in Indian Country

"Republic. I like the sound of the word. It means people can live free, talk free, go or come, buy or sell, be drunk or sober, however they choose. Some words give you a feeling. Republic is one of those words that makes me tight n the throat—the same tightness a man gets when his baby takes his first step or his first baby saves and makes his first sound as a man. Some words can give you a feeling that makes your heart warm. Republic is one of those words."

—*The Alamo* (John Wayne, 1960)

Chorei, Satyr-Drama, and the Birth of Tragedy in John Ford's *Cheyenne Autumn* (1964)

SUE MATHESON

An under-appreciated Western, John Ford's *Cheyenne Autumn* has been disparaged, respectfully ignored, or defended as being either an historically inaccurate representation or a sentimental account of the Northern Cheyenne Exodus.[1] Richard Oulahan of *Life* magazine labeled *Cheyenne Autumn* "a turkey"; Stanley Kaufman of the *New Republic* described it as a "pallid" version of the best Ford, its cast "beyond disbelief"; and *Newsweek* declared "Ford has apparently forgotten everything he ever knew, about actors, about cameras, about Indians, and about the West."[2] In *Mad Magazine*, Larry Siegel and Mort Drucker satirized the movie as "*Cheyenne Awful*."[3] Released on the 3rd of October 1964, *Cheyenne Autumn* was a box office flop in the United States, carrying a net loss at September 1966 of $5.7 million.[4] Only John Ford thought *Cheyenne Autumn*, "a good story."[5] Mark Haggard, in a letter to the editor of *Newsweek*, found it a "good and competent" film, and Bosley Crowther of *The New York Times* deemed it "a stark and eye-opening symbolization of a shameless tendency that has prevailed in our national life—the tendency to be unjust and heartless to weaker peoples who get in the way of manifest destiny."[6]

Today, *Cheyenne Autumn* is seen as a film "powerful enough to start a real re-examination of popular American history" that paved the way for Ralph Nelson's *Soldier Blue* (1970) and Arthur Penn's *Little Big Man* (1970).[7] Before *Cheyenne Autumn*, news stories and history reminiscences couched the Northern Cheyenne Exodus in melodramatic stereotypes of savages reclaiming their homeland.[8] Ford, who thought the Exodus "a tragic story,"[9] turned his back on the melodramatic value offered by the band of 89 Northern Cheyenne warriors and 246 Northern Cheyenne women and children returning to their homelands near the Great Lakes.[10] Pat Ford's memoranda reveal that his grandfather planned the movie *without* heroes or villains, specifying that the U.S. Army be "an underpaid, undermanned force trying to maintain a virtually impossible peace" and the "Cheyennes are not to be heavies."[11] As McBride remarks, *Cheyenne Autumn* offers the viewer "both sides of the epic."[12] Ford himself reminded Peter Bogdanovich, there "are *two* sides to every story,"[13] and in *Cheyenne Autumn*, there are: the Cheyenne's and the U.S. Cavalry's. Without heroes or heavies, *Cheyenne Autumn* is an Everyman tale. During its preproduction, Ford stipulated that the Cheyenne "serve" as a "Greek Chorus."[14] Notably, its pursuing cavalrymen are another.

According to Heather H. Bacon, "[c]horal participation in dramatic action ranges from mere observation and sympathetic comment to necessary ritual gesture and direct involvement as important or principal actors."[15] The presence of a chorus is not only "a sign of the wider significance of an enacted event," she remarks, "Dramatic choruses [*choreogoi*] should be seen as an integral part of the action, and not, as many modern readers and critics and most theatrical directors tend to see them, as a source of interludes and peripheral lyrical commentary on an action performed by the actor."[16] "Whatever the nature of their participation," she says, "[A]ll dramatic choruses are deeply involved, in the sense that their [members'] attitudes or lives will be permanently affected by the outcome of the action."[17]

Every Cheyenne is deeply affected by his or her participation in the Exodus. Some die; others live to rebuild their culture in their ancestral homeland. Dignified and stately, their flight from Indian Territory is orchestrated as a choral procession (πομπή), expressing itself as a dithyramb in the desert, conveyed in what T.B.L. Webster would recognize as walking or stately time.[18] Harry Carey, Jr., remembers that during the shooting of *Cheyenne Autumn*, Victor Jory, Dolores del Rio, Gilbert Roland, and Ricardo Montalbán marched and marched "across the red sand of Monument Valley. Every so often, one of them would say something as though it were a world-shattering statement, and then they would continue to march, stop, make another announcement, and march, march" (194). Here, Ford's emphasis on the actors' movement again draws our attention to the stage in ancient Greece of which "the kernel or centre of the whole was the orchestra, the circular dancing place of the chorus, and, as the orchestra was the kernel and centre of the theatre, so the chorus, the band of dancing and singing men—this chorus that seems to us so odd and even superfluous—was the center and kernel and starting-point of the drama."[19] Beginning the action, the Cheyenne's *parodos* (entering procession) introduces and establishes the action of the Exodus. Their decision to jump the reservation leads to the action that takes place in Monument Valley. Resembling the circular movement of the ancient chorus, the Cheyenne travel in a huge circle of over 700 improbable miles in what is a *theatron* of the American Southwest.

The Cheyenne's specialized use of languages also borrows heavily from another important feature of classical tragedy. As Ian C. Storey and Arlene Allan point out, the members of a Greek chorus use the normal Attic (Athenian) dialect and their speech is no different from that of the actors when they take part in an episode; when they process into the orchestra, they chant in the usual Attic dialect. But when the ancient chorus performs a standing-song (*stasimon*) or engage in a lyric exchange with a character (*kommos*), its members' language switches to a quasi-Doric dialect, an artificial construct which would have sounded different to the audience. Throughout the Exodus, Ford's Cheyenne use "normal" and "artificial" languages. Archer's (Richard Widmark) voice-over in English at the beginning of the film, which the audience would recognize as "normal," serves as a *lingua franca*. When the Cheyenne engage in song, or converse with one another, or speak in soliloquy, they often use an "artificial" language, which seems to the uninitiated to be Plains Algonquian but is Navajo. English is also used to teach the viewer Cheyenne culture. Spanish Woman is often the mediator in such instances. For example, when Tall Tree sings his death song in his native tongue, Spanish Woman alerts the audience to the content of the elder's song, exclaiming, "No! No!"; when Little Wolf speaks in Navajo to order his "*natani*" into battle,[20] Spanish Woman then explains to Wright in English that the Cheyenne are preparing for war.

These "artificial" and "normal" languages not only distinguish *Cheyenne Autumn*'s social aggregates; they support an ancient protocol that drives the film's narrative. As Bacon remarks, a group speaking with a single voice about an issue of common "is a natural human phenomenon [the alteration between 'I' and 'we'] that occurs in some form in many societies, including our own, as well as in that of ancient Greece."[21] Ford's use of "artificial" and "normal languages" during the Cheyenne's decision to divide itself into two groups highlights this aspect of choral mentality. This sequence begins with its male members speaking heatedly in "Algonquin Plains" and standing in the middle-ground of Ford's wide shot in what have would been the center of the ancient stage that was reserved for actors. In the foreground of the shot, Wright and Spanish Woman, at first unidentifiable in their blankets, act as choral members, being seated at what would be in the *theatron* the edge of the orchestra space, that area of the stage that is closest to the audience. Sitting with their backs to the film's viewers, Wright and Spanish Woman mirror the actual audience members seated behind them.

Deborah Wright (Carroll Baker) and Spanish Woman (Dolores Del Rio) mirror the actual audience members seated behind them. Little Wolf (Ricardo Montalbán, left) and Dull Knife (Gilbert Roland, right) stand before them. *Cheyenne Autumn* **(Warner Bros., 1964).**

Detaching themselves from the actors in the middle ground, Dull Knife and Little Wolf step into the foreground. As they do, their exchange is heated. The dispute in English assimilates the audience into the exchange. Dull Knife addresses Wright who is sheltering a child in her blanket, "Fort Robinson is near here. If we go there…," but is interrupted by Little Wolf who exclaims, "You are saying there is no hope of victory. We will die before we reach our homeland. There was hope in your heart when we started. Where has it gone?" Dull Knife's lyric reply (another choral convention), is also delivered in English: "Maybe the hunger clawing at our bellies has clawed my hope away too." Little Wolf then shows Dull Knife the Sacred Bundle and asks, "Why was I given this? Why?" before stating, "To lead our people home."

As they continue to talk, Little Wolf and Dull Knife transition from being actors in a drama (the thing staged and watched) to participants in an ancient *dromenon* (the thing done).[22] Creating a play-within-a-play on screen, Ford's camera abruptly cuts to a 180-degree point of view shot as Wright interrupts the men's argument, addressing both with the statement, "[i]f we go on, the children will die." In the following point of view shot, Dull Knife leans forward to reply. Doing so, he breaks the fourth wall, also addressing the audience seated in the movie theater. When Wright agrees to speak for the Cheyenne at Fort Robinson, she invites the viewer to support her response. Actors and audience are included in the chorus. When Little Wolf and Dull Knife can no longer agree, this group splits in half. Those who think like the war chief go to the Black Hills of what is now South Dakota; the others *and* the audience follow Dull Knife to Fort Robinson.

The cavalry soldiers who pursue the Cheyenne also function like a composite character, participating in and commenting on the action at hand. Ford uses wide shots to distance the viewer from and encourage contemplation of the cavalry troop and its leader. At times, close tracking shots are used to create a tightly-knit relationship between Archer and his cavalrymen and the audience, including the viewer as the troop moves in pursuit of its prey by blurring barriers that separate the audience from the stage. While the cavalrymen pursue the Cheyenne, the camera rides alongside the blue bellies as the Cavalry's dithyramb proceeds at a much quicker tempo than the Cheyenne's, moving on horseback at what T.B.L. Webster would recognize as a striding or dance time.[23]

Many of *Cheyenne Autumn*'s ironies are produced by the variety of its choruses' overlapping tempos during the cavalry's pursuit of the Cheyenne. Despite the cavalry's quicker tempo, they prove themselves unable to catch the slow-moving women and children before them. The Cheyenne evade Archer and his men, at times using fire to keep the cavalry away and remaining stationary beneath railway trestles, making their pursuers pass by them. Ironically, what prevents the Congressional Committee from meeting with the Cheyenne is its members' need to rest up for the faster pace of the waltzes at the Officers' Ball.

As in ancient drama, in *Cheyenne Autumn* the action of each chorus in the larger political world is essential to its dramatic role. As Bacon observes, in ancient drama, male choruses deal with "questions of political morality, of revolution, of the relationship between the ruler and subject or between citizen and state,"[24] thirled to the masculine. The Cheyenne and the cavalry's shared conditions give them a common interest in questions of revolt and political morality, while each retains its separate identity. The cavalrymen, in particular, are prime examples of shared conditions and individual action. Their uniforms express their commonality. Their professional training, the commonality that welds them into an effective fighting unit, is also immediately established at the start of the film. When the Congressional Committee does not review the Cheyenne's desperate situation, Deborah Wright (Carroll Baker) requests that Maj. Braden (George O'Brien), the commanding officer of the reservation outpost, act outside his orders and "plead for justice." As a professional soldier, Braden refuses to break ranks with his fellows. He replies, "Miss Wright, my responsibility to the Indians is only to guard them. When you have reached my age, you will have realized that it pays to stick to your knitting. That's exactly what I intend to do." Notably, every chorus leader is a professional. Tall Tree, Little Wolf, and Dull Knife who lead the Cheyenne are soldiers from the moment they are born. Braden is a veteran of the Cheyenne Indian Wars. Capt. Thomas Archer (Richard Widmark), another seasoned veteran, acts as his troop's *choryphaeus*, speaking for his constituents' views and taking stands that represent those of his community.

The choral members' individual natures are also emphasized. As Helene Foley remarks, *choreutai* (chorus members) often express opposition to tragic leaders, especially when those leaders are wrong or unjust, noting that the chorus of Ajax criticizes Menelaus.[25] Being servants of the state, Archer, Scott, the Senior First Sergeant (Mike Mazurki), and Capt. Wessels (Karl Malden), support the interests of corporate America and further the annihilation of the Cheyenne whose actions impede the progress of profit. However, Archer's critique of the United States government's policies asserts that in America the moral worth of the individual can make political and social change possible. After the massacre of Dull Knife's band at Fort Robinson, Archer challenges not only the authority of Wessels, the fort's commanding officer, but also that of his divisional commander in Omaha, before traveling to Washington to discuss the plight of the imprisoned Indians with the Secretary of the Interior Carl Schurz (Edward G. Robinson). Archer's disagreements with his superior officers about the treatment of the Cheyenne at Fort Robinson do not signal disrespect, because doing one's "duty" is not a matter of unquestioning obedience on the part of the officer. When making decisions, officers are expected to discriminate between the demands of situations in the field and those thought out before.

In *Cheyenne Autumn*, *choreogoi* and their *choreutai* compete for their viewers' attention, gravitating towards what Foley recognizes as "traditional wisdom even when such wisdom is misapplied or only crudely fits the situation at hand."[26] The Cheyenne's authoritative cultural memory guides them. It ensures that they pray before meeting with "the white chiefs from Washington." When Tall Tree (Victor Jory) chooses Little Wolf to be the group's *choryphaeus*,[27] he gives the younger man the Sacred Bundle, which denotes him being the group's leader. The cavalry also acts in accordance with its own gnomic wisdom. Falling back on well-known military adages, the experienced Archer reminds the younger, hot-headed 2nd Lieutenant Scott (Patrick Wayne) that "[t]he job of this army is to keep the peace" and to remember that "the trick to being brave is not to be too brave."

In ancient drama, female choruses "focus on domestic issues of natural interest to this group or to the female protagonist with whom they are bound by ties of sympathy or friendship; they would be out of line if they took a predominantly political interest in the action."[28] Throughout *Cheyenne Autumn*, there is no female chorus per se. However, it is important to note that the film's gender divisions respect ancient choral protocols. While Ford's male *choreutai* concern themselves with issues of the body politic, the mature women, Deborah Wright, a Quaker schoolteacher who joins the Cheyenne's Exodus, and Spanish Woman (Dolores del Rio), Dull Knife's wife, busy themselves with domestic concerns. Neither Wright nor Spanish Women's interest is the political well-being of the Cheyenne. Wright is particularly concerned about the welfare of the Cheyenne children. Spanish Woman also recognizes the importance of educating and caring for the children. In short, both women symbolize the spirit of their communities while participating in the political reality of the state. Wright and Spanish Woman transmit the emotional response of those who believe in natural justice. Wright's decision to join the Cheyenne in their decision to defy the U.S. government marks the Exodus in the same way that the Mycanean women mark Electra's actions in Sophocles' *Electra*—"as right and just, approved by society and the gods."[29]

Ford's refraction of choral principles in *Cheyenne Autumn* is also found in his presentation of Carl Schurz, the Secretary of the Interior. Demonstrating the American

Character as a progressive force, Schurz, who represents the American government, is yet another *choryphaeus*, being a spokesperson of the American people. Like the "leader of leaders" in Walt Whitman's "By Blue Ontario's Shore," Schurz supports "the idea of perfect and free individuals" comprising the nation,[30] and after hearing Archer's concerns, addresses the portrait of Abraham Lincoln, America's quintessential "leader of leaders," hanging in his office. "Old friend … old friend," he asks, "What would you do?" Directing the viewer to the moral and political dimensions of the Cheyenne's situation, Schurz's face, reflected in the glass protecting the portrait, doubles Lincoln's. *The Battle Hymn of the Republic* playing in the background signals the politician, who is a moral individual, will follow Lincoln's example and unite a divided nation. Accordingly, at the end of *Cheyenne Autumn*, Schurz assures Dull Knife and Little Wolf that "a new tradition" of trust and reconciliation between the Cheyenne and the United States government is possible. Linking the two populations, he promises the Cheyenne that he will tell all the nation's people what happened at Fort Robinson.

According to Joseph McBride, *Cheyenne Autumn's* "Dodge City War" has baffled audiences and reviewers alike.[31] Ford's borrowing from ancient drama, however, points to this sequence, designed to relieve the emotional tension generated by the Exodus, being a Western satyr-drama, At the City Dionysia in ancient Greece, each tragedian concluded the production of his three tragedies with a satyr play that parodied what preceded. In seems that "the Dodge City War's" lampooning of the Western hero and Manifest Destiny, located before the movie's intermission, suffers from being mislaid. In 1964, *Daily Variety* reviewer Whitney Williams found the satirical offering "simply out of place," generating "laughs [that] project no valid reason for their presence."[32] In 2017, Mark Ayala, as puzzled as Williams, thought the sequence its own "intermission." Bewildered when *Cheyenne Autumn* leaves the vastness of the desert to visit a Western town, Ayala finds things go "haywire" in Dodge when "pandemonium erupts" over the fear of the Cheyenne invading the city—"everyone proves to be useless and misdirected," and the sequence ends "with a moment connected to the antics of silent movie comics, complete with a lady's undergarments being exposed."[33]

A comedy of character and values, "the Dodge City War" marks the beginning of a bacchanalia in the Wild West with the arrival of Guinevere Plantagenet (Elizabeth Allen) and her prostitutes in red dresses at the Crystal Saloon, a house of ill repute and high living. There, townsfolk and riders of the range behave like Pratinus' satyrs—drinking, gambling, and consorting with saloon girls. Boasting champagne, slugs of rye, a honky-tonk piano, a lascivious oil painting of an alluring half-naked woman sprawled on a settee, well-dressed banjo players, card games, and a crap table, the saloon caters to every appetite of its patrons, smartly dressed in expensive jackets, respectable ties, and flashy felt hats. In satyr-drama, satyrs, wild and unregulated, intrude on and disrupt a conventional myth. This gives the satyr-play's dramatic action a clear structure.

"The Dodge City War" kids (and corrects) the legend of Wyatt Earp—the Old West lawman and gambler in Cochise County, Arizona Territory, and deputy marshal who cleaned up Tombstone with Bat Masterson and Doc Holliday.[34] As Les Carpenter points out, "Wyatt Earp was a character that only the Wild West could invent—part lawman, part myth—with a saloon-keeper moustache and a taste for the cards … a real live gunslinging hero, shooting those cattle rustling cowboys at the OK Corral … he built his name one boomtown at a time riding out of the dust with a pistol and a past."[35] Earp has long been lauded as good badman, a man of integrity and principle in the Western. Since

Passin' Through (Douglas Fairbanks) curbed his "evil" outlaw ways in Allan Dwan's *The Good Bad-Man* (1916) to help some children,[36] this "courageous, moral, tough, solid and self-sufficient, maverick" with an independent, honorable attitude, has been remarkable for standing alone and facing down anti-social antagonists.[37] Ford's Earp, however, is not an epic figure. Smoking an outsized (and obviously phallic) cigar, he is, as McBride observes, "a mean-spirited egoist."[38] Unable to "protect a lady from an insult," he "can hardly be bothered to look up from his poker game to perform his functions as town marshal."[39]

Sharply contrasted with Little Wolf, Dull Knife, and Archer (who are all intent on saving lives), the aging Earp is interested only in enjoying himself, protecting his income, and saving his own skin. Throughout, Stewart offers "escapist counterbalance, some humor and fun."[40] His diverting banter during the poker game, like that of old Silenus in the satyr play, lightens the tension caused by the Cheyenne's misfortune. Ford's middle-aged crimefighter conveniently claims to be as "blind as a bat" while playing poker—and also hard of hearing, refusing to acknowledge the hysterical Mayor's announcement that the town must arm itself against the marauding Cheyenne. Hilariously, Earp has no problem hearing there are only fifty-one cards in the deck that they riffle despite the noise in the bar. Although he claims to be short-sighted, Earp, like Silenus,[41] is wise. The wily gambler does not trust his fellow gamblers, for the community of satyrs playing poker at the saloon is an anti-community. Because the "friendly game of poker" in which he is engaged is a matter of every man for himself, Earp ensures honesty at the table by carefully placing his burning cigar with its long ash on top of the silver dollars stacked on his cards. When Blaire asks what will happen if the ash falls off the cigar "by mistake" while the marshal is gone, Holliday replies, "Wyatt might shoot you, by mistake." Earp's romantic adventures are also simple matters of gratification—as Guinevere discovers to her dismay, the gambler, driven by the most basic and animalistic part of his personality, is incapable of remembering her face or the scarlet dress she flaunts.

In general, "the Dodge City War's" comic dithyramb is that of a rabble—when this choral ensemble leaves the saloon and the war begins, the sequence's disorganized action, galloping out of control, proceeds at a frenzied tempo. What T.B.L. Webster would recognize as the *choregoi*'s fastest movement[42] overturns the legend of the good badman setting the West to rights. Taking the Mayor's place at the head of the Dodge City Army to defend his gambling interests instead of the lives of the citizens of Dodge City, Wyatt Earp becomes the boom town's *choryphaeus*, a "field marshal" who purposefully leads his "motley army" and the women who "follow the flag" in the wrong direction. His plan of campaign is to flee northeast before "bloodthirsty Cheyenne savages" who are approaching from the southwest. Overturning the popular press's myth of the Cheyenne as white murderers, Earp's unlikely cavalry devolves into mob of drunken louts, shouting "There they are! Indians!," as they chase one lonely Cheyenne warrior who wears a war bonnet and rides a pinto pony. Wanton, impertinent, and insolent, Guinevere Plantagenet loses her skirt when the carriage she is riding in overturns. As the saloon girl runs frantically in her knickers past Earp in his buggy, the *choryphaeus* instructs his partner to "grab" her. When Holliday unceremoniously dumps the Western *maenad* in the buggy at Earp's feet, Earp, with his chin lodged between her ankles, looks up her legs at her bloomers and exclaims, "By golly, I did know her in Wichita." Mocking the action of the Western, the dance of this chorus consists of a fantastic skipping and jumping as horses rocket by the camera and wagons become airborne while cresting ridges before overturning. Notably, the solemn marching of the Cheyenne and the highly organized dithyramb of the pursuing cavalry are replaced by the whooping saloon girl's *sicinnis*, as she first runs, then hops and skips through the desert, losing her shoe (but not her parasol) while chasing the lone Cheyenne warrior with the townsfolk.

Guinevere Plantagenet (Elizabeth Allen) hops through the desert during her *sicinnis*. *Cheyenne Autumn* (Warner Bros., 1964).

Remarkably, the clowning that takes place during "the Dodge City War" does not depend so much on the action itself (as would be the case in comedy) as it does on the relation of the members of the Dodge City army to the war at hand. Like satyrs, theirs is a certain primitive cunning. Driven by the pleasure principle, the Saloon's denizens, intent on satisfying their appetites, go to war carrying their creature comforts. Foaming mugs of beer are served from the bar loaded on a wagon, and the heroic defense of the city, the brainchild of four thirsty trailhands, becomes a rollicking tailgate party on horseback. Instigating fear, the cowboys' leader, Joe (Ken Curtis), uses the choral singular when he announces, "*We* just fought off them murderin' devils southeast of here. *We* showed 'em how a cow eats a cabbage, didn't *we boys*? ... After they killed poor Pete, *we* was like the Lord and the avengin' sword" (italics mine). A concerned group is generated by fake news as the saloon's sophisticated, upscale clientele quickly bond with the Texans.

Like the choral members of Aeschylus' *Suppliants* and Euripides' *Suppliants*, Dodge City's *choreogoi* have as many and varied functions on screen as people would have in real life.[43] Each man's hat, for example, signals his individual nature. At the poker table, Earp wears the headgear of a Southern gentleman. His white, low-crowned, wide-brimmed town hat was the favorite civilian headgear of one of most powerful and civilized of America's men, Confederate General Robert E. Lee. Holliday's stylish brown felt derby also lends him the façade of respectability. He too looks like a refined, upper-class, well-dressed gentleman. Blaire's stovepipe was the most common men's hat of the 19th century, worn by all classes, for any occasion, at any time of the day. Aptly, despite his hat's elegant, imposing, and dramatic appearance, Blaire is no gentleman. A common thief, he is the only man at the poker table to lighten the deck by a card.

The Texans' hats also distinguish their owners. No diamond in the rough, Joe's low character is signaled by the dirty brown felt Open Road Stetson that he wears, and his immature nature is signified by the ornamental, leather saddle stitching around the edge of its brim that resembles the stitching found on children's cowboy hats. Two of his companions sport different versions of the Open Road which are equally filthy. Curiously, it is Joe's wingman who signals his individuality with a Boss of the Plains. Remarkably, the cylindrical crowns of all these hats have not been peaked, suggesting the men never take them off. Fittingly, Joe's wide brim has been curled only on one side—denoting dysfunction. Men who work outside with cattle usually bend up both sides of the brims of their hats so their headgear will not be knocked off when they are swinging a rope, while the front and back of their brims remain flat to shade their eyes and necks.

The cavalrymen's creased crowns, on the other hand, are individually peaked and highly functional. Form following function, the cavalrymen's drab 1889 campaign hats (popular from the closing of the frontier to the Second World War) are Bosses of the Plains, designed to protect their wearers on the frontier.[44] These hats also signal their wearers' individuality. Reflecting their owners' preferences and personalities, some are curled in front, others on the sides. Only one hat indicates dysfunction on the part of its wearer. Like the Boss of one of Frederic Remington's Tenth Cavalry Buffalo soldiers in *A Campfire Sketch* (1889), both Scott's front and back brims are turned up to expose his face and neck to the sun and wind. As Scott's hat suggests, its wearer is not ready to be a Boss. Scott is not only inexperienced, he is also immature. Indeed, when he disobeys Archer's orders, the older, experienced artillery men ask one another, "What is that *kid* doin'?" (italics mine). Scott's ineptitude is a stunning critique of the cavalry legend that began with Custer and his "glorious" 7th Cavalry. In *Regeneration Through Violence: The Mythology of the American Frontier 1600–1860*, Richard Slotkin argues that the structuring metaphor of the frontier psychology of America's recent past and long heritage has been "the myth of regeneration through violence."[45] Notably, in *Cheyenne Autumn*, Scott's ill-advised cavalry charge revitalizes military action belonging in the past. Notably, his actions create the very situation that led to his father's demise and encourage the running gunbattle that is the Exodus to continue.

According to Jane Ellen Harrison, "in the heroic saga, the individual is everything, the mass of the people, the tribe, or the group are but a shadowy background which throws up the brilliant, clear-cut personality into a more vivid light," but in "the old ritual dance," the individual is nothing, "the choral band, the group, everything."[46] As Bacon would agree, Scott's failure proves Plato's observation that choral, not individual, acts give events the coherence and meaning that constitute civilization.[47] Ford emphasizes this truth in what Fujiwara terms *Cheyenne Autumn*'s "most ambiguous scene."[48] On his return to his homeland, Little Wolf (Ricardo Montalbán) re-establishes his personal honor by killing Red Shirt (Sal Mineo). Because of this act, he is stripped of his virtue and sent into exile, for "a war chief of the Cheyenne can only raise his hand against the enemy." Last seen moving along on the horizon into the sunset, Little Wolf is the film's last and most memorable good badman, positioned as the composition's vanishing point in Ford's final one-point perspective. Visually, literally, and metaphorically a "Vanishing American," Little Wolf invites comparison with Nophaie (Richard Dix) in George B. Seitz's *The Vanishing American* (1925), which was shot in Monument Valley. But unlike Nophaie, Little Wolf does not die or assimilate. Ford leaves the war chief suspended on the screen at the film's end, riding not into the sunset but along it—in perpetual exile. Little Wolf's personal εξοδος or *exodus* (exit process), produces the audience's *catharsis* and serves as a curtain closing on the story. It is here, in this personal εξοδος, that tragedy in *Cheyenne Autumn* finally arises, aptly as "Aristotle has told us, from the leaders of the Dithyramb, the leaders of the Spring dance."[49] Exiled, Little Wolf becomes a tragic figure, experiencing his *peripetia* and *anagorisis* at the film's conclusion. Distanced and presented as a mere silhouette, he ends as only a part of the background into which he rides. Ford's last, tragic vision of the individual unable to return H-O-M-E radically revises the stereotype of the indigene in the Western. Remarkably, the war chief, not the cavalryman, rides off into the sunset.

In final analysis, *Cheyenne Autumn's* brilliant return to choral richness complicates and sophisticates the Western. As Harrison observes in *Ancient Art and Ritual*, the Dithyramb, performed in ancient Greece, was "a Spring song, a song of Bull-driving, a song of dance of second Birth ... the Song and Dance of the New Birth."[50] Framed in the frontier's birthing of America, the Northern Cheyenne nation's rebirth, conveying tragedy's "peculiar, incommunicable beauty,"[51] embodies what Nietzsche terms "*the Dionysian spirit* in our modern world."[52] As the Cheyenne are settled and re-settled, ordered and coordinated, the viewer learns that, as in Greek tragedy, "the individual [is] nothing, the choral band, the group, [is] everything."[53] And as *Cheyenne Autumn* demonstrates, the Western's motive power is generated by the individual's conflicted relationship with his or her community. Borrowing from antiquity, *Cheyenne Autumn* breaks new ground as a tragic story *and* a choral Western, critiquing American political, diplomatic, military actions and deceptions while complicating its audience's expectations of the Western. *Cheyenne Autumn* also cautions Americans, raised on legends of frontier heroes, that they, like the ancient Greeks, also are a "race of men, well-fashioned, beautiful, envied, life-inspiring"[54] and as such may be subject to tragedy. You have to hand it to John Ford—at sixty-nine, the American master continued to be a filmmaker on the cutting edge.

Notes

1. Bernard Smith remarks that "*Cheyenne Autumn* was a great hit in Europe, but was disappointing here…In Europe they were waiting for it; in America it was ahead of its time"—in Scott Eyman's *Print The Legend: The Life and Times of John Ford*, 483. In *Searching for John Ford: A Life*, Joseph McBride points out on page 658 that "[t]he American public in 1964 was not in the mood for the melancholy history lesson Ford offered them in *Cheyenne Autumn*." See Toshi Fujiwara's comments regarding *Cheyenne Autumn's* critical reception in "The People. Who Will Tell Them? Who Will Tell The People?," at http://fipresci.hegenauer.co.uk/undercurrent/issue_0509/cheyenne.htm.

2. In Joseph McBride's *Searching for John Ford: A Life* (New York: St. Martin's Press, 2001), 659.

3. Larry Siegel and Mort Drucker, "Cheyenne Awful," *Mad Magazine* Vol. 97 (September 1965): 9.

4. In Scott Eyman, *Print the Legend*, 484. Eyman also points out that Warner Bros carried the negative cost of *Cheyenne Autumn* at $7.37 million although the picture grossed $3.1 million domestically and $6.3 million worldwide. In *Searching for John Ford*, Joseph McBride observes because of the "relatively high cost of making and distributing the picture, [*Cheyenne Autumn*] failed to show a profit" (659).

5. See Carey, Harry, Jr. *Company of Heroes: My Life as an Actor in the John Ford Stock Company* (Lanham MD: Rowman & Littlefield, 2013), 193.

6. See Mark Haggard, "A New Direction," 42; Bosley Crowther's "Screen: John Ford Mounts Huge Frontier Western: Cheyenne Autumn' Bows at Capitol 3 Other Films Open at Local Cinemas." Also see Joseph McBride's account of Mark Haggard's defense of John Ford and *Cheyenne Autumn* in *Searching for John Ford*, 659.

7. See Dwight Logan's "Films that tell true stories of Indian massacres" in *DHT: dailyheraldtribune.com* 27 March 2013, https://www.dailyheraldtribune.com/2013/03/27/films-that-tell-true-stories-of-indian-massacres/wcm/172f1a8e-6631-1c07-621d-32e9d97c21d1.

8. James N. Leiker and Ramon Powers deconstruct these stereotypes of the Cheyenne in *The Northern Cheyenne Exodus in History and Memory*.

9. Peter Bogdanovich, *John Ford* (Berkeley: University of California Press, 1978), 106.

10. The Northern Cheyenne Exodus, which began on September 9, 1878, was a running battle as the band travelled across Kansas and Nebraska. Contemporary records report that the Cheyenne's contact with whites was not harmonious and often bloody. One group of drovers, for example, lost 80 head of cattle, and isolated settlers (including 40 men and boys in Oberlin, Kansas) lost their lives as well as their livestock. Close to ten thousand soldiers and three thousand settlers chased the Northern Cheyenne through Nebraska, the soldiers being a mixed command from the 19th Infantry and 4th Cavalry under Lt. Colonel William H. Lewis and by men from Fort Wallace, Fort Hays, Fort Dodge, Fort Riley, and Fort Kearney.

11. McBride, *Searching for John Ford*, 645.

12. *Ibid.*, 648.

13. Bogdanovich, *John Ford*, 104.

14. McBride, *Searching for John Ford*, 645.

15. Bacon, 9.

16. Helen H. Bacon, "The Chorus in Greek Life and Drama," *Arion: A Journal of Humanities and the Classics* Vol. 3, No. 1 (Fall 1994/Winter 1995): 8; 7.

17. *Ibid.*, 18.

18. T.B.L. Webster, *The Greek Chorus* (London: Methuen & Co Ltd, 1970), 200.

19. *Ibid.*, 123.

20. In Navajo, "natani" means warrior.

21. *Ibid.*, 6.

22. Harrison, *Ancient Art and Ritual*, 35. According to Harrison, collectivity and emotional tension turn simple reaction into the *dromenon* or rite, "a thing done," Ritual becomes drama when the dance that revive an event, enabling participants and spectators to re-enact emotion produced in the past (35–45).

23. T.B.L. Webster, *The Greek Chorus*, 200.

24. Cynthia P. Gardiner, *The Sophoclean Chorus: A Study of Character and Function* (Iowa City, IA: University of Iowa Press, 1987), 163.

25. Helene Foley, "Choral Identity in Greek Tragedy," *Classical Philology* Vol. 98, No. 1 (January 2003): 22.

26. *Ibid.*, 20–21.

27. Historically, Little Wolf, a war chief of the Cheyenne was also one of the four "Old Man" chiefs among the Council of Forty-four and the Northern Cheyenne's Sweet Medicine Chief. A master strategist, Little Wolf was recognised as a talented leader. His able command skills elevated him to leadership within the prestigious Elk Society.

28. Foley, "Choral Identity in Greek Tragedy," 20. Considering the female chorus of *Electra*, Cynthia P. Gardiner remarks, "If Sophocles had made this a chorus of men, he would have had to deal with the questions of political morality, of revolution, of the relationship between the ruler and subject or between citizen and state. In consequence, the focus of the play would very likely be shifted from Electra's behavior to the males as the true body politic" (163). See Cynthia P. Gardiner's *The Sophoclean chorus: a study of character and function*, 163.

29. Gardiner, *The Sophoclean Chorus*, 163.

30. See Walt Whitman's "By Blue Ontario's Shore" in *Leaves of Grass and Selected Poems and Prose* (270) in *The Walt Whitman Archive*.

31. See McBride's discussion of the "Dodge City War" in *Searching for John Ford*, 659–60.

32. *Ibid.*, 659. According to McBride "[t]hat advice from the trade paper was heeded by Warner Bros. In the opening road-show engagements, Warners broke the sequence into two parts to make room for an intermission. The second part, showing 'the Battle of Dodge City,' was cut from the film before its wider American release. Ford and Smith were unhappy about this mutilation, as well as with prior cutting done by the studio in the Fort Robinson massacre sequence and other parts of the film, but they had no recourse, since their contract with Warners, like most of Ford's other contracts in the later years of his career, gave the studio the final cut. Warners restored the missing Dodge City footage for the 1990 home-video release, although only in the pan-and-scan format. The entire sequence was final seen in the letter boxed format on the American Movie Classics cable television network which aired the restoration without fanfare in its August 1999 Ford festival" (660).

33. Mark Ayala, "*Cheyenne Autumn,*" *Beverly Cinema*, May 14, 2017, http://thenewbev.com/blog/2017/05/cheyenne-autumn/.

34. After the closing of the frontier, Earp furthered his legend in silent films, working as "an unpaid technical consultant on Hollywood Westerns [and] drawing on his colorful past to tell flamboyant matinee idols like William Hart and Tom Mix how it had really been" (see "Wyatt Earp dies in Los Angeles" in History.com editors *This Day In History*, January 9, 2020, https://www.history.com/this-day-in-history/wyatt-earp-dies-in-los-angeles). Andrew C. Isenberg also points out that the deputy marshal, now considered a "con-man man and horse thief who consorted with prostitutes and murdered his enemies," became larger than life on screen (see *Wyatt Earp: A Vigilante Life*).

35. Les Carpenter, "The forgotten story of … Wyatt Earp and the 'fixed' heavyweight title fight," *The Guardian*. July 22, 2015, https://www.theguardian.com/sport/2015/jul/22/wyatt-earp-botched-heavyweight-boxing-championship.

36. More information regarding *The Good Bad-Man* (1916) is available at *IMDb*, https://www.imdb.com/title/tt0006736/.

37. See Tim Dirks' discussion of the Western's film narrative at the *AMC filmsite*.

38. Ibid.

39. McBride, *Searching for John Ford*, 657.

40. See Scott McGee's "Cheyenne Autumn," *TCM Special Theme: Directed by John Ford*, *TCM: Turner Classic Movies*, 2020, http://www.tcm.com/this-month/article.html?isPreview=&id=1576417%7C296726&name=Cheyenne-Autumn.

41. In satyr-drama, the satyrs would call Silenus "father."

42. T.B.L. Webster, *The Greek Chorus*, 200.

43. Ibid., 17–18.

44. See the discussion regarding the inception and development of the Stetson at https://www.cardenashats.com/evolution-of-the-cowboy-hat.html which identifies the "Boss of the plains" as "the first lightweight all-weather hat designed for the demands of the American West. It was durable, waterproof and elegant. Just as the Winchester became synonymous with rifles, and Colt with pistols, the inventor John B. Stetson's name became interchangeable with the then unnamed cowboy hat. The Boss had a high crown to provide insulation on the top of the head where most body heat is lost. It had a wide stiff brim to provide shelter from the sun, rain and snow on your face, neck and shoulders. The Boss was waterproof so that they could carry water. And they were made durable and extremely lightweight, because you were going to carry it on your head for a long, long time. And as you know it had a simple band, a liner, and a bow on its sweatband for no real reason at all. Except to make it the most elegant hat in the West."

45. Richard Slotkin, *Regeneration Through Violence: The Mythology of the American Frontier 1600–1860*, 5.

46. Harrison, *Ancient Art and Ritual*, 139.

47. See Bacon's discussion of choral performances making events meaningful in "The Chorus in Greek Life and Drama," 18.

48. Toshi Fujiwara, "The People. Who Will Tell Them? Who Will Tell The People?."

49. Aristotle, *Poetics*, IV,12; Bacon, 143; also see Harrison's discussion in *Ancient Art and Ritual*, 76.

50. Ibid., 118

51. Ibid., 122; 174.

52. Friedrich Nietzsche, *The Birth of Tragedy or Hellenism and Pessimism*, 150; at https://www.gutenberg.org/files/51356/51356-h/51356-h.htm.

53. Jane Ellen Harrison, *Ancient Art and Ritual* (New York: Henry Holt and Company, 1913), 159.

54. Ibid., 2.

Filmography

Cheyenne Autumn. Dir. John Ford. Warner Bros., 1964.
The Good Bad-Man. Dir. Alan Dwan, Fine Arts Film Company, 1916.
Stagecoach. Dir. John Ford. Walter Wanger Productions, 1939.
The Vanishing American. George B. Seitz. Paramount Pictures, 1925.

Works Cited

Aristotle. *Poetics*. In *Aristotle in 23 Volumes*. Vol. 23, trans. W.H. Fyfe. Cambridge, MA: Harvard University Press; London: William Heinemann Ltd., 1932; also at http://www.perseus.tufts.edu/hopper/text?doc=Perseus%3Atext%3A1999.01.0056%3Asection%3D1456a.

Ayala, Mark. "Cheyenne Autumn," *Beverly Cinema*, May 14, 2017. http://thenewbev.com/blog/2017/05/cheyenne-autumn/.
Bacon, Helen H. "The Chorus in Greek Life and Drama." *Arion: A Journal of Humanities and the Classics* Vol. 3, No. 1 (Fall 1994/Winter 1995): 6–24.
Bogdanovich, Peter. *John Ford*. Berkeley, CA: University of California Press, 1978.
Carpenter, Les. "The forgotten story of…Wyatt Earp and the 'fixed' heavyweight title fight." *The Guardian*. July 22, 2015. https://www.theguardian.com/sport/2015/jul/22/wyatt-earp-botched-heavyweight-boxing-championship.
Carey, Harry, Jr. *Company of Heroes: My Life as an Actor in the John Ford Stock Company*. Lanham, MD: Rowman & Littlefield, 2013.
Cheyenne Autumn (1964). *IMDb*. https://www.imdb.com/title/tt0057940/?ref_=fn_al_tt_1.
Crowther, Bosley. "Screen: John Ford Mounts Huge Frontier Western: Cheyenne Autumn's Bows at Capitol 3 Other Films Open at Local Cinemas." *The New York Times* December 24, 1964. At https://www.nytimes.com/1964/12/24/archives/screen-john-ford-mounts-huge-frontier-western-cheyenne-autumn-bows.html.
Davis, Ronald L. *John Ford: Hollywood's Old Master*. Norman: University of Oklahoma Press, 1995.
Dirks, Tim. "Westerns: Part 1." *AMC filmsite*. At https://www.filmsite.org/westernfilms.html.
"Evolution of the Cowboy Hat." *Cardenas Hats Quality Hats Since 1960*. May 7, 2015. https://www.cardenashats.com/evolution-of-the-cowboy-hat.html.
Eyman, Scott. *Print The Legend: The Life and Times of John Ford*. New York: Simon & Schuster, 1999.
Foley, Helene. "Choral Identity in Greek Tragedy." *Classical Philology* Vol. 98, No. 1 (January 2003): 1–30.
Flickinger, Roy Caston. *The Greek Theatre and its Drama*. Whitefish, MT: Kessinger Publishing, LLC, 2007.
Fujiwara, Toshi. "Who Will Tell Them? Who Will Tell The People?" *undercurrent* Vol. 5 (2009). At http://fipresci.hegenauer.co.uk/undercurrent/issue_0509/cheyenne.htm.
Gardiner, Cynthia P. *The Sophoclean Chorus: A Study of Character and Function*. Iowa City: University of Iowa Press, 1987.
The Good Bad-Man (1916). *IMDb*. https://www.imdb.com/title/tt0006736/.
Haggard, Mark, "Letter" *Newsweek*, February 1, 1965, 42.
Harrison, Jane Ellen. *Ancient Art and Ritual*. New York: Henry Holt and Company, 1913.
History.com Editors. "Wyatt Earp dies in Los Angeles." *This Day in History*. At https://www.history.com/this-day-in-history/wyatt-earp-dies-in-los-angeles.
Isenberg, Andrew C. *Wyatt Earp: A Vigilante Life*. New York: Hill and Wang, 2013.
Kauffman, Stanley. "No Ford in Our Future." *New Republic*. January 23, 1965, 36.
Leiker, James N., and Ramon Powers. *The Northern Cheyenne Exodus in History and Memory*. Norman: University of Oklahoma Press, 2011.
Logan, Dwight. "Films that tell true stories of Indian massacres." *DHT: dailyheraldtribune.com*. 27 March 2013. At https://www.dailyheraldtribune.com/2013/03/27/films-that-tell-true-stories-of-indian-massacres/wcm/172f1a8e-6631-1c07-621d-32e9d97c21d1.
Matheson, Sue. *The Westerns and War Films of John Ford*. Lanham, MD: Rowman & Littlefield, 2016.
McBride, Joseph. *Searching For John Ford: A Life*. New York: St. Martin's Press, 2001.
McGee, Scott. "Cheyenne Autumn." *TCM Special Theme: Directed by John Ford*, *TCM: Turner Classic Movies*. 2020. At http://www.tcm.com/this-month/article.html?isPreview=&id=1576417%7C296726&name=Cheyenne-Autumn.
Nietzsche, Friedrich. *The Birth of Tragedy or Hellenism and Pessimism*. Project Gutenberg. March 4, 2016. At https://www.gutenberg.org/files/51356/51356-h/51356-h.htm.
Oulahan, Richard. "John Ford's Trojan Horse Opry." *Life 27* (November 1964): 19.
Remington, Frederic. *A Campfire Sketch* (1889). *Fineartamerica*. https://fineartamerica.com/featured/a-campfire-sketch-frederic-remington.html.
Siegel, Larry, and Mort Drucker, "Cheyenne Awful." *Mad Magazine* Vol. 97 (September 1965): 9–13.
Slotkin, Richard. *Regeneration Through Violence: The Mythology of the American Frontier 1600–1860*. Norman: University of Oklahoma Press, 1973.
Stagecoach (1939). *IMDb*. https://www.imdb.com/title/tt0031971/?ref_=fn_al_tt_1.
T.B.L. Webster, *The Greek Chorus*. London: Methuen & Co Ltd, 1970.
The Vanishing American (1925), *IMDb*. https://www.imdb.com/title/tt0016480/?ref_=fn_al_tt_2.
Whitman, Walt. "By Blue Ontario's Shore." *Leaves of Grass*. In Ed Folsom and Kenneth M. Price, eds. *The Walt Whitman Archive*, 267–76. At https://whitmanarchive.org/published/LG/1891/poems/197.
Williams, Whitney. "Cheyenne Autumn." *Daily Variety*. December 31, 1964. At https://variety.com/1964/film/reviews/cheyenne-autumn-1200420666/.
"Wyatt Earp Dies in Los Angeles." In History.com editors, *This Day in History*. January 9, 2020. At https://www.history.com/this-day-in-history/wyatt-earp-dies-in-los-angeles.

Peckinpah and the Problem of Catharsis; or: How Well Does *The Wild Bunch* Fit Aristotle's *Poetics*?

Martin M. Winkler

Sam Peckinpah's *The Wild Bunch* (1969) was one of the most controversial films of its time but later became a classic in the Western genre and an acknowledged masterpiece of American cinema. In Jim Kitses' apt phrase: "*The Wild Bunch* is America."[1] Its complete version is often considered Peckinpah's most accomplished work. The film was initially notorious for its graphic violence, a feature in this and other films that overshadowed Peckinpah's entire career. He became known as "bloody Sam," "artist of death," and "master of violence."[2] But as Stephen Prince has pointed out: "Peckinpah's images of violence are remarkably discrete [*sic*]. This discretion follows from his regard for the sensibilities of the viewer that he did not wish to bludgeon and destroy."[3] This is in strong contrast to screen violence after Peckinpah. Prince also stated: "The radical thrust of Peckinpah's experiment with graphic screen violence takes the concept of catharsis as its impetus and justification."[4] This catharsis is Aristotelian.

1. Peckinpah and the Greeks

Cordell Strug published an article in 1975 whose title posed an intriguing question and which eventually entered the pantheon, as it were, of Peckinpah criticism: "*The Wild Bunch* and the Problem of Idealist Aesthetics, or, How Long Would Peckinpah Last in Plato's Republic?"[5] Strug, like virtually all critics of *The Wild Bunch*, defenders and detractors alike, focused on the explicit violence in the film. Strug defended it but proceeded from the familiar, if erroneous, view that Plato was hostile to poetry.[6] It seems more advisable to examine the film's violence from the perspective of Aristotle, Plato's most famous disciple, and in connection with the workings of tragedy as described in Aristotle's *Poetics*. Peckinpah knew the *Poetics* from his days as a drama student. His wife at the time, recalling his obsession with classical and classic American authors, said about the former:

> he was also interested in the Greeks, philosophy—he read a lot of Plato and Aristotle too. Aristotle's *Poetics* was something that seemed to grab him and he was constantly referring to it ... it always seemed amazing, because he'd have his Greeks and the others in one hand and his cowboy books and detective stories in the other.[7]

Peckinpah referred to Aristotle's *Poetics* on numerous occasions, in particular to the idea of catharsis as a defense of the explicit violence in *The Wild Bunch*. In a 1972 interview he stated:

> I'm a great believer in catharsis ... the old basis of catharsis was a purging of the emotions through pity and fear. People used to go and see the plays of Euripides and Sophocles and those other Greek cats. The players acted it out and the audience got in there and kind of lived it with them.[8]

This is a vague summary of how Greek tragedy affected its audiences, but it is in keeping with the traditional understanding of catharsis as a process of purgation, promulgated in 1857 by Jacob Bernays and now largely abandoned.[9] In 1971 Peckinpah had said about *The Wild Bunch*:

> It's about the violence within all of us.... I intended it to have a cathartic effect. Someone may feel a strange, sick exultation at the violence, but he should then ask himself, 'What is going on in my heart?' I wanted to achieve a catharsis through pity and fear.[10]

This is significantly closer to the true nature of the matter. The more startling, then, is Peckinpah's complete reversal, which had occurred by 1976. In an interview broadcast on BBC television, he retracted everything:

> I made *The Wild Bunch* because I still believed in the Greek theory of catharsis, that by seeing this we would be purged by pity and fear and get this out of our system. I was wrong.... Catharsis only works in certain—as Theodor Lipps once said, it depends upon the viewer and his situation and the artist, and I was a total failure.[11]

A fundamental question now arises: how reliable are artists when they describe their own works? Here is what Robin Wood once observed about Alfred Hitchcock:

> the chief obstacle in the way of a serious appraisal of Hitchcock's work for many people is Hitchcock's own apparent attitude to it; and it seems worth insisting ... on the fundamental irrelevance of this. What an artist says about his own work need not necessarily carry any more weight than what anyone else says about it: value can only be assessed by the test to which one must subject all criticism or elucidation, the test of applying it to the art in question and asking oneself how much it contributes toward either understanding or evaluating it. The artist's own utterances are more likely to have an indirect relevance, by telling us something further about his personality and outlook.

Wood's comment about Hitchcock's *The Birds* (1963) reinforces our context:

> whether or not Hitchcock consciously intended these interpretations [i.e., those Wood advances and, by implication, any others] is quite immaterial: the only question worth discussing is whether they are sufficiently *there*, in the film ... there is no need to suppose them consciously worked out.[12]

Seen from such a perspective, it does not matter whether Peckinpah was right or wrong, although it is sensible to agree with his comments whenever a close analysis of his films bears them out. Prince, for example, contrasts Peckinpah's often glib and superficial statements with the evidence provided in the films themselves.[13] Still, Peckinpah was fully capable of eloquent insights when he wished to be.

Prince, a specialist in screen violence, has argued the case for Peckinpah's reversal and against Aristotelian catharsis at considerable length.[14] Prince fully agrees with Peckinpah's statement in the BBC interview.[15] His overall conclusion is this: "A defense of Peckinpah's work through appeals to catharsis is a dead end."[16] Is Prince right?

The answer must be *No*. The most obvious reason is that Prince marshals sufficient research and scholarship on modern psychology, social science, screen violence, and related topics to support his conclusion—in which he is not alone—but not a single work of scholarship on Aristotle or ancient conceptions of catharsis, e.g., in Greek medical writings. This is a crucial omission. After all, Aristotle was not a social or behavioral scientist *avant la lettre*. So the subject deserves a re-evaluation: not with the intention of overturning Prince's or anybody else's arguments but in order to deepen our understanding of *The Wild Bunch*.

Despite Peckinpah's recantation, the concept of catharsis seems to refuse to die in publications about his films. Scholars still refer to it, usually briefly and superficially and often quoting the earlier Peckinpah with approval. Here are three representative examples. Bernard Dukore speaks of Aristotelian *hamartia* ("mistake, error") in connection with catharsis in regard to Peckinpah's portrayals of flawed heroes, especially in *The Wild Bunch*. He vitiates his argument at the outset by a bizarre statement:

> Like the heroes of Greek tragedy, notably Oedipus (also a murderer) and Antigone, like Hamlet (another murderer, who kills without regret) and Lear, the four members of the Bunch … do not employ halfway measures but go all the way to accomplish their goals.[17]

John Simons and Robert Merrill mention Aristotle and catharsis on a few occasions. They state early on: "our critical sympathies [with Peckinpah] are Aristotelian in nature."[18] But they do not offer any extended analysis. Cordell Strug is on surer ground on a different occasion but adduces Aristotle merely in preparation for comments which proceed from Christian ethics.[19]

Unintentionally, such instances provide sufficient justification to call upon Stephen Halliwell, today's leading scholar of the *Poetics*, as a corrective. Halliwell reminds us of a fundamental characteristic of this work: "many of its ideas and arguments are hints and pointers, not fully elaborated theses.… All dogmatic readings of the work, whether *pro* or *contra*, should be regarded as suspect."[20]

2. On Catharsis

Aristotle's definition of tragedy, with a few comments added for clarification, is this: "the representation [*mimêsis*] of an action which is serious, complete, and of a certain magnitude—in language which is garnished [with rhythm and melody] in its various parts—in the mode of dramatic enactment, not narrative [as in epic] and through the arousal of pity and fear effecting the *katharsis* of such emotions."[21] What this catharsis is, however, remains largely unclear: "the most notorious and vexed feature of the *Poetics*, its unexplained concept of catharsis," is "arguably now the most famous/notorious, as well as enigmatic, concept in the entire history of Western poetics."[22] As a result, "a definitive understanding of catharsis will always (in the absence of new evidence) elude us."[23] This is in strong contrast to how the term has generally been dealt with: "The catharsis controversy of the past century and a half [i.e., since Bernays] has been marked by a display of confidence on the part of many interpreters that stands virtually in inverse ratio to the quality of evidence available on the subject."[24] Concerning spectators' feelings of pity and fear, Halliwell observes:

> When an audience is drawn into intense fear and pity for the characters of tragedy, Aristotle supposes that it is not simply having its feelings exposed to a kind of nervous excitation.

Rather, the emotions ... both reflect and help to shape how spectators grasp and see the underlying patterns of significance in a plot's structure of action and suffering.[25]

Pity is felt "for one whose misfortune is undeserved, fear for one who is 'like (us),' [*Poetics*] 1453a3–7"[26]—that is to say, someone who is not worse than ourselves but whose misfortunes may remind us of the precarious nature of our existence.[27] In this, emotion and intellect are inseparable because "Aristotle ... looks to poetry, even to the mythically magnified domain of tragedy and epic, for an imaginative vividness which can sustain an audience's cognitive and emotional engagement."[28] From this twofold engagement there arises the mental process of catharsis in the spectator:

> tragic catharsis can plausibly be connected to the *transformation* of normally painful experiences (pity and fear) into a rewarding and gratifying experience (the special pleasure of tragedy [at *Poetics* 1448b9–19]) ... we can enjoy viewing otherwise painful objects when they are effectively depicted in (visual) art, because we are able in this context to understand them and learn from them in ways that (for most people) would not be possible under the exigencies of real-world situations.... On Aristotle's model of tragedy ... spectators of the finest plays are induced, at supreme moments of *ekplêxis* ["stunning emotional impact"], to experience strong surges of pity and vicarious or 'sympathetic' fear.[29]

The result: "A feeling of release, of uninhibited psychological flow, both during and after strong surges of emotion, is a suitable adjunct to the type of aesthetic experience that Aristotle takes to generate catharsis in the tragic theatre.... Catharsis ... is Aristotle's description for the benefit that is felt in and through the heightened arousal of the emotions by artistic stimulations of the human world."[30]

3. Styles and Dramatic Uses of Violence

The Wild Bunch has often been regarded as epic, and so it is, not least in the Homeric explicitness of its violence. Peckinpah himself referred to Homer more than once.[31] But his film is at the same time tragic. So is Homer's *Iliad*.[32] Mythic-heroic epic is by nature violent. French philosopher Simone Weil famously characterized the *Iliad* as "the poem of force."[33] The myths dealt with in Homeric epic provided the tragic playwrights with their greatest source of inspiration. While the violence (and everything else) in epic is verbal, not visual, Homer and later epic poets made sure that listeners or readers get the full impact of what they describe. The rhetorical concept of *enargeia* ("vividness") is appropriate here: listeners and readers were to see with their mind's eye what they heard or read. This is a chief reason why Homer in antiquity was sometimes regarded as a painter, even as the greatest of all.[34]

Violent acts in Greek tragedy took place off-stage, partly for aesthetic and partly for technical reasons. The playwrights were their own producers and directors and not only the authors that most people today, even theatergoers, understand them to be. In Greek drama, the verbal and the visual are inseparable, as the literal meaning of the Greek word *theatron* tells us: "viewing space."

A Greek playwright had various ways to drive home the impact of acts of violence. One of these were messenger speeches: reports, often in gruesome detail, of what has happened elsewhere. Death screams, as those of Agamemnon in Aeschylus' *Agamemnon* or of Medea's children in Euripides' *Medea*, powerfully worked on the audience's imagination as well. This verbal side was reinforced visually. The backdrop of the Greek theater, a building from which actors enter and into which they exit, contained a rolling platform (*ekkyklêma* or *eccyclema*), which could be wheeled out onto the actors' area. This platform displayed a violent act or its immediate aftermath in a kind of *tableau vivant*.[35] A case in point is, once again, Aeschylus' *Agamemnon*, in which the spectators presumably saw Clytemnestra, blood-splattered and with axe raised, standing above the corpses of Agamemnon and Cassandra. Clytemnestra then gloats, in horrific detail, over her deed:

> I struck him twice. In two great cries of agony
> he buckled at the knees and fell. When he was down
> I struck him the third blow....
> Thus he went down, and the life struggled out of him;
> and as he died he spattered me with the dark red
> and violent driven rain of bitter savored blood
> to make me glad....[36]

Even before the *ekkyklêma* appeared and the audience heard about Clytemnestra's deed from her own mouth, Cassandra had uttered a prophetic vision of blood-soaked doom in a speech meant to heighten the impending horror. The *ekkyklêma* of *The Libation Bearers* showed the dead bodies of Clytemnestra and Aegisthus, her accomplice, both killed by Agamemnon's son, Orestes. An ancient commentator on Sophocles' *Ajax* reports: "There is an *ekkyklema* so that Ajax can appear.... For these things also shock the spectator; spectacle is deeply emotive. He [Ajax] is shown carrying a sword, covered in blood, sitting among the sheep."[37] A modern scholar comments on this moment: "This gory *nature morte* captures with shocking, unalleviated directness the extent of Ajax's disaster."[38] The shock value of this and comparable scenes conforms to Aristotle's concept of *ekplêxis* ("stunning impact") in the *Poetics*.[39]

Despite obvious differences, the emotional function of the *ekkyklêma* may be considered in analogy to the tableaux in Peckinpah's films. Prince has drawn appropriate attention to this stylistic feature, especially in his Westerns.[40] He describes these tableaux as "striking scenes and images presented formalistically so that they are detachable from the immediate narrative context." This fits the purpose of the ancient *ekkyklêma* quite closely although, given the nature of cinema, screen tableaux are not usually as static as those on a theatrical stage. Peckinpah "incorporated the tableau image or scene as an enduring feature of his own work, most often used as a means for commenting explicitly on the nature and place of violence in human life."[41] Close again. Although it is unlikely that Peckinpah was aware of the classical stage in this particular regard, the parallels are worth keeping in mind when we discuss his Aristotelianism. Prince's comments can profitably be read in this context; they also make further discussion unnecessary here. Instead, the verbal explicitness with which Greek tragedians could present the horror of violence is crucial. It comes to fore in the two messengers' speeches in Euripides' final play, *The Bacchae*, the quintessential tragedy on the subject of violence. Aristotle called Euripides the "most tragic" of playwrights.[42] A commentator explains: "taken in its context, this famous aphorism must mean that Euripides excels in arousing pity and fear."[43] Aristotle knew a lot more about all those Greek cats than we do.

The Bacchae demonstrates the two sides of Dionysus' religion, its elevating beauty and the opposite: deadly violence. The god's cult has frequently been regarded as an illustration of the irrational and destructive nature of man, the Dionysian as opposed to the

Apollonian.[44] The play's titular women are adherents of Bacchus (Dionysus), who possesses their minds; their alternate collective name of Maenads ("Raging Women") indicates that the god can instill furious madness in them. The Bacchae engage in ecstatic but peaceful rites, primarily singing and dancing in the mountains, and then sleep off their exhaustion. When they are disturbed, however, either by animals or non-initiates, they set upon these and tear them apart. Dismemberment (*sparagmos*) of animals and, in extreme cases, of humans is an integral part of Bacchic frenzy. Ecstatic bliss and violent destruction are the parameters of Dionysian religion. Euripides' play demonstrates the god's power by showing Dionysus' revenge on Pentheus, the young king of Thebes, who has resisted the god. Driven by Dionysus, the Bacchae, chief among them Pentheus' mother Agave, tear him apart.

Two messenger speeches tell the audience about the Maenads' devastating fury. The first messenger informs Pentheus about the effect Dionysus can have on human minds. This speech is intended to prepare the audience for the king's horrific fate. The messenger's essential lines, without direct quotations within his speech or specific geographic and supernatural details, summarize, first, the change of the Bacchae from quiet to fury:

> There they lay in the deep sleep of exhaustion....
> But your mother heard the lowing
> of our hornèd herds, and springing to her feet,
> gave a great cry to waken them from sleep....
> Unarmed, they swooped down upon the herds of cattle
> grazing there on the green of the meadow. And then
> you could have seen a single woman with bare hands
> tear a fat calf, still bellowing with fright,
> in two, while others clawed the heifers to pieces.
> There were ribs and cloven hooves scattered everywhere,
> and scraps smeared with blood hung from the fir trees.
> And bulls, their raging fury gathered in their horns,
> lowered their heads to charge, then fell, stumbling,
> to the earth, pulled down by hordes of women
> and stripped of flesh and skin....
> Everything in sight they pillaged and destroyed.[45]

The shocking details of the Maenads' frenzy correspond to what on screen would receive a series of close-ups, presented with rapid editing. As has been well said about Euripidean messenger speeches in general: "The perspective frequently alternates between a wide-angled view of the whole scene and close-ups of particular details." And: "Pictorial contrast ... is a means of rendering action exciting."[46]

Euripides could rely on his audiences' familiarity with the myth, so the messenger's report heightens their dread of what they know will happen. We may compare Anton Chekhov's dramatic principle that a gun introduced early in a story or play must in due course go off; its first appearance necessitates a climactic moment later on. Aristotle had made virtually the same point.[47] In *The Bacchae*, a second messenger reports on Pentheus' death. Dionysus roused the Maenads and alerted them to Pentheus' presence among them. The Maenads pelted the king, perched on the top of a tree, with stones and branches, then tore out the tree by its roots:

> down, down
> from his high perch fell Pentheus, tumbling
> to the ground, sobbing and screaming as he fell,

> for he knew his end was near. His own mother...
>   fell upon him
> first....
> But she was foaming at the mouth, and her crazed eyes
> rolling with frenzy. She was mad, stark mad,
> possessed by Bacchus. Ignoring his cries of pity,
> she seized his left arm at the wrist; then, planting
> her foot upon his chest, she pulled, wrenching away
> the arm at the shoulder—not by her own strength,
> for the god had put inhuman power in her hands.
> Ino, meanwhile, on the other side, was scratching off
> his flesh. Then Autonoë and the whole horde
> of Bacchae swarmed upon him. Shouts everywhere,
> he screaming with what little breath was left,
> they shrieking in triumph. One tore off an arm,
> another a foot still warm in its shoe. His ribs
> were clawed clean of flesh and every hand
> was smeared with blood as they played ball with scraps
> of Pentheus' body.
>   The pitiful remains lie scattered,
> one piece among the sharp rocks, others
> lying lost among the leaves in the depths
> of the forest. His mother, picking up his head,
> impaled it on her wand.[48]

The two messenger speeches are powerful dramatic devices: first an introductory presentation of an awesome force; then the climactic release of that force. They may be compared to the two episodes in *The Wild Bunch* involving a machine gun. Before it is first tested, none of the characters on screen understands its lethal potential, just as only a few, if any, in the theater will have had any practical experience with such a weapon. When it goes off without proper handling, the gun becomes a demonic force with a destructive will of its own, spraying bullets randomly. Miraculously, however, no one receives even a scratch; only inanimate objects like flowerpots, water jugs, and clay utensils are shattered. Slow-motion photography intensifies viewers' observation of such deadly power. Peckinpah drives home the point by dividing this sequence into two

Lyle Gorch (Warren Oates) experiences the ecstasy of agony in *The Wild Bunch* (Warner Bros.–Seven Arts, 1969).

parts, separated by a brief interval during which the characters on screen and the viewers in the theater breathe a sigh of relief that the danger is now over—which it is not. Even more daringly, Peckinpah injects a humorous note when he tops off this sequence with General Mapache's know-it-all command: "Put it on a tripod!" We have just seen Mapache lying on his back, as if wrestled to the ground by the machine monster. Now that we know what havoc it *can* wreak, we anticipate the havoc it *will* wreak. Given its complete bloodlessness, the scene is in stark contrast to the bloody deaths of the animals in Euripides' first messenger speech, but the Greek audience is unlikely to have considered these deaths with any concern or outrage. They will have been as indifferent to the fate of the animals as we are to the fate of pots and pans.

All this changes when the machine gun goes off in earnest at the film's climax. Slow motion interspersed with photography at normal speed and the extremely rapid editing for which *The Wild Bunch* is famous are the cinematic means that drive home the full impact of the carnage; they are the equivalent of the gruesome details reported by

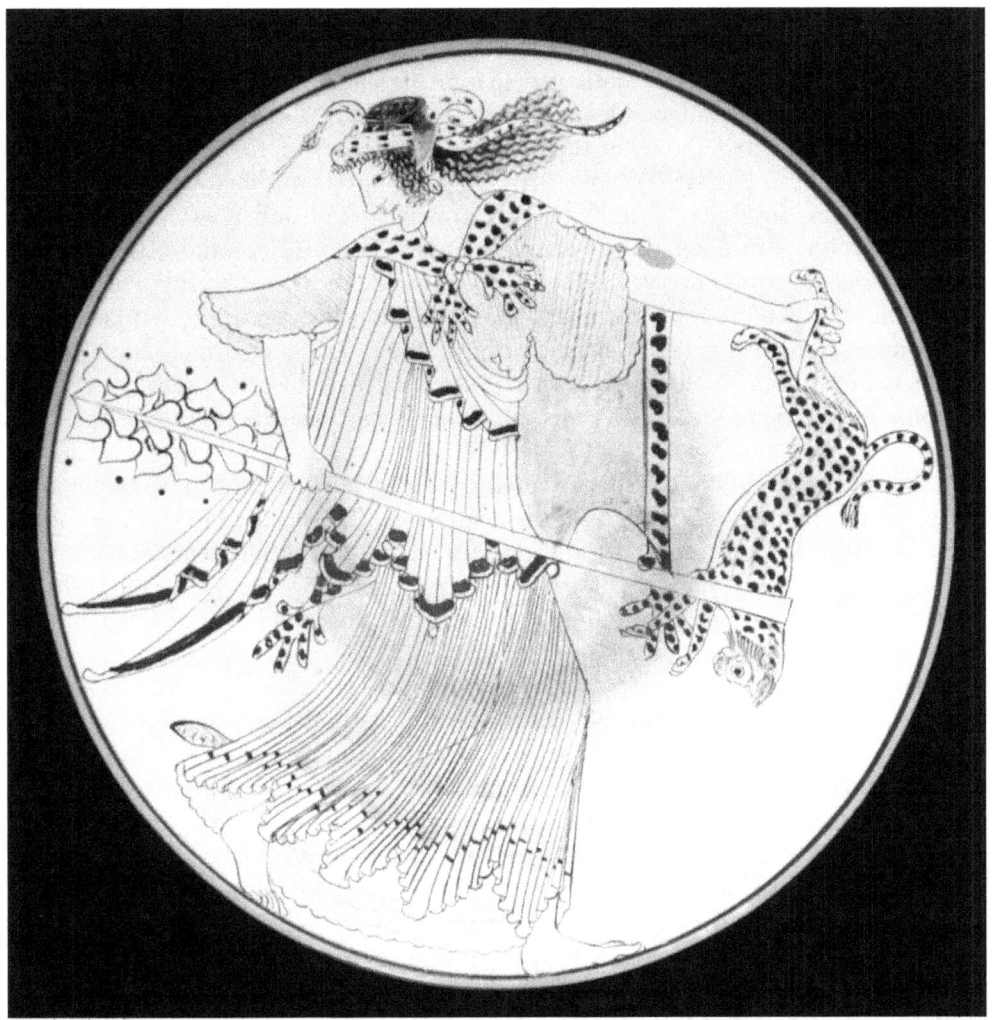

Beauty and ecstasy: dancing Maenad by the Brygos Painter.

Euripides' second messenger. Both the ancient verbal and the modern visual vividness ensure maximum effect on audiences' emotions. From this perspective it hardly matters that in *The Bacchae* only one man dies while hundreds are killed in *The Wild Bunch*. The two sequences in either work arouse a profound sense of pity and fear.

4. Violence and Ecstasy: The Complexity of Ambivalence

The most harrowing single moment in *The Wild Bunch* occurs when Lyle Gorch, one of the Bunch, is firing the machine gun. As if possessed by its superhuman power, he screams in simultaneous agony and ecstasy. The prolonged scream has often been described as an orgiastic, even orgasmic, release—a kind of emotional and psychological, if non–Aristotelian, catharsis. It is a moment both repellent and beautiful, which remains mesmerizing even after repeated viewings. The American cinema has never achieved its equal. It is often remembered on its own, detached from its immediate context and the story in which it occurs. Peckinpah carefully prepared his viewers for this moment. Just before the opening massacre, a member of the railroad posse had kissed the barrel of his rifle in almost erotic anticipation of slaughter.

We may again consider, at least as partial analogy, Peckinpah's use of tableaux. Prince's words, quoted above, fit the messenger speeches in *The Bacchae* and Lyle's ecstatic moment in *The Wild Bunch*. Prince rightly points out that, to Peckinpah, an "ambivalent response" was "a fundamental characteristic of audiences watching screen violence." As he elaborates—and here we should keep Euripides and Maenadism in mind as well, even if not everything in Peckinpah is identical to everything in *The Bacchae*: "the tableau announces the mixture of attraction and repulsion that Peckinpah had come to recognize as the essential attribute of the spectator's response to violence, in life and on screen."[49] The result is this: "Peckinpah's best work produces a crisis of response for the viewer because it pulls the viewer's emotional and cognitive responses in different directions."[50]

One of the most famous tableaux in *The Wild Bunch* is that of children playfully torturing scorpions and killer ants at the beginning. "The children in the film," it has been observed, "embody innocence and evil, beauty and corruption, gentleness and brutality."[51] These terms are apropos for our context, especially in regard to the childlike gentleness of the Maenads as described by the first messenger and their unstoppable violence as reported by the second.

The Bacchae fully demonstrates that ambivalence is integral to Greek Maenadism, both in its nature and in the response it calls forth in its audience. A famous Greek vase painting illustrates the duality of Dionysus' cult in one single image. It appears on the inside of a white-ground Attic drinking cup (*kylix*) dating to ca. 490 BC. It is the work of the potter Brygos and an anonymous painter, today called the Brygos Painter.[52] This ideal depiction of Maenadism shows a Maenad in her ecstasy, dancing toward the viewer's right but looking back to her left. In her right hand she is holding a *thyrsos*, the giant fennel stalk tipped with a pine cone that is characteristic of Maenadism; in her left she is holding a young leopard by a hind leg. The animal and a leopard skin she is wearing as a cloak indicate a past and a future *sparagmos*. She also has a serpent knotted around the locks on her head. While these animals point to the destructive side of Dionysus' cult, the beatific expression on the Maenad's face, seen in profile, reveals her devotion to her

Peckinpah and the Problem of Catharsis (Winkler)   75

"The high air hushed" in *The Wild Bunch*. Pike Bishop (William Holden, back to camera), flanked by Lyle Gorch (Warren Oates, center), his brother Tector (Ben Johnson, left), and Dutch Engstrom (Ernest Borgnine, right), moments before starting the final bloodbath that none of them will survive. *The Wild Bunch* (Warner Bros.–Seven Arts, 1969).

god and the elevating feelings it evokes. The image is simultaneously dark—figuratively: death and dismemberment—and light: literally in its colors, whose current faded state only reinforces the positive side of ecstasy, and figuratively in the beauty of the dance. The attractive and elegant swing of the Maenad's pleated dress emphasizes the scene's extraordinary quality even more. Bliss and destruction are inseparable. What we today tend to keep apart as incompatible opposites are two sides of the same phenomenon.

The simultaneous attraction to and repulsion by screen violence are comparable to Euripides' and the Brygos Painter's portrayals of Maenadism. The ecstasy of the dancing Maenad may be juxtaposed to that of Lyle Gorch, if in opposite modes of presentation. The serenity of the Maenad's expression is nothing like the contortion of Lyle's features. Violence is only implied in the painting but fully expressed in the film. Still, the underlying emotional and psychological complexities, while not identical, at least invite comparison.

One other feature of *The Bacchae* is important here. This is the moment of calm before the storm. The following lines appear immediately before those quoted above in the second messenger's speech:

> The high air hushed, and along the forest glen
> the leaves hung still; you could hear no cry of beasts.
> The Bacchae heard that voice but missed its words,
> and leaping up, they stared, peering everywhere.
> Again that voice. And now they knew his cry,
> the clear command of god.[53]

A modern commentator has observed that the first two of these lines "describe wonderfully the hush of nature at the moment when the pent-up forces of the supernatural break through."[54] *The Wild Bunch* contains a comparable moment. Pike Bishop, the Bunch's leader, has just shot and killed Mapache in almost instinctive retaliation for the latter's murder of Angel, a Mexican member of the Bunch. As if in disbelief, the others and Mapache's soldiers have become immobile, as if rooted to the ground. And there is complete silence: "The high air hushed." Pike and the others then "stared, peering everywhere." Pike now rises somewhat from his crouched position (cf. "leaping up"), takes aim, and shoots the Prussian officer who had been the Mexicans' military adviser. Pike thus intentionally precipitates the massacre that will finish all of the Bunch and most of the enemy. "Again that voice" in *The Bacchae*; here: again that gun. As did the double cry of Dionysus, so do Pike's two shots tell the followers of either what is to come next: "now they knew … the clear command." As one Peckinpah scholar has put it: "They smile knowingly at one another."[55] The result is an *ekplêxis*: "The shock that Peckinpah has been preparing us for is the moment before the killing starts, when, with chilling serenity, a middle-aged man resolves to go to hell and take a few people with him."[56] The moment here described is equivalent to Aristotle's principle of *peripeteia* ("reversal") and connected to that of *anagnôrisis* ("recognition"), both characteristic of complex tragic plots. The moment of *anagnôrisis* in *The Wild Bunch* ("Let's go!"—"Why not?") had occurred a little earlier as culmination of the scene with Pike, the Gorch brothers, and two prostitutes.[57]

The two massacres in *The Wild Bunch* serve to frame and put into greater relief a heroic tale that is largely non-violent. Such a tale is *The Bacchae*, too. And that is why these works have preserved their emotional power. What Strug once explained about Peckinpah's film can be applied to Euripides' play, with obvious differences kept in mind:

> *The Wild Bunch* achieves its wonder by its form. There is violence that is gripping not because of graphic images but because it touches fear and sacrifice and because it is filmed to show its pain and its amoral beauty. We see its attraction and we see its destruction…. There is ambiguity that comes from the obvious savagery of the gang and the equally obvious qualities of courage, guilt, and loyalty they possess and are possessed by.
>
> The battles are stunning … because … carefully choreographed and shot, and because each one … has internal developments that bring out or resolve tensions in the characters…. *The Wild Bunch* [is] an unusually powerful, unusually complex statement of ambiguity and of honor won in the face of ambiguity.[58]

As Peckinpah himself put it: "The strange thing is that you feel a strange sense of loss when these killers reach the end of the line."[59] Tellingly, he does not call them heroes. The more remarkable is our emotional attachment to a gang of ruthless outlaws and their eventual fate. Peckinpah has carefully prepared this effect in one crucial scene. The pastoral idyll of the Bunch taking their farewell from Mexican villagers has made our attachment possible. In Peckinpah's words: "If you can ride out with them there and feel it, you can die with them and feel it."[60] Their ride from the village is briefly, and appropriately, reprised as the film's final shot.

The two sides of violence in *The Wild Bunch*, its attraction and beauty on the one hand and its carnage on the other, may well come closest to illustrating the concept of catharsis that is possible in modern art. Whether such a catharsis is Aristotelian or not hardly matters. Here two statements by Peckinpah about *The Wild Bunch* are important. In 1971, as quoted, he referred to Aristotelian catharsis. His decisive words are worth repeating: "Someone may feel a strange, sick exultation at the violence, but he should then ask himself, 'What is going on in my heart?'" Earlier, in 1969, he was not thinking about catharsis when he said:

> Actually, it's an anti-violence film. I use violence as it *is*. It's ugly, brutalizing, and bloody fucking awful…. And yet there's a certain response that you get from it, an excitement, because we're all violent people; we have violence within us…. It's important to understand

it and the reason people seem to need violence vicariously.... It's a disturbing film; people who've seen it call it a *shattering* film.... I'm exhausted when I see it, I'm literally exhausted for hours.[61]

Both statements complement each other. They come close to demonstrating the very beauty and terror classical tragedy evokes. So it is surprising that the dramatic and emotional affinities of *The Wild Bunch* to *The Bacchae* have not previously been noticed.[62] But there is more. Peckinpah's expression "sick exultation" is a virtual restatement of Greek sophist Gorgias' term "pleasurable sickness" (*nosos hêdeia*). It describes the feeling we get from looking at works of art in contrast to witnessing actual carnage. The latter is a "terrible sickness" (*deinai nosoi*).[63]

5. *Peckinpah: Aristotelian Despite Himself*

Aristotle adduced epic for his analyses of tragedy as a matter of course.[64] While *The Wild Bunch* is primarily American, its dramatic structure, its emotional power, and the characterization of its hero relate it to classical epic and tragedy. Regardless of how we decide about Aristotle's and Peckinpah's conceptions of catharsis, any analysis of the film from the perspective of Greek literature and culture can only deepen our understanding and appreciation, the very *raison d'être* of scholarly criticism. We can now also answer, in just two words, the question posed in the title of this essay: *Very well*. In the course of time, Aristotle's *Poetics* has been applied to the arts at large.[65] Dorothy Sayers, for example, considered it a virtual manual for writers of detective fiction. Today, screenwriting teachers routinely refer their students, who include professionals, to it as well.[66]

Peckinpah was right to say that he had been wrong about catharsis, mainly because of the standard modern views of it, which are wrong or at least questionable but which Peckinpah followed. Nonetheless, Peckinpah was also right to say that he consciously intended to call forth pity and fear in viewers. Peckinpah evinced an instinctive dramatic and poetic grasp of the creative process to express in a modern medium an ancient emotional and aesthetic concept. Together with his collaborators, especially his co-writer, cinematographer, editor, and actors, Peckinpah perhaps unconsciously worked out a tragic epic in such a way that parallels to Greek tragedy with its moments of *ekplêxis*, *peripeteia*, and *anagnorisis* evoke strong pity and fear. This results from his careful structuring of the plot in *The Wild Bunch*, which switches from moments of calm to bursts of shocking action. So did *The Bacchae*, e.g., in its choral odes and messenger speeches. We might contrast the virtually non-stop violence and extremely simple structure in Zack Snyder's *300* (2007), another film about the last stand of a killer elite facing overwhelming odds. It is doubtful that *300* can call up in audiences even a tiny fraction of the emotions that *The Wild Bunch* has always elicited, to say nothing of the earlier film's enduring power. After all, "Peckinpah's savage poetry was informed by an abiding moral perspective on its violence."[67] So Peckinpah may be regarded as having been astonishingly Aristotelian, regardless of his own or his critics' understanding of catharsis.

The last word ought to be Peckinpah's. It is intended to provide a kind of synthesis to his own thesis (catharsis) and antithesis (no catharsis). Before he said in his BBC interview that he had been wrong, he stated, matter-of-factly, something with which every sensitive viewer and critic can agree: "I deal in violence as ... very sad poetry."

Notes

1. Jim Kitses, *Horizons West: Anthony Mann, Budd Boetticher, Sam Peckinpah: Studies of Authorship within the Western* (London: Thames and Hudson/British Film Institute, 1969), 168. The expanded edition—*Horizons West: Directing the Western from John Ford to Clint Eastwood* (London: BFI Publishing, 2004)—is marred by academic jargon; the quotation now appears at 223.

2. Cf. the titles of Marshall Fine, *Bloody Sam: The Life and Films of Sam Peckinpah* (1991; rpt. New York: Miramax, 2005); Terrence Rafferty, "Artist of Death," *The New Yorker* (March 6, 1995), 127–129; Max Evans, *Sam Peckinpah, Master of Violence: Being the Account of the Making of a Movie and Other Sundry Things* (Vermillion: Dakota Press / University of South Dakota, 1972). The film referred to in Evans's title is *The Ballad of Cable Hogue* (1970), Peckinpah's first film after *The Wild Bunch*.

3. Stephen Prince, *Savage Cinema: Sam Peckinpah and the Rise of Ultraviolent Movies* (Austin: University of Texas Press, 1998; rpt. 2010), 231.

4. Prince, *Savage Cinema*, 104–105.

5. Cordell Strug, "*The Wild Bunch* and the Problem of Idealist Aesthetics, or, How Long Would Peckinpah Last in Plato's Republic?" *Film Heritage*, 10 no. 2 (Winter, 1974–1975), 17–26; rpt. in Michael Bliss (ed.), *Doing It Right: The Best Criticism on Sam Peckinpah's* The Wild Bunch (Carbondale: Southern Illinois University Press, 1994), 80–89.

6. That this is far from true has recently been shown, if not for the first time, by Stephen Halliwell, *Between Ecstasy and Truth: Interpretations of Greek Poetics from Homer to Longinus* (Oxford: Oxford University Press, 2011), 155–207 (chapter titled "To Banish or Not to Banish? Plato's Unanswered Question about Poetry"). Strug's term "totalitarianism" for Platonic thought seems indebted to Karl Popper, *The Open Society and Its Enemies*, vol. 1: *The Spell of Plato*, first published in 1945.

7. Quoted from Paul Seydor, *Peckinpah: The Western Films—A Reconsideration* (Urbana: University of Illinois Press, 1997; rpt. 1999), 341 (statement to author). An earlier edition of the book had appeared in 1980 (without the title's last phrase).

8. William Murray, "Playboy Interview: Sam Peckinpah," *Playboy* (August 1972), 65–66, 68, 70, 72–74, 192; rpt. in Kevin J. Hayes (ed.), *Sam Peckinpah: Interviews* (Jackson: University Press of Mississippi, 2008), 96–120; quotation at 68 (original) and 102–103 (rpt.).

9. Jacob Bernays, *Grundzüge der verlorenen Abhandlung des Aristoteles über Wirkung der Tragödie* (Breslau: Trewendt, 1857), frequently reprinted and translated. On this see, e.g., Halliwell, *Between Ecstasy and Truth*, 236–238, 245–246, and 253. Bernays was an uncle of Sigmund Freud's by marriage and exerted a strong influence on Freud's psychoanalysis. On Bernays and Freud see now Marie-Christin Wilm, "Die Grenzen tragischer Katharsis: Jacob Bernays' *Grundzüge der verlorenen Abhandlung des Aristoteles* (1857) im Kontext zeitgenössischer Tragödientheorie," and Günter Gödde, "Therapeutik und Ästhetik—Verbindungen zwischen Breuers und Freuds kathartischer Therapie und der Katharsis-Konzeption von Jacob Bernays," both in Martin Vöhler and Dirck Linck (eds.), *Grenzen der Katharsis in den modernen Künsten: Transformationen des aristotelischen Modells seit Bernays, Nietzsche und Freud* (Berlin: De Gruyter, 2009), 21–50 and 63–91.

10. Chris Hodenfield, "Sam Peckinpah Breaks a Bottle," *Rolling Stone* (May 13, 1971), 18.

11. Barry Norman's interview with Peckinpah was broadcast on BBC One on December 1, 1976; it is available online at, e.g., https://www.youtube.com/watch?v=quT0SLvqQLY. Peckinpah scholars occasionally misdate it to 1979. Presumably Peckinpah was in Britain at that time working on the postproduction of *Cross of Iron*, a British-German production released early in 1977. German philosopher and psychologist Theodor Lipps, too, influenced Freud.

12. Robin Wood, *Hitchcock's Films Revisited*, rev. ed. (New York: Columbia University Press, 2002), 61 and 171.

13. Prince, *Savage Cinema*, 134, speaks of Peckinpah's "customary verbal stupidity when granting public interviews."

14. Prince, *Savage Cinema*, 105–119. On explicit violence as depicted in ancient texts and images see, e.g., Susanne Muth, *Gewalt im Bild: Das Phänomen der medialen Gewalt im Athen des 6. und 5. Jahrhunderts v. Chr.* (Berlin: De Gruyter, 2008), and Martin Zimmermann (ed.), *Extreme Formen von Gewalt in Bild und Text des Altertums* (Munich: Utz, 2009).

15. Prince, *Savage Cinema*, 109, with erroneous date.

16. Prince, *Savage Cinema*, 118.

17. Bernard F. Dukore, *Sam Peckinpah's Feature Films* (Urbana: University of Illinois Press, 1999), 95–96; quotation at 95.

18. John L. Simons and Robert Merrill, *Peckinpah's Tragic Westerns: A Critical Study* (Jefferson: McFarland, 2011), 4 (cf. 31, where they dismiss Prince's view). Their first chapter ("Peckinpah's Tragic Vision," 3–32 and 197–198 [notes]) includes discussions of other directors' works, among them John Ford's *The Searchers* (1956) at 11–13. Their points about this film are intended (197 note 5) as a rebuttal of my "Tragic Features in John Ford's *The Searchers*." They do not know its expanded and revised version—"Tragic Features in John Ford's *The Searchers*," in Martin M. Winkler (ed.), *Classical Myth and Culture in the Cinema* (New York: Oxford University Press, 2001), 118–147—and are cavalier about the spelling of Aristotle's term

peripeteia (correct at 6, incorrect at 184). Nor do they get my name right. So I take only a dim view of their argument.

19. Cordell Strug, "Human Striving, Human Strife: Sam Peckinpah and the Journey of the Soul," in Michael Bliss (ed.), *Peckinpah Today: New Essays on the Films of Sam Peckinpah* (Carbondale: Southern Illinois University Press, 2012), 137–146, at 137–138. He primarily discusses *The Killer Elite* (1975) and *Cross of Iron* (1976).

20. Halliwell, *Between Ecstasy and Truth*, 220. Below, page references to this book appear in brackets directly following quotations.

21. Aristotle, *Poetics* 1449b24–28 (in Chapter 6); quoted from Stephen Halliwell, *The Poetics of Aristotle: Translation and Commentary* (London: Duckworth / Chapel Hill: University of North Carolina Press, 1987; rpt. 2006), 37; commentary on this at 88–92. By mimesis, a fundamental term in Plato and Aristotle, we should understand "representation," not the narrower concept of "imitation" (its traditional translation). On mimesis see Halliwell, *The Aesthetics of Mimesis: Ancient Texts and Modern Problems* (Princeton: Princeton University Press, 2002), especially Chs. 5–8 on Aristotle. Andrew Ford, "The Purpose of Aristotle's *Poetics*," *Classical Philology*, 110 (2015), 1–21, is a useful introduction, suitable for non-specialists as well.

22. Halliwell, *Between Ecstasy and Truth*, 222, 210.

23. *Ibid.*, 237.

24. *Ibid.*

25. *Ibid.*, 233–234.

26. *Ibid.*, 245.

27. Cf. Martha C. Nussbaum, *The Fragility of Goodness: Luck and Ethics in Greek Tragedy and Philosophy*, rev. ed. (Cambridge: Cambridge University Press, 2001).

28. Halliwell, *Between Ecstasy and Truth*, 235.

29. *Ibid.*, 248, 249.

30. *Ibid.*, 258.

31. E.g. at Murray, "Playboy Interview: Sam Peckinpah," 72 (original) and 109 (rpt.).

32. Cf. the title of James M. Redfield: *Nature and Culture in the* Iliad: *The Tragedy of Hector*, 2nd ed. (Durham: Duke University Press, 1994; rpt. 2004).

33. Cf. James. P. Holoka (ed.), *Simone Weil's* The Iliad, or, The Poem of Force: *A Critical Edition* (New York: Lang, 2003; rpt. 2008). Weil's text first appeared in 1939.

34. On *enargeia*, Homer, and cinema see Martin M. Winkler, *Classical Literature on Screen: Affinities of Imagination* (Cambridge: Cambridge University Press, 2017), 21–40 (chapter titled "The Classical Sense of Cinema and the Cinema's Sense of Antiquity").

35. Eric Csapo and William J. Slater, *The Context of Ancient Drama* (Ann Arbor: University of Michigan Press, 1995; rpt. 2005), 270–272 (78A-79A), collect ancient descriptions. See further Oliver Taplin, *Greek Tragedy in Action* (1978; rpt. New York: Routledge, 2015), 101–121 and 189 (notes; chapter titled "Tableaux, Noises and Silences").

36. Aeschylus, *Agamemnon* 1384–1386 and 1388–1391; quoted from Richmond Lattimore (trans.), *Aeschylus I:* Oresteia (Chicago: University of Chicago Press, 1953), 80. The translation was first published in 1947.

37. Quoted from Csapo and Slater, *The Context of Ancient Drama*, 271 (78D, with source reference). Ajax will soon be dead by his own hand, shamed by his realization that, in a fit of madness, he has killed a flock of sheep rather than his enemies.

38. Taplin, *Greek Tragedy in Action*, 108.

39. Halliwell, *Between Ecstasy and Truth*, 6. Cf. Halliwell, 230: "the piercing psychological 'shudder' of *ekplêxis* (which suggests an acute emotional impact)."

40. Prince, *Savage Cinema*, 170–184.

41. Prince, *Savage Cinema*, 169 and 172.

42. Aristotle, *Poetics* 1453a29–30 (in Chapter 13).

43. D.W. Lucas (ed. and comm.), *Aristotle*: Poetics (Oxford: Clarendon Press, 1968; several rpts.), 147.

44. Cf. on this the classic and still fundamental work by E.R. Dodds, *The Greeks and the Irrational* (Berkeley: University of California Press, 1951; several rpts.).

45. Euripides, *The Bacchae* 683, 689–691, 735–746, and 753–754; quoted from David Grene and Richmond Lattimore (eds.), *The Complete Greek Tragedies: Euripides V: Electra, The Phoenician Women, The Bacchae* (Chicago: University of Chicago Press, 1959; several rpts.), 185–187. The translator is William Arrowsmith.

46. Shirley A. Barlow, *The Imagery of Euripides: A Study in the Dramatic Use of Pictorial Language*, 3rd ed. (London: Bristol Classical Press / Duckworth, 2008), 63; quoted in reverse order.

47. Aristotle, *Poetics* 1451a34–35.

48. Euripides, *The Bacchae*, 1111–1115 and 1122–1141; Arrowsmith, 203–204. Ino and Autonoë are Agave's sisters and Pentheus' aunts.

49. Prince, *Savage Cinema*, 171 and 172.

50. Prince, *Savage Cinema*, 249.

51. Stephen Farber, "Peckinpah's Return," *Film Quarterly*, 23 no. 1 (Fall, 1969), 2–11; quotation at 5. This

article is reprinted in Bliss (ed.), *Doing It Right*, 31–45; quotation there at 36–37. Prince, *Savage Cinema*, 173–175, examines the opening tableau in detail.

52. Staatliche Antikensammlungen, Munich: J332 (previously 2645) = Beazley Archive 2.371.15 (no. 203914).

53. Euripides, *The Bacchae* 1084–1089; Arrowsmith, 203.

54. Euripides, *Bacchae*, edited and comments by E. R. Dodds, 2nd ed (Oxford: Clarendon Press, 1960; several rpts.), 213.

55. Garner Simmons, *Peckinpah: A Portrait in Montage*, new ed. (New York: Limelight, 1998), 96.

56. Rafferty, "Artist of Death," 129.

57. Cf. on this the brief comments in Martin M. Winkler, "Classical Mythology and the Western Film," *Comparative Literature Studies*, 22 (1985), 516–540, at 523.

58. Cordell Strug, *Lament of an Audience on the Death of an Artist (1985)* (St. Paul: Ytterli Press, 2008), 21–22. The text of this slim volume was written in the year given in its title. Peckinpah died in 1984. Cf. in this context Weddle, "*If They Move…Kill 'Em!*" 377.

59. Quoted from Farber, "Peckinpah's Return," 9 (original) and 42 (rpt.).

60. David Weddle, "*If They Move…Kill 'Em!*" *The Life and Times of Sam Peckinpah* (New York: Grove Press, 2000), 342.

61. Quoted from Farber, "Peckinpah's Return," 8 and 11 (original); 40–41 and 45 (rpt.).

62. An exception is Peter Borden, "A Shared Vision: Euripides' *The Bacchae* and Peckinpah's *The Wild Bunch*" (undated, unpublished), a seminar paper written for "Violence and Catharsis: From Greek Epic and Tragedy to Modern Cinema," a course I began teaching in the mid-1980s. I am pleased to acknowledge my student's work even after all the years that have passed.

63. Gorgias, *Encomium of Helen* 18 and 17. Cf. on this Halliwell, *Between Ecstasy and Truth*, 279, with note 30 on the textual emendation to *nosos*. The translations of Gorgias' terms are Halliwell's. Gorgias was born almost exactly a century before Aristotle. Gorgias' adjective *hêdys* ("pleasurable") literally means "sweet." Cf. Sir Philip Sidney's famous dictum about "the sweet violence of a tragedy" in *An Apology for Poetry* or *The Defense of Poesy*, ed. Geoffrey Shepherd; 3rd ed. by R.W. Maslen (Manchester: Manchester University Press, 2002), 98.

64. Cf., e.g., Aristotle, *Poetics* 1462b-16-17. He states there, at the conclusion of our surviving text, that he has been dealing with fundamental features of both genres. The second book of the *Poetics* (on comedy) is lost.

65. Cf. the title of S.H. Butcher, *Aristotle's Theory of Poetry and Fine Arts, with a Critical Text of* The Poetics, 4th ed. (1907; rpt. New York: Dover, 1951; several rpts.). Specifically against Butcher's view of catharsis: Bernd Seidensticker, "Die Grenzen der Katharsis," in Vöhler and Linck (eds.), *Grenzen der Katharsis in den modernen Künsten*, 3–20, at 16–17. Seidensticker, 20, concludes that Aristotelian catharsis applies only to tragedy and only in limited ways.

66. Cf. Dorothy L. Sayers, "Aristotle on Detective Fiction," in Sayers, *Unpopular Opinions: Twenty-One Essays* (New York: Harcourt Brace, 1947), 222–236 (the essay was first published in 1935); Pedro L. Cano, *De Aristóteles a Woody Allen: Poética y retórica para cine y televisión* (Barcelona: Gedisa, 1999); Michael Tierno, *Aristotle's Poetics for Screenwriters: Storytelling Secrets from the Greatest Mind in Western Civilization* (New York: Hyperion, 2002). Robert McKee, *Story: Substance, Structure, Style, and the Principles of Screenwriting* (1997; rpt. London: Methuen, 2014), refers to Aristotle and the *Poetics* throughout. Most often Aristotle is cited as ultimate authority on plot construction (the three unities, generally misunderstood) and progression, e.g., by Syd Field, *Screenplay: The Foundations of Screenwriting*, rev. ed. (New York: Delta, 2005), and *The Screenwriter's Workbook*, 5th ed. (New York: Delta, 2006), passim.

67. Prince, *Savage Cinema*, 246.

Filmography

The Birds. Dir. Alfred Hitchcock. Alfred J. Hitchcock Productions, 1963.
Cross of Iron. Dir. Sam Peckinpah. Anglo-EMI Productions, ITC Entertainment, 1976.
The Killer Elite. Dir. Sam Peckinpah. Omnilab Media, Mascot Pictures Wales, 1975.
The Searchers. Dir. John Ford. C.V. Whitney Pictures; Warner Bros, 1956.
300. Dir. Zack Snyder. Warner Bros., 2007
The Wild Bunch. Dir. Sam Peckinpah. Warner Bros.-Seven Arts, 1969.

Works Cited

Aeschylus. *Aeschylus I: Oresteia*. Translated by Richmond Lattimore. Chicago: University of Chicago Press, 1953.
Aristotle. *Poetics*. Edited and comments by D.W. Lucas. Oxford: Clarendon Press, 1968.

Barlow, Shirley A. *The Imagery of Euripides: A Study in the Dramatic Use of Pictorial Language.* 3rd ed. London: Bristol Classical Press/Duckworth, 2008.
Bernays, Jacob. *Grundzüge der verlorenen Abhandlung des Aristoteles über Wirkung der Tragödie.* Breslau: Trewendt, 1857.
Butcher, S. H. *Aristotle's Theory of Poetry and Fine Arts, with a Critical Text* of The Poetics. 4th ed. New York: Macmillan, 1907; rpt. New York: Dover, 1951.
Cano, Pedro L. De Aristóteles a *Woody Allen: Poética y retórica para cine y television.* Barcelona: Gedisa, 1999.
Csapo, Eric, and William J. Slater. *The Context of Ancient Drama.* Ann Arbor: University of Michigan Press, 1995; rpt. 2005.
Dodds, E.R. *The Greeks and the Irrational.* Berkeley: University of California Press, 1951
Dukore, Bernard F. *Sam Peckinpah's Feature Films.* Urbana: University of Illinois Press, 1999.
Euripides. *Bacchae.* Edited and comments by E. R. Dodds. 2nd ed. Oxford: Clarendon Press, 1960.
Evans, Max. *Sam Peckinpah, Master of Violence: Being the Account of the Making of a Movie and Other Sundry Things.* Vermillion: Dakota Press/University South Dakota, 1972.
Fine, Marshall. *Bloody Sam: The Life and Films of Sam* Peckinpah. New York: Primus/ Donald I. Fine, 1991; rpt. New York: Miramax Books, 2005.
Ford, Andrew. "The Purpose of Aristotle's *Poetics,*" *Classical Philology* vol. 110 (2015): 1–21.
Farber, Stephen. "Peckinpah's Return." *Film Quarterly* vol. 23, no. 1 (Fall, 1969): 2–11.
_____. "Peckinpah's Return." In Michael Bliss, ed., *Doing It Right: The Best Criticism on Sam Peckinpah's* The Wild Bunch, 31-45. Carbondale, IL: Southern Illinois University Press, 2005.
Field, Syd. *Screenplay: The Foundations of Screenwriting.* Rev. ed. New York: Delta, 2005.
_____. *The Screenwriter's Workbook.* 5th ed. New York: Delta, 2006.
Gödde, Günter. "Therapeutik und Ästhetik—Verbindungen zwischen Breuers und Freuds kathartischer Therapie und der Katharsis-Konzeption von Jacob Bernays." In Martin Vöhler and Dirck Linck, eds., *Grenzen der Katharsis in den modernen Künsten: Transformationen des aristotelischen Modells seit Bernays, Nietzsche und Freud,* 63–91. Berlin: De Gruyter, 2009.
Grene, David, and Richmond Lattimore, eds. *The Complete Greek Tragedies: Euripides V: Electra, The Phoenician Women, The Bacchae.* Chicago: University of Chicago Press, 1959.
Halliwell, Stephen. *The Aesthetics of Mimesis: Ancient Texts and Modern Problems.* Princeton: Princeton University Press, 2002.
_____. *The* Poetics *of Aristotle: Translation and Commentary.* London: Duckworth/Chapel Hill: University of North Carolina Press, 1987; rpt. 2006.
_____. "To Banish or Not to Banish? Plato's Unanswered Question about Poetry." In *Between Ecstasy and Truth: Interpretations of Greek Poetics from Homer to Longinus,* 155–207. Oxford: Oxford University Press, 2011.
Hodenfield, Chris. "Sam Peckinpah Breaks a Bottle." *Rolling Stone* (May 13, 1971): 18.
Holoka, James. P., ed. *Simone Weil's* The Iliad, or, The Poem of Force: *A Critical Edition.* New York: Lang, 2003; rpt. 2008.
Kitses, Jim. *Horizons West: Anthony Mann, Budd Boetticher, Sam Peckinpah: Studies of Authorship within the Western.* London: Thames and Hudson/British Film Institute, 1969.
_____. *Horizons West: Directing the Western from John Ford to Clint Eastwood.* London: BFI Publishing, 2004.
McKee, Robert. *Story: Substance, Structure, Style, and the Principles of Screenwriting.* New York: It Books, 1997; rpt. London: Methuen, 2014.
Murray, William. "Playboy Interview: Sam Peckinpah." *Playboy* (August 1972): 65–66, 68, 70, 72–74, 192.
_____. "Playboy Interview: Sam Peckinpah." In Kevin J. Hayes, ed., *Sam Peckinpah: Interviews,* 96–120. Jackson: University Press of Mississippi, 2008.
Muth, Susanne. *Gewalt im Bild: Das Phänomen der medialen Gewalt im Athen des 6. und 5. Jahrhunderts v. Chr.* Berlin: De Gruyter, 2008.
Norman, Barry. "Sam Peckinpah – Interview (January 12, 1976)." *YouTube,* BBC One on December 1, 1976. At https://www.youtube.com/watch?v=quT0SLvqQLY.
Nussbaum, Martha C. *The Fragility of Goodness: Luck and Ethics in Greek Tragedy and Philosophy.* Rev. ed. Cambridge: Cambridge University Press, 2001.
Popper, Karl. *The Open Society and Its Enemies,* Vol. 1: The Spell of Plato. London: Routledge, 1945.
Prince, Stephen. *Savage Cinema: Sam Peckinpah and the Rise of Ultraviolent Movies.* Austin: University of Texas Press, 1998; rpt. 2010.
Rafferty, Terrence. "Artist of Death." *The New Yorker* (March 6, 1995): 127–129.
Redfield, James M. *Nature and Culture in the* Iliad: *The Tragedy of Hector.* 2nd ed. Durham: Duke University Press, 1994; rpt. 2004.
Sayers, Dorothy L. "Aristotle on Detective Fiction." In *Unpopular Opinions: Twenty-One Essays,* 222–236. New York: Harcourt Brace, 1947.
Seidensticker, Bernd. "Die Grenzen der Katharsis." In Martin Vöhler and Dirck Linck, eds. *Grenzen der*

Katharsis in den modernen Künsten: Transformationen des aristotelischen Modells seit Bernays, Nietzsche und Freud, 3–20. Berlin: De Gruyter, 2009.
Seydor, Paul. *Peckinpah: The Western Films—A Reconsideration.* Urbana: University of Illinois Press, 1997; rpt. 1999.
Sidney, Philip. *An Apology for Poetry or The Defense of Poesy.* Edited by Geoffrey Shepherd. 3rd ed. Edited by R. W. Maslen. Manchester: Manchester University Press, 2002.
Simons, John L., and Robert Merrill. *Peckinpah's Tragic Westerns: A Critical Study.* Jefferson, NC: McFarland, 2011.
Simmons, Garner. *Peckinpah: A Portrait in Montage.* New ed. New York: Limelight, 1998.
Staatliche Antikensammlungen, Munich: J332 (previously 2645) = Beazley Archive 2.371.15 (no. 203914).
Strug, Cordell. "Human Striving, Human Strife: Sam Peckinpah and the Journey of the Soul." In Michael Bliss, ed., *Peckinpah Today: New Essays on the Films of Sam Peckinpah,* 137–146. Carbondale: Southern Illinois University Press, 2012.
_____. *Lament of an Audience on the Death of an Artist* (1985). St. Paul: Ytterli Press, 2008.
_____. "*The Wild Bunch* and the Problem of Idealist Aesthetics, or, How Long Would Peckinpah Last in Plato's Republic?" *Film Heritage,* vol. 10, no. 2 (Winter, 1974–1975): 17–26; rpt. in Michael Bliss, ed., *Doing It Right: The Best Criticism on Sam Peckinpah's The Wild Bunch,* 80–89. Carbondale: Southern Illinois University Press, 1994.
Taplin, Oliver. *Greek Tragedy in Action.* New York: Routledge, 1978; rpt. 2015.
Tierno, Michael. *Aristotle's* Poetics *for Screenwriters: Storytelling Secrets from the Greatest Mind in Western Civilization.* New York: Hyperion, 2002.
Weddle, David. *If They Move...Kill 'Em!: The Life and Times of Sam Peckinpah.* New York: Grove Press, 2000.
Wilm, Marie-Christin. "Die Grenzen tragischer Katharsis: Jacob Bernays' *Grundzüge der verlorenen Abhandlung des Aristoteles* (1857) *im Kontext* zeitgenössischer Tragödientheorie." In Martin Vöhler and Dirck Linck, eds., *Grenzen der Katharsis in den modernen Künsten: Transformationen des aristotelischen Modells seit Bernays, Nietzsche und Freud,* 21–50. Berlin: De Gruyter, 2009.
Winkler, Martin M. "Classical Mythology and the Western Film." *Comparative Literature Studies* vol. 22 (1985): 516–540.
_____. "The Classical Sense of Cinema and the Cinema's Sense of Antiquity." In *Classical Literature on Screen: Affinities of Imagination,* 21–40. Cambridge: Cambridge University Press.
_____. "Tragic Features in John Ford's *The Searchers.*" In Martin W. Winkler, ed., *Classical Myth and Culture in the Cinema,* 118–147. New York: Oxford University Press, 2001.
Wood, Robin. *Hitchcock's Films Revisited.* Rev. ed. New York: Columbia University Press, 2002.
Zimmermann, Martin, ed., *Extreme Formen von Gewalt in Bild und Text des Altertums.* Munich: Utz, 2009.

Euripidean Sunsets
Tragedy, the Western, and Conflicts Within
Maria Cecília de Miranda N. Coelho

It is well-known that only thirty-three tragedies have survived from the three greatest Greek playwrights, Aeschylus, Sophocles, and Euripides. With only around ten percent of their production available, we are still struggling to define what Greek tragedy is, and, consequently, its reception in the Western. Nonetheless, the Western is a genre in which several tragic elements can be identified, such as a heroic protagonist dying in a singular, dignified, and arresting duel that he could not avoid or leaving the scene (a house, a village) alone, as a scapegoat, after establishing order. In some Westerns, the reason for the battle is not—as it is the case in ancient tragedies—to deal with gods or forces of the world that are beyond our control. Many times, the opponent is simply a bad man or a group of bad men. There are films that are much more complex, and, in many of these, the conflict within the protagonist himself defines both the plot and the *mise-en-scène*. Elements of these dramatic Westerns are often accompanied by those of another genre, like *film noir*. This, of course, has created a cinematic minefield: what is classified as a Western (or a *noir*), like Greek tragedy, is not a homogeneous, easily characterized set of works. Rather than discussing definitions, I propose to use a common-sense approach to consider certain parallels between the Western and Greek tragedy in order to understand (and better appreciate) the richness and complexity of the Western genre and to explore a case of the reception of classics—a field that is currently exploding—in cinema. In particular, this essay will examine personal dilemmas and inner conflicts in four exemplary films: *The Gunfighter* (1950), *Track of the Cat* (1954), *The Lonely Man* (1957), and *Decision at Sundown* (1957). Other films will also be briefly mentioned and compared with those above.

To begin, a note on Euripides—specifically, on tragedy and the tragic. In Aristotle's *Poetics*, Euripides is referred to as "the most tragic of the tragedians" (1453a29); even other criticisms that Aristotle directs at the poet[1] within his influential work do not obscure this daring and challenging statement. Nietzsche's influential accusation that Euripides caused the death of tragedy is also famous, in part, because the playwright brought philosophical arguments to the stage because of his relationship with Socrates.[2] The reason for Euripides' daunting reputation is summed up best by Terence Irwin's solid argument that compares the work of the dramaturge with the fragility of human decisions even when they are guided by rational arguments. As Irwin points out:

> We might suppose that the dangers to us are external—from the gods or other aspects of the world beyond our control—or that they result from mistaken beliefs and values. If we

are optimistic, we will claim that mistaken beliefs and values make us vulnerable to external disaster, from the world and from the gods, and that the right views protect us from these hazards. This aim is accepted, with qualifications, by Aeschylus, Sophocles, and Socrates. Euripides rejects it.[3]

With this in mind, it is not surprising that Euripidean heroes like Heracles in the play named after him or Eteocles in *The Phoenician Women* are examples of an internal force acting against the individual (for example, Heracles' madness diminishes his rationality). Medea and Phaedra think they are acting properly but also struggle with their "non-rational desires." That (Greek) tragedy means confrontation or conflict is almost a truism.[4] When internalized, Greek tragedy's dramatic conflict onstage is even more disturbing. Hence, many of Euripides' plays are confusing to those who believe in the rationality of human agency and the universe.

Here, it is important to note that, by the end of the 19th century a sort of hermeneutic duel began concerning rationalism[5] versus irrationalism[6]—a debate that continues to this day, as Nicole Loraux argues, affirming that Euripides is the most misunderstood of the poets.[7] In connection with the death of ancient tragedy, modern discussions of tragedy today (or more generally in modern times) are complex. George Steiner, for instance, in his ground-breaking work on the subject, when analyzing the characteristics of Greek tragedy and the traditions that followed it, argues that even the plays of Shakespeare (an author more closely related to Euripides than Euripides was to his Greek colleagues) should not be seen as an extension of variant of ancient drama.[8] If this is the case, how can we—or directors like Anthony Mann, to note an outstanding case[9]—identify parallels between Greek tragedy and Westerns? Happily, help is available, first, through critical works like Martin Winkler's 1991 analysis of tragic features within Ford's *The Searchers*. Masters of *noir* also offer valuable psychological insights into tragedy, as the films we will consider radically confront the darker side of human nature. Jean-Pierre Melville, for example, is an indispensable help when bridging genres and then bridging the ancient and the contemporary. When asked the question, "What do gangsters represent for you?" he answered:

> Nothing at all. I think they're pathetic losers. But it so happens that the gangster story is a very suitable vehicle for the particular form of modern tragedy of film *noir* which was born from the American detective novels. It is a flexible genre. You can put whatever you want into it, good or bad. And it is a fairly easy vehicle to use to tell stories that matter to you about individual freedom, friendship, or rather human relationships, because they're not always friendly. Or betrayal, one of the driving forces in American crime novels.[10]

Here, the concepts related to "loser" (but also "gangster" and "flexibility of the genre") are also connected to Westerns and their protagonist(s). In both types of modern tragedy, such characters view themselves (and/or are viewed by others) as outlaws. Like the gangster, the Western gunfighter or gunslinger is also a "killer of men,"[11] with all the glory and doom that this entails at the conclusion of his story. This paradox results from his being at once a civilizer and a murderer, someone who cannot absent himself from any sort of excess. The *topos* of such a protagonist's loneliness is highly significant and recurrent in the genre.[12]

Associated with tragic figures in many ancient texts, the powerful image of the sunset and the end of light (as a form of life) appears in Euripides' *Helen*, where it is said that Menelaus was not dead or "gone to the land of shadows (*melamphaes*) where darkness takes the place of light,"[13] when the daughter of Oedipus claims she is on her last journey, "looking at [her] last sunlight,"[14] or when Iphigenia who, before being sacrificed, protests: "No more for me the light of day! No more these beams of the sun!"[15] Another striking example is found in Ajax's words, in the Sophoclean play named after him. Before his suicide, he remarks:

> And you, Helios, whose chariot-wheels climb the steep sky, when you see the land of my fathers, draw in your rein spread with gold and tell my disasters and my fate. [...] But you, beam of the present bright day, I salute you and the Sun in his chariot for the last time and never again. O light! [...] The rest he will tell to the shades in Hades.[16]

In Westerns, these types of sunsets also express inner dilemmas and the human paradox, transmitting the pessimism related to human beings' ability to know and control their own behavior. In short, the Euripidean sunset confirms the impossibility of the protagonist being with others.[17]

Keeping this in mind, let us now discuss some elements of the films I have selected, in chronological order. All of these belong to the same decade—a highly prolific period for the genre.[18] Henry King's *The Gunfighter* (1950) opens with its credits over the silhouette of a man riding quickly, followed by an intertitle that notes how famous men made their names from their ability with a gun: "the difference between death and glory was often but a fraction of seconds." It ends with a religious funerary service, in which the well-known hymn *Rock of Ages*,[19] by Augustus Toplady, is sung. While we hear the words "cleft for me, Let me hide myself in Thee," the same scenes of the rider, Jimmy Ringo (Gregory Peck), from the beginning, are shown, glorifying him.

> In *The Death of Tragedy*, George Steiner remarks that "[i]n the drama of Christian life, the arrow beats against the wind but points upward. Being a threshold to the eternal, the death of a Christian hero can be an occasion for sorrow but not for tragedy. [...] The Christian view knows only partial or episodic tragedy. Within its essential optimism there are moments of despair; cruel setbacks can occur during the ascent toward grace. But, as a Portuguese proverb has it, *Deus escreve direito por linhas tortas*."[20] Although Steiner insists that the Christian and pagan worlds are incompatible, there are instances in which they mingle. *The Gunfighter* is one of them. This Christian memorial to Ringo co-exists with the heroic temperament of Greek tragedy. Ringo's last words reveal a catastrophic vision of the world.

In *The Gunfighter*, Ringo, a famous but aging killer, is shown trying to meet his wife Peggy (Helen Westcott) and son to rebuild his life in a Christian way. Such a destiny, however, is doomed in this "psychological western."[21] In the village of Cayenne, in the few hours he has left,[22] Ringo, with the help of his old pal Mark (earlier, his fellow outlaw but now a marshal, played by Millard Mitchell), desperately attempts to demonstrate that he is more than just a gunfighter. But he is cursed by his reputation as fastest on the draw. When he arrives at the saloon, the more he tries to avoid conflict, the more he seems to lose (although he wins his unwanted duels). Ringo and Mark share a remarkable scene with a group of women: they talk to Ringo without knowing who he is about the necessity of expelling the gunfighter (himself), demonstrating that his reputation is greater than his actual presence. Although the scene has a comic mood, Ringo is greatly affected when he discovers his name has become anathema. Even as he tries to dispel his notoriety, he cannot establish a new life—something his wife recognizes before he does.

Peck's somber and subdued comportment (comparable to that of his later Atticus Finch in Robert Mulligan's *To Kill a Mockingbird* [1962]), with Arthur Miller's remarkable black and white cinematography, magnifies the tension between his desire to change and his ability to do so during his encounter with his wife (living *incognito* in Cayenne). When Peggy (a dedicated school teacher, in sharp contrast with the nomadic outlaw[23]) asks him where he got the idea of returning to try a new life, he says, "All of a sudden you look at things different than the way ya did five years ago. All of a sudden I knew this was the only thing in the world I wanted." His childish expression—trying to convince her he has changed, that he is "different"—contrasts with her grave face, which reveals the implacability of life. Ringo cannot run from his past—there is no refuge for him, even in his wife's heart, when she says she will wait for him as he promises to return in a year.[24] Unlike Jim Douglass (also played by Peck for the same director) in *The Bravados* (1958) or Chris Danning (Randolph Scott) in *Coroner Creek* (by Ray Enright, 1948), Ringo cannot find solace in a moral lesson with people singing at a funeral. There is also no answer to why those like Mark enjoy this comfort while others like himself and the young gunslinger Hunt (Skip Homeier) cannot.

In the end, after meeting his son, the aging gunslinger is murdered—not in a duel, but shot from behind by Hunt, who just wants to be famous as "the one who killed Ringo." Surprisingly, Ringo's last request is that the marshal free his killer. His final words not only ensure that his legendary persona continues, but they also punish Hunt.

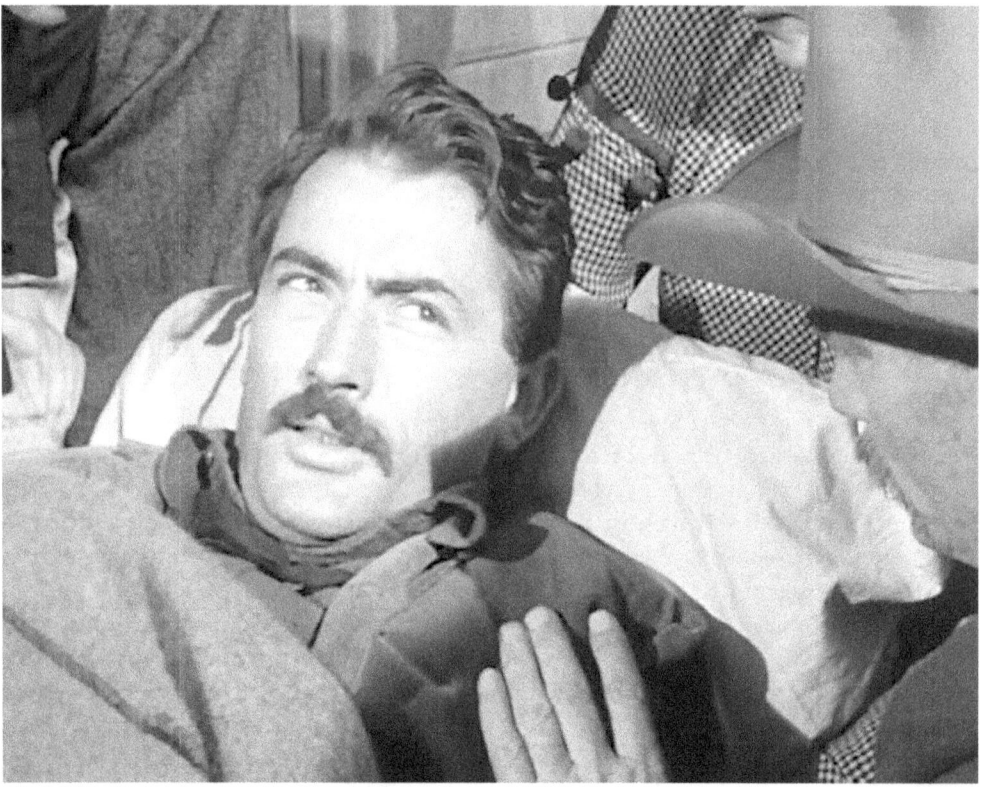

Predicting his killer's arrival, Ringo (Gregory Peck) says, "You will see what I mean … just wait." *The Gunfighter* **(20th Century–Fox, 1950).**

Being set free is not a favor, as Hunt assumes. Saying he does not want the killer to be hanged but wants to live "to see what it means to live like a big tough gunny," Ringo curses his murderer—demonstrating how tragic his lonely life (and that of others like him) is and revealing anger, not Christian forgiveness.

When Ringo speaks about his loneliness, in the context of the film, it means more than a characteristic that could be attributed to many people who live isolated or in solitude. We could compare him, for instance, to Orestes in Euripides' *Electra*. *Mutatis mutandis*, Ringo, like the son of Agamemnon, is an avenger and cannot live with those he came to help. Orestes, after killing his mother, has to depart for a long process of purification, however, Electra will be safe having his best friend, Pylades, as her husband. Even if Orestes is not dead, he feels as if he were when he asks his sister to embrace him and sing a threnody (*Electra*, 1325–6), and even if his act was done in obedience to Phoebus's oracle, he is cursed by the Erinyes (incidentally, this is seen by the *Dioskouroi* as not fair, *Electra* 1241–48). In a similar way, Ringo dies, and Peggy and his friend Mark will be together, with his son. Although Ringo is not pursued by the Furies, his final words act as a curse—Hunt will be persecuted and lonely for his whole life. Complicating this revenge story, there are (at least) two perspectives in the film, and, as some scholars have argued, this was common in Greek drama: the audience was not monolithic, and the dramas also contained many voices. In *The Gunfighter*, the people who go to church and end singing the salvific hymn find consolation. But for Ringo, there is only anger, solitude, and death. In "The Mutability of Fortune in Euripides," Michael Lloyd remarks that "one of Euripides's most distinctive features is his portrayal of human beings *in extremis*, and his examination of what they can find, over and above mere endurance, to set against their circumstance."[25] Isolated and unable to find consolation, Ringo's sensibility is tragic and Euripidean. As Mary R. Lefkowitz points out, "despite the frequency Euripides portrays in his dramas the gods and their actions, he is thought of as the poet who more than any other asks his audiences, ancient and modern, to question the nature of the gods and even their existence."[26]

The Track of the Cat is the second work to be considered here. Just as some scholars have questioned (out of prejudice) whether Euripidean plays like *Helen* or *Alcestis* truly are tragedies, this film has also been seen as not fitting into its genre. In the audio commentary accompanying Paramount Home Video's Special Collector's edition of *The Track of the Cat*, the director's son, William Wellman, Jr., recalls that the studio did not know what to with this production by the Wayne-Fellows Company, advertising it as an "unusual western."[27] As Josh Anderson (2013) notes, *The Track of the Cat* followed other genre experiments, *The Ox-Bow Incident* (1943), *Yellow Sky* (1948), and *Westward the Women* (1951), in which William A. Wellman (again) "recklessly dash[ed] our conceptions of what westerns can be, should be."[28]

In *The Track of the Cat*, the bareness and cold of the snowy landscape contrast with the tumultuous emotions of the dysfunctional Bridges family, who are menaced by a black panther (that is never seen) on their property. Based on the novel by Walter Van Tilburg Clark, this film features Curt (Robert Mitchum), who is favored by his parents, Ma (Beulah Bondi) and Pa (Philip Tonge), yet dominates his brothers Hal (Tab Hunter) and Arthur (William Hopper), both of whom are more resigned to his abusive behavior than his sister Grace (Teresa Wright). There is also the peculiar presence of a ranch hand, Chief Sam (Carl Switzer), whose wife and daughter were killed by a black cat.

The mysterious panther and Hal's sweetheart Gwen (Diana Lynn) are the disruptive forces that change the family. The fear (*phobos*) and pity (*eleos*) that, according to Aristotle, characterize tragedy also surround the characters (and the spectators) among the highly theatrical scenery of the ranch which acts as a stage and enhances the confrontation. William Clothier's photography, which intensifies the film's psychological struggle, is further reinforced by the colors associated with Curt and Gwen, whose red and yellow clothes form, respectively, a vivid contrast against the otherwise dominant black and white.[29]

To hunt and kill the animal that is attacking the family's cattle is only one level of the film's deeply symbolic plot. In the course of stalking the big cat, the hunters become the hunted, Arthur and Curt are its victims, and Hal is the only brother to survive. Paralleling the external menace, the family's internal struggle becomes apparent as everyone argues bitterly, revaluating their traumatized lives: Grace and Arthur argue with Curt, Pa with Ma, and Gwen with Curt and Ma. Curt and Hal must also fight against themselves. Violence is manifested in the first scene when Sam, perceiving the presence of the animal on a windy dawn, goes to wake the brothers. When Sam shows a wooden image of the panther, carved by Arthur, Curt lashes out angrily, criticizing Sam's native *spiritual* practices and his brothers' weakness. Amid discussions with an ireful Grace, alcoholic Pa, and unpleasant Ma (who judges Sam's beliefs and Gwen and Hal's behavior partly on the basis of her repressive Christianity), Curt and Gwen's scenes are particularly instructive.

When they track the cat in the valley, Arthur asks Curt to be fair to Hal and less egocentric in respect to the Bridges' property. Curt, filled with disdain for Hal's feelings and plan and upset because the cat has killed four animals (including his bull), leaves Arthur in the valley, returning to the ranch to better prepare for the hunt. After he arrives at the ranch, Curt speaks three times about killing the cat and giving its skin to Gwen as a blanket (if it is black, not yellow) as a wedding gift to warm her bed, insinuating that her husband will be a "bashful kid." Each time he jokes, in a scene of no more than five minutes, there are sexual innuendoes. When reprimanded by Grace for not changing his clothes in the living room, Curt teases Gwen, saying that, if the cat's skin is small, she can use it as a costume for a special wedding dance. After she sternly answers that she "is not much of a dancer," he stands imposingly in front of Gwen, saying he will show her how. In contrast, Curt calls Arthur a monk, and later, when Arthur dies, Ma asks to wrap his body in a bedspread that he liked as a child. It has a unicorn (similar to the famous Cluny tapestry, surrounded by other animals), a symbol of chastity. That Gwen's blouse is yellow is also meaningful. It is the only color besides Curt's red coat to contrast with the film's black and white monotones, suggesting her sexuality is as disruptive to the family as is the panther.

When Arthur speaks in favor of Hal (who needs his blessing to get married), Curt, who presents himself as the strongest member of the family, says that, if it were not for him, "there wouldn't be any valley. Any stock ... the cat and the Indians would have it all." Curt says he "built it all" and will continue to do so: "I'd whip this valley into shape." Curt's insolence (*hubris*) contrasts with his actions, for he spies on Gwen and Grace through their bedroom window and shows weakness when he is alone hunting the cat. After he finds Arthur's body and places his red coat on him (to avoid the horse smelling the panther on his brother's coat, which has the same pattern as the bull that was killed), Curt's tragic denouement takes place. While the horse carries Arthur home, his fortunes unravel. Curt wanders in the storm, dressed like his brother. Finally, he enters a cave and before a small fire (which is as yellow as Gwen's blouse), he talks to the carved panther Arthur kept in his pocket, saying he will defeat and kill her, take her skin to Gwen, and will make her pay his price. He thinks he has time and food. Suddenly, however, he realizes he has lost the food and becomes angry and throws the sculpture into the fire. Trying to calm himself, he browses the book by John Keats that Arthur had carried with him. In a close-up, we see and hear him reading the first line: "When I have fears that I may cease to be."[30] Driven to desperation, he starts crying and speaking words at random. The scene then cuts to Hal digging a grave for Arthur and the fighting among the other Bridges. When we next see Curt, he is outside the cave, lost, trying to make another fire, even using the pages from the book, insolently saying that he will give them a better home. Flurries of snow extinguish the fire. Again desperate, while listening for the cat, he shoots erratically (having earlier been praised by Pa for his marksmanship) and falls down a chasm.

Reading an ode by John Keats, Curt (Robert Mitchum) recites, "When I have fears that I may cease to be." *The Track of the Cat* (Warner Bros., 1954).

Central to this scene, the line from Keats' poem reveals the fragility and fear of a man who was once so proud of his strength. A vitally important emotion discussed in Aristotle's *Rhetoric* and *Poetics*, fear is a key concept in the characterization of tragedy. In *Rhetoric*, Aristotle defines fear as "pain or agitation derived from imagination of a future destructive or painful evil."[31] One of the problems related to fear (*phobos*) is how the emotion can be stimulated in the audience and how and why the emotion suffered by the actor is perceived by the audience. Notably, after reading Keats' line, Curt reacts violently. Read, the word, "fears" triggers a chain of reactions that, at the end, takes him to his death. He trembles (*tromos*) like Megara in Euripides' *Heracles*, feels alarmed, like Hector, when he meets Achilles, in front of the gates of Troy, and flees (*phobethai*).[32] Instead of challenging an enemy without, Curt fights against himself, his fear signified by the strangeness of nature and the black cat. When Hal and Sam find his body, the native says that it was not the panther that killed Curt but his fear. Unlike Curt, Hal, who kills to become a man, listens for the cat, tracks and kills her, and is praised by Sam: "now you marry." This seemingly happy ending, however, does not make up for the family's losses, and Sam's words—"not the panther, the world is devil"—are disturbing. As Rush Rehm remarks, in tragedy "the sins, crimes, and obsessions of parents break out again in their offspring, usually with destructive consequences."³³ Aptly, the family makes a huge fire so Hal and Joe can find their way home in a stylized (man-made) sunset.

Commenting on Greek tragedy's treatment of dysfunctional families and transgenerational inheritance, Rehm also notes that the role that fear plays "trades on the public and cultural far more than the private and personal."³⁴ This connection, however, is more complex and much stronger than Rehm suggests. *Hippolytus* and *Medea* are good examples that blur such distinctions. Like Greek tragedy, *The Lonely Man* and *Decision at Sundown* also deal with family quarrels and traumas which involve the entire community. The first, directed by Henry Levin, focuses on a gunfighter who tries to gain the confidence of his son after leaving fourteen years earlier.³⁵ Riley Wade (Anthony Perkins) hates his father Jacob (Jack Palance), whom he sees as being responsible for his mother's suicide five years earlier. The son follows his father on a journey, a vengeful decision to make the father remember his mother's suffering and death every time he sees him. Jacob's resentment is evident when, before departing, he sets fire to the ranch where he once lived with his wife and son. After wandering from place to place and being banished for gunfighting, Jacob takes his sick son to the ranch where he lived with the young and thoughtful Ada (Elaine Aiken). The tension among these three, which is exacerbated by old enemies who unexpectedly arrive, is enhanced by cinematography (from Lionel Lindon) and the soundtrack (by Nathan van Cleave). Like Jimmy Ringo, Jacob wants to live in peace with his son. However, because of his former connections with outlaws and his fading sight (it could be argued that there is also an Oedipal element here), Jacob has only a short time to try to set Riley's life on the right track. The fight between them, as well as their personal demons, is symbolized by their efforts to collect and break the spirit of wild horses, particularly a white mare. Ada's interposition in the family dysfunction proves to be a double-edged sword, and the characters' dilemmas contribute to a gloomy fate that even a final redemptive death cannot dispel.

Lucy (Karen Steele) scolds Bart (Randolph Scott), saying, "The truth isn't an easy thing to face up to." *Decision at Sundown* (Columbia Pictures, 1957).

Besides Ada, Ben (Robert Middleton), an old friend of Jacob's gang, is also living on the ranch when he arrives. He tells the rebellious Riley what happened between his parents and changes the son's image of them. Jacob sets his and his son's fate in motion, when he kills a sheriff in self-defense while cutting wires placed by cattle barons. This could have been avoided if he had persuaded his wife Ruth to let the place; however, she—unlike the biblical Ruth, as is pointed out by Ben—refused to follow Jacob, even though he returns for her three times. When Ben's machinations alienate Jacob, Ada, and Riley, Ada defends Riley after he disappears (having argued with his father, he tries to tame the wild white mare), and Jacob accuses him of fleeing. When Ada finds Riley, hurt after being dragged by the mare he roped, she holds him, and they kiss passionately. However, the return of King Fisher (Neville Brand), Jacob's enemy and Ada's former lover, spoils Ada and Riley's plans. In a final showdown, with the help of his son (who is aware of his father's blindness), Jacob dies but also kills King. While external facts bring about a solution, Jacob's loneliness and tragic fate have no rational explanation. Simply trapped by passion, Ada is not a bad person, and Jacob dies in spite of always doing the right thing.

Decision at Sundown, one of the most famous of Budd Boetticher and Randolph Scott's collaborations, follows the same pattern—the Phaedra motive, one might say—as *The Lonely Man*. In this film, wrong actions also cause an erroneous perception of reality, in this case, of a woman. The psychologically affected Bart (Scott) attributes the suicide of his wife to the unscrupulous Tate Kimbrough (John Carroll) and decides to take revenge, helped by his friend Sam (Noah Beery, Jr.) on Tate's wedding day. From the church to the livery stable, most of the action takes place in a claustrophobic space within a single day. During this time, Bart not only affects many of the decisions of the citizens (who are controlled by Tate and his allies) but is also himself affected by finding out that his wife had numerous affairs. Most strikingly, Lucy (Karen Steele) and Ruby (Valerie French), respectively Tate's fiancée and former lover, reveal to Bart something he does not want to hear, as is made clear by Lucy's words: "Look, when you're in love the way you must have been, the truth isn't an easy thing to face up to. No man, including Tate Kimbrough, can take another man's wife away from him unless she really wants to be taken." In the end, the showdown does not occur. Tate and Bart leave Sundown, the former supported by Ruby, who shoots him in the shoulder to prevent his death. Bart, after a raucous scene in the saloon, rides off drunk into the sunset (like a prosaic Euripidean Heracles, who destroys everything around him), deflated after a frustrated and senseless revenge, albeit one that helped to clean the city. Observing the cowardice of the men confronting Tate, Otis (James Westerfield), a saloon keeper, confides to Doctor Storrow (John Archer): "If you'd been tending bar as long as I have, you wouldn't expect so much out of the human race." At the end, Storrow says to Lucy: "unfortunately, there's nothing we can do for him. I'll tell you one thing, none of us will ever forget the day that Bart Allison spent in Sundown." In the end, Bart seems to be condemned to duel with himself, as he did not seem to accept the blindness (*ate*) and intemperance (*hubris*) he had shown.

At the beginning of this essay, I was going to explore only four films which demonstrate how Westerns dialogue with ancient Euripidean drama, exhibiting their cultural inheritance. But I cannot end this essay without making reference to three other films in which the heroes also conform to this pattern of inner conflict. The first is Samuel Fuller's *Run of the Arrow* (1957), which offers a very revealing example of a man divided against himself. O'Meara (Rod Steiger), a Confederate veteran, leaves his family and culture after Appomattox to go West and ends up living as a Sioux. At the conclusion of the film, his native wife, Yellow Moccasin (Sara Montiel) helps O'Meara see that he cannot be a Sioux. He himself remarks, "I will live as a Sioux.... I will hunt as a Sioux.... I will fight and I will even die as a Sioux. But my God is a Christian God. I can't serve your Great Spirit." A reversal of Euripides' *Medea*, the conclusion of *Run of the Arrow* offers its viewer an internal clash fought out between the civilized and the savage and a tragic decision.[36]

Riley (Anthony Perkins, left) asks Jacob (Jack Palance), "Who are you?" Jacob answers, "I am your father." *The Lonely Man* (Paramount Pictures, 1957).

Arguably, the two best examples of the tragic character of the Western are embodied in Ethan Edwards in John Ford's *The Searchers* and Link Jones in Anthony Mann's *Man of the West*. Both films feature protagonists who, like Euripidean characters, accomplish what they think is necessary but are torn between opposing impulses in their natures. Their final screen images reveal lonely and internally scarred men, complex protagonists constrained to cross moral limits and to vacillate between civilization and savagery.

Identifying parallels between Greek tragedy and Westerns enables us to understand (and better appreciate) the richness and complexity of the Western genre. In this case of classical reception, surprising similarities in character portrayals of Euripides and King's *The Gunfighter* (1950), Wellman's *Track of the Cat* (1954), Levin's *The Lonely Man* (1957), and Boetticher's *Decision at Sundown* (1957) highlight the fragility of the human condition, inviting philosophical questions regarding the rationality of human agency and the universe and convey the tragedy, pessimism, and loneliness of the human condition. Bridging the modern and ancient worlds, the Western's Euripidean sunsets, transmitted by the artificial light of a film projector, are aesthetic and ethical (vicarious) experiences as moving and disturbing as those the ancient Greeks experienced under the sun (their theatrical performances were performed during the day), affecting their audiences deeply and forging their beliefs. Because Westerns are such suitable vehicles for tragedy and the conflict within, I hope that my readers feel, while they are wandering and wondering with the Western, that they should come away as Jean-Pierre Melville would have them, "unsure whether they understood." Westerns with Euripidean sunsets should "leave them wondering."[37]

Notes

1. Including the irrelevance of his choruses, *Medea*'s lack of artistic merit, and its use of *ex machina* or badly constructed characters, such as the depraved Menelaus or overly philosophical women, like Melanippe. For information on the uses and misuse of Aristotle, see pages 8–12 of Mark Ringer's *Euripides and the Boundaries of the Human*.

2. As is well-known, Euripides occupies third position after Aristophanes (*Frogs* 1470–1523), but his

damnatio came mainly after Schlegel brothers' studies and Nietzsche's criticism of his rationalism, in spite of the appreciation the German philosopher had for the *Bacchae*. See August Schlegel's *Cours de Litterature Dramatique* (1885), Frederick Nietzsche's *O Nascimento da Tragédia O Nascimento da Tragédia* (1992), Peter Burian's "Myth into *Mythos*: The Shaping of Tragic Plot" (1997), and Maria Cecília de M.N. Coelho's *Filosofia e Arte na Grécia Antiga* (2011).

3. Terence H. Irwin, "Euripides and Socrates," *Classical Philology* Vol. 78 (1983):196.

4. See the long chapter on Confrontations in Edith Hall's *Greek Tragedy: Suffering under the Sun*, pages 105–55, or the brief but incisive comment in Peter Burian's "Myth into *Mythos*: The Shaping of Tragic Plot," 181–82.

5. See Arthur W. Verrall's *Euripides the Rationalist: A Study in the History of Art and Religion* (Cambridge: Cambridge University Press, 1895).

6. See Eric R. Dodds' "Euripides the Irrationalist," *Classical Review* Vol. 43 (1929): 102–10.

7. Mark Ringer, *Euripides and the Boundaries of the Human* (Lanham, MD: Lexington Books, 2018), 1–6.

8. On elements of tragic experience in practice and theory, following Steiner's *The Death of Tragedy* (1961), see Williams' *Modern Tragedy* (1966) and, resuming the vexed question, see Eagleton's *Doce violência: A idéia do Trágico* (2012). For the latter, it is not only tragic drama that is considered, but also novels and philosophical works, which represent a variety of definitions of tragedy itself and expand on the idea of the tragic world as including the universe as a whole, without rational order.

9. See Christopher Wicking and Barrie Pattinson's "Interview with Anthony Mann," *Screen* Vol. 10, No. 4 (1969): 41–44.

10. Jean-Pierre Melville, "Interview (1970)," *YouTube*, 11 Sept. 1970, https://www.youtube.com/watch?v=Avz45nU-AJg&fbclid=IwAR2xHRVcK3AKkmVVRWL44tQ98MNGDo83hTHm-Mz6uxkO-V8ewkpYd0hBNTc. More recently, Bertrand Tavernier, commenting on *Coroner Creek* (a production by Sidonis Calysta, in 2015, released as a special feature in de Brazilian DVD edition of the film) pointed to the aspects of *noir* in this film and others from the Fifties. It is also worth remembering the parallels between the hero and the gangster pointed by Warshow (1948).

11. The famous expression came from Warshow in his classical essay *The Westerner*, as pointed by Winkler, 1991: 187.

12. It is worth noting the great number of Westerns in which terms like lonesome, lone, and lonely occur.

13. See Euripides' *Helen*, translated by E.P. Coleridge, 517–20.

14. See *The Antigone of Sophocles*, edited with introduction and notes by Sir Richard Jebb, 810.

15. See Euripides' *Iphigenia in Aulis* in *The Plays of Euripides*, translated by E.P. Coleridge, 1281–83.

16. See *The Ajax of Sophocles*, edited with introduction and notes by Sir Richard Jebb, 845–65.

17. See E. Segal's "Euripides: Poet of Paradox" (1983), C. Segal's *Euripides and the Poetics of Sorrow Euripides and the Poetics of Sorrow* (1993), and Seidensticker's "Peripeteia and Tragic Dialetic in Euripidean Tragedy" (1996).

18. On page 2 of *Cowboys as Cold Warriors: The Western and U.S.*, Stanley Corkin informs us that, from 1947 to 1950, Westerns made up 30% of the total output of major Hollywood studios and, in 1958 alone, more than 50 Westerns were made. For information about how the genre is connected to U.S. ideology and political agenda, see Corkin, in particular his "Introduction" and Chapters Three and Four, which focus on the Fifties. Also see McGee's *From* Shane *to* Kill Bill: *Rethinking the Western* (2007) and Loy's *Westerns in a Changing America, 1955–2000* (2014). On this approach to Greek Tragedy, *contra* the hegemony of Nietzschean perspective, see Winkler and Zeitlin's *Nothing to Do with Dionysus? Athenian Drama in Its Social Context* (1990).

19. Played also in *The Doolins of Oklahoma* (1949), *How the West Was Won* (1962), and *Hang 'Em High* (1968).

20. George Steiner, *The Death of Tragedy* (New York: Albert A. Knopf, 1961), 225.

21. Graham Fuller, "The psychological western," *Sight & Sound* (16 May 2016), www.bfi.org.uk.

22. Will Kane (Gary Cooper) in Fred Zinnemann's *High Noon* (1952) and Ben Wade (Glen Ford) in Delmer Daves' *3:10 to Yuma* (1957) are also found in similar situations.

23. See Clint Eastwood's *Unforgiven* regarding this contrast between the couples. On Ringo as a Homeric (but not tragic) hero, see Myrsiades, 2009.

24. Likewise, in *The Last Sunset*, Bandon (Kirk Douglas) tries to convince his former sweetheart, Belle (Dorothy Malone), now a self-assured woman, that he has changed in an inverted Oedipal story.

25. See Michael Lloyd's "The Mutability of Fortune in Euripides" in *Tragedy and Archaic Greek Thought*, 222–23.

26. In Mary R. Lefkowitz's "'Impiety' and 'Atheism' in Euripides' Dramas," 103.

27. Released June 6, 2006, Paramount Home Video's Special Collector's Edition of *The Track of the Cat* (1954) contains audio commentary (Dolby Digital 2.0) by William Wellman, Jr., Tab Hunter, and Frank Thompson.

28. Josh Anderson, "Westward Wellman," *Senses of Cinema* Vol. 67 (2013), http://sensesofcinema.com/2013/feature-articles/westward-wellman/.

29. For more information about the use of physical phenomena or landscapes to indicate emotions, or conflict framing mindsets and feelings in Greek tragedy, see Padel's *In and Out of the Mind: Greek Images of the Tragic Self* (1992).

30. An Elizabethan sonnet by John Keats, "When I Have Fears That I May Cease To Be" was published posthumously in *Life, Letters, and Literary Remains, of John Keats* (1848) by Richard Monckton Milnes.

31. Aristotle, *Rhetoric*, 1382a21–3. A detailed analysis of the function of fear in tragedy can be seen in *Tragic Pathos—Pity and Fear in Greek Philosophy and Tragedy*, in which Munteanu discusses theoretical approaches by Gorgias, Plato, and Aristotle and also some occurrences of the term and plays by Aeschylus, Sophocles, and Euripides, and Rehm, who has a whole chapter, "Fear and Tragedy" in *Radical Theatre: Greek Tragedy in the Modern World* dedicated to the theme.

32. See Euripides' *Heracles*, 627, and Homer's *Iliad*, 22, 136. Curt's death also recalls the last scene of *Prometheus Unbound*, by Aeschylus, in which the protagonist disappears complaining about the fear Zeus instilled in him (*ll*.1089–90).

33. Rush Rehm, *Radical Theatre: Greek Tragedy and the Modern World* (London: Duckworth, 2003), 59.

34. *Ibid.*, 63.

35. I do not include *Shane* (George Stevens, 1953) here, as it seems to be highly optimistic. The final words of Shane (Alan Ladd) to Joey Starrett (Brandon De Wilde) suggest order can be achieved: "Tell her [your mother] everything's all right. And there aren't any more guns in the valley…. You go home to your mother and father and grow up to be strong and straight."

36. A similar reversal can also be found in *Faccia a Faccia* by Sergio Sollima.

37. My heartfelt thanks to Andy Redwood for reviewing the first draft of this paper and to Sue Matheson for careful editing and very helpful suggestions. I owe special gratitude to Martin M. Winkler, an inspiring and admirable professor, whose chapter quoted here was my first contact (in the Nineties) with a scholarly text on Westerns and a turning point in my research. Later on, I learned a great deal from Martin, not only from his vast publication record but also from the many lectures he gave in Brazil.

Filmography

The Bravados. Director Henry King. 20th Century Fox, 1958.
Coroner Creek. Director Ray Enright. Columbia, 1948.
Decision at Sundown. Director Budd Boetticher. Columbia, 1957.
Faccia a Faccia. Director Sergio Sollima. PEA Produzioni Europee Associati /Tulio Demicheli S.L. 1967.
The Gunfighter. Director Henry King. 20th Century Fox, 1950.
The Last Sunset. Director Robert Aldrich. Universal, 1961.
The Lonely Man. Director Henry Levin. Paramount, 1956.
Man of the West. Director Anthony Mann. Aston Productions; Walter Mirisch Productions, 1958.
Resa dei Conti. Director Sergio Sollima. PEA Produzioni Europee Associati /Tulio Demicheli S.L. 1966.
Run of the Arrow. Director Samuel Fuller. RKO/Universal, 1957.
The Searchers. Director John Ford. C.V. Whitney Pictures; Warner Bros., 1956.
Shane. Director George Stevens. Paramount, 1953.
The Track of the Cat. Director William A. Wellman. Wayne/Fellows Production Co., 1954.
Unforgiven. Director Clint Eastwood. Warner Bros., 1992.

Works Cited

Anderson, Josh. "Westward Wellman." *Senses of Cinema* Vol. 67 (2013). At http://sensesofcinema.com/2013/feature-articles/westward-wellman/.
Aquila, Richard. *The Sagebrush Trail: Western Movies and Twentieth-Century America*. Tucson: University of Arizona Press, 2015.
Aristotle. *On Rhetoric*—a theory of civic discourse intro., transl. and notes, George A. Kennedy. Oxford: Oxford University Press. 1991. *Digital Library*, https://www.perseus.tufts.edu/hopper/.
Basinger, Jeanine. *Anthony Mann*. Middletown, CT: Wesleyan University Press, 2007.
Burian, Peter. "Myth into *Mythos*: The Shaping of Tragic Plot." In Pat Easterling, ed. *The Cambridge Companion to Greek Tragedy*, 178–210. Cambridge: Cambridge University Press, 1997.
Coelho, Maria Cecília de M.N. "O princípo—trágico!—de terceiro excluído: Eurípides entre a Retórica e a Filosofia entre antigos e modernos." In Izabela Bocayuva, ed. *Filosofia e Arte na Grécia Antiga*, 115–37. Rio de Janeiro: Hexis/Nau, 2011.
Coelho, Maria Cecília de M.N. "'We been haunted a long time'—Raped Women in Westerns." In Sue Matheson, ed. *Women in Westerns*. Edinburgh: Edinburgh University Press (2020): 187–200.

Corkin, Stanley. *Cowboys as Cold Warriors: The Western and U.S. History*. Philadelphia: Temple University Press, 2004.
Dodds, Eric R. "Euripides the Irrationalist." *Classical Review* Vol. 43 (1929): 102–10.
Eagleton, Terry. *Doce violência: A idéia do Trágico*, trad. Alzira Allegro. São Paulo: Ed. UNESP, 2012.
Euripides. *Helen*, trans. E.P. Coleridge. New York: Random House, 1938. At the *Perseus Digital Library*, https://www.perseus.tufts.edu/hopper/.
_____. *Iphigenia in Aulis*. In E.P. Coleridge, trans. *The Plays of Euripides*. Volume II. London: George Bell and Sons. 1891. Also at the *Perseus Digital Library*, https://www.perseus.tufts.edu/hopper/.
Fuller, Graham. "The Psychological Western." *Sight & Sound* (16 May 2016). At www.bfi.org.uk.
Godi, Giovanni, and Carlo. *La tempesta del mio cor: il gesto del melodramma dalle arti figurative al cinema*. Milano: Mazzotta, 2001.
Goldhill, Simon. "Modern Critical Approach to Greek Tragedy." In P.E. Easterling, ed. *The Cambridge Companion to Greek Tragedy*, 324–347. Cambridge: Cambridge University Press, 1997.
Gregory, Justina. *Euripides and the Instruction of Athenians*. Ann Arbor: The University of Michigan Press, 1997.
Hall, Edith. *Greek Tragedy: Suffering Under the Sun*. Oxford: Oxford University Press, 2010.
Henderson, Brian. "*The Searchers*: An American Dilemma." In Arthur M. Eckstein and Peter Lehman, eds. *The Searchers: Essays and Reflections on John Ford's Classic Western*, 47–74. Detroit: Wayne State University Press, 2004.
Irwin, Terence H. "Euripides and Socrates." *Classical Philology* Vol. 78 (1983):183–97.
Lefkowitz, Mary R. "'Impiety' and 'Atheism' in Euripides' Dramas." In Judith Mossman, ed. *Euripides*, 102–121. Oxford: Oxford University Press, 2003.
Lloyd, Michael. "The Mutability of Fortune in Euripides." In Douglas Cairns, ed. *Tragedy and Archaic Greek Thought*, 205–226. The Classical Press of Wales, Swansea, 2013.
Loy, Phillip R. *Westerns in a Changing America, 1955–2000*. Jefferson, NC: McFarland, 2014.
Matheson, Sue. *The Westerns and War Films of John Ford*. Lanham, MD: Rowman & Littlefield Publishers, 2016.
McGee, Patrick. *From Shane to Kill Bill: Rethinking the Western*. Malden, MA: Blackwell, 2007.
Melville, Jean-Pierre. "Interview (1970)." *Youtube*. 11 September 1970. At https://www.youtube.com/watch?v=Avz45nU-AJg&fbclid=IwAR2xHRVcK3AKkmVVRWL44tQ98MNGDo83hTHm-Mz6uxkO-V8ewkpYd0hBNTc.
Munteanu, Dana LaCourse. *Tragic Pathos—Pity and Fear in Greek Philosophy and Tragedy*. Cambridge: Cambridge University Press, 2012.
Myrsiades, Kostas. "Reading 'The Gunfighter' as Homeric Epic." In Kostas Myrsiades, ed. *Reading Homer: Film and Text*, 229–252. Madison/Teaneck, WI: Fairleigh Dickinson University Press, 2009.
Nietzsche, Friedrich. *O Nascimento da Tragédia*, trad. Jacob Guinsburg. São Paulo: Cia das Letras, 1992.
Padel, Ruth. *In and Out of the Mind: Greek Images of the Tragic Self*. Princeton, NJ: Princeton, 1992.
Rehm, Rush. *Radical Theatre: Greek Tragedy and the Modern World*. London: Duckworth, 2003.
Ringer, Mark. *Euripides and the Boundaries of the Human*. Lanham, MD: Lexington Books, 2018.
Schlegel, August. *Cours de Litterature Dramatique*, trad. N. de Saussure. Paris: Librairie internationale Lacroix, Verboekhoven et Co., 1865.
Segal, Charles P. *Euripides and the Poetics of Sorrow*. Durham, NC: Duke University Press, 1993.
Segal, Erich. "Euripides: Poet of Paradox." In Erich Segal, ed. *Oxford Readings in Greek Tragedy*, 244–53. Oxford: Oxford University Press, 1983.
Seidensticker, Bernd. "Peripeteia and Tragic Dialectic in Euripidean Tragedy." In Michael Silk, ed. *Tragedy and the Tragic*, 377–96. Oxford: Clarendon, 1996.
Sophocles. *The Ajax of Sophocles*, ed., intro., notes, Sir Richard Jebb. Cambridge: Cambridge University Press, 1893. Also at the *Perseus Digital Library*, https://www.perseus.tufts.edu/hopper/.
_____. *The Antigone of Sophocles*, ed., intro., notes Sir Richard Jebb. Cambridge: Cambridge University Press. 1891. At the *Perseus Digital Library*, https://www.perseus.tufts.edu/hopper/.
Steiner, George. *The Death of Tragedy*. New York: Albert A. Knopf, 1961.
Verrall, Arthur W. *Euripides the Rationalist: A Study in the History of Art and Religion*. Cambridge. Cambridge: at the University Press, 1895.
Warshow, Robert. "The Gangster as a Tragic Hero." *Partisan Review* (February 1948): 240–244.
Wicking, Christopher, and Barrie Pattinson. "Interview with Anthony Mann." *Screen* Vol. 10, No. 4 (1969): 32–54.
Williams, Raymond. *Modern Tragedy*. London: Chatto & Windus, 1966.
Winkler, John, and Froma Zeitlin (eds). *Nothing to Do with Dionysus? Athenian Drama in Its Social Context*. Princeton: Princeton University Press, 1990.
Winkler, Martin M. "Tragic Features in John Ford's *The Searchers*." In Martin M. Winkler, ed. *Classics and Cinema*, 185–208. London: Associated University Presses, 1991.

Cowboys and Catharsis

"Every night and every morn, some to misery are born. Every morn and every night, some are born to sweet delight. Some are born to sweet delight/ some are born to endless night."
—*Dead Man* (Jim Jarmusch, 1998)

Pharmakos and the Bad Citizen *Topos* in Charles Marquis Warren's Westerns

Trooper Hook, Tension at Table Rock *and* Charro!

Fernando Gabriel Pagnoni Berns

Will Wright argues in *The Wild West: The Mythical Cowboy and Social Theory* that the cowboy myth lies at the core of the social origin of community and civil society.[1] Western films are often informed by common themes, among them, freedom, rationality, equal opportunity, and market competition. Heavily and morally codified, the Manichean dichotomy of good and evil is also very much in evidence, commonly found in costumes in Westerns, a well-known example being the genre's discursive and visual politics of "white hats/black hats.": "Everyone knows, good guys wear white hats and bad guys wear black," Sarah Laskow remarks in "The Counterintuitive History of Black Hats, White Hats and Villains": "[I]n *Gangsters of the Frontier*, for instance, a group of four bad guys comes in wielding guns; hero Tex Ritter, wearing a white hat intervenes…. It's always easy to image that the past was simpler, and modern films sometimes use white hat/black hat symbolism in a heavy-handed way, as an homage to this imagined past. In *3:10 to Yuma*, for instance, Christian Bale's good guys wears a white hat, while Russell Crowe's bad guy wears a black one."[2] Another familiar trope lies in the Western's building of borders, articulating sameness and difference, separating community from outcasts, right from wrong. Enter Charles Marquis Warren, an overlooked Western auteur obsessed with the figure of the innocent citizen who is caught within the cracks of his town's internal tensions and contradictions and used by that community as a scapegoat for what went wrong.

In the United States, the 1950s were a period dominated by McCarthyism, witch hunts, and a disregard for civil liberties. Parodying human aspirations towards justice and mocking the supposition that men can understand, let alone control, their fates, Warren made the scapegoat a leitmotif in his Westerns. In *Trooper Hook* (1957), for example, Barbara Stanwyck plays a woman who has been kidnapped and raped by an Indian chief. Although she has been rescued from the tribe that had held her prisoner, she is abhorred by many in her community, which mostly wants to return her. In *Charro!* (1969), the community wants to sacrifice Jess Wade (Elvis Presley). Wade is an innocent man who is unjustly accused of a crime. Like him, Wes Tancred (Richard Egan) is also expelled by his community in *Tension at Table Rock* (1956). Throughout Warren's Westerns, which were made when filmmaking in Hollywood was dominated by black lists and ideological persecution, scapegoats (and scapegoating) draw upon the ancient, yearly ritual of *pharmakos*. In Greece, yearly observances of the *pharmakos* ritual purified towns of their defilement by driving out or sacrificing selected scapegoats. Sensitive to the crossroads of the *pharmakos* ritual, classical literature, and the dilemmas of citizenship, this essay will elucidate the ways in which the flawed resolutions portrayed in Warren's westerns inform the borders separating community from the scapegoat.

Shunned by the townspeople, Cora Sutliff (Barbara Stanwyck) becomes the perfect scapegoat. *Trooper Hook* (United Artists, 1957).

The Scapegoat Figure and Hollywood in the 1950s

Guilt and the figure of the scapegoat have always been inextricably linked. The scapegoat as a concept was coined by William Tyndale for his 1530 translation of the Bible in which two goats were inscribed with the sins of the people[3] and set free outside the community. From that point on, the term suffered shifts of meaning and lexical confusions until the scapegoat became a figure of victimization, as attested by David Dawson in *Flesh Becomes Word: A Lexicography of the Scapegoat, or the History of an Idea*. As a verb in common usage, "to scapegoat" means "to blame or persecute, and this meaning has little to do with the Leviticus ritual, which lacks a punitive aspect,"[4] as is now over-generalized by Sir James Frazer's *The Golden Bough* and the anthropological theory of René Girard.

Here it is important to note that the meanings of the scapegoat can be traced back to the Greek rites of the *pharmakos*, which does not involve goats but human beings. The most telling testimony derives from a passage in Harpocration's dictionary, where the *pharmakos* ritual was described in some detail:

> They used to lead out at Athens two men to be purifications for the city at the Thargelia, the one for the men, the other for the women (...). The word derives from a proper name, Pharmakos [Scapegoat], and that he stole the sacred bowls of Apollo, and was caught and stoned by Achilles' men and that the rites performed at the [festival of the] Thargelia are a representation of this.[5]

Rituals involving scapegoats took place at the Thargelia, "a festival of Apollo celebrating the first fruits at the beginning of harvest,"[6] and it was linked "to rid the city of scum, discarded elements, useless and dirty people."[7]

> The Athenians kept a stock of potential scapegoats, all of whom were characterised [sic] by being ugly or deformed in some way. These degraded and so-called 'useless' individuals were maintained at public expense, fed and cared for, but when catastrophe threatened they were haled forth to propitiate the gods. First they were beaten on the genitals with branches of wild fig, then driven through the city streets and stoned to death or near death and then burnt.[8]

The *pharmakos* is offered in times of crisis by a community in Ancient Greece, as a gesture of purification, to cleanse and free the place from guilt. The individual scapegoated was called the "offscouring," and "the procedure was seen as catharsis, purification."[9] By exiling someone labeled as impure, the city, then, become pure. What unites the image of goats with the classic Greek rituals of cleansing? The fact that the goat heaped with the sin of a community cleanses the people who live there, as it is expelled from their city. Today, scapegoating, persecution and the shifting of blame onto the shoulders of a propitiatory victim is one and the same. In the contemporary convention, the deflection of culpability onto a scapegoat is always undeserved, as the punishment justly owed to others.

To date, reliable information on the *pharmakos* ritual has been extracted from classical literature such as the *Bibliotheca* of Photius, and Greek theater. Essentially rooted to the notions of myth and ritual, Greek dramas were staged in a religious context and their themes borrowed from legends, myths, epic cycles and local traditions.[10] In *The Liberated Gospel: A Comparison of the Gospel of Mark and Greek Tragedy*, Gilbert Bilezikian argues that "almost every tragic hero has the traces of the *pharmakos* in him—he bears some pollution and he dies for the sins of others."[11] But, as Ian Storey and Arlene Allan explain in their *A Guide to Ancient Greek Drama*, the actual ritual of the *pharmakos* is often more of a subtext framing these texts than fully realized: "Characters such as Oedipus (*Oedipus at Kolonos*), Pentheus (*Bacchae*), Eteokles (*Seven*) do die at the end of their dramas, but that does not make them into the scapegoat of Greek society. In fact, no play that we possess fits this theoretical model" completely.[12] However, they note that some Greek dramatic works do mention the *pharmakos* ritual explicitly. Aristophanes' *Frogs*, for example, refers to these sacrificial victims when the chorus complains that good men are now passed over in favor of newcomers "whom our city, years ago, scarcely would have used as scapegoats [*pharmakoi*]."[13] They find the most impressive description of the *pharmakos* in Greek drama is found in the figure of Sophocles' Oedipus who, to atone for the evil that he unwillingly triggered and to rid the land from a curse, blinds himself and is driven out from the community.

It was René Girard who introduced *pharmakos* to the anthropological world and united this Greek ritual with the image of goats. In Girard's view, all the world's values are based on a primal tragedy now unveiled, which reached its climax in the ultimate tragedy: the rejection and murder of Jesus Christ. Girard uses examples of Greek drama when discussing the presence of the *pharmakos*, in part, modeling our values. Girard also cites Shakespeare and Corneille, among others, to argue that the history of western society was built on the veiled, invisible ritual of the scapegoat. Girard concludes that "once the basic mechanism is revealed, the scapegoat mechanism, that expulsion of violence by violence, is rendered useless by the revelation."[14] Great poets, such as Sophocles or Euripides, come close to uncovering the presence of this ritual, he says, for *pharmakos* "is a theme or motif in Greek culture."[15] He also notes "if it appears at all in the tragedy, its appearance is problematic" because Sophocles "suspects something"—that civilization depends on this sacrifice.[16]

Girard's theory of the scapegoat rests the nature of sacrifice in the religious system. According to Girard, the origins of cultural order reside in recurring acts of violence against an innocent victim who is not a member of the community. This individual, in effect, becomes a scapegoat for the community of which he or she is not a part, and thereby becomes a vessel for the community's destructive energies. To function properly, a community needs to subdue its individuals to keep them from running wild, and it does so by directing violence against a victim chosen because of some particularity and whose sacrifice deflects violence outward and away from the group. Violence, like that committed, for example, in Aeschylus' *Oresteia*, pollutes and threats the civic community, inviting moral censure and some form of communal stability through the *pharmakos* ritual.

Charles Marquis Warren uses scapegoating and the ritual of the *pharmakos* and the scapegoat to critique violence and the community. In *Trooper Hook*, a female outcast, a woman tainted by racial difference (Stanwyck), is a textbook scapegoat. In *Tension at Table Rock* and *Charro,* Tancred and Jess Wade, temporary replacements of the law, arguably act as surrogates of "the king." The recurrence of scapegoats and themes privileging the idea of community structuring itself through the expulsion of any being who can highlight its internal contradictions in Marquis Warren's Westerns leads one to ask why this leitmotif, why this obsession with the figure of a sacrificial, polluting victim when other filmmakers, such as Alfred Hitchcock, used and re-used the well-known motif of the wrongly accused man? In Marquis Warren's world, the man/woman accused of a crime is not a citizen who is mistaken as a criminal by the law. Instead, this individual is on the run, trying to prove his or her innocence to the entire community, which seems to have a pleasurable time punishing and expulsing its victim. Sometimes there is not even a particular crime to lay on the victim's shoulders. In *Trooper Hook* and *Charro!* there is no crime per se, merely deviance from the proper norms of citizenship. The sacrificial victims in these films are despised merely because the community deposits its disgust, guilt, and hypocrisy on them.

Warren's obsession with sacrificial victims in his Westerns may be attributed to America's political and social climate during the Cold War. After World War II, America was gripped by paranoia. Sustained by anticommunism and the blacklisting led by

Joseph McCarthy, a witch hunt began. People were publicly denounced as "reds" and charged with unfounded crimes. Many in America projected their personal fears on innocent victims or on people who were "guilty" of their political convictions. These people suffered loss of employment, unjust trials, legal harassment, imprisonment, and expulsion. "Upon the altar of anticommunism, domestic Cold War crusaders undermined civil liberties, curtailed equality before the law, and tarnished the ideals of American democracy."[17] During the Second Red Scare, the House Committee on Un-American Activities (HUAC) "was a minotaur in search of *sacrificial victims*."[18]

It is not surprising in a social and cultural climate in which people were charged with being "anti–American" and stripped of their full citizenship that Warren's films depicted communal guilt offloaded onto the innocent, showcasing the figure of the sacrificial victim and the ritual of the *pharmakos*.

Ambiguous Citizenship in Trooper Hook

Like Greek drama, classic Western films rest on myth. Built on the mythology of the American frontier, Westerns contain perfect scenarios in which variations on the ritual of the *pharmakos* may be enacted. As Richard Maynard points out in *The American West on Film: Myth and Reality*, "two of the staple figures of our Western mythology are the gunfighter and the outlaw,"[19] signaling the boldly drawn boundaries found in traditional Westerns between law and criminality, the community and the outcast. In Warren's Westerns, however, there is hardly any manifestation of a Manichean dyad of good (wearing white hats) versus evil (wearing black). The world is populated not with the good and the bad; instead it is polluted with social outcasts.

Trooper Hook takes place in the Southwest, where Apache warriors execute a group of cavalry soldiers on a cliff, with the whole Indian community observing the action much as spectators at the temple of Apollo in Leucas watched criminals thrown over the cliff into the sea every year as *pharmakos*.[20] The film opens with a close shot of the soldiers' legs while slowly walking to the border of a cliff. One of them even has an arrow piercing throughout his leg. They walk slowly, painfully, marked by defeat. The camera cuts to an aerial view: American soldiers stand still at the border of the cliff, the Apache coming closer. A close shot of the face of Indian Chief Nanchez (Rudolfo Acosta) reveals a triumphant smile. Next, the soldiers are executed by the Apache, falling from the cliff as they die.

The scene establishes a common theme in Western films: Indians as evil characters. The scene is particularly cruel as the American soldiers were unarmed and completely defenseless. Any Manichean dichotomy, however, is promptly swiped away. Part of a reciprocal never-ending spiral of cruelty, the Apache kill the soldiers for past sins: through a report, audiences know that the soldiers killed in the opening scene were sent to Apache territory to catch Indian Chief Nanchez "living or dead." Even if not showed, it is easy to presume that the soldiers engaged in their own acts of senseless violence against the Apache previous to their execution. This particular scene is lacking, its absence structuring the whole initial sequence while speaking of the ideologies shaping traditional Westerns: the blood and fire that comes with the conquest of Apache territory remains unseen, as white men in Westerns only kill, apparently, to defend themselves and their loved ones.

The Apaches are then subdued, in turn, by another troop of soldiers, led by Sgt. Clovis Hook (Joel McCrea). The cavalrymen torch the Apaches' village in revenge and send them to an Indian Reservation. The burning of the village is a very brief glimpse of white men's cruelty, here "justified" by the "irrationality" of the Apaches' violence that opened the film. There is even a close up shot of the angst-ridden face of Sgt. Hook when he sees the bodies of his fallen comrades. Still, even if Warren keeps some acts of violence unseen, the intention is clear: there are no good versus bad characters here, but an escalade of violence on the part of both adversaries.

As Girard points out while analyzing Euripides' *Ion*, revenge is a form of "bad violence" which can be stopped with the "good violence"—universally embodied in the practice of the cathartic scapegoat sacrifice which interrupts escalating revenge with the powerfully diverting experience of the expulsion and/or sacrifice.[21] Clearly, the society illustrated in *Trooper Hook* is in need of a sacrificial victim to release some of the tensions, and the white community finds the perfect one in Cora Sutcliff (Barbara Stanwyck), who was taken captive in a raid some years ago on a journey to join her rancher husband. Raped by Chief Nanchez, she is mother of the Chief's son. The soldiers consider her just "Indian's leavings," but Hook wants to take her back to the white community. After Hook returns Sutcliff to the white world, the film traces two paths: Hook's struggles to reintegrate Cora to the community and the anger that her presence awakes in those around her, as she rapidly becomes recipient of blame and injustice. Although audiences understand from the beginning that Sutcliff was taken against her will and that she had no love for Nanchez, she is treated nevertheless by the white community as one who should have had at least the decency to kill herself before submitting to an Apache and being mother of his bastard son. People are quick to point out that she is no longer a white woman, but one of "them." Citizens deny her and her son clothes, food, shelter and respect. Fred (John Dehner), Cora's husband, brutally rejects her during the film's climax: he can "forgive her" for her relationship with an Apache, but he cannot tolerate the child. When Nanchez escapes, some members of the community ask that she be given back to him, rather than have the town suffer Apache violence. It is clear that she is tainted, a threat to the town, a "thing of scorn."

Here it should be noted that Cora is not persecuted because she is different, but because she threatens the system of differences within the community. She is at once one of Them and one of Us—destroying social constructs and natural boundaries. Revealing that race is, basically, "a matter of performance,"[22] not an essential reality, Cora relates that Nanchez hit her "once" but that the main problem were the Apache women until she became "one of them." As Cora points out, the white community hates the Apaches but "they hate me even more." Racially different from her captors, she is nevertheless potentially polluting when rescued. She is the embodiment of a truth that the "civilized" world wants to reject: there is no gap separating dark-skinned Apaches from the world of the white men, only a set of cultural rules and behavior.

As the film's escalating violence introduces the need for a scapegoat, the threat of the pollution linked to Sutcliff points to the need for *pharmakos*. As Jennifer Cooke in *Legacies of Plague in Literature, Theory and Film* would doubtless agree, *Trooper Hook*, like Greek ritual, "is not concerned with guilt or innocence, sin or its atonement; it is concerned with contagion, pollution and disease."[23] The community's racial anxieties placed upon Cora's shoulders are a way to put those fears at rest. A scapegoat, Cora answers the politics of the classical *pharmakos*: she is "the ugliest" of town. She, however, is not sacrificed. Instead, the film ends in equilibrium: Nanchez and Fred, both "fatherly" figures of Cora's son, kill each other. Only Hook, the man who never mistreats her, remains to take care of both Cora and her son, maybe triggering the end of conflicts through racial acceptance.

The King Surrogate: Tension at Table Rock *and* Charro!

Besides being "the ugliest" man of town, the historical scapegoat could also be the king. In the case of Sophocles' *Oedipus Rex*, the polluting agent is the king himself. As Jean-Pierre Vernant points out, in ancient Greece, the tyrant borrows some traits from the hero, since both figures are not tied by the rules that shape their community; neither is a "common" citizen.[24] "Inscribed in the religious and social practice of the Greeks," the dyad of king/scapegoat was created by "two characters who in their opposition appear symmetrical and in some respects interchangeable."[25] When the polluting citizen was the king, a scapegoat was chosen to adopt this role (momentarily) and later, was sacrificed as a surrogate figure. In Warren's *Tension at Table Rock* and *Charro!*, the hero/king is replaced by a good-hearted criminal/sheriff before becoming a *pharmakos*.

The narrative of *Tension at Table Rock* traces the tragic destiny of Wes Tancred (Richard Egan), a bandit with a conscience. A follower of Sam Murdock (Paul Richards) since they rode with Quantrill during the Civil War, Tancred decides to pull out of the outlaw's gang. Murdock has killed a wounded gang member while fleeing a posse, and Cathy, his girlfriend (Angie Dickinson), has been flirting with Tancred. Wes decides to avoid tragedy leaving the couple behind; fate, however, does not let him go. Cathy creates more distrust between the two men, and Wes is obliged to kill his best friend just as the posse arrives. Tancred's decision to escape sets in motion a plot that could have been lifted from the classical Greek drama. Cathy tells the posse that Tancred shot Murdock in the back. Polluted, Tancred is broken by forces which he can neither fully understand nor overcome. Although he receives a complete pardon from the governor (because Sam was a wanted criminal), wherever he goes, his corrupted reputation accompanies him: Tancred is known as a coward, the man who shot his best friend in the back. Wherever he goes he hears "The Ballad of Wes Tancred," a song that tells of cowardice and treason.

As an outlaw and a lawman, Tancred takes part in the community's *pharmakos*. When the sheriff gives Tancred the reward for killing the wanted man, the former does not hide the scorn in his voice because the outlaw killed his best friend. Clearly, representatives of the law also acknowledge that friendship comes first. Embodiment of the hypocrisy of the community, which tolerates delinquency as long as the criminals leave the community untouched, Tancred is both polluted and polluting. Not surprisingly, the town seems to take a special pleasure in mocking, taunting, and psychologically torturing Tancred. People sing about his cowardice and refuse to share the same room with him. He is quickly expelled from their town and obliged to live elsewhere. Forced to take on an alias, he finds some peace working at kindhearted Ed Burrows (Joe DeSantis) and his little son Jody's (Billy Chapin) farm. Trouble follows him, however, and Ed is killed in a shootout when three cowboys try to rob a stagecoach. Responsible for Jody, Tancred takes the child to the town of Table Rock, where Fred Miller (Cameron Mitchell), Jody's uncle, works as the sheriff. He plans to leave Jody in his uncle's care. The communal ties forgive delinquency but not treason (arguably, a minor crime). Like Cora, Wes is polluting and like the woman, he is coded as different: Cora dresses up to the middle of the film as an Indian and Wes wears black, the code for evilness even if he is a reformed man.

When Tancred arrives in Table Rock, the social tension is unbearable. Some of its citizens want their sheriff to take more aggressive approach to a group of cowboys from a cattle drive who are heading to town; others agree to shelter the bullies in the town's midst, if that means a peaceful existence. Fred, however, has become "ineffective" having been traumatized by past unseen violence. Both the criminals and corrupt citizens boss Fred around. Unable to enforce the law and surrounded by unhappy citizens, it appears that their useless sheriff, a nervous wreck, is fast becoming the community's scapegoat and destined for *pharmakos*.

Responding to the community's dilemma, Tancred becomes, in effect, a surrogate king. Deputized, he helps Fred fight back, and, in doing so, regains a more pro-active attitude. Ironically, Tancred does so no through acts of violence but speaking the truth, pointing out the hypocrisy within the town's borders. In the middle of a crooked trial where a guilty man will probably be declared innocent in good measure thanks to Fred's inactiveness, Tancred reveals to everyone his real name and identity. It is this act, seemingly, what takes Fred to a more active attitude and to embrace real justice rather than scapegoating. After the sequence of the trial, there is no scene of Tancred engaging in any act of violent bravado. In the climax, however, Fred helps Tancred to defeat Jim Breck (DeForest Kelley), a man who has been paid to kill the sheriff. Since the sheriff is nowhere to be seen after the trial, audiences only can speculate that his change of heart was motivated by Tancred's dismissal of his own fame as a coward rather than any depiction of "manly" bravery. In this view, Tancred's main feat is truth rather than fisticuffs that could prolong the town's history of violence.

In the end, however, a sacrifice is needed to cleanse the community of its deficiencies and restore its psychic health. Given Fred's ineffectiveness, it is clear that he should be "off-scoured," but it is Tancred who becomes the *pharmakos*, leaving town once his past is revealed by himself. He has been a good surrogate for the king and helped Fred regain his proper status. If he stays, however, his bad reputation will pollute the town again, so he must leave.

Warren returns to the Western's criminal/sheriff device of the bad-guy-going-straight in *Charro!* Written and directed by Warren, *Charro!* begins in 1870, when reformed outlaw Jess Wade (Elvis Presley) is tricked into believing that his former girlfriend Tracy (Ina Balin) urgently needs to see him in a small Mexican border town. Captured by the band of outlaws that he had abandoned in order to lead an honest life, Wade is taken to the gang's mountain hideout and shown the legendary Victory Gun (the cannon that fired the last shot against Maximilian and won freedom for Mexico), and a counterfeit poster proclaiming that he is wanted dead or alive by both Mexico and the United States for the theft of the cannon. The Hackett brothers, Vince (Victor French) and Billy Roy (Solomon Sturges), brand Wade to substantiate rumors that have been spread about the thief being a dark-haired young man with a visible neck-scar; part of the plan of the Hackett brothers involves branding with a white-hot poker a scar in Wade's neck.

Wade manages to escape and seek safety in the village of Rio Seco, where Tracy operates the local saloon and Sheriff Ramsey (James Almanzar) is a trusted friend. Soon, Billy Roy appears in town. In the ensuing fight with the Hacketts and their gang,

Wade takes on the role of sheriff when Ramsey is badly wounded. As sheriff, he subdues and drags Billy Roy off to Jail. Vince attempts to rescue his brother, several gang members are killed, and Billy Roy dies when the wagon holding the cannon breaks loose and crushes him. At the climax of the fighting, the townsfolk want to give not only Billy Roy but also Wade to the Hacketts' gang to appease them, but after Billy Roy dies and Vince is arrested, the grateful inhabitants of Rio Seco ask Wade to remain on as sheriff. Wade declines, stating that he must take Vince and the cannon back to Mexico.

In Rio Seco, Wade is a prime candidate for scapegoating. He is a foreigner, a criminal, and a person of interest. Like West Tancred in *Tension at Table Rock*, Wade becomes, in effect, a surrogate king. A good surrogate, he ensures that the town survives its crisis, but in the end a sacrifice is needed to cleanse the community of its deficiencies and restore social balance. Wade must leave to restore his reputation, and before riding out of town, he promises Tracy that he will send for her.

In *Tragedy and Enlightenment: Athenian Political Thought and the Dilemmas of Modernity*, Christopher Rocco points out that equality to the gods and equality to nothing marks Oedipus.[26] Like Oedipus, both Tancred and Wade are expelled from the towns that they had saved, because they had exceeded the upper limits of equality—having become sheriffs, they have risen to the top of the West's social order—and because they have fallen to the bottom of order by being criminals. Their identity doubled, they are at once the saviors of their towns and their town's potential destroyers. Generally, *Charro!* presents itself as an adaptation of *Oedipus*, in which the sheriff (as the law) is king. Replacing Ramsey, Wade is a doppelganger. As Vernant remarks, "Such is the *pharmakos*: double of the king."[27] First a criminal, later the embodiment of law, and, finally, a sacrificial victim, Wade is many things in *Charro!* but never a common citizen.

Conclusion

Rife with self-negation, communities in *Trooper Hook*, *Tension at Table Rock*, and *Charro!* run the risk of facing ugly truths about themselves. Their citizens decide it is better to scapegoat and expel individuals who are threatening their stability than resolve their town's inner contradictions. In *Trooper Hook*, Cora, who blurs the community's prohibitions regarding race and sex, is an explicit embodiment of the scapegoat. She is a mark of difference within the homogeneity of the white town, her blood-mixed son a haunting of cohabitation of Apache with "civilized" citizens. If she and her son are accepted within, this will mean integration. Better to send her off to keep the divided spheres as mutually excluding.

In *Tension at Table Rock* and *Charro!* Wes Tancred and Jess Wade are criminals who act as personifications of the surrogate king, momentarily taking on the role of lawmen. Their hypocritical neighbors who are willing to cohabit with criminals are happy to sacrifice them to maintain their community's status quo. The conclusions of these movies, however, each reveal the will to end what is a cycle of violence for not only the scapegoated individuals involved but also for the nation. In this regard, it is striking that Sgt. Hook wears the blue soldier's kepi, and Mr. Trude (Royal Dano), the other man to treat Cora with open-minded kindness, wears gray—Union and Confederate team up to protect a harassed woman. The union of colors and different ideologies points, again, to the potentiality of peace that comes with integration.

In *Tension at Table Rock*, Tancred is steadfast in his desire to end any cycle of violence. When Jody mentions how good Tancred is with a gun, the man asks the boy not to mention the topic never again. As Tancred explains, when word spreads that someone is "pretty fast with the gun, there is always someone who wants to prove that he is faster." Thus, Tancred rather prefers a low profile. It is noticeable that Warren keeps the violence in the film to a minimum: after coming to Table Rock and before the duel at the climax, Tancred only fights once, to protect Jody, an uncharacteristically approach to a Western's hero.

Charro! ends in a peculiar fashion: during the climatic fight between Jess and the Hackett's gang, Billy Roy is killed. Vince, rather than being hell-bent on vengeance, gives up and accepts being arrested to avoid more bloodshed. The cost of his beloved brother has been too much for him. It is interesting that in the end of the film the camera frames both Jess Wade and Vince Hackett in the classical duel position, both men facing each other, hands on their guns. Vince, however, just drops his gun. Arguably, he has no bullets left in his revolver, but still, there is no attempt to defend himself in any other fashion. The death of his brother has killed his desire for violence and, implicitly, he agrees with the sentiment of putting bloodshed to a halt rather than prolonging it. Later, they are framed walking to the town one next to the other, now companions in grief and tiredness rather than adversaries.

In final analysis, each of these films reveals that the scapegoats are blameless and that the communities that expel them act resentfully. The *pharmakos* ritual was a perfect vehicle for Charles Marquis Warren to speak of hypocrisy, silence and the attitude of "look the other way" in an era dominated by paranoia and witch hunts where the "land of freedom" was anything but. Both in the films and in real America, the social and communal fabric were approaching a point in which the threat of self-exposure as hypocrite would include a revelation of national fears about ideological homogenization and oppression. The communities, fictional and real, become uncomfortable with "their collective badness," and because of this, they "searched for ways in which, with minimal cost to themselves, they could discharge this badness."[28] Consciously or not, Warren tapped into the zeitgeist of the era through the resource of bringing back a classical form of a cleansing ritual. In an era dominated by blacklists and ideological persecution, it is hard to deny the deep effect that the scapegoat holds in a community dominated by fears of the evil of communism.

Notes

1. Will Wright, *The Mythical Cowboy and Social Theory* (Thousand Oaks, CA: SAGE, 2001), 13.
2. Sarah Laskow, "The Counterintuitive History of Black Hats, White Hats, and Villains," *Atlas Obscura* January 27, 2017, https://www.atlasobscura.com/articles/the-counterintuitive-history-of-black-hats-white-hats-and-villains.
3. David Dawson, *Flesh Becomes Word: A Lexicography of the Scapegoat, or the History of an Idea* (East Lansing: Michigan State University Press, 2014), x.
4. *Ibid.*, xi.
5. Cited in Sarah Johnston's *Religions of the Ancient World: A Guide*, 35.
6. Grace Jantzen, *Foundations of Violence* (New York: Routledge, 2004) 218.
7. Dawson, xi.
8. Tom Douglas, *Scapegoats: Transferring Blame* (New York: Routledge, 2003), 37.
9. Jantzen, *Foundations of Violence*, 218.
10. Jean-Pierre Vernant, *Myth and Society in Ancient Greece* (New York: ZoneBooks, 1996), 213.

11. Gibert Bilezikian, *The Liberated Gospel: A Comparison of the Gospel of Mark and Greek Tragedy* (Eugene, OR: Wipf & Stock, 2010.), 25.
12. Ian Storey and Arlene Allan, *A Guide to Ancient Greek Drama* (Hoboken, NJ: Blackwell, 2005), 31.
13. *Ibid.*, 56.
14. René Girard, *The Scapegoat*, trans. Yvonne Freccero (Baltimore, MD: John Hopkins University Press, 1986), 189.
15. *Ibid.*, 122.
16. *Ibid.*
17. Phillip Deery, *Red Apple: Communism and McCarthyism in Cold War New York* (New York: Fordham University Press, 2014.), 1.
18. Bernard Dick, *The Screen Is Red: Hollywood, Communism, and the Cold War*, 74 (emphasis mine).
19. Richard Maynard, *The American West on Film: Myth and Reality* (New York: Hayden Book Company, 1974). 1.
20. Christopher Tuplin, "Greek Racism? Observations on the Character and Limits of Greek Ethnic Prejudice," in Gocha Tsetskhladz, ed. *Ancient Greeks West and East* (Leiden, Netherlands: Brill, 1999), 53.
21. Girard, 32.
22. See Ewa Bogdanowska-Jakubowsk's discussion that race is a metaphor, performance, or acting in "Communicating Emotions Related to Racial Identity Issues: A Case Study," *Approaches to Conflict: Theoretical, Interpersonal, and Discursive Dynamics*, 207.
23. Jennifer Cooke, *Legacies of Plague in Literature, Theory and Film*, 82.
24. See Jean-Pierre Vernant's discussion of the two faces of Oedipus as symmetry, the divine king and *pharmakos*, in "Ambiguity and Reversal: on the Enigmatic Structure of *Oedipus Rex*," 489–91.
25. Lucien Scubla, "Hesiod, the Three Functions, and the Canonical Formula of Myth," in Pierre Maranda, ed. *The Double Twist: from Ethnography to Morphodynamics* (Toronto: University of Toronto Press, 2001), 146.
26. Christopher Rocco, *Tragedy and Enlightenment: Athenian Political Thought and the Dilemmas of Modernity* (Berkeley: University of California Press, 1997), 47.
27. Jean-Pierre Vernant, 489.
28. See Douglas, 79.

Filmography

3:10 to Yuma. Dir. James Mangold. Relativity Media; Treeline Film, 2007.
Charro! Dir. Charles Marquis Warren. National General Pictures, 1969.
Gangsters of the Frontier. Dir. Elmer Clifton. Producers Releasing Company, 1944.
Tension at Table Rock. Dir. Charles Marquis Warren. Sam Wiesenthal Productions, 1956.
Trooper Hook. Dir. Charles Marquis Warren. Filmaster Productions, 1957.

Works Cited

Andrew, Dudley. *Concepts in Film*. Oxford: Oxford University Press, 1984.
Aristophanes. *Frogs*. George Allen and Company, 1912.
Bilezikian, Gilbert. *The Liberated Gospel: A Comparison of the Gospel of Mark and Greek Tragedy*. Eugene, OR: Wipf & Stock, 2010.
Bogdanowska-Jakubowska, Ewa. "Communicating Emotions Related to Racial Identity Issues. A Case Study." In Barbara Lewandowska-Tomaszczyk et al, eds. *Approaches to Conflict: Theoretical, Interpersonal, and Discursive Dynamics*, 193–216. Lanham, MD: Rowman & Littlefield.
Cooke, Jennifer. *Legacies of Plague in Literature, Theory and Film*. New York: Palgrave Macmillan, 2009.
Dawson, David. *Flesh Becomes Word: A Lexicography of the Scapegoat, or the History of an Idea*. East Lansing: Michigan State University Press, 2014.
Deery, Phillip. *Red Apple: Communism and McCarthyism in Cold War New York*. New York: Fordham University Press, 2014.
Dick, Bernard. *The Screen is Red Hollywood, Communism, and the Cold War*. Jackson: University Press of Mississippi, 2016.
Douglas, Tom. *Scapegoats: Transferring Blame*. New York: Routledge, 2003.
Frazer, James George. *The Golden Bough: A Study in Magic and Religion*. 3rd ed. London: Macmillan, 1913.
Girard, René. *The Scapegoat*, trans. Yvonne Freccero. Baltimore, MD: John Hopkins University Press, 1986.
_____. *Violence and the Sacred*, trans. Patrick Gregory. Baltimore, MD: John Hopkins University Press, 1979.

Jantzen, Grace. *Foundations of Violence.* New York: Routledge, 2004.
Johnston, Sarah (ed.). *Religions of the Ancient World: A Guide.* Cambridge, MA: Belknap Press, 2004.
Laskow, Sarah. "The Counterintuitive History of Black Hats, White Hats, and Villains." *Atlas Obscura* January 27, 2017. At https://www.atlasobscura.com/articles/the-counterintuitive-history-of-black-hats-white-hats-and-villains.
Maynard, Richard. *The American West on Film: Myth and Reality.* New York: Hayden Book Company, 1974.
Rocco, Christopher. *Tragedy and Enlightenment: Athenian Political Thought and the Dilemmas of Modernity.* Berkeley: University of California Press, 1997.
Scubla, Lucien. "Hesiod, the Three Functions, and the Canonical Formula of Myth." In Pierre Maranda, ed. *The Double Twist: from Ethnography to Morphodynamics*, 123–155. Toronto: University of Toronto Press, 2001.
Storey, Ian, and Arlene Allan. *A Guide to Ancient Greek Drama.* Hoboken, NJ: Blackwell, 2005.
Tuplin, Christopher. "Greek Racism? Observations on the Character and Limits of Greek Ethnic Prejudice." In Gocha Tsetskhladz, ed. *Ancient Greeks West and East*, 47–75. Leiden, Netherlands: Brill, 1999.
Vernant, Jean-Pierre. "Ambiguity and Reversal: on the Enigmatic Structure of *Oedipus Rex.*" *New Literary History* Vol. 9, No. 3 (1978): 475–501.
Vernant, Jean-Pierre. *Myth and Society in Ancient Greece.* New York: ZoneBooks, 1996.
Wright, Will. *The Mythical Cowboy and Social Theory.* Thousand Oaks, CA: SAGE, 2001.

"Scratched blood"
The Erinyes and Anthony Mann's The Furies

Kelly MacPhail

The Furies, the massive, eponymous ranch that forms the main setting of Anthony Mann's *The Furies* (1950), becomes the focal point of the multiple actions of treachery and vengeance that characterize both the film's plot and its historical setting. The original reason the ranch is called the Furies is never explained, but the name clearly references the Furies of Classical Greek myth. The Greek term for these chthonic sister goddesses is the Erinyes, but later in the mythological cycle, as a sign of fearful respect, they were referred to by euphemistic terms including the "Eumenides" ("gracious ones") and "Semnai Theai" ("venerable goddesses"). The term Furies comes from their Latin name, "Furiae," by which they were known by the Romans. Though representations vary, the Erinyes are divine figures who typically act in vengeance and retribution following murder within families, broken oaths, betrayal, or other violations of personal obligation. They unflaggingly pursue their prey and avenge violently and without mercy. By framing *The Furies* through the motif of the Classical Erinyes, Mann reconsiders the American mythology of the Old West by exposing the violent consequences of broken oaths, familial betrayal, and the overriding quest for personal vengeance.

The Erinyes are variously represented by different Classical writers. Importantly, different treatments and presentations of these figures reveal how the myths surrounding them developed through different stages.[1] Although it is the Greek tragedians, Aeschylus, Sophocles, and Euripides, the poets, Homer and Hesiod, and the mythographer Apollodorus who first and most compellingly recount the oral myths of the Erinyes in their poetry, later Latin writers, including Virgil, Ovid, and Statius, also make use of the sister goddesses in their verse. As the Classicist Robert Graves draws a composite picture of the Furies from multiple ancient sources, the Erinyes are called upon to "hear complaints brought by mortals against the insolence of the young to the aged, of children to parents, of host to guests, and of householders or city councils to suppliants—and to punish such crimes by hounding the culprits relentlessly."[2] Physical descriptions again vary, but some common attributes include long claws on their hands and feet, snake hair, dog faces, black bodies, bat wings, bloodshot eyes, and brass-studded scourges with which to torture their victims. Walter Burkert notes that the Erinyes are invoked in an oath formula in Homer's *Iliad* (8th century BCE) and are described as those who punish dead men in the underworld, specifically "whoever has sworn a false oath," meaning that they are primarily "an embodiment of the act of self-cursing contained in the oath."[3]

In connection with this theme of familial betrayal, Hesiod's *Theogony* (c. 700 BCE) details that they were born when the Titan Kronos castrated his father Ouranos and threw his genitals into the sea.[4] This act occurred because Ouranos (the Sky) mated with Gaia (Mother Earth) but rejected the Titans, the twelve children who were born to them. As each child was born, Ouranos would push him or her back into Gaia, causing her pain. Eventually, she crafted a sickle and convinced Kronos, the youngest Titan, to avenge his father's wrongdoing. After the castration, some drops of blood fell on Gaia, and the Erinyes emerged. From their very inception, therefore, the Erinyes have to do with toxic family relationships, retaliatory violence, and the protection of mothers. They are thus even more ancient than the Olympian gods, so their interventions in human affairs are based on a prehistoric norms of moral and honorable behavior based in primary relationships. Interestingly, Edith Hamilton argues that while other "monsters" from this period were driven away from the earth, the Erinyes could not be banished "[a]s long as there was sin in the world."[5] The Erinyes take it as their duty ruthlessly to pursue and punish evildoers, and they are frequently seen to drive their prey to insanity through guilt and physical torture, as happened to Orestes. Yet, as Timothy Gantz asserts, while it is true that the Erinyes claim to protect all blood relationships ("blood congenital") in Aeschylus' *Eumenides* (line 605), they do not address Agamemnon's earlier sacrifice of his daughter Iphigeneia.[6] Indeed, they are not even asked about it in the play, which may indicate the need for a wronged party to plead with them first to enact vengeance. Likewise, argues Gantz, the actual punishments meted out by the Erinyes are left "lamentably unclear" in many of the myths.[7] Nonetheless, the Erinyes represent the need to uphold familial moral conventions, operate as a plausible threat, and embody the desire for vengeance on the part of victims.

A change in their representation occurs with Euripides, who, in *Trojan Women* (415 BCE), indicates that they are three sisters instead of the undetermined number of earlier sources. Later, they even had names, as shown for instance by Virgil's specific mention of them in the *Aeneid* (c. 29–19 BCE): Alecto, "the Unceasing One," Tisiphone, "the Avenger of Murder," and Megaera, "the One Who Holds a Grudge." Conversely, William Hansen offers a distinction between these particularly named Erinyes and the "personal Furies that each person has."[8] Examples from Classical mythology that use the term Erinyes in such a way include Homer's *Odyssey* (8th century BCE), in which the mother of Oedipus hangs herself and leaves to her son "the world of horror a mother's Furies bring to life."[9] The *Odyssey* also notes that beggars have their own gods and Furies,[10,11] much as Aeschylus has the Erinyes assert in *Eumenides* that so do strangers (545–49). Also, in Hesiod's *Theogony*, Rhea takes revenge upon her spouse, Kronos, to pay the Erinyes of Ouranos (his father whom he castrated) and of his own children whom he had swallowed as they were born (lines 472–3). The difference is between a general sense of impersonal justice on one side and a keenly personal vendetta on the other.

Though the Erinyes play a role in several ancient mythological sources, they appear most centrally as the eponymous leads in *Eumenides*, the third play of Aeschylus' fifth-century-BCE trilogy *The Oresteia*. The trilogy narrates the murder of Agamemnon and then of Clytemnestra and the subsequent trial of Orestes. In *Eumenides*, the Erinyes are urged by the ghost[12] of Clytemnestra to pursue Orestes to punish him for murdering her, his mother, even though this was in retaliation for her murder of Agamemnon, his father and her husband.[13] Through the protection of Apollo, Orestes is able to escape to Athens where Athena sets up a judicial trial including a jury of twelve who try Orestes for his deeds. After a split vote, Athena casts the deciding vote and declares that he will not be punished. The Erinyes, meanwhile, feel that justice has not been served according to their notions and so threaten the destruction of Athens. They must be placated by Athena, who wins them over and convinces them of the need for an independent judiciary as opposed to personal vendettas of revenge. As Hugh Lloyd-Jones posits, a part of Athena's argument is to compare "the function of the Erinyes in the universe with that of her newly established council in the government of Athens," by which he links the play to "the actual legal practice of the city."[14] Indeed, this denouement includes the promise that all future murderers will be tried by the Court of Areopagus, which indicates the emergence of Athenian democracy and rule of law over against vigilante or mob justice.

Another notable representation of the Erinyes is by the first-century-CE Roman poet Statius in his epic *Thebaid*. The background of the poem is that Oedipus, having discovered that he has been wed to his own mother and has fathered several children by her, is overcome with grief and guilt and so blinds himself though his grief is displaced by anger at his subsequent maltreatment by his two sons, Eteocles and Polyneices. Oedipus in a rage calls out in prayer to Tisiphone to punish them. The poem then moves to the center of the earth, to the lowest realms of Hades, and to Tartarus itself, where Tisiphone reigns as Queen.[15] Statius records a frightening character in his Tisiphone (1: lines 55–127). When she hears Oedipus' prayer, Tisiphone slowly allows her fury to build up against the two evil sons who treated their father so badly. Her "hair" of a hundred living, writhing snakes is loosed that they might drink from the sulfuric river of the dead. Her steely red eyes drip blood. Her skin is taut and poisonous. Her lips are black, and she breathes out fiery vapors that bring disease, hunger, thirst, and death. She carries a funeral torch in one hand and a huge, living water snake in the other that she uses as a whip. When she hears Oedipus' prayer, she does not rest until she comes to perch above the gates of Thebes, from whence she begins her plan for the downfall of the brothers, its two rulers.

Tisiphone is presented as the prime mover of the ensuing civil war, siege, and eventual fall of Thebes. She is always in the background, never visible to the men fighting but known, nonetheless, by her actions that keep the blood flowing until her ends are met. She summons her sister, Megaera, and they each take the side of a brother to ensure that they will come together in single combat and kill one another. Two other divine beings, Pietas and Fortuna, arrive in hopes of arranging for a peaceful settlement, but the two Erinyes fight them off so that they can complete their task of driving the brothers to kill one another on the battlefield. Indeed, for C.S. Lewis, this is a milestone in allegorical poetry in that "the human (and Olympian) action of the poem stays suspended and the personified good and evil of the human soul contend, not through their human representatives, but, face to face, with each other."[16] In other words, Lewis takes both Tisiphone and Pietas as allegories for contrasting human states of mind: rage and mercy. Ultimately, Tisiphone finds victory by avenging Oedipus, finally satiating herself with the mutual fratricide of the brothers.

Certainly, the Classical sources paint a fiery picture of the Erinyes and their violent treatment of familial betrayal, and this is just the image taken up in *The Furies*. The central plotline follows the relationship of T.C. (Walter Huston) and his adoring yet fiercely independent daughter, Vance, played by the inestimable Barbara Stanwyck. T.C. has promised Vance that she will run and inherit the Furies. Her name indicates a masculine strength admired in the context of the Old West, and it is clear that she will be not only preferred but also more effective than her brother as the inheritor and boss of the Furies ranch. However, T.C.'s oaths to her are broken through his entanglements with bankers and his courting of Flo (Judith Anderson), an unscrupulous widow who admits that she mainly desires him for his money. The film's climax arrives when Flo usurps Vance's role and insists that she leave the ranch; Vance, embodying both the violence and the vengeance of the Greek Furies, lashes out at Flo with a pair of sharp, long scissors, permanently disfiguring the once beautiful woman. T.C. casts out Vance and, in retribution, hangs Juan, Vance's former lover. This lynching sets in motion Vance's extended plan for revenge that ruins T.C. and returns possession of the Furies to her.

The Classical resonances of the film originate in Niven Busch's novel *The Furies* (1948). Busch remains well known for penning the classic Western *Duel in the Sun* (1944; filmed in 1946) and the original screenplay for 1947's *Pursued*, the first noir Western. In his novel, Busch directly appeals to the body of myth surrounding the Erinyes. Although the extent to which Busch sought to incorporate particular aspects from Classical sources about the Erinyes remains uncertain, he consciously made them the symbolic center of his novel through the overriding craving several characters exhibit for personal or familial vengeance. It is also Busch who contributed undeniable elements from film noir, from Freudian psychology, and from two key source texts, namely Shakespeare's *King Lear* (1605/6)[17] and Dostoyevsky's *The Idiot* (1874), to Mann's film. Several crucial plot points clearly come from Dostoyevsky, most notably the stacks of money and T.C.'s questionable I.O.U.s.[18] To this, Anthony Mann's direction adds his controlled sense of violence to an open landscape that strengthens both Busch's film noir[19] approach and the epic Greek nature of the film.

To *The Furies*, Mann brought a lifelong passion for Classical drama. As is well known, Mann grew up at Lomaland, a commune founded by the Theosophical Society in 1900 near San Diego. The commune's founder, Katherine Augusta Westcott Tingley, avidly sponsored the dramatic arts, and Mann (then known as Emile Anton Bundsmann) would have participated in both ancient Greek and Shakespearean plays as a youth.[20] Indeed, in 1901, the commune became the site of the first Greek style amphitheater built in North America. When Mann's career took him to Hollywood, this early exposure to Greek drama shaped the direction of his great films, from noir to Westerns and historical epics. It seems obvious that Mann would turn to the Western, given its dominance as a popular film form in the 1940s and '50s. However, it was Mann's background that equipped him to change the Western drastically by adding to it psychological elements that redefined its characters and stories, which in turn allowed him to challenge and deconstruct popular notions regarding the American character of the Old West, racial interactions, gender roles, and cinematic storytelling itself.

Under Mann's direction, the popular genre of the Western could integrate the high art of Classical drama by adopting its epic sweep and its deep concern with the complexities of human life. In a 1967 BBC interview with Paul Mayersberg, Mann makes his stance on the Western hybrid quite clear:

> You can take any of the great dramas—it doesn't matter whether it's Shakespeare, doesn't matter whether it's Greek plays, or what—you can always lay them in the West, and they somehow come alive, and they [have] this kind of passion and this drama. You can have patricide … every kind of 'cide, you know, in a Western, and you can get away with it because it's sort of where all action took place.[21]

During the climactic argument with Flo (Judith Anderson), Vance (Barbara Stanwyck) clutches her mother's shears behind her back, poised to hurl them at her antagonist. Mann uses mirrors aptly to parallel Vance's inner turmoil with the fragmentation of her image. *The Furies* (Paramount, 1950).

1950 proved to be a critical year for Mann's career, as he directed the first three of his eventual eleven Westerns that year. These three films are *Devil's Doorway*, *The Furies*, and the classic *Winchester '73*, the first of six Westerns that Mann made with Jimmy Stewart. Importantly, certain themes circulate between these three films. *Devil's Doorway* follows a Shoshone Native American who wins the Medal of Honor during the Civil War but whose people are steadily dispossessed of their lands through racism and greed, a situation echoed by the Herrera subplot in *The Furies*. Familial betrayal and vengeance also frame *Winchester '73*, in which Stewart's character pursues and eventually kills an outlaw who is only then revealed to be his own brother whom he must kill out of revenge for patricide, the brutal murder of their father.

A central action of *The Furies'* storyline, then, is to demonstrate why there is a need for vengeance and to establish the manner of frontier justice. Although the film and the ranch are both named for the Erinyes, Busch's novel is more nuanced in his approach to encoding the Classical references. In the novel, the home ranch is instead named the Birdfoot, and T.C.'s holdings are in fact so large that they encompass three separate tracts of land totaling nearly a million acres. The Erinyes remain implicitly present; the Birdfoot brand, for example, is an approximation of a double spur next to three claws from the talons of a bird.[22] Images of scratching and clawing are frequent, and all indicate the lurking and threatening presence of the Erinyes.

Although the main plot centers on the multiple acts of familial betrayal between

T.C. and Vance, the whole story is grounded in injustice. T.C. Jeffords has developed a modern day feudal empire with himself as a king who sits enthroned, feared, and adored. He is so unchallenged that he even produces his own money, referred to as "T.C.s," which are nothing more than I.O.U.s.[23] Given his capitalist bluster, T.C.'s seemingly impressive acts of creation are achieved at the expense of other, weaker individuals. One such family opposed by T.C. is that of Rip Darrow (Wendell Corey), whose father's life and land were taken outright by T.C. It is hinted that T.C. used dirty dealings by manipulating the judicial ruling of a territorial court to take the choice land, the so-called "Darrow Strip," for himself. In the novel, Rip is simply a gambler who sets up a saloon in town; Charles Schnee's screenplay thus compounds the character's desire to see T.C.'s downfall and to participate in it actively. A subtle change is that Busch's character is called Curley Darragh. The family name Darragh is typically Irish whereas Darrow is a Scottish spelling of the same name; both refer to a Celtic god of the Underworld, which further invokes the chthonic Erinyes. Likewise, Schnee's choice to change "Curley" to "Rip" again makes explicit his participation in the revenge plot against T.C. As Vance approvingly asserts, the nickname "Rip" "fits you—like a blade cutting right through." He too has something of the Erinyes about him and a familial grudge to settle with T.C.

Others ill treated by T.C. include the Mexican Herrera family, Latinos who live in a natural fortress at the top of a small mountain on the land T.C. now owns and whom he castigates as mere squatters. Given the 1870s setting of the film, the Herreras clearly echo the aftermath of the Mexican-American War twenty years earlier. This war was controversial and unpopular, as many Americans believed it to be fueled by an unethical expansionism that would also extend the reach of slavery. When T.C. violently forces the Herreras off the ranch, partially to please his bankers and partially to punish Vance, he breaks yet another oath to her that is compounded when he unjustly hangs her friend and former love interest, Juan. At the end of the film, T.C.'s actions ultimately bring about yet another act of vengeance when Juan's mother (Blanche Yurka), the so-called "Herrera witch," shoots and kills T.C. In a wider sense, Busch and Mann may also be reminding viewers of the broken oaths to Latinos from the U.S. government that contravened the Treaty of Guadalupe Hidalgo (1848) during and after the settlement of former Spanish territories.

Given the importance of this historical context to the film, a perhaps overlooked Classical reference occurs as the film moves into the first scene. Victor Milner's camerawork takes the perspective of the domestic sphere through the point of view of the massive Jeffords ranch house surveying a part of the likewise massive expanse of the Furies. Superimposed on the opening shot is an establishing message that reads like a scroll, giving viewers the background information necessary to enter the film with a basic understanding of the when and where of the setting and of who the central characters are. Through taken for granted by viewers, this opening is in fact indebted to the innovations of early Greek playwrights and their use of a chorus to set the stage with background information and to interact with the action of the play as it proceeded. In *Agamemnon* (458 BCE), for example, Aeschylus uses a chorus of the elderly men of Argos to inform the audience of the events surrounding the siege of Troy as they relate to Agamemnon and his return; the chorus then acts as both a collection of characters who interact with and comment on the actions of the central characters. In *The Furies*, the scrolling text that takes the place of a literal chorus informs us that the story is set in 1870s New Mexico territory, and, as the text scrolls over the image of a lone rider approaching against the open range, we are told that this is a new land where "men created kingdoms out of land and cattle ... and ruled their empires like feudal lords." T.C. Jeffords is noted as the author of "this flaming page" in the history of the West. Again with the Classical resonance, a chorus returns to end the film, though in this case it is a literal, all male choir that sings the range song composed about T.C.'s big roundup and that deifies him, for "there never was a man like old T.C. when he was in his prime." Here it should be noted that there is a definite shifting of focus in the film, for Mann's main interest quickly becomes T.C.'s daughter, Vance. Indeed, a significant problem with the novel arises in how it moves between celebrating both Vance and T.C. while they are in conflict. Neither is expected to remain on top of the Classical Wheel of Fortune forever, of course, but Vance is certainly the dominant character until the antepenultimate section that follows T.C. alone and glowingly portrays his fortitude in making deals to save the Birdfoot through the massive roundup of 20,000 head of cattle. As Jim Kitses observes in his audio commentary to the Criterion Collection edition of the film, Mann himself claimed in 1967 that "*The Furies* failed because he deviated from his favorite narrative: the single minded pursuit of a goal: 'Nobody in it cared about anything. They were all rudderless, rootless, and haters.'" Yet, insists Kitses, these characters "all pursue obsessive agendas."[24]

Whether Vance or T.C. is truly the central character of the narrative remains unsettled in Busch's novel, but in Mann's film it is immediately apparent that Vance is the character who is foregrounded. She is not only preferred by her father but is, in fact, more aggressive and capable than he is in running the ranch. In the camera's first view of Vance, she is playing at being the lady of the house by trying on her dead mother's white dress, the same dress that the dead woman wears in her portrait. While speaking to her brother Clay, Vance implicitly references the switching of their gender roles while giving play to their sibling rivalry. As Vance insists: "you're T.C.'s son, and he despises anything he can beat. I never let him beat me. Why do you always let him get the best of you?" A part of Vance's claim is that Clay is T.C.'s offspring and should be tougher simply because of his genealogy. T.C. shares this sentiment; at the film's denouement, he proudly claims that only he could have bred a daughter as smart, beautiful, and fiery. A second aspect of Vance's claim is that Clay is just that: clay that is unformed and too easily manipulated or too easily overcome, like the biblical metaphor of a statue with feet of clay. Vance, conversely, bears an androgynous name that clearly references the male name Vince, fittingly derived from the Latin *vincere*, meaning "to conquer." Clay, Vance further asserts, alone understood their mother, which for her points to Clay as a proverbial momma's boy who is not fit to run the Furies. Vance next innocently picks up her mother's very large pair of scissors, symbolically indicating Clay's relative castration[25] and foreshadowing the violence that is to come much later in the film. Not only does T.C. despise Clay because he knows he can beat him—Vance knows that she too can beat her brother and despises him for the same reason.

T.C. is a big man, larger than life, but he is clearly more at ease on the range and travelling than he is at home. As Clay notes, he spends an hour alone in his wife's room when he returns and when he leaves the Furies.[26] Indeed, the film plays between the threats represented by the shadow and mirror-lined interior of the house and the different threats represented by the open spaces, tall phallic cacti, and mountain peaks of the harsh surrounding landscape. For T.C., the domestic sphere is the realm of his dead wife and a symbol of his dysfunctional family. At the same time, his great ranch house is palatial, roomy, and comfortable. In particular, the great winding staircase represents the wealth and extravagance of the Furies, and Mann several times uses the staircase as a prop for Vance's appearances, both in grace and in disgrace. T.C.'s study, however, a firmly masculine space, is lined with hunting trophies, his chair is made of horns, and his desk is flanked by busts of Napoleon and of himself. His admiration for Napoleon is further solidified by his claim that he "started from scratch and built himself an empire."

For T.C., Vance is intimately and positively linked to the future of that empire. When they reunite upon his return, T.C. is at first taken aback by Vance wearing her mother's dress, evidence that she had broken the taboo of entering the dead mother's bedroom and touching her things. After a moment's hesitation, she descends the staircase toward T.C., and they kiss full on the mouth. T.C.'s main desire is that his daughter scratch his "sixth lumbar vertebra" for him. This request, and Vance's gleeful scratching, raises several concerns. As T.C. recounts several times, he was wounded by an Osage arrow many years earlier, so this is an old wound from battle that reminds him how close he came to death.[27] Further, Vance's scratching foreshadows her role as a potential Fury, in that her nails substitute for their long sharp claws; in this case, at least, T.C. loves it. Also, the specific naming of T.C.'s sixth lumbar vertebra is peculiar for two reasons. First, 90 percent of people have only five lumbar vertebrae, meaning T.C. (if there was any reliable way he could actually know he had the extra vertebra) is set apart by this small physical difference. Second, the sixth lumbar vertebra is located directly over the coccyx, or tailbone. Hence, although the camera only shoots this back scratching from particularly safe angles, Vance's hands are touching her father in a rather sensitive and intimate place.

Thus, sex remains a troublesome subject in the story. At the heart of the issue, T.C. and Vance encode a strong Electra complex, yet another Classical allusion. A part of Vance's sexual identity is her inability to find a mate who can stand up to her father or equal him—at least in her own mind. Vance, on the other hand, knows her sexual power and is able to manipulate most men. For Vance, the notion of not respecting—and of not loving—what and whom you can beat continues. Following a meeting with the bank's representative, T.C. sets out his claims to whom Vance will marry and promises her $50,000 for a dowry but insists that he has already spoiled most men for her in comparison with himself. In an intensely close two shot, Vance declares, "You sound like you'd like if I never married" and that "You think you're top man on God's green earth, don't you?" At this, she begins scratching his back at his request once again, clearly suggesting the sexual tinge of their near incestuous relationship.

Two other male characters are possible matches for Vance. Juan Herrera and Vance remain friends after a hinted at love affair in the past.[28] Following a flirtatious ride and run up to high ground with Juan, Vance brags about beating him every time they race. He recalls that the one time she lost, she was so angry that she "scratched blood," and he points out the scar on his chin. She smiles and remarks, "It's the Furies' brand on you, all right." "No, Vance," replies Juan, ""Not the Furies. Yours." "No difference" is Vance's quick response. Thus, although Juan remains a confidant for Vance and in fact dies for her stoically when T.C. orders him hanged, he is himself too effeminate and romantic for Vance, who, to the contrary, is often pictured in the film with her hands planted aggressively on her hips. Though they kiss in parting, Juan remarks sadly that it is but "the kiss of a good friend."

Later, at Clay's wedding, Rip Darrow and Vance approach each other as possible sexual conquests. Rip verbally jousts with T.C., which leads Vance to assume that perhaps he is the one who is finally man enough to stand up to T.C. and provide her with a suitable match. Indeed, dancing with Rip, she even recycles the same line about him thinking himself "top man on God's green earth" that she earlier used on her father. Jeanine Basinger goes so far as to argue that Corey and Anderson were cast as "lookalike actors" to echo the physical resemblances of Huston and Stanwyck in order to strengthen the Electra connection between Vance and T.C., as if they both chose sexual partners who physically and temperamentally resembled the father or daughter they subconsciously wanted but could not have.[29][30] As they begin courting, Rip offers Vance a ride in his buckboard. She demands, "Do you mind if I take the reins? I like to know where I'm going," thereby asserting the traditional masculine role of driving the horses and of determining the pace and direction of the emerging relationship. She drives him to the Darrow Strip, the land previously owned by his father, who was killed by her father. Though Rip is somewhat taken aback by her forwardness, Vance demands, "When you know what you want, why waste time?" right before she kisses him and insists that he come calling at the house that Saturday night.

Rip, wisely acknowledging that T.C. will try to ruin him, does not call at the Furies, forcing an angry visit from Vance. Rip responds with immediate violence that reflects his fear of what might happen if T.C. hears that she has come to his bedroom. He slaps her, grabs her, and pushes her face into a bowl of water. Busch's novel makes this scene even more violent: Vance threatens to kill him, and there is an implicit threat of rape, but in the end, Vance stays and gets drunk on whiskey for the first time, and the two become lovers.[31] Theirs is a troublingly sadomasochistic sexual relationship that at least partially stems from Vance's relationship with her father. The bowl of water, strikingly, is another departure from the novel. Tellingly, as Mann's daughter Nina recounted in a 2008 interview, she had "a sort of jolt" when she saw the scene because her father had told her about an abusive schoolmaster at the Lomaland commune who similarly "would pick him up by his feet and dunk his head in a pail of water until he knocked it over, which was pretty horrific"; Nina's reaction was "Oh, okay, I get that one. I know where that came from."[32]

For Vance, love is difficult. Repeatedly, she and other characters adopt equine metaphors to describe her falling in love, as if, in Rip's words, she were "a filly that never had a rope around her neck." Vance later takes up the same equine metaphor while speaking with Juan: "I don't think I like being in love. It's like having a bit in my mouth." A major upset occurs when Rip is offered a choice by T.C.: Vance's hand in marriage without a dowry or $50,000 in cash if he leaves her alone for good. Of course, he takes the money.[33] Indeed, the one character, it seems, who does not pay for his or her sins is Darrow. He hits Vance and behaves not at all like the chivalrous gentleman she expects. This leads to a seesawing of the power structure of their romantic relationship that parallels their business negotiations.

Not only is Vance's romantic life problematic but her previously impregnable hold on T.C. falters when the new character of Flo Barnett is introduced. A beautiful and refined older widow, she is a love interest for T.C. and a definite rival for Vance. She alone calls T.C. by his given name, "Temple," and she shows her power by connecting him to the President. Yet Flo's usurpation of Vance is most clearly seen when she scratches T.C.'s back in front of Vance, as if she were literally marking her territorial claim. In Clay's words, again using the sexual equine metaphor, it is Flo alone who has "brought [Vance] to halter" because Vance has found herself fighting against another woman for the first time.

The tension between Vance and Flo steadily increases until it, quite expectedly for a Mann film, erupts violently. Flo weasels into the ranch's business affairs and claims Vance has failed by allowing the squatters to return. At the film's climax, Flo, who has now claimed the room of Vance's mother, announces to Vance that she is marrying T.C. and will have the mother's room redone to suit herself. She boldly admits to marrying T.C. for his money and out of loneliness, and she recounts that T.C. had already given her $50,000. When T.C. enters the room, Flo further advises Vance that she has hired a new experienced manager for the ranch. She proclaims that the Herreras and other squatters should be moved off the land forcibly. She has convinced T.C. to send Vance away to tour Europe and to refine herself as a proper lady as opposed to a living like a masculine ranch hand. Flo thus seeks to force onto Vance a particular frame of femininity rooted both in traditional gender roles and in her understanding of class. Finally, she remarks in a trenchant manner to Vance that "there'll always be room for you at the Furies. There'll always be room, won't there, Temple?" She thus repeatedly and forcefully claims her territory. These threats to the integrity of the ranch result in Vance, embodying the role of the Erinyes, taking matters into her own hands.

Here, Vance faces a choice in dealing with this usurper. The viewer watches this choice unfold in another mirror shot that shows T.C. and Flo's faces toward Vance. We see Vance from behind and notice her hands grasp at the same pair of scissors that she picked up in the first scene. The scissors, or shears as Busch describes them, belonged to Vance's dead mother and are very long, very sharp, and pointed like daggers. Whether premeditated or instinctual, Vance, in her tight fitting black blouse, grasps the pair of scissors tightly behind her back and then throws them directly at Flo, hitting her hard and directly in the face. Blood immediately begins to pour out of two long gouges in the right side of Flo's face. In perhaps the most compelling scene of the film, T.C. declares to his once beloved daughter, "If she dies, I'll kill you." As in a noir, Vance slowly walks down the grand staircase with complete composure as if she were a sleepwalker in the midst of the house's intense chaos. As she walks to the front door, the light against the railings and the bars of the staircase create long shadows against her body akin to the bars of a jail cell, figuring her entrapment in the cycle of familial violence and retribution.

The appearance of sudden violence is certainly characteristic of Mann. In the novel's version, conversely, Vance waits to attack a sleeping Flo after her bold and vulgar suggestion that T.C. needed a woman of a different sort than a daughter, namely, the type of woman who could satisfy him in the bedroom. The violence takes us in several directions in the film. The Classical resonance is clear: Vance is acting as the Erinyes here, using the claw like scissors to lash out at this rival and to punish both T.C. and Flo for their disloyalty to her and their threat to push her off the Furies. As Kitses posits, this violent action makes Vance a template for latter Mann heroes: "Stanwick's character, huge eyes blazing, is every bit as righteous, vicious, magnificent as the male heroes of the latter films. She is at once the Furies, the Noir anti-heroine, and Western hero, at once affirming her identity, facing off with evil, and saving the ranch." However, the violence does give viewers pause in their regard for Vance, though she is somewhat recuperated when T.C., seeking his own revenge, soon kills Juan in front of her in retribution. Likewise, Flo, now victimized and brutalized, suffers permanent partial paralysis and disfigurement that goes deeper than the flesh. In Busch's words, "What had been impaired was the soul: its tissues, not the body's, were what Vance had slashed with the shears."[34] Flo, consequently, must now be seen in a more sympathetic light.

For T.C., Vance is now a "cancer to be cut out." He decides to force the Herrera clan off the ranch immediately, knowing that Vance has taken refuge with them. After a long gun battle and the use of dynamite, T.C. promises that the Herreras can leave with their lives, but he breaks his oath and hangs Juan, claiming that he was a horse thief. Vance knows that T.C. "means me to beg—to beg him for your life" and that he is executing Juan to hurt her. Powerless, and symbolically facing T.C. next to a long fence, Vance declares, "Now I hate you in a way I didn't know a human could hate. Take a good long look at me, T.C. You won't see me again until the day I take your world away from you."[35]

Exiled from the ranch, Vance determines a course of vengeance that will see her come to own the Furies outright and thus dethrone her father. Again, the central Classical linkage that Busch and Mann focus on is the guilt of T.C., who has broken several sworn oaths and family obligations to his daughter. In her Erinyes-like quest for revenge, Vance realizes T.C.'s biggest weakness. Cunningly, she starts touring nearby states to buy up his now almost worthless I.O.U. bills. At one stage in her business dealings, for example, she acquires $37,502.00 in T.C.s for $3475.60 USD, buying them in a "bear run" for 5 or 10 cents on the dollar.

Vance now partners up with Rip because she needs more money to destroy T.C. and get back the Furies. Rip reveals that he has kept the $50,000 dowry "for you" all those years, but he quickly becomes concerned and insists, "You've found a new love in your life, haven't you, Vance? You're in love with hate."[36] Nonetheless, he agrees to help but asks for the Darrow Strip in return, meaning she would give up 10 percent of the ranch to save 90 percent. Again, unknowingly indicating Vance's relation to the Erinyes and her loyalty to the land, Rip observes, "Look at you: just the thought of losing part of the Furies and you're ready to claw and scratch." Without a better option, she makes the deal. Much later, after considerable work on their part to buy as many T.C.s as possible, Vance and Rip discuss how to manipulate Mr. Anaheim, the banker. A part of the secret of Vance's success is that she needs the bank to extend T.C.'s loan so that he can be manipulated into rounding up and selling the Furies' cattle. Rip, somewhat perturbed, questions Vance's confidence that she is so "sure you can handle any man." She, in fact, while wearing an evening gown and long gloves, then handles him promptly while suggestively eating a chicken wing:

"You'd like to hit me right now, wouldn't you?"
"I would."
"Go ahead." [He does.]
"Now you'd like to kiss me, wouldn't you?"
"Yes, I would."
"What's in it for me? Is it worth the Darrow Strip to you?"

Though he does not reply verbally, they do kiss, after which she abruptly leaves with the parting shot that he "Sleep well." Later, as the denouement of Vance's plans arrives, she and Rip rekindle their love with their third trip to the Darrow Strip. Inserting sexual innuendo into their conversation, Rip insists that if they marry then he will tell her if she is wrong, whereas, if he is wrong, she "will keep her little mouth shut." "Mr. Darrow, sir," she replies, "I hope you can chew what you just bit off." Kitses notes this sexual wordplay and asserts that Mann sought to evade Hays Code censor control through such veiled connections between sex and food. Most tellingly, this sexual-culinary coding is revealed by the courting cake, the bread used for the ritual parting with Juan, the large chicken wing held by Vance's whited gloved hand, and her assertion to Rip that she hopes he "can chew what you just bit off."

Meanwhile, T.C.'s fortunes worsen, and he takes desperate measures to stave off foreclosure, keep the Furies intact, and prove himself still equal to his reputation. In order to get money to pay his debts, T.C. accepts an offer to sell 20,000 cattle to an anonymous buyer. He is given 90 days to complete the massive task of rounding up that many head across his massive holdings.[37] Despite his age, T.C. works harder and longer than the rest of the men to the extent that someone composes a range song about his manly exploits. One evening during the roundup, a cowboy refers to a wild old bull he sees as "the king of the Furies." T.C., who is himself referred to several times as a bull,[38] takes the comment personally and sets out to rope the bull and wrestle him to the ground. The challenge echoes both ancient Greek bullfighting and the bull as a Classical and Western icon of manhood. Having shown his domination over the creature, T.C. insists once again, "I'm still the King of the Furies." Unfortunately, this scene does not come off well, beginning with the fact that the film, intentionally or not, depicts T.C. as a clown and so does not approach the novel's sincere rendering of this Herculean task.[39] Most strikingly, the novel's massive, dangerous, wild Longhorn bull is represented in the film by a young steer. A stunt double, trick ropes, and continuity errors are clearly visible. This scene, frankly ridiculous, stands in for what in the novel is a climactic and meaningful sequence.

As the novel's narrator describes the beautiful ferocity of the bull, T.C. looks at him with "admiration" and "even affection." But then, T.C. feels a more complicated kinship with the bull: "He got the idea that this ancient, crafty bull was his own fate. This outlaw had grown strong and happy while he, T.C. Jefford, had been pestered and chivvied, driven by his creditors, deserted by his children, and plagued by his worries."[40] He becomes convinced that he "couldn't enjoy his range while an animal lived on it who was his superior. He wanted personal combat with this bull."[41] In yet another Classical allusion, T.C. can be said to be the victim of his own success, a man who suffers from the hamartia or tragic flaw of his own strength that makes him at once successful and bullheaded. Anticipating success, T.C. takes it as "an omen—it would be powerful proof that he, T.C., could whip anything, even his personal Furies, the murderous unknown shapes in the sky."[42] In this, the novel's only mention of the literal Erinyes, T.C. acknowledges the threatening presence of external forces that he cannot control. However, rather presumptuously, T.C. believes that if he is able to whip the bull then he can take it as a sign that he has indeed whipped the Furies too. Busch has his T.C. go off alone after the massive old bull—*toro a toro*—and successfully rope and wrestle him to the ground, though this is due in great measure to T.C.'s intelligent cutting horse, Salty. There is no cheering crowd, only two bulls—human and bovine—who battle one another for supremacy. Crucially, although T.C. gets the animal to the ground, he is left in somewhat of a stalemate in that he cannot let go of the bull for fear of his violent reaction upon being released. If we accept his assertion that he, in throwing the bull, has symbolically whipped the Furies, then, obviously, this is only a momentary victory that leaves him grasping the tail of a very dangerous creature. Clearly, more troubles are to come. T.C., as the bigger and stronger bull in this interaction, may be pictured not only as bullheaded and macho but also as a threatening Minotaur whom Vance must overcome and destroy—not through physical strength or the gun but through her superior cunning.

When T.C. finally meets the buyers for his herd, he anticipates getting paid $145,600 USD in return for his 20,000 head of cattle—enough to end all his money troubles and more. However, when he comes face to face with the buyers, he finds Vance and Rip. The next surprise is that they have paid him with his own I.O.U.s, the now completely worthless T.C.s. This, then, is the "legal tender" that Rip and Vance bought, partially with the $50,000 given to Rip not to marry Vance. Looking at the image of the girl riding the bull on his stylized I.O.U.s, T.C. exclaims, "Lulu of a girl ridin' a bull. I knew it was art, but I'll be double dogged—I never thought a girl could really ride a bull. But you did it, Vance. You rode me proper, and you throwed me proper." Although he is now financially ruined, T.C. is impressed with what his daughter has done. To him, she has been able to throw and ride him, just as surely as he threw the Longhorn bull. However, the image undoubtedly reasserts the Electra complex and the threat of incest by invoking the Classical myth of Europa and Zeus, who took the form of a white bull when he abducted her. That T.C.'s downfall is caused by his own I.O.U.s is not only pleasantly ironic. It again accesses the character's hamartia in that his great strength is his word of honor, but that same strength brings him low when he is not able to uphold the bond between his promise and following through by paying off his debts with real money. Once again, the Erinyes are invoked to punish the broken oaths represented by T.C.'s worthless financial promises.

As opposed to celebrating her long-fought victory over her father, Vance reconciles with T.C. Bursting with pride, he exclaims, "She's smart, and she's a beauty, and she's full of lick and fire. She's one in a nation, I tell ya." Taking Vance in his arms, he claims partial credit for her success: "No one could have bred her but T.C. Jeffords." Returning to the most frequently used metaphor for T.C., Vance replies happily, "You're an old rogue bull, T.C., and you'll always prance wild." At that, T.C. signs the cattle and, therefore, the land over to her, but, again using Erinyes imagery, he looks forward to starting again: "I'm back to scratch. That's when I had my fun—startin' from scratch." The term scratch here offers multiple puns, as it references the several earlier literal back scratches, the figurative scratches of violence, the idea of money as scratch, and of course the pugilistic sense of being up to scratch and toeing a scratched line to begin a fight. He burns the large pile of T.C.s and, imperturbable in his self confidence, is eager to move ahead toward what he assumes can only be future successes.

In the film's penultimate scene, all three walk off to celebrate new beginnings. Suddenly, Juan Herrera's mother emerges from the shadows and shoots and kills T.C. She has already proved herself to be a fierce fighter, but Mann goes further by portraying her as yet another female Fury seeking and obtaining revenge. Busch's novel instead has the mother killed in the assault on the Herreras and her death and Juan's hanging avenged by the three remaining brothers—another approximation of the three Erinyes sisters. With his dying breath, and again with Classical resonance, T.C. blesses the union of Vance and Rip but, still full of oversized male bravado, insists they not name their son T.C. because "That's too heavy a pack for him to carry. He'll have too much to live up to. 'Cause there'll never be another like me." As T.C. dies with a saloon piano playing the round-up song composed in his honor, Vance replies that now they would "take him home … to the Furies." With the vengeance of the Erinyes seemingly served and T.C.

124 Cowboys and Catharsis

now forgiven, a more just future is envisioned through the coming marriage of Vance and Rip. As they return to the ranch, the couple agrees that they will name his grandson T.C. just the same, indicating that justice has been served and T.C.'s kingdom will continue.

Notes

1. For more on these stages of development, see Hugh Lloyd-Jones' "Erinyes, Semnai Theai, Eumenides."
2. Robert Graves, *The Greek Myths*, Vol. 1 (London: Penguin, 1960), 122.
3. Walter Burkert, *Greek Religion*, trans. John Raffan (Cambridge, MA: Harvard UP, 1985), 197–8. In *Works and Days*, Hesiod writes that the Erinyes assist at the birth of Horkos (Oath), which reflects their interest in punishing perjury. See pages 803–4.
4. See lines 133–87 in Hesiod's *Theogony*. Other sources, including Aeschylus (*Eumenides* line 321), Virgil (*The Aeneid* 6: line 250), and Ovid (*Metamorphoses* 4: line 453), hold that the Erinyes were daughters of Nyx (Night).
5. Edith Hamilton, *Mythology* (New York: Black Dog & Leventhal, 2017), 7.
6. Timothy Gantz, *Early Greek Myth: A Guide to Literary and Artistic Sources* (Baltimore, MD: Johns Hopkins UP, 1993), 14; 681.
7. Ibid., 13–14.
8. William Hansen, *Classical Mythology* (*Classical Mythology*. Oxford: Oxford UP, 2004), 155–6.
9. See lines 279–80 in Homer's *The Odyssey: Book 11*.
10. See line 475 in Homer's *The Odyssey: Book 17*.
11. For further examples drawn from Homer, see Lloyd-Jones, "Erinyes, Semnai Theai, Eumenides," 91–2.
12. One view of the Erinyes holds that they first represented the ghosts of murdered relatives returning for revenge on their kin. For more on this reading, see pages 214–17 in Jane Harrison's *Prolegomena to the Study of Greek Religion*.
13. In the *Eumenides*, provokingly, Aeschylus makes the Furies themselves the play's chorus. In the *Oresteia* trilogy, Clytemnestra murders Agamemnon because he had in turn killed and sacrificed their daughter Iphigenia in order to propitiate the goddess Artemis, whom he had offended and who had altered the winds so as not to allow his ships to leave for the war in Troy. The trilogy also gives rise to the Electra Complex, named for Orestes' sister, who joins with him in avenging the murder of their father by plotting the murder of their mother and her lover.
14. Hugh Lloyd-Jones, "Erinyes, Semnai Theai, Eumenides," in *The Further Academic Papers of Sir Hugh Lloyd-Jones* (Oxford UP, 2005), 96.
15. Hamilton posits that there is a notable difference here between the Greek poets, who picture the Erinyes "chiefly as pursuing sinners on the earth," and the Romans, like Statius, Ovid, and Virgil, who place them in the underworld where they punish evildoers (37). Also see Ovid's *Metamorphoses* (4: lines 416–562) for his rendering of the Athamas and Ino story, in which Tisiphone appears in much the same guise as she does in Statius.
16. C.S. Lewis, *The Allegory of Love* (Oxford: Oxford UP, 1936), 54.
17. As argued by Wood, aspects of *King Lear* appear in at least two other Mann Westerns: *The Man from Laramie* (1955) and *Man of the West* (1958). Wood notes that *King Lear* fascinated Mann, who was working on a cinematic adaptation of the play called *The King* when he died (10).
18. As Mann later recounted, "*The Furies* was *The Idiot*. In fact, Niven Busch began with Dostoyevsky's novel, turned it into a western, and made a few changes, thinking nobody would notice. When he brought me his script, I told him that this was *The Idiot*, and he had to admit it. So I told him that given a choice between *The Furies* and *The Idiot*, I would have rather made *The Idiot*!" (Bitsch and Chabrol 30).
19. Kitses notes that Mann shot *The Furies* in black and white instead of Technicolor, as would have been expected for a 1950 Western. Furthermore, Milner's camerawork includes several dark scenes filmed at night. These choices undoubtedly recall film noir cinematography.
20. Max Alvarez, *The Crime Films of Anthony Mann* (Jacksonville, MS: University Press of Mississippi, 2014), 10–13.
21. See Paul Mayersberg's 1967 BBC interview with Mann found in the Special Features section of The Criterion Collection's 2008 release of *The Furies*.
22. Niven Busch, *The Furies*, 1948 (Criterion Collection, 2008), 33–4; 238.
23. Naming the bills "T.C.s" is a clever addition of the screenplay; in the novel, they are simply printed I.O.U.s akin to the I.O.U.s in Dostoyevsky's *The Idiot*.
24. Kitses observes in his audio commentary to the Criterion Collection edition of the film that Mann himself claimed in 1967 that the characters obsessively followed their agendas.

25. The family name of Clay's fiancée, Weadick, further suggests the effeminate character of Clay, the presumptive heir who is passed over for his younger sister. In the film and novel, Clay appears instead to run and inherit the LX, the smaller, less desirable ranch of his wife's family.

26. In the film, T.C. honors the memory of his deceased wife frequently and with great passion. In Busch's novel, however, T.C. has been cruel to Vance's mother—not through physical or sexual violence but rather as a result of his distant travels and dalliances with other women.

27. Though the film does not mention it, T.C.'s battle with the Osages is a pivotal moment because it is the only time he truly feels fear and because his father, Old Dan, dies during the attack, which provokes an abiding guilt in T.C. (199–200).

28. The novel makes their affair explicit but begins with Vance breaking it off on the morning of T.C.'s return. Likewise, Kitses argues that Juan was meant to be a former lover in the film as well but that the edited version eliminated that connection.

29. Jeanine Basinger, *Anthony Mann* (Woodbridge, CT: Twayne Publishers, 1979), 94.

30. For Basinger, Huston and Corey are similar facially and "almost identical in height, carriage, and body type" while Stanwyck and Anderson "bear a striking resemblance" not only physically but also vocally and in similar acting ranges made apparent by their abilities to play their roles as both sympathetic and unsympathetic (94).

31. Busch, 69–73.

32. Quoted in Alvarez, *The Crime Films of Anthony Mann*, 14.

33. Busch writes a much more complex scene in which T.C. tests Curley (Rip in the film) by throwing the dowry packet of $50,000 into the stove and saying he can have it if he pulls it out with his hand; Vance sees Curley's reaction and realizes his greed, so she retrieves the money and sends him away with the singed packet while openly despising him (83–9). This test, T.C. notes, he heard was once used by "some Roosian gal," who, of course, is a character from Dostoyevsky's *The Idiot*. In the story, Nastassya measures Ganya's greed against his pride by throwing a packet of 100,000 rubles into the fire and offering them to him if he will humiliate himself by pulling them out with his bare hand.

34. Busch, 211.

35. Though this condensed sequence is workable, Busch's novel raises the stakes by having Juan rescue a dying Vance, marry her, and then be hanged by her father after he is set up for stealing a bull calf.

36. Vance is in considerable danger of adopting hate as her permanent emotional state. In the novel, she thinks, "Hate was a real thing too—as real as love. If you let it soak into yourself long enough you didn't want love. For love was a delicate thing, easily spoiled. Hate was tough: it could last forever" (182).

37. Busch's novel makes a further connection between T.C. and Napoleon by linking T.C.'s 90 days to Napoleon's Hundred Days in 1815 (227).

38. Even Mother Herrera, while waiting patiently for T.C. to come into her rifle sights, several times urges him, "Come, my toro."

39. Busch, 228–232.

40. *Ibid.*, 229.

41. *Ibid.*, 230.

42. *Ibid.* 230.

Filmography

Devil's Doorway. Dir. Anthony Mann. Nicholas Nayfack, 1950.
The Furies. Dir. Anthony Mann. Hal Wallis Productions, 1950.
Winchester '73. Dir. Anthony Mann. Aaron Rosenberg, 1950.

Works Cited

Aeschylus. *Aeschylus II: The Oresteia: Agamemnon, The Libation Bearers, The Eumenides, Proteus (Fragments)*, trans. Richmond Lattimore. 3rd Edition. Chicago: University of Chicago Press, 2013.
Alvarez, Max. *The Crime Films of Anthony Mann*. Jacksonville: University Press of Mississippi, 2014.
Basinger, Jeanine. *Anthony Mann*. Woodbridge, CT: Twayne Publishers, 1979.
Bitsch, Charles, and Claude Chabrol. "Interview with Anthony Mann." *Cahiers du cinéma* March 1957. In *The Furies* (Booklet). The Criterion Collection, 2008, 17–32.
Burkert, Walter. *Greek Religion*, trans. John Raffan. Cambridge, MA: Harvard University Press, 1985.
Busch, Niven. *The Furies*. 1948. Criterion Collection, 2008.
Dostoyevsky, Fyodor. *The Idiot,* trans. Constance Garnett. New York: Barnes & Noble Classics, 2004.
Gantz, Timothy. *Early Greek Myth: A Guide to Literary and Artistic Sources*. Baltimore, MD: Johns Hopkins University Press, 1993.

Graves, Robert. *The Greek Myths*. 2 Vols. London: Penguin, 1960.
Hamilton, Edith. *Mythology*. New York: Black Dog & Leventhal, 2017.
Hansen, William. *Classical Mythology*. Oxford: Oxford University Press, 2004.
Harrison, Jane. *Prolegomena to the Study of Greek Religion*. 3rd Edition. Princeton, NJ: Princeton University Press, 1991.
Hesiod. *Theogony* and *Works and Days*, trans. M.L. West. Oxford University Press, 1988.
Homer. *The Iliad*, trans. Robert Fagles. London: Penguin, 1990.
_____. *The Odyssey*, trans. Robert Fagles. London: Penguin, 1996.
Kitses, Jim. "Audio Commentary." In *The Furies*. The Criterion Collection, 2008.
Lewis, C.S. *The Allegory of Love*. Oxford: Oxford University Press, 1936.
Lloyd-Jones, Hugh. "Erinyes, Semnai Theai, Eumenides." In *The Further Academic Papers of Sir Hugh Lloyd-Jones*, 90–99. Oxford University Press, 2005.
Mayersberg, Paul. "Action Speaks Louder Than Words: An Interview with Anthony Mann." *The Movies*. BBC Two England. February 20, 1967. In *The Furies*. The Criterion Collection, 2008.
Statius, Pablius Papinius. *Thebiad*, trans. Jane Wilson Joyce. In *Masters of Latin Literature Series*. Ithaca, NY: Cornell University Press, 2008.
Virgil. *The Aeneid*, trans. Robert Fagles. London: Penguin, 2006.
Wood, Robin. "Man(n) of the West(ern)." *CineAction* Vol. 90 (Winter 2013): 6–12.

The Splendor of Bart Allison
Antigone and the Tragic Western Hero
Christopher Minz

Budd Boetticher's 1957 film *Decision at Sundown* is a striking work amongst Westerns and stands out even with those tallied on its director's slate. While Boetticher made effective and compelling use of the Cinemascope technology in many of his works, *Decision at Sundown* has none of the sweeping wide shots and panoramic Western landscapes that mark that style, and is instead a deeply intimate film, its framing often uncomfortably tight, signifying the collapsing internal psychology of its protagonist. The town of Sundown itself is defined by a compact mise-en-scene, the vast majority of which is depicted through a single, relatively narrow street between the stable in which Bart Allison (Randolph Scott) is holed up for much of the film, and the hotel in which his quarry, the petty tyrant Tate Kimbrough (John Carroll) is waiting. The film follows a familiar pattern for a Boetticher film, shadowing Bart Allison on a quest to avenge his dead wife. Bart travels to the town of Sundown to kill Tate Kimbrough, whose rape of Mary led to her suicide. Elsewhere in Boetticher's films, the wife character exists in ellipsis, a gap in the films, that is palpably and affectively felt. She is never even offered a flashback. In *Decision at Sundown*, this ellipsis is taken a step further: not only does Mary Allison not exist within the visual structure of the film, she is considered by those in the film a fantasy created by Bart.[1] This becomes clear as the film progresses, despite repeated attempts by Bart to repress his knowledge that Mary was neither raped nor faithful in any way to him when he was away at the war. Her suicide is intimated to be the result of her own depravity. Throughout the film, the gap between the chaste symbolic fantasy that Bart builds and the sexually promiscuous reality of his wife acts as a site at which Mary's lascivious specter threatens to erupt. Revenge is often empty in any sense. The payback Bart seeks, based on an entirely false premise, is one he must insist on believing, for it defines his identity. Kimbrough, however, is saved by a saloon girl, who rides off with him, and Bart is left to wallow without reprisal—his ability to fully repress what he considers to be Mary's sexual proclivity evaporates with Kimbrough's survival and exit. Bart ends the film drunk. Slumped on his horse, he rides off as the townsfolk watch with a palpable impotence, lamenting only that his memory will remain with them. A deeply tragic structure underpins the complete moral certitude that Bart Allison insists upon and culminates with his social diminishment. Riding away in ruins, Bart leads alongside him the unridden horse that belonged to the friend whom he got killed in his obsessional mission. The empty saddle signals an open space for the return of the repressed.

In general, it is not a complicated, nor particularly controversial, assertion that the Western enacts the tragic.[2] It is the Western's connection with the Greek tragic tradition that is more of a reach until its classical models and underpinnings are recognized. Like Sophocles' Antigone, the hero of the Boetticher Westerns exists in *até*, that space in which the living dead exist. This essay examines the relationship of *Decision at Sundown* with Sophocles' *Antigone* and offers salient psychological insights into Bart Allison's situation. Like Antigone, Allison's choice is not one to be envied or emulated—he also lives beyond human sanctions.

To begin, *Antigone* is the text with which psychoanalysis is able to fully make an ethical turn. Being Oedipus and Jocasta's daughter,[3] Antigone lives in a space, a textual prison, from which she strives to remove herself. Yet the legacy of her parentage flows through like poisoned wine, and her only choice is to find herself fully embraced in the incestuous lineage of her family. Her situation is particularly applicable to the Western so often defined by John Ford, who certainly thrives on tragic figures like Ethan Edwards. Ford always seems to maintain that a community can arise from the remainders of the tragic hero's journey and catharsis. *The Searchers* is a foundational work vis-à-vis the tragic figure in the Western, even though Ford allows a sort of moral legibility that is often absent from tragedy. While the interior may remain dark in the finale of *The Searchers*, there is a warmth in that darkness that Ethan will never know. And much as in Shakespeare's *Hamlet* outside the cold confines of Elsinore Castle, the world is functioning as it should—"Rosencrantz and Guildenstern are dead" as they must be, by decree, no matter how falsified. Yet Budd Boetticher, Jr., creates films that seem to lack the moral legibility in their structure that tends to inhabit Ford's or even Anthony Mann's films. Boetticher's films leave the hero in a space that defies society's symbolic order (as he never couples, never rejoins the social, nor actively rejects it).

As Jacques Lacan argues, Antigone "is required to sacrifice her own being in order to maintain that essential being which is the family *até*, and that is the theme or true axis on which the whole tragedy turns. Antigone perpetuates, eternalizes, immortalizes that *até*."[4] *Até* signifies the boundary *and* the space beyond that limit which the human beings, if they wish to remain human, should not cross. One becomes increasingly inhuman, the more one passes beyond that limit. Lacan explains that in *Antigone*, *até* "is an irreplaceable word. It designates the limit that human life can only briefly cross. Beyond this *até* one can only spend a brief period of time, and that's where Antigone wants to go."[5] Antigone's radical decision to reject the comfort and symbolic order of Creon's house (both the actual house and his "house" defined by the law and the edict against her brother's burial), enables her to go beyond, to *até*, and self-consciously dwell there. The chorus says a person cannot exist in the state of *até* for long, but Antigone in her defiance opts to stay not only too long, but perpetually. Her decision renders her into something not human. Lacan warns us "she is inhuman. But we shouldn't situate her at the level of the monstrous."[6] *Até* is a space in which the living dead can exist.

Eternalized, the hero of the Boetticher Westerns also exists in and aesthetically exemplifies *até*. The very structure of the cinema itself and these particular films aid this process, freezing the hero within the confines of the cinematic need to conclude. Thus, when we see Ben Brigade (Randolph Scott) in the striking finale of *Ride Lonesome*, he burns as emotionally hot and destructive as the hanging tree he has set on fire. The camera pulls back, until the figure of the hero is nearly indistinguishable from that of the burning tree. Brigade is poised immobile and immortal between the wood and the ash.

His fixed immobility defines this moment in a broader notion of tragedy: in the Nietzschean sense, Apollonian (social) structuring is abandoned in the Dionysian, the wild conflagration, as the hero holds his immortal vigil over the dead.[7] Lacan observes that "in the end tragic heroes are always isolated, they are always beyond established limits, always in an exposed position and, as a result, separated in one way or another from the structure."[8] In *Decision at Sundown*, Bart Allison is also contrasted against that which constitutes what is human. Bart's friend Sam (Noah Beery, Jr.), for example, expresses the desire to get something to eat, and talks about the grumbling of his stomach repeatedly. This very human need only draws grim looks from Bart, who is already in *até*, that space beyond. As the film progresses, Bart's own vestiges of humanity are stripped from him, until the end when he has even lost the ability to shoot properly with his hand bandaged and mangled. Bart's participating in *até* reveals our corporeal fragility and the infinite beyond.

Decision at Sundown (and truly all Boetticher Westerns) also houses a hero for whom the race is run. Like Antigone, Bart is an example of the living dead. The traumatic event for both Antigone and Bart Allison (Randolph Scott) occurs before we are introduced to them. Polyneices has died on the battlefield and Creon has decreed that he remain uninterred and left to the dogs, and Bart Allison's wife Mary has committed suicide after apparently being raped while Bart was fighting in the Civil War. Both narratives begin their action at a point where the heroes are reacting to rather than facing trauma itself. Both are burying and refusing to bury their dead. Antigone is acting in a philosophical oscillation: while she insists on burying Polyneices, she is at once immortalizing him in that familial *até*. Bart Allison has buried his wife, but in his quest to seek revenge upon her violator, he refuses to let her rest in peace. His refusal begins to unravel the truth, which, much like Antigone's cursed father Oedipus, leads to his ruin.

Here it is important to note that one of the key features that Lacan ascribes to the Apollonian/Dionysian structure of the Sophoclean tragedies is the pre-existence of the traumatic event: "for all his heroes the race is run."[9] Oddly, this discounts *Oedipus Rex*, wherein the traumatic event is the discovery of the nature of his existence. In a sort of rejoinder to the nobility of the search for truth, Oedipus's search for the truth of his lineage, despite Jocasta's admonishments to accept life as it is, leads to the discovery of Jocasta's, and by relation his own, identity. Had Oedipus left well enough alone, he might have died fat and content as the king of Thebes. Nietzsche offers a foundational basis for this line of thought, arguing that the Dionysian wisdom, an unbridled wisdom in contradistinction to Apollonian intelligence, is set against the natural. "The myth seems to wish to whisper to us that wisdom, and particularly Dionysian wisdom, is an unnatural abomination: that he who by means of his knowledge plunges nature into the abyss of destruction must also suffer the dissolution of nature in his own person."[10] Thus Oedipus is damned not for his breaking of the incest prohibition, but by his desire for wisdom and truth which exposes the abomination. The exposure of the act becomes the crime rather than the act itself. Antigone has no such pre-life, bound and firmly entrenched in a limited space before the play that bears her name even begins. Explaining this during an exchange shortly after the third choral ode, the chorus admonishes Antigone who is on her way to the tomb in which she is being interred: "[b]ut in this ordeal thou art paying, haply, for thy father's sin." To this, Antigone retorts, "Thou hast touched on my bitterest thought,—awaking the ever-new lament for my sire and for all the doom given to us, the famed house of Labdacus. Alas for the horrors of the mother's bed! alas for the wretched mother's slumber at the side of her own son,—and my sire! From what manner of parents did I take my miserable being! And to them I go thus, accursed, unwed, to share their home. Alas, my brother, ill-starred in thy marriage, in thy death thou hast undone my life!"[11] Here, Antigone recognizes that her *até* is one already inscribed by her fate because of the very structure of her pre-existence. It is the legacy of her formation that leads to her need to express such unyielding devotion to her brother. To paraphrase another psychoanalytic assertion, her desire is not her own, it is the desire of the other.

Both Antigone and Bart Allison are defined by desire external to themselves, Antigone by the desire of her parentage and her brother's transgression against the state of Thebes and Bart by the desire of his wife, which he represses deeply to maintain his sense of righteousness and connection to human order. Cecilia Sjoholm explains that such desire is made more palpable by the transgression: "the prohibition against touching the dead brother's body only reinforces the incestuous overtones of Antigone's desire."[12] For Bart, Mary, of course, is not related by blood to him, but desiring her is transgressive, because she is dead, something beyond, something that exists only as an idea, a form devoid of substance. She is therefore forbidden, and her desire is tabooed, because it does not comply with Bart's reification of her. Bart's desire for his dead wife (evidenced in the burial/refusal) is also related to *até*. As Sjoholm explains, "the limit of *até* engenders the wish to embrace the forbidden things that lie beyond it."[13] In short, Mary stimulates Bart's *até*. But what he desires, her primal form, exists in his head. Antigone claims to love her brother as he is, in his simple being, but he too engenders a beyond, something wherein being is not bound by the symbolic structures that deem him forbidden and traitorous. *Até*, this beyond, is represented in both *Decision at Sundown* and *Antigone* by visual absences.

Buried and unburied, the dead exist in a visual gap. Polyneices' and Mary's non-existences point to a notable feature of *Antigone* and *Decision at Sundown* that seems to escape mention in most attempts to analyze them. Both the play and the film construct themselves aesthetically around a vacant space.[14] In the play, Polyneices is a phantom. He is dead before the structure of the narrative begins, as is Bart Allison's wife, Mary. This lack of concrete representation enables Antigone and Bart to infuse themselves with their own concerns while being confined by the desire of a spectral center that is never revealed. This desire threatens both Antigone and Bart because it erupts in their actions.

The *até* experienced by Antigone is established as penetrable long before her ill-conceived birth and is fomented by the desire, not of her illicit father-brother Oedipus, but of her mother-grandmother Jocasta. It is key here to recall that nearing the climax of *Oedipus Rex,* when Jocasta discerns from a messenger's words who Oedipus truly is (while Oedipus himself remains unknowing), rather than revealing, or fleeing to avoid more potential incestuous relations, her response is to beg Oedipus not to pursue the matter further. Her desire for her son overtakes her rejection of the incest prohibition. Sjoholm argues that, by way of *até*, the limit that the law prescribes, "from this perspective, the founding crime is not the incest of Oedipus, but the desire of the mother Jocasta."[15] Slavoj Zizek takes this notion one step further arguing that it is precisely Oedipus's unknowing that bolsters his mother-wife's desire and associates this situation with Lacan's ontological concept of women, saying "the source of her enjoyment was precisely Oedipus's ignorance…. Woman enjoys insofar as her *other* (man) does not know."[16] In *Decision at Sundown*, Mary, in her absence, stands in for Polyneices, but because of her desire, which becomes the cruel reality Bart must face, and which he, to his ruin, refuses to face, she becomes like Jocasta. Mary's desire, a transgressive *jouissance* that breaks social boundaries, is a horror which Bart must repress at all costs, for it motivates his *até* (what both Aeschylus and Aristotle would say was his Ruin) and erupts in his violence and crazed behavior as the film continues.

Até in both *Antigone* and *Decision at Sundown* is disclosed by radical acts of speech that begin the unraveling of Antigone and Bart and mark them willing to transgress beyond the boundaries of simple legality. Antigone not only buries her brother against Creon's decree; she also insists her act be spoken. When her sister Ismene, the only Oedipal child to survive (perhaps the most tragic fate of all), says that she will not betray Antigone by confessing her knowledge of the deed, Antigone lashes out, "Oh, denounce it! Thou wilt be far more hateful for thy silence, if thou proclaim not these things to all." As Judith Butler explains, "Antigone wants her speech act to be radically and comprehensively public, as public as the edict itself."[17] It is her declaration of her act that pushes the crime to *até*. "Antigone ... acknowledges her deed," Butler says, "[B]ut the verbal form of her acknowledgement only exacerbates the crime. She not only did it, she had the nerve to *say* she did it."[18]

The action of *Decision at Sundown* begins in earnest, when Bart disrupts the state-sanctioned edict of a wedded union. In this scene, the staging of the church is tight and maintains the insistent claustrophobia of the entire film. Denoting Bart's existence in a collapsing symbolic world, the tightness of the camera's framing creates an affective squeeze. As the entire wedding turns to face Bart, he tells the bride-to-be, "If you marry this man, you'll be a widow by sundown." Like Antigone, he insists on making his intent verbal and assertively public. And, like Antigone, his behavior is questioned by a close compatriot. Standing in for Ismene is Bart's friend Sam (Noah Beery, Jr.) who is bewildered by Bart's nerve: "Bart, I think you done a fool thing," he says, "After all that searching around, it seems like you would have been satisfied to just kill him on sight." Tellingly, Bart replies, "Even a rattler gives a warning." As unshakeable as Antigone's, Bart's declaration rests on his ethics, and demonstrates that the law itself is powerless in the face of the *até* in which he resides.

Lacan argues that another of the key elements that defines the tragic and alienating nature of Antigone is her beauty which is manifested in various ways. For Lacan, Antigone illustrates "a line of sight that defines desire" that reaches beyond the specifics of the narrative: he says, "it is Antigone herself who fascinates us, Antigone in her unbearable splendor. She has a quality that both attracts us and startles us, in the sense of intimidates us; this terrible self-willed victim."[19] Self-willed victimhood truly is what separates Antigone from so many tragic heroes, who go unknowingly through their hubris to their fates. Antigone not only exists as a member of the living dead in the play, she desires living death. Her longing, however, is a reflection of the dead Polyneices's desire (and perhaps, as mentioned earlier, that of her incestuous desiring mother). Cecilia Sjoholm aptly describes this situation: "Antigone confused the *rights of the dead* with *the desire of the dead*—contaminated by their desire going one step beyond the piety of sisterly duty because the signifier she claims as the cause of her action, the rights of the dead, is the desire of her dead brother operating in her."[20] When Creon posts guards over Polyneices' body, the leader of the guards is also confused, asking why their presence is necessary, since the edict demands death for transgression, and commenting that "No man is so foolish that he is enamored of death."[21] And indeed, no man is. But Antigone exists beyond this, not only in the sense of being a woman, but in the sense that she has passed through and lingered in *até*.

Antigone's inhuman beauty, her terrible splendor, is caused by her transgression. Her splendor is uncanny, recognizable in its attraction and horrific in its rejection of the symbolic and the natural order. Not physically dead, she becomes a creature of being, not meaning, nearly animal as the guard who apprehends her re-burying her brother Polyneices claims she wailed the "sharp cry of a bird in its bitterness,—even as when, within the empty nest, it sees the bed stripped of its nestlings."[22] Bart Allison functions in much the same way. There is something beautiful yet intimidating about him. He is dirty, forlorn, and less put-together than the Randolph Scott characters in other films, even in other Boetticher films. And at the end he, like Antigone, is imprisoned. His confusion also muddies the rights of the dead with his desire for his wife. Trapped in a small stable, he too becomes nearly animal.

Settings associated with both characters further reinforce Sophocles' and Boetticher's associations of female desire with the uncanny. Referring to her prison as a "bridal-chamber, eternal prison in the caverned rock, whither I go to find mine own, those many who have perished," Antigone creates a signifying chain from what she bemoans as the "horrors of the mother's bed," to her own place in the tomb.[23] Sjoholm calls Sophocles' leitmotif "a womb of disaster which finds a metaphorical exponent in the cave where Antigone dies."[24] A more humble expression of the womb, Bart's stable brings to mind the feminine's animal nature and attributes to descent and debasement. Imprisoned in the dark, cramped space, Bart, confined by Mary's horrifying (to him) unnatural lasciviousness, is, at base obsessed with his dead wife's sexual organs. Oddly, the tight, bound up mise-en-scene of the stable, the abode of the inhuman, is at once comforting and imprisoning. And like those who enter the tomb where Antigone is shut up, those who attempt to enter the stable where Bart is hiding must be excised. If any stay, they must end like poor pathetic Haemon, who loves Antigone, and attempts to join her in death. Standing in for Haemon, the ever too human Sam[25] (Noah Beery, Jr.) perishes as ignominiously for his time in the stable and his love of Bart Allison. Bart, however, wrapped in splendor and beauty, refuses to leave the stable and return to the town's symbolic order to recognize his dead wife's true desire. Mary's libidinal drives repel him as a magnet is repelled by another with the same pole. The more her desire is revealed in relation to his, the more he is repulsed, and the more he withdraws into the womb that the stable provides.

Realization of Mary's jouissance also deprives Bart of any sort of satisfaction of his own. As Lacan explains "phallic jouissance is the obstacle owing to which man does not come (*n'arrive pas*) ... to enjoy woman's body precisely because what he enjoys is the jouissance of the organ."[26] Well beyond the limit drawn by *até* and long past his departure date, Bart eventually comes to grips with his wife's polymorphous perversity. In the end, Antigone takes her own life, but Bart visually collapses in stature. While he does not die, the camera begins to distance itself from him, often shooting him as diminished in two-shots, and from behind in the final sequences of the film. When the camera finds his face again, it never lingers long, as though even the aperture cannot bear the inhuman anguish that is there.

In short, Bart and Antigone are both *deinon*, a term that in Greek denotes both the wonderful and the terrible and is reflected in the chorus's declaration that "[w]onders (*ta deina*) are many and none more wondrous (*deinoteron*) than man"[27] Wonders may also be terrors. We stand in awe[28] of Bart and Antigone, because they both attract and repel us. We all desire to transgress, but achieving that transgression leads to the fates of Bart and Antigone—and their splendor. Judith Butler points out that our fascination in watching this splendor is "constitutive of desire itself. In the theatre we watch those who are buried alive in a tomb, we watch the dead move, we watch with fascination as the inanimate is animated."[29] Perhaps this is what makes Bart all the more unbearable in his splendor than Antigone. She, at least, has the luxury of death, while Bart slips out of view, damned to an existence without release. In the sense of the Apollonian, as Nietzsche describes it, our Western hero must remain stoic and poised. However, Dionysian eruption, with its unbearable splendor and jouissance (in this case, Mary's repressed feminine sexual desire) unseats the need for uncomplaining heroic suffering. The chorus of *Antigone* in the fifth choral ode cries out for Bacchus (Dionysus): "Come you master of the dancing, fiery breathing pulsing stars, steward of the midnight voices, son of Zeus appear! Bring your train of Maenads raving, swirling round you, round you dancing, through the night and shouting 'Bacchus, giver of all blessings, Bacchus! Bacchus, oh come!"[30] The song seems (on the surface) to be joyous, but Lacan reminds us that while this invocation is rapturous, it is also about something also beyond, a jouissance that brings with it a terrible potential cost. He remarks that those who know "what Dionysus and his savage followers represent realize that the hymn breaks out because the limits of the field of the conflagration have been breached."[31]

Finally, via the chorus an emotional release is facilitated, and by way of conclusion, it is via the chorus that we will lastly pass. The results of the hero's actions in the surrounding community are generally apparent in Westerns, but communities in the Western often do not function chorally. Generally, the members of the Western's towns comprise a background, are a mass waiting to inhabit the space created by the hero's actions even as these actions destroy the tragic figure. However, in the films of Budd Boetticher, townspeople or surrounding characters do not simply wait to take the tamed space once it is civilized by the Randolph Scott hero. They are the conduit through which the viewer knows the hero, or more rightfully, is told how to regard him. Lacan explains in *The Ethics of Psychoanalysis* that we should resist the urge to think of the chorus as the public or as a stand-in for the audience. As Lacan points out, the chorus consists of "people who are moved." The chorus exists to feel for the spectator: "your emotions are taken charge of by the healthy order displayed on stage. The chorus takes care of them. The Emotional commentary is done for you ... therefore you don't have to worry; even if you don't feel anything, the chorus will feel in your stead."[32] In *Decision at Sundown*, the townspeople act as a chorus that has been "moved" in this way. They pontificate about the nature of the events happening, and they philosophize and question. They feel for the audience, and the camera keeps them unified in staged clumps all through the film to its end. When they do attempt act, in an extremely modest way, their actions are not lauded but derided.

Is the tragic a neurotic tic that helps to structure existence? As Bart Allison growls, you don't need "a big to-do when a man acts the way a man's supposed to act." After all, in *Birth of Tragedy*, Nietzsche most famously declares that "it is only as an *aesthetic phenomenon* that existence and the world are eternally *justified*."[33] Tracing the deeply tragic nature of human experience, *Antigone* and *Decision at Sundown* both insist on the necessity of transgressive behavior; moreover, this tic, *até*, in both works invites moral legibility. Boetticher's radical treatment of *até*, in particular, marks an important psychoanalytic turn as the return of the repressed reveals not a monster but the "other" at work in *Decision at Sundown*. Nietzsche, of course, would agree that the splendor of Bart Allison demonstrates tragedy and justifies our lives. If we accept that *até* is indeed a limit, it is an aesthetic phenomenon since all limits are. Something appears as one thing, and then is suddenly not what it was. We do not recognize one thing is different from another other until a change registers their difference. When water boils, it is not boiling, then it is. In precisely this way, the limits of the Apollonian and the Dionysian also affect and justify existence in the world. Abandoning the Apollonian, Bart Allison, like Antigone, chose *até*. Like Antigone, he lives beyond human sanctions. Social creatures, we ourselves are not privy to what happened to cause that; we simply experience the results of such transgressions aesthetically and visually and aurally. We see their living deaths and hear their adamant declarations. And we marvel and shudder at their insistent ethical, eternally justified presences.

Notes

1. See my extended discussion of the wife as an ellipsis in Boetticher's Westerns, "You Were Married, But You Never Had a Wife," may be found in *ReFocus: The Films of Budd Boetticher*, Gary D. Rhodes and Robert Singer, eds. (Edinburgh: Edinburgh University Press, 2017), 166–87.

2. In my current expanded work, I am in the process of exploring how the tragic nature of the Western Hero is made more unbearable by being situated in the melodramatic structure of most American media and how this creates an impossibility in the aesthetic of the Western itself.

3. The importance of Sophocles' *Oedipus Rex* and the mythology surrounding cannot be overstated in its vitality and impact. This is particularly true when one is invested in the theories and clinical practices of psychoanalysis. Sigmund Freud posits Oedipus, or more precisely the structure of the Oedipal narrative, as the foundational form of human development, and furthermore the architectural schema for mapping out human desire. However, what becomes apparent when delving further into psychoanalysis, and its relation to Oedipus, is that *Oedipus Rex* is itself a sort of failed Oedipal story. As Lacan puts it in his *Seminar VII*, "in a sense Oedipus did not suffer from the Oedipus Complex, and he punished himself for a sin he did not commit" (304). Essentially, Oedipus is unaware that he has broken that most potent and structuring of taboos in having incestual relations with his mother Jocasta. In his mind, he was actively freeing the parents he knew (his adoptive parents) from the fate of the Oracle's prophesy, and in his flight kills his actual father and finds and weds Jocasta. All none the wiser. Unlike other tragic figures, Hamlet foremost among them, Oedipus desires not beholden to the Oedipal, conscious or unconscious. Oedipus's transgression is applied *après-coup* as it were, and the true tragedy of his existence flows through his issue and defines the fates of his children.

4. Jacques Lacan, *The Seminar of Jacques Lacan, Book VII: The Ethics of Psychoanalysis*,
ed. Jacques Alain-Miller, trans. Dennis Porter (New York: Norton & Co., 1992), 283. It is important for a broader understanding that *até* is also a root for the term, atrocious.

5. *Ibid.*, 262–3.

6. *Ibid.*, 263.

7. For Nietzsche, the tragic erupts from the tension between two separate impulses. The underlying, that which becomes the sort of remnant and reminder of a time of blissful, near orgasmic, agony, is the Dionysian. It could be argued, though one must beware of equation, that the Dionysian is a more closely natural state, or perhaps less tied to what Lacan would call the symbolic (akin to the super-ego for Freud). In this, we have recourse not only to Nietzsche, but also to Freud and psychoanalysis. For Freud, and later Lacan, there is a state pre-ego, what Freud refers to, borrowing from a poet friend, "the oceanic feeling." Freud explains, "it is a feeling which he (Freud's friend) would like to call a sensation of 'eternity,' a feeling as of something limitless, unbounded, as it were, 'oceanic.'" Freud himself describes it further, saying "it is a feeling of an indissoluble bond, of being one with the external world as a whole" (24, 25). This Oceanic feeling is what exists in the days before the child begins to understand itself as distinct. In these moments there is an undifferentiated mass of which consists as a source of pure flow. This Oceanic sensation is the pool of pure id. The world of nothing but drives and libidinal saturation. The animal world before meaning occurs, where simply being suffices. This is the Dionysian par excellence. As Nietzsche describes it, "under the charm of the Dionysian not only is the union between man and man reaffirmed, but nature which has become alienated, hostile, or subjugated. Celebrates once more her reconciliation with her lost

son" (37). Essentially, Nietzsche is describing a return to an undifferentiated state, a union of man and man with nature. A frenzy of flows and excitements that are exemplified in the rupture of the social that occurs during Dionysian festivals. Like Freud who sees the Oceanic perpetually exciting us from the unconscious, and later Lacan who sees The Real ever flickering through the symbolic, Nietzsche too sees the sensorial Dionysian as a constant threat to the near-rational, intellectualized Apollonian.

    8. *Ibid.*, 271.
    9. *Ibid.*, 272.
    10. Nietzsche, "The Birth of Tragedy," 69.
    11. Unless specified elsewhere, all quotes from *Antigone* are from R.C. Jebb's translation.
    12. Cecilia Sjoholm, *The Antigone Complex: Ethics and the Invention of Feminine Desire* (Stanford: Stanford University Press, 2004), 105–06. Oddly, Lacan is reticent about the incestuous or sexual nature of Antigone's relation to her brother, although Judith Butler attempts to address this, as does Joan Copjec, differently.
    13. *Ibid.*, 105–06.
    14. There is a sense of repression in this lack especially in *Decision at Sundown*. While Antigone is incredibly prone to discussing Polyneices, Bart repeatedly shoots down any attempt by friend or foe to mention Mary. The film echoes this aesthetically by cutting her completely from the film, via quick cuts and shots of a glaring Bart whenever she arises.
    15. For more information regarding the vacant space in *Antigone*, see Sjoholm, 106.
    16. Slavoj Zizek, *Enjoy your Symptom! Jacques Lacan in Hollywood and Out* (New York & London: Routledge, 1992), 143.
    17. Judith Butler, *Antigone's Claim: Kinship Between Life and Death* (New York: Columbia University Press, 2000), 28.
    18. *Ibid.*, 34.
    19. Jacques Lacan, *Book VII*, 247.
    20. Sjoholm, 104.
    21. Sophocles, "The Antigone," in *The Plays and Fragments*, Part III, trans. R.C. Jebb (Cambridge: At The University Press, 1891), 220.
    22. *Ibid.*, 423–25.
    23. *Ibid.*, 891–93.
    24. Sjoholm, 106.
    25. Who immediately rushes to get food! How deeply human!
    26. Lacan, *The Seminar of Jacques Lacan, Book XX: Encore: On Feminine Sexuality, the Limits of Love and Knowledge*, ed. Jacques Alain-Miller, trans. Bruce Fink (New York: Norton, 1998), 7.
    27. This oscillation is apparent in the poetic claims of Sophocles and evident when regarding *deinon* within the text itself. The reactions of students at Harvard to this oscillation were also helpful. See https://kosmossociety.chs.harvard.edu/?p=13357.
    28. Awe itself is a term that has both positive and horrific etymological grounding.
    29. Butler, 49.
    30. Here I am using the Paul Roche's translation of *Antigone* rather than Jebb's that has been used in other quotes from *Antigone*. Roche's translation gives a more fevered and frenzied interpretation that also captures some of the underlying sexual connotations of the Bacchanalia. See Sophocles, "Antigone," in *The Oedipus Plays of Sophocles*, trans. Paul Roche (New York: Plume, 1996), 1148–52.
    31. Lacan, *Book VII*, 269.
    32. *Ibid.*, 252.
    33. Nietzsche, "The Birth of Tragedy: Out of the Spirit of Music," in Walter Kaufman, trans. *Basic Writings* (New York: Modern Library, 2000), 52.

Filmography

Decision at Sundown. Dir. Budd Boetticher. Producer-Actor Corporation; Scott-Brown Productions, 1957.
Ride Lonesome. Dir. Budd Boetticher. Ranown Pictures, 1959.
The Searchers. Dir. John Ford. C.V. Whitney Pictures: Warners Bros., 1956.

Works Cited

Butler, Judith. *Antigone's Claim: Kinship Between Life and Death*. New York: Columbia University Press, 2000.
Copjec, Joan. *Imagine There's No Woman: Ethics and Sublimation*. Cambridge: MIT Press, 2002.
Freud, Sigmund. *Civilization and its Discontents*. Trans. James Strachey. New York & London: Norton, 2010.

Lacan, Jacques. *The Seminar of Jacques Lacan, Book VII: The Ethics of Psychoanalysis*, ed. Jacques Alain-Miller, trans. Dennis Porter. New York: Norton & Co., 1992.

———. *The Seminar of Jacques Lacan, Book XX: Encore: On Feminine Sexuality, the Limits of Love and Knowledge*, ed. Jacques Alain-Miller, trans. Bruce Fink. New York: Norton, 1998.

Minz, Christopher. "You Were Married, But You Never Had a Wife." In Gary D. Rhodes and Robert Singer, eds. *ReFocus: The Films of Budd Boetticher*, 166–87. Edinburgh: Edinburgh University Press, 2017.

Nietzsche, Friedrich. "The Birth of Tragedy: Out of the Spirit of Music." In Walter Kaufman, trans. *Basic Writings*, 1–144. New York: Modern Library, 2000.

Sjoholm, Cecilia. *The Antigone Complex: Ethics and the Invention of Feminine Desire*. Stanford: Stanford University Press, 2004.

Sophocles. "Antigone." In Paul Roch, trans. *The Oedipus Plays of Sophocles*. New York: Plume, 1996.

———. "The Antigone." In R.C. Jebb, trans. *Sophocles: The Plays and Fragments*, Part III. Cambridge: Cambridge University Press, 1891.

Zizek, Slavoj. *Enjoy Your Symptom! Jacques Lacan in Hollywood and Out*. New York & London: Routledge, 1992.

———. *How to Read Lacan*. New York: Norton, 2006.

Homer on Horseback

"Is this the face that wrecked a thousand ships / and burned the towerless tops of Ilium?"

—*Stagecoach* (John Ford, 1939)

Homer's *Odyssey* and Cattle Drive Westerns

ANDREW HOWE

Perilous journeys are a familiar trope in the Western, with cattle drives providing a common narrative backdrop for such drama. The fact that a comic Western—*City Slickers* (1991)—employed a modern-day cattle drive as the set-up for the film's humor demonstrates this narrative's familiarity. The distant origins of such a tale extend back through several channels. Douglas Pye identifies John Ford's *The Searchers* (1956) as a grail quest modified by overtones of the Israelite journey to Canaan,[1] illustrating how both British and Judeo-Christian narratives resonate with a genre predicated on dangerous quests set in the wilderness. Martin Winkler, however, identifies more classical origins for Ford's masterpiece, noting in some of the character dynamics resonance with Achilles and the *Iliad*.[2] Thematically, however, *The Searchers* best counts the *Odyssey* as its spiritual antecedent, both in the nature of the perilous, and indirect, journey undertaken, but more importantly in the complex notion of "home," a concept as illusory as it is essential. More so than Arthurian legend or Judeo-Christian derivations, classical mythology seems best suited as a prism through which to understand many Westerns. Specific identifications of such in genre criticism have been made, but usually are focused on individual films. Kostas Myrsiades, for instance, links *The Gunfighter* (1950) to both the *Iliad* and the *Odyssey*.[3] As a journey of self-revelatory wandering for protagonist William Blake, Jim Jarmusch's *Dead Man* (1995) enjoys a spiritual connection to the *Odyssey*. The fact that Blake's Indian guide goes by the name "Nobody" constitutes a specific reference, taking the name Odysseus used to fool the Cyclops (multiple Spaghetti Westerns play off of the "Nobody" stranger motif, including "The Man with No Name" in the Dollars Trilogy, "Harmonica" in *Once Upon a Time in the West*, and even the entire film *My Name Is Nobody*). The film *Cyclops* (1957) features a 50-foot tall, one-eyed monster that, like Polyphemus, lives in a cave, although created by radiation rather than sired by Poseidon. This B-film has most often been denoted as Horror or Sci-Fi, although it does have Western genre elements.

As a sub-category of the Western, cattle drive films resonate strongly with classical themes in the *Odyssey*. Numerous episodic intersections can often be discovered, including the following: saloons and opium dens where cowboys deaden their senses (Land of the Lotus Eaters); myopic land owners or other sources of institutionalized or private authority who must be tricked in order to keep the drive going (Polyphemus); cowboys turned cattle rustlers who prey on their own kind (Laestrygonians); individual women who attract the attention of the protagonist, threatening to distract from his mission (Circe); prostitution as a threatening diversion to the rank and file cowboys (Sirens); and the dangers inherent in water crossings (Scylla & Charybdis and the Journey to Hades). Such literary and cultural touchstones encompass more than just one-to-one textual relationships, however. Plot and character parallels often serve larger narrative projects, coming together in a cinematic bricolage informed by classical texts and in service of issues relevant to modern audiences—larger, thematic topics, particularly those involving what constitutes home and anxiety regarding change, allow such films to intimately display their resonance with Homer's *Odyssey* and other classical texts. Numerous Westerns feature cattle drives, including: *Cattle Drive* (1951), *The Tall Men* (1955), *Cowboy* (1958), *The Last Sunset* (1961), *Will Penny* (1967), *The Cowboys* (1972), and *The Culpepper Cattle Co.* (1972). This essay examines two such films—*Red River* (1948) and *Lonesome Dove* (1989)—in exploring specific points of convergence between the Western genre and the *Odyssey*, particularly as they present a bricolage of plot devices and character tropes encompassing themes relevant to journeys of discovery.

In July 1893, historian Frederick Jackson Turner declared the American frontier closed in an address given at the annual meetings of the American Historical Association. Among other dimensions of what would become known as his "Frontier Thesis," Jackson noted the sentimental hold that the 19th century and its western frontier would continue to enjoy on 20th-century American identity. Little did Turner realize that several months prior, on May 9, 1893, the aesthetic vehicle of this sentimentality—with apologies to Zane Grey, Louis L'Amour, and other genre authors—had taken its first bow when Thomas Edison publicly screened one of his Kinetoscope films, *Blacksmith Scene*. In the next few years Edison featured several cattle themed shorts—including *Cattle Fording Stream* and *Lassoing Steer* (both 1898). When fictional shorts began to find favor with audiences, some of the first were Western-themed, including *A Bluff from a Tenderfoot* (1899), *The Great Train Robbery* (1903), and *Cowboy Justice* (1904). As shorts gave way to more extended narratives, western themes continued to grow in popularity, culminating in what would become the dominant cinematic genre from the mid–1920s through the 1960s. Even though the frontier had evaporated by the beginning of this era, many of the events were still fresh in the minds of viewers, with many of the players still living. The Johnson County War—fought over grazing rights and water access—ended in 1893, and Butch Cassidy's Wild Bunch robbed banks into the early part of the 20th century. Buffalo Bill Cody, the creator of a series of Wild West shows which sold out on two continents, performed as late as 1908, and Annie Oakley 1924. Wyatt Earp even befriended "cowboy" actors Tom Mix and William S. Hart and directors John Ford and Raoul Walsh, routinely visiting them on their film sets. Even before the ascendancy of the Western genre, cattle drives began to serve as narrative backdrops not only for perilous physical journeys, but also for psychological and philosophical transformations. Several such films during the silent era—including *Wagon Tracks* (1919) and *North of 36* (1924)—were progressive in nature, the latter featuring a white criminal who assaulted a Comanche girl given by the U.S. Cavalry to her tribe for punishment.[4]

The theme of cattle driving in cinema, which spans from Edison's 1898 short to, at the time of this writing, the 2019 documentary *Cowboys*, evidences a longevity of interest that far outstrips it subject material. The era commonly associated with frontier cowboys and cattle driving was fairly attenuated, sparked by the end of the American Civil War and major east/west rail line completion during the mid- to late 1860s and greatly reduced by the completion of north/south rail lines during the mid–1880s, as well as by barbed wire and tick-borne Spanish Fever. As Jeremy Agnew notes: "Following the Civil War, depressed economic conditions in the South and an increased demand for beef in the Northeast gave several entrepreneurs the idea of rounding up some of the wild cattle and selling them."[5] Prior to the war, the annexation of Texas had resulted in huge tracts of land that some entrepreneurs, such as Richard King, used for cattle ranching. By 1865, Texas held so many free-range Longhorns that they could only fetch $4 a head in-state. However, the price could be up to ten times that amount in Chicago, St. Louis, and Kansas City,[6] in part to feed the appetites of larger and larger waves of immigrants flooding eastern cities. Overnight, dusty towns that served as terminus points for the railroad or that lay close to stock trails extending south into cattle rich country—such as the Chisholm, Western, and Santa Fe trails—transformed into economic hubs for the beef industry. These included Dodge City and Abilene in Kansas and Sedalia in Missouri. Stock trails could be dangerous, with cowboys subject to adverse weather, perilous river crossings, and hostile indigenous tribes. Bandit groups formed out of ex-Civil War units also pestered droving routes, although the rewards for those who made it through with a full herd could be extreme. The cattle towns boomed—Abilene alone went from shipping 35,000 cattle east in 1867 to 700,000 in 1871[7]—and so did vice, which in turn led to increased criminal activity and the need for law enforcement. A generation of villains such as Billy the Kid rose to prominence, as well as heroes such as Wyatt Earp, many of whom provided much narrative fodder for the early Hollywood industry. As Lee Clark Mitchell points out, however, Hollywood's romantic image differed greatly from prevailing views of the time:

> Even in the cowboy's own vocational world, it was ranchers and cattlemen who were regarded as the industry's heroes—shrewd mercantile-capitalists like Richard King, Charles Goodnight, Nelson Story, and John Iliff, who made sharp speculative ventures to earn windfall profits. If anyone warranted the distinction, these were the Western individualists, who moved fast, risked fortunes, and ended by transforming the West through innovative ideas and marketing practices. By contrast, cowboys in the peak years of the 1880s were essentially seasonal laborers whose modest skills earned them barely more than the average industrial worker.[8]

Cattle droving was dangerous, repetitive, and poorly paid, although rudimentary unions existed and work stoppages even occurred, as chronicled in Mark Lause's recent book *The Great Cowboy Strike* (2017). The mythology of the Western genre, however, focused not on the land baron but instead the cowboy, the cattle drive proving grounds for masculinity and endurance, teamwork and honor, and other such character features that have fascinated mankind since the time of Homer.

Many consider Howard Hawks' *Red River* (1948) the quintessential cattle drive film, replete with a series of themes straight out of the *Odyssey*: a dangerous voyage with many digressions; tests of skill between those on the journey; omens and fate; and a search for home. The film begins in 1851 when Thomas Dunson (John Wayne) splits off from a wagon train to scout some land. His fiancée, who stays with the main group, subsequently perishes in an Indian attack, leaving Dunson embittered. It's almost as if he is Odysseus without the direction of a return to Penelope to center him. He eventually settles on land just north of the Rio Grande, but never views it as home. In order to secure this land, he shoots one of the hired guns of Don Diego, a Mexican land baron who lives 400 miles to the south. As Janet Walker notes, Dunson's act although violent is ironic when one considers that Don Diego certainly stole the land from one indigenous group or another.[9] The Frontera region of South Texas encompasses much complexity when it comes to the politics of ownership, with Dunson just the latest to usurp the land through right of violence. John Cawelti notes that the frontier as a space offers "liberation from moral and social restraint," but that the genre hero often resists that tendency.[10] Dunson is not the film's hero, however, instead autocratic with everyone around him, most notably Matthew Garth (Montgomery Clift), a young boy who survived the attack on the wagon train and who grows into adulthood off-camera during the Civil War. The narrative picks up in 1865, Garth having returned from the war. Dunson operates one of the largest cattle ranches in the United States but is broke. He decides to drive his cattle north to Sedalia, Missouri, and the railroad that will send his beef east.

The film's bulk features the cattle drive itself, with Dunson doing a slow burn as the pressures of the trail become too much for him. From Comanche attacks to a stampede, torrential rain to dangerous river crossings, and a lack of food to the chaos that reigns in the wake of the Civil War, the enterprise exists in constant danger. The Red River itself plays very little role in the film, although it is the first river Dunson and Garth forded on their way south in 1851 and the last they cross on their way north fourteen years later. Suzanne Liandrat-Guigues notes the danger that this specific river crossing posed for cattle drovers: "The reputation of this crossing-point was due as much to the majesty of the 'merciless' river whose high red banks color the water as it is to its torrents which were capable of swelling rapidly and drowning many a 'trail man.'"[11] The film's stampede scene, and not the river crossing, serves as the film's most memorable, in part due to the use of medium shots to establish viewer claustrophobia and cameras placed at ground level to make the audience feel as if they are about to be trampled.[12] A stampede provides an important plot point in just about every cattle drive film, although the cause never seems to be the same. Rustlers in *The Culpepper Cattle Co.*—including one with a single eye, calling to mind Polyphemus—use rattlesnakes to spook the cattle; in *City Slickers*, it's a battery-powered coffee bean grinder! The stampede in *Red River*, caused by a sweet tooth cowpoke who accidentally knocks over kettles while trying to steal sugar, contains classical overtones in the omens evident with the character of Dan Latimer (Harry Carey, Jr.), trampled to death right after telling Dunson that he will surprise his wife by using his wages to buy her a pair of red shoes. This scene references both the Land of the Lotus Eaters and Cattle of the Sun episodes of the *Odyssey*, with the chuckwagon providing cowboys a break from the saddle and in the punishment that results from the theft of sugar. The stampede serves to bring together several episodes of Homer's epic and introduces fate as a theme.

Dunson becomes increasingly sullen—even when things are going well—and violent when tested. He shoots several cowboys who force a conflict with him and prepares to lynch two deserters before Garth leads a mutiny, banishing Dunson from his own drive, akin to Telemachus wresting power away from instead of helping restore it to Odysseus. As Scott Simmon notes, *Red River* stands as a rare case where in a John Wayne vehicle the actor exists as an anti-hero against whom a younger, and more sympathetic, character competes.[13] David Lusted, however, promotes a different perspective, situating the cattle drive within the life stages of each of the two leads: "The epic cattle trail they will embark on is a rite of passage for Matthew, but for Dunson it represents a legacy, as much emotional as financial."[14] Dunson may be autocratic, but he has the larger picture in mind. Indeed, after Garth takes over and turns the herd onto the untested Chisholm Trail, he very nearly ruins everything by involving the company in an Indian attack upon a wagon train. Although they maintain a sort-of adversarial father/son relationship and Dunson represents experience to Garth's innocence, it would be a mistake to view Dunson as Odysseus and Garth as Telemachus. As a journey of self-revelation, the cattle drive represents Garth's narrative more than Dunson's. Both characters resonate with Odysseus, in so doing establishing a bricolage redistributing Homer's classical themes across multiple characters and rewriting the nature of the father/son relationship. This recombination allows the son to wander and to experience some of the plot devices not accorded to Telemachus in Homer's work.

The wagon train episode introduces one narrative element with resonance to the *Odyssey* and brings another into sharp relief. Nearly all cattle drive films contain the diversion of women, either in nearby towns or groups they pass in transit, usually (but not always) in the form of sex workers. In such films, women—who not only represent sexuality but also civilization and, most importantly, human connection—serve as the Sirens distracting the drovers from their journey. In most of these films, the Siren figures are prostitutes or dance hall girls. In *The Tall Men*, the character of Nella Turner (Jane Russell) represents the quintessential Siren figure, serving as a distraction in her accompaniment of a cattle drive run by Ben Allison (Clark Gable). At one point, a stagecoach driver asks Allison if Nella is a dance hall girl. The taciturn drover replies "No. Prospector" before following that up with a clarification: "Gold digging." More than a few cattle drive films involve women on the banks of, or even swimming in, rivers, a clear reference to the Sirens of the Aegean. In *The Tall Men*, Nella bathes in rivers, gets thrown into a river, and at night—when camped too far away from a river—bathes in a special tub that she has had installed in her wagon, all the time singing while the drovers listen in silence. Such plot devices involving water are not always realistic, so the majority of these narratives involve women that the drovers meet in town. The Siren in *Red River* differs from this general formula, however. Several days after parting ways with Dunson, one of the scouts Garth sends ahead returns shouting: "Women! Women and coffee, I tell you! I seen them! I had some! I tell you, I had pie and biscuits and beans and coffee and whiskey." This drover reduces an entire gender to just another commodity for consumption, and without Dunson's stern leadership Garth suspends the drive, fortunate in that when he and his group reach the train they find it besieged by Indians, whom Garth along with his friend Cherry Valance (John Ireland) drive off due to their shooting prowess.

Garth and Valance, as the only two men in the Frontera region as quick on the draw as Dunson, have a friendly competition that runs throughout the film, reminding one of the tests of skill that occur throughout the *Odyssey*, such as when Odysseus strings the bow and shoots an arrow through twelve axe heads. In one scene, the two gunslingers alternate shooting a can back and forth in the air. Although not as consequential as the Greek hero revealing himself in Ithaca, the scene demonstrates their skill and suggests something about their identity as potential competitors to Dunson. It's almost as if the young suitors travel with Odysseus on his journey, subsequently banishing him from it when they take over the cattle drive. The classical allusions in this relationship extend beyond just the *Odyssey*, however. The homoerotic tension in the scene where Garth and Valance admire each other's guns reminds one of Achilles and Patroclus in the *Iliad* and other classical texts—including those by Plato and Aeschylus—whose relationship runs the gamut from male bonding to romantic connection. Valance never takes on Garth's

Matt Garth (Montgomery Clift) finds himself wooed by a Siren, Tess Millay (Joanna Dru). *Red River* **(United Artists, 1948).**

identity, as Patroclus does in the *Iliad* by wearing Achilles' armor. However, as bricolage the sub-plot pulls in multiple texts, investing *Red River* with classical overtones.

Garth strikes up a relationship with Tess Millay (Joanne Dru), who represents a Siren figure in the threat she poises in diverting him from his mission but also Circe in that she and Garth care for and respect one another. Millay asks him to stay, but unlike Odysseus (who lingers for an entire year) Garth only spends a single night with her before returning to his cattle. He doesn't fill his ears with beeswax or drink a potion that makes him immune to her charms; he has taken on the role of leader, and much work remains to be done. Several days later, when Dunson arrives with a posse, Tess plays the role of the Siren distraction as well, even offering to bear his son after he tells her he yearns for an heir. She makes this offer not out of love or desire but instead as a chip with which to bargain for Garth's life. Dunson declines, in so doing establishing a closer parallel to Odysseus in that he resisted Millay's charms. Resonance with the Circe episode also occurs in this scene. Millay does not turn anyone into swine, as Circe does with Odysseus' men. However, Dunson acts swinishly toward her, as he does with pretty much everyone else throughout the film.

After turning down her advances, he eventually catches up with Garth. The latter has brought nearly all of the cattle into Abilene, Kansas, securing a sum approaching $180,000 (over $2.8 million in 2020 dollars), a good portion of it separated out in a check bearing Dunson's name. Despite the turmoil experienced and the men lost, the journey has been lucrative. It's in this moment of triumph, however, that Dunson arrives, keen on revenge. He and Garth brawl, though they make up following Tess' intervention—she empties a gun at them to get them to stop fighting—with Dunson acknowledging Garth as his heir. The film re-establishes paternal law and order and allows Dunson to be re-habilitated. Odysseus does not require such re-habilitation, his murder of Penelope's 108 suitors justified in the *Odyssey* due to their boorish behavior and plans to murder Telemachus. Joseph McBride notes that Howard Hawks made two basic types of westerns, ones involving origins and pioneers before the establishment of law, and those about the enforcement of law and order.[15] Clearly, *Red River* belongs to the former category, although with the last scene occurring in 1865 it will not be long before the great cattle cities of the American Midwest witness the rise of lawmen such as Bat Masterson and Wyatt Earp.

Although it ends in a cattle town on the verge of becoming a city, *Red River* represents a tale of the frontier. Michel Perez situates the film in the aesthetic legacy of—among other authors who focused upon the frontier—Mark Twain.[16] Huck Finn's journey can be interpreted as a sort of late 19th-century *Odyssey*, populated by strange peoples and numerous obstacles and with a tension between individual drives on one hand and the allure of civilization on the other. This dichotomy plays a particularly significant role in both Twain's and Hawks' portrayals of home and belonging. Law and order came more grudgingly to the frontier, with rustlers and Jayhawkers—anti-slavery partisans in Kansas who viewed cattle ranching as enriching the southern economy, and who supported farmers in the fight against cattle interests after the war—making life difficult for those operating outside the sphere of the emergent lawmen. As Suzanne Liandrat-Guigues perceptively notes, such lack of accountability informs this film:

> In *Red River*, it is clear that whatever the crimes committed during the course of the adventure, no sheriff or man of law ever intervenes to establish a notion of culpability or to pass judgment. The loneliness of the individual who plays the leading role of Tom Dunson (John Wayne) therefore arises from the fact that he is accountable to no one for a large part of his existence.[17]

For Odysseus, the lack of accountability leads him to acts—including his crew turning into cattle rustlers when they encounter Helios' sacred herd—that incur the wrath of the gods, resulting in years of wandering. Dunson's driven nature translates into an autocratic demeanor that nearly leads him to kill his adopted son. Despite their intense physical and psychological journeys, both men must find their center if they are going to adapt, and thus survive. Whether it entails surviving the chaos that follows in the wake of the Trojan War or the economic morass following the American Civil War, eventually life has to return to normal and order must reign. Odysseus and Dunson/Garth must, and do, come home, although it means very different things to each of them.

Lonesome Dove, the 1989 CBS mini-series adaptation of Larry McMurty's epic novel, perhaps more fully even than *Red River* plumbs the depths of the cattle drive as a backdrop for notions of what constitutes home. As in Hawks' film, the narrative involves a round trip taken during the economic collapse of Texas following the American Civil War, centered upon a cattle drive teeming with danger in the form of water moccasins, swollen rivers, dust storms, drought, lightning, stampedes, horse rustlers, indigenous groups, and a true monster in the form of Blue Duck (Frederic Forrest), a Mexican/Indian bandit who coldly murders anyone who gets in his way. A key difference in the specific makeup of the round trip quickly makes itself manifest. In *Red River*, Dunson and Garth head south first to establish their ranch and, years later, back north with the cattle for profit. In *Lonesome Dove*, however, the journey north combines both the establishment of a ranch in Montana and the seeds for future profit, with the return trip to Texas a journey of commemoration. Mary Bandy notes that television provided an excellent canvas for such an epic journey,[18] and indeed the run time of 384 minutes allowed for numerous explorations of both the journey itself and of the concept of home, not only for the main characters but also minor ones. Instead of just one river crossing, the mini-series features numerous ones—Rio Grande, Nueces, Red, Canadian, Platte, Powder, Yellowstone, Missouri, Milk—each an invitation for the cowboys to reflect upon just how far away from home they have come, with the realization eventually coming that home is a place to which they will never return. Indeed, only one character returns to the tiny Texas town of Lonesome Dove. Augustus McCrae (Robert Duvall) and Woodrow F. Call (Tommy Lee Jones) anchor the narrative as dual protagonists, aging former Texas Rangers who decide to embark on one final adventure. Both men have loved, and lost, and Call has a son—Newt (Ricky Schroder)—although one whom he does not recognize as his own. In this tale, it is almost as if a two-headed Odysseus, bored at the end of his life and following the death of Penelope, decides to go on one final journey with Telemachus. Call and McCrae start the Hat Creek Cattle Company, whose motto—"Uva Uvam Vivendo Varia Fit"—literally translates into "a grape ripens when it sees another grape." Indeed, the narrative hinges on maturity and perspective and how these factors allow one to deal with time, change, and trauma. Mary Bandy notes that this mini-series "initiated a cycle of performances by Robert Duvall that provide an evolving portrait of the westerner as an older, sagacious, feisty cowpoke who still can handle a gun and drive a herd with the best of them."[19] In this case, as Odysseus analogues these two men approach a home of a different kind, although they are determined to go out not with a whimper but a bang. Despite their age, Call and McCrae aspire to be the first to drive cattle from Texas to Montana.

The two set out with a whole host of cowboys, many of whom will perish along the way. Multiple character journeys occur in *Lonesome Dove*, passages both physical and psychological. July Johnson (Chris Cooper), a sheriff from Arkansas, attempts to track down his wife, who although in late-term pregnancy has run off to find an ex-lover, leaving behind not only July but also her son. When he loses everything except his newborn son, Johnson finds peace at the home of Clara Allen (Anjelica Huston), who, although we never see her away from her home, attempts to find her way in the wake of her husband's death. Many of these journeys are metaphysical in nature, but the cattle drive provides the narrative spine for the mini-series. Although thematic links to the *Odyssey* are the most relevant, numerous episodic similarities exist. Much as Odysseus sacrifices to his honored dead, so too do the drovers, clustered around one makeshift gravestone or another, men of action and of few words who still find the time to memorialize. In San Antonio, much as with Odysseus upon his return to Ithaca, no one recognizes McCrae and Call. As with the Greek adventurer, too much time has passed for anyone to remember these Texas Rangers who at one point in time were legends. Practical as always, Call says: "The reason they forgot us is we never got killed." Unlike Achilles in the *Iliad*, Odysseus—and McCrae and Call—lingered too long for full enshrinement as a hero during his lifetime.

Although in the twilight of their lives, McCrae and Call are still quite capable. In several towns they visit each enjoys a moment of violence, although decidedly more muted than Odysseus slaughtering Penelope's suitors: McCrae pistol-whips a surly bartender in San Antonio, and in Ogalalla Call savagely beats a scout from the U.S. Cavalry who attempts to steal some of their horses. John Cawelti notes that the very makeup of a cattle drive, with weeks of hard work on the trail followed by the release of tension in cities, leads to a descent into various forms of vice and, inevitably, violence.[20] Vice in such films involves alcohol and/or drugs ("Land of the Lotus Eaters") and women ("Sirens"). In *Lonesome Dove*, distraction comes in the form of prostitution, depicted in some form or another in just about every town the drovers visit. Upon first drawing wages, several of the young cowpokes fortify themselves with liquid courage before visiting a brothel. Lorena (Diane Lane) is the character who perhaps best represents a Siren, however, in the disruption that she introduces into the company. A sex worker from Lonesome Dove who accompanies the drive as far as Nebraska, she loves McCrae, has entered into a relationship with McCrae's former Texas Ranger compatriot Jake Spoon (Robert Urich), and is the object of infatuation of a third member of the company. In particular, the seeds for discord are sown between the Texas rangers when Spoon finds out that, after initiating his relationship with Lorena, McRae tricked her into having sex with him. Later, Blue Duck and his outlaw gang kidnap and brutally assault Lorena, an unfortunate narrative punishment for a character standing in the way of male bonding. As a character, Lorena serves as a victim representing the role of women on a frontier dominated by chauvinistic, lawless, and violent men. However, when one compares the mini-series to the *Odyssey*, it becomes clear that Lorena's sexuality establishes her as a Siren character introducing added tension to an already dangerous journey. Much as the Sirens' music threatened to divert classical sailors from their course, so too does Lorena's presence result in a loss of focus upon mission and potentially drives a wedge between multiple members of the cattle drive. As in *Red River*, the true power of the classical antecedents as incorporated into *Lonesome Dove* lie not in the one-to-one parallels to Homer's epic, but in the thematic resonances established through bricolage.

Much as it was for Odysseus, the notion of home for both Call and McCrae is an illusory and complex thing. Unlike their mythological progenitor, as well as Dunson and Garth, these two former Texas Rangers encounter a bittersweet ending. They are forced to hang Spoon—a sort of Odysseus figure who ended up on the wrong side of the law—after he joins a group of murderous horse rustlers. In explaining to a forlorn Newt why they had to hang their former colleague, McCrae denotes him a wanderer, noting that "Any wind can blow him," a clear reference to Odysseus. Later, McCrae reunites with Clara Allen, the constant love of his life, who waits at her farm near the Platte River in Nebraska. During his short visit, he sees what might have been had he chosen Clara over a life of adventure. In a brief conversation with Call, Clara laments that she had so little time with McCrae compared to his Texas Ranger compatriots. Penelope's claim on Odysseus similarly stands broken, first by the Trojan War and then by 20 years with no news while her husband wandered all over the classical world. Unlike in the *Odyssey*, no happy ending is accorded this couple. Toward the end of the mini-series McCrae returns to Clara's farm, but this time in a coffin being taken south by Call for burial. From the outset, McCrae understood that this last adventure revolved around the journey, not the destination—at one point stating: "Up north ain't a place … it's a direction"—but Call is the one who must complete the drive and build a ranch. Before dying the previous autumn from sepsis when he refused to have both legs amputated after taking several arrow wounds, McRae realized that his friend would need to make a return journey in order to be made whole again after, for the first time since their youth, approaching life without his best friend at his side. Before he dies, McCrae makes Call swear that he will take his body for burial in San Antonio, the place where he cut his teeth as a lawman and courted Clara. He also knows that, going as far south as San Antonio, Call will be compelled to return to Lonesome Dove, and that this journey will give Call, who in his relentless practicality suffers from extreme tunnel vision, the philosophical distance he needs in order to understand the fullness of what he has accomplished.

Before he dies, McCrae says: "I'm giving you a reason to go off on another adventure," and that's exactly what happens. Call takes his friend 2000 miles south, a reverse odyssey with just as many hardships, including a wagon that throws a wheel; raging rivers (one of which sweeps the coffin away); vultures that worry his friend's body; and getting stranded without a wagon in the middle of a desert. He also gets to witness the death of the notorious criminal Blue Duck—who kidnapped and killed members of their party—suggesting that, much like the *Odyssey* signals the twilight of the classical hero, in *Lonesome Dove* the age of the frontier with its heroes and villains nears its conclusion. At the end of the narrative, Call stands in the empty streets of Lonesome Dove, speaking at cross-purposes with a reporter, admitting that he has "one hell of a vision," not in the foresight of establishing the first cattle ranch in Montana but in his memories of those—some living, most dead—with whom he made the voyage of life. Call experiences a homecoming, not in the warmth of hearth and bosom of Penelope as does Odysseus, but in the knowledge that McCrae knew would flood his friend's consciousness when Call returned to the dusty town on the banks of the Rio Grande. It doesn't matter where you make your home. As long as you are surrounded by good friends and make the most of the time you have with them, that's home enough for anyone.

The central classical image of the Western genre is that of the modern centaur, with John Wayne or Randolph Scott or Clint Eastwood cutting an imposing figure on horseback, seemingly as tall as the buttes of Monument Valley and mythologized into something that never really existed in the first place. Odysseus has nothing on the journeys of endurance and self-discovery typified in this genre, with wanderers as diverse as Ethan Edwards (John Wayne) in *The Searchers* and Mitch Robbins (Billy Crystal) in *City Slickers* discovering exactly where they fit in or don't, as in the case of Ethan, when it comes to notions of home and how to get there. Not all cattle drive films are equally rooted in the *Odyssey*, as some can be more clearly linked to other quest narratives, a case in point being *The Cowboys*. In this film, a group of green schoolboys (some as young as 13), assist Wil Anderson (John Wayne, in one of his last films) on his cattle drive. Despite clear classical references—such as a hilarious scene where the boys run into a group of sex workers out for a picnic, and would like to be diverted by these alluring Sirens but have no idea what to do—the film is primarily modeled on Moses taking the children across Sinai, including an ending where Anderson dies before he can reach the promised land. It is in Homer's masterpiece, however, that the cattle drive finds its closest spiritual forebear. Although in the following quote Suzanne Liandrat-Guigues specifically references *Red River*, she could very well be talking about all cattle drive films, or the *Odyssey* for that matter: "What we have is a more cyclical time, distinct from the normal temporality of the advancing herd, a mythical time during which beings are dislocated and reassembled by virtue of this new modality of movement to-and-fro."[21] Most cattle drive narratives occur in the political and economic chaos that followed in the wake of the American Civil War, setting the table for journeys both physical and meta-physical in nature. The cattle drives give directionality to chaos, allowing those who have signed on to the most solitary of professions to find their way home. Such narratives contain numerous impediments to the goal of finding one's way home, whether it be in the *Odyssey* with a home in Ithaca, or in *Red River* with a reformulated family, or in *Lonesome Dove* with an awareness of a life well-lived.

Notes

1. Douglas Pye, "The Western (Genre and Movies)," in Barry Keith Grant, ed. *Film Genre Reader II* (Austin: University of Texas Press, 1997), 199.
2. See Martin Winkler's "Homer's *Iliad* and John Ford's *The Searchers*." In Arthur M. Eckstein and Peter Lehman, eds. *The Searchers: Essays and Reflections on John Ford's Classic Western* (Detroit: Wayne State University Press, 2004),145–170.
3. See Kostas Myrsiades's "Reading *The Gunfighter* as Homeric Epic," in Kostas Myrsiades, ed. *Reading Homer: Film and Text* (Madison, WI: Fairleigh Dickinson University Press, 2009), 229–252.
4. Scott Simmon, *The Invention of the Western Film: A Cultural History of the Genre's First Half-Century* (Cambridge: Cambridge University Press, 2003), 86.
5. Jeremy Agnew, *The Old West in Fact and Film: History Versus Hollywood* (Jefferson, NC: McFarland & Company, 2012), 30.
6. *Ibid.*, 28.
7. *Ibid.*, 29.
8. Lee Clark Mitchell, *Westerns: Making the Man in Fiction and Film* (Chicago: University of Chicago Press, 1996), 25.
9. Janet Walker, "Captive Images in the Traumatic Western," in Janet Walker, ed. *Westerns: Films Through History* (New York: Routledge, 2001), 245.
10. John G. Cawelti, *Mystery, Violence, and Popular Culture* (Madison, WI: University of Wisconsin, 2004), 150.
11. Suzanne Liandrat-Guigues, *Red River*, Nick Coates, trans. (London: BFI, 2000), 16.
12. Mary Lea Bandy, *Ride, Boldly Ride: The Evolution of the American Western* (Berkeley: University of California Press, 2012), 138.
13. Simmon, 129.
14. David Lusted, *The Western* (Harlow, Essex: Pearson Longman, 2003), 170.
15. Joseph McBride, *Hawks on Hawks* (London: Faber & Faber, 1996), 138.
16. Michel Perez, "Howard Hawks and the Western," *Presence du Cinema* Vol. 2, No. 3 (1960): 44.
17. Liandrat-Guigues, 11–12.
18. Mary Lea Bandy, 271.
19. *Ibid.*, 272.
20. Cawelti, 147.
21. Liandrat-Guigues, 24.

Filmography

Blacksmith Scene. Dir. William K.L. Dickson. Edison Manufacturing Company, 1893.
A Bluff from a Tenderfoot. Cinematographer Frederick S. Armitage. American Mutoscope & Biograph, 1899.
Cattle Drive. Dir. Kurt Neumann. Universal Pictures, 1951.
Cattle Fording Stream. Dir. James H. White. Edison Manufacturing Company, 1898.
City Slickers. Dir. Ron Underwood. Columbia Pictures, 1991.
Cowboy. Dir. Delmar Daves. Columbia Pictures, 1958.
The Cowboys. Dir. Mark Rydell. Warner Bros., 1972.
Cowboy Justice. American Mutoscope & Biograph, 1904.
The Culpepper Cattle Co. Dir Sergio Leone. Paramount, 1972.
Cyclops. Dir. Bert I. Gordon. Allied Artists, 1957.
The Great Train Robbery. Dir. Edwin S. Porter. Edison Manufacturing Company, 1903.
The Gunfighter. Dir. Henry King. Twentieth Century Fox, 1950.
Lassoing Steer. Dir. James H. White. Edison Manufacturing Company, 1898.
The Last Sunset. Dir. Robert Aldrich. Universal, 1961.
Lonesome Dove Dir. Simon Wincer. CBS, February 5–8, 1989.
My Name Is Nobody. Dir. Tonino Valerii. Titanus, 1973.
Once Upon a Time in the West. Dir. Sergio Leone. Paramount Pictures, 1968.
Red River. Dir. Howard Hawks. Monterey Productions/United Artists, 1948.
The Searchers. Dir. John Ford. Warner Bros., 1956.

The Tall Men. Dir. Raoul Walsh. 20th Century Fox, 1955.
Will Penny. Dir. Will Gries. Paramount, 1967.

Works Cited

Agnew, Jeremy. *The Old West in Fact and Film: History Versus Hollywood*. Jefferson, NC: McFarland, 2012.
Bandy, Mary Lea. *Ride, Boldly Ride: The Evolution of the American Western*. Berkeley: University of California Press, 2012.
Cawelti, John G. *Mystery, Violence, and Popular Culture*. Madison: University of Wisconsin, 2004.
Lause, Mark. *The Great Cowboy Strike*. London: Verso, 2017.
Liandrat-Guigues, Suzanne. *Red River*, Nick Coates, trans. London: BFI, 2000.
Lusted, David. *The Western*. Harlow, Essex: Pearson Longman, 2003.
McBride, Joseph. *Hawks on Hawks*. London: Faber & Faber, 1996.
Mitchell, Lee Clark. *Westerns: Making the Man in Fiction and Film*. Chicago: University of Chicago Press, 1996.
Myrsiades, Kostas. "Reading *The Gunfighter* as Homeric Epic." In Kostas Myrsiades, ed. *Reading Homer: Film and Text*, 229–252. Madison, WI: Fairleigh Dickinson University Press, 2009.
Perez, Michel. "Howard Hawks and the Western." *Presence du Cinema* Vol. 2, No. 3 (1960): 45–47.
Pye, Douglas. "The Western (Genre and Movies)." In Barry Keith Grant, ed. *Film Genre Reader II*, 187–202. Austin: University of Texas Press, 1997.
Simmon, Scott. *The Invention of the Western Film: A Cultural History of the Genre's First Half-Century*. Cambridge: Cambridge University Press, 2003.
Walker, Janet. "Captive Images in the Traumatic Western." In Janet Walker, ed. *Westerns: Films Through History*, 219–251. New York: Routledge, 2001.
Winkler, Martin. "Homer's *Iliad* and John Ford's *The Searchers*." In Arthur M. Eckstein and Peter Lehman, eds. The Searchers: *Essays and Reflections on John Ford's Classic Western*, 145-170. Detroit: Wayne State University Press, 2004.

Lonesome Dove

Uva uvam vivendo varia fit and Tragic Elements in a Western Epic

BENJAMIN HUFBAUER

Larry McMurtry's Pulitzer Prize-winning 1985 novel *Lonesome Dove* and the Emmy Award-winning miniseries closely based on it both feature a mangled Latin quote that is not translated for the reader or viewer: "*Uva uvam vivendo varia fit.*" This Latin motto is carved on the sign of the Hat Creek Cattle Company in Texas by Augustus "Gus" McCrae (played by Robert Duvall) because he thinks it will add "dignity" to his jointly-owned ranch, even though he does not know what it means.[1] His partner Woodrow Call (Tommy Lee Jones) makes fun of his friend Gus for this highfalutin' and yet ignorant pretension. Hidden in plain sight, the translated phrase, "a grape changes color [ripens] when it sees another grape," is a theme of *Lonesome Dove*, highlighting the growth that these characters experience together during their sometimes humorous but more often tragic journey. *Lonesome Dove* is an epic that draws upon three elements of Greek tragedy to tell its Western tale: *hamartia*, the character flaws that drive the narrative; *anagnorisis*, the eventual recognition by the protagonists of their own tragic flaws; and, finally, *catharsis*, the emotional release—the purging of pity and fear—that Aristotle identified as the essential function of tragedy.

In *Comanche Moon*, one of two prequels to *Lonesome Dove*, McMurtry emphasizes the connection the *Lonesome Dove* series has to classical literature by having the classically-educated Indian-battler Inish Scull (who has named his horse "Hector,") say: "Ever hear Greek read, boys? It's a fine old language—the language of Homer and Thucydides, not to mention Xenophon."[2] Scull even carves a passage from Homer's *Iliad* into a cliff in the original Greek. Scull's Greek passage, like Gus's Latin, is somewhat mangled and is never translated for the reader. But it is reminiscent of classic Western imagery as it tells of a beautiful night landscape with "stars: crowds of them in the sky" as "men warmed their hands by the flames of each fire," while their "horses champed white barley."[3] The classical world is a cultural cornerstone that characters in McMurtry's Westerns literally carve into wood and rock to proclaim their links to the ancient world. The parallels between the ancient Greeks and the American West is strong in the work of McMurtry, who in his youth was a real-life cowboy, sometimes riding horses in the vast spaces of the West under the stars.[4]

McMurtry's Career of Fusing Classical Literature with Westerns

Born in rural Texas in 1936, McMurtry grew up in an environment that had not yet changed dramatically from the late-19th-century setting of *Lonesome Dove*, or in some ways even from the conditions of the ancient world. As McMurtry writes, 1936 was "well before electricity had arrived in rural parts of the country,"[5] and he remembered that his father "was haunted all of his life by the privation his mother endured as a frontier woman. He never forgot the sight of her carrying water from the spring to the cabin they lived in when he was a boy."[6] When electricity finally did come to the McMurtry household in the early 1940s it was a huge change, but daily existence was still a struggle, and storytelling was an essential part of coping. McMurtry recalled that "In the evening, once the chores were done, people sat on the front porch (if it was summer) or around the fireplace (if it was winter) and told stories."[7] This oral storytelling tradition eventually found its way into the texture of *Lonesome Dove*'s prose. But the young McMurtry also read widely, including various adaptations of the *Iliad* and *The Odyssey*.[8] Like Homer's originally oral epics, McMurtry's *Lonesome Dove* portrays flawed characters experiencing tragedies in an elemental and yet heroic past. Captain Call's epic and traumatic journey in *Lonesome Dove*, during which he loses most of his comrades, but in the end returns to where he started, parallels the journey of Odysseus.

Most Western novels are relatively short, but *Lonesome Dove* is 864 pages long, which is about the combined length of the *Iliad* and the *Odyssey* in the one-volume Modern Library edition that the young McMurtry read and re-read. McMurtry consciously transcended the pulp novel tradition of the Western when he wrote *Lonesome Dove*, and William Wittliff, who wrote the screenplay for the *Lonesome Dove* miniseries, and Simon Wincer, who directed it, were also deliberately creating a Western that would be a cinematic epic. The *Lonesome Dove* miniseries is six hours long, making it perhaps the longest classic Western movie made, and it won huge ratings for CBS in 1989. The *Houston Chronicle* called it "[t]he best Western ever made," and if we assume that they meant the best *television* Western, then they were right.

Lonesome Dove was also inspired by Cervantes' 17th-century epic *Don Quixote*. McMurtry writes that "[t]he first book I read that belonged indubitably to world literature was *Don Quixote*.... Probably I was about thirteen, a ranch boy who had never had a really good book to read before."[9] McMurtry writes that he "responded to the classic opposition of types, Don Quixote and Sancho Panza, the visionary and the practical man,"[10] because "the crazy old knight and the peasant pragmatist were an essential pair, the ultimate source of Gus and Call in *Lonesome Dove*."[11] By drawing on *Don Quixote*, McMurtry was at the same time drawing on the ancient classics that inspired Cervantes, for, as Howard Mancing writes, "Among the classical writers who appear to have most influenced Cervantes are the Greeks[,] Homer and Heliodorus, and the Romans[,] Virgil, Ovid, and Apuleius."[12]

Lonesome Dove borrows some of its narrative structure from Homer, some of its character types from Cervantes, and is also connected with the emotional function of drama as understood and experienced by the Greeks. As a student at Rice University, McMurtry was exposed to Aristotle's landmark analysis of drama, *The Poetics*. As McMurtry writes, he was "engrossed by literary theory when it applied to the novel,"[13] and he highlights *The Great Tradition* by F.R. Leavis and *Studies in Classic American*

Literature by D.H. Lawrence, both of which use Aristotle's concepts. McMurtry's understanding of Greek drama's tragic catharsis—with its emotional release—was key to *Lonesome Dove*'s success, both as a novel and as a miniseries. As McMurtry writes, "*Lonesome Dove* satisfies its huge public emotionally."[14]

McMurtry's earlier classically-influenced tragic Western novels, which were also adapted into Hollywood movies, paved the way for his career-defining *Lonesome Dove*. His first novel, the contemporary Western *Horseman, Pass By* (1961), tells the story of an older rancher—significantly named "Homer"—who loves the land, the animals, and the people of the West, but who discovers that his amoral son, Hud (played in the film by Paul Newman), does not share his values. *Hud* was a box office hit and won three Oscars, and film critic Tom Milne noted that "The film sometimes seems to be busting its britches to attain the status of Greek tragedy."[15] Later, while teaching literature at Rice University, McMurtry wrote the semi-autobiographical novel *The Last Picture Show*, set in a mythological Texas town with the Greek name of Thalia (meaning Muses). Published in 1966, *The Last Picture Show* is also like a Greek tragedy set in the post–World War II West, and in 1971 it became the basis for a successful and critically-acclaimed film directed by Peter Bogdanovich.

The Odyssey of Making Lonesome Dove: *From Screenplay to Novel to Miniseries*

Because of McMurtry's success at fusing Westerns with classical tragedy, Warner Bros. hired McMurtry and Bogdanovich to write an original screenplay for a Western movie to be set in the 19th century. This screenplay, begun in the early 1970s, eventually became *Lonesome Dove*. McMurtry and Bogdanovich imagined the movie as featuring three of the biggest stars of Hollywood Westerns—John Wayne as Captain Call, James Stewart as Augustus, and Henry Fonda as Jake Spoon, their one-time friend who goes bad. McMurtry writes that when the screenplay was finished, "the draft was welcomed by the studio, but not the three actors. This was a story about aging men. Eventually Stewart and Fonda came around because they weren't working that much. Wayne was working right up until he dropped, but he didn't like it and wouldn't do it."[16] As Don Graham, a professor of English at the University of Texas at Austin explains, "John Wayne wasn't going to lend himself to a total critique of the genre he had been working on for forty years."[17] As McMurtry later wrote, "John Wayne could have been Captain Call in *Lonesome Dove*, though what he turned down was a very different story from the *Lonesome Dove* that was eventually made."[18]

Western movies and TV shows were an integral part of American cultural identity in the 1950s and 1960s, but declined in importance in the 1970s during the time the original *Lonesome Dove* screenplay was being written. And in 1980 director Michael Cimino dealt the Western an almost fatal blow, for, as McMurtry writes, "*Heaven's Gate*, his interesting but ill-fated epic—a film so expensive to make, at least as Cimino made it … sort of took down the genre called Westerns for some while."[19] When McMurtry vainly tried to pitch new Western movie ideas to Hollywood executives, he found that they had "never heard of Westerns such as *The Searchers* or *Red River*."[20]

With the Western in Hollywood almost dead in the early 1980s, McMurtry bought back his unproduced Western screenplay from Warner Bros. for $35,000 (Spong 42).

McMurtry had never before written a novel about the 19th-century West, and in using his screenplay as the basis for his novel he wanted it to contrast with the romantic view of the West that had long been popular. McMurtry points out that "Readers don't want to know and can't be made to see how difficult and destructive life in the Old West really was. Lies about the West are more important to them than truths, which is why the popularity of the pulpers—Louis L'Amour particularly—has never dimmed."[21] McMurtry worked on the novel steadily, and one day driving in rural Texas he saw a sign that gave him his title:

> I happened to notice an old church bus parked beside the road, and on its side was written: Lonesome Dove Baptist Church. If ever I had an epiphany it was at that moment: I had, at last, found a title for the trail driving book.... Why did I so instantaneously conclude that *Lonesome Dove* was my title? I think it is because there is a kind of lonesome dove in the story, Captain Call's unacknowledged son, Newt.[22]

The often tragic story of *Lonesome Dove*, reflected in its title, contrasts with the more usual romantic myths about the West. *Lonesome Dove* fuses the frequently painful real history of the West with McMurtry's understanding of Greek tragedy. As McMurtry writes, "The book is permeated with criticism of the West from start to finish," including references to how whites "exterminated the Indians" and "ruined the landscape."[23]

The Lonesome Dove *Miniseries: Hamartia, Tragedy, and Catharsis*

In the miniseries, Captain Gus McCrae and Captain Woodrow Call are both examples of what Aristotle in *The Poetics* calls the "tragic hero."[24] According to Aristotle, a tragic hero is a generally good—but flawed—character who commits, without truly evil intent, wrongs that lead to sorrow both for themselves and for others.[25] At a key moment in the drama, the tragic hero comes to the realization (*anagnorisis*) of how he or she made the mistake that led to their fate, but by then it is already too late to correct their mistake and change their destiny. Hubris, the excessive pride and ambition that goes before a character's fall in classic drama, is part of Gus's and Woodrow's characters. In fact, *Lonesome Dove* is driven by their hubris—Gus and Call's reckless decision to leave their somewhat pathetic, but also more-or-less comfortable and safe existence in the tiny mythological town of Lonesome Dove to move up to Montana. Gus recognizes this hubris—though he does so without using the term—even before their journey starts.

Gus and Call's friend Jake Spoon (Robert Ulrich) plants the seed for their wanderlust. After fleeing the law because he accidentally killed a man in Arkansas, Jake says to them that Montana is the "prettiest land there ever was," claiming that if they went up there with some cattle, "We'd be rich in no time." Gus is suspicious of this idea and, foreshadowing his own fate, worries about the dangers of the Indians: "We ain't seen you in ten years, and now you come riding in here want us to pack up, go North, and get scalped?" But Jake waves this aside and says, "We whupped 'em down here, didn't we?" Gus hopes the idea has died, but just a few days later Call says to Gus, "Why not go up to Montana? It's a cattleman's paradise, to hear Jake tell it." Gus replies, "It sounds like a damn wilderness if you ask me." But in spite of the deep doubts Gus has, they all leave for Montana. Jake and his girlfriend, the sometime-prostitute Lorie (Diane Lane), come with them as they herd their mostly stolen cattle and come face to face with hardships brought about by their hubris. As they ride into San Antonio, Woodrow remarks how much the city has grown in the years since they were last there as Texas Rangers. Gus answers, "Of course it's all growed up, Woodrow. We killed all the Indians and the bandits so the bankers could move in."

These basically good, but flawed, characters, who eventually recognize the mistakes they have made in life, correspond with Aristotle's guidelines for dramatic tragedy:

> for the finest form of Tragedy, the Plot must be not simple but complex; and further, that it must imitate actions arousing pity and fear, since that is the distinctive function of this kind of imitation [of life]. It follows, therefore, that there are three forms of Plot to be avoided.[26]

According to Aristotle, the dramatic forms to be avoided are first, when a completely good person through no fault of their own meets with terrible misfortune, because, as Aristotle states, this is just depressing, and does not give the audience the catharsis of the best kind of tragedy; the second form of drama to avoid is that of the bad character who triumphs, which is "the most untragic" imaginable, because "it does not appeal to either the human feeling in us, or to our pity, or to our fears"[27]; and the third form to avoid is a drama focused on a completely bad character who has a tragic end, because, for almost all audience members, this kind of evil character is not "like ourselves."[28] In contrast to all this, Aristotle writes, for a highly effective drama, an "intermediate kind of character" should be central—more good than bad, but flawed, and whose misfortune is brought on by "some error of judgment."[29] Outside of San Antonio, Gus's and Call's errors of judgment are revealed. Call finds Gus sitting by a river bank, clearly having an emotional moment. This exchange is worth quoting in detail, because in it Gus reveals not only his own tragic flaw, but Call's as well:

> CALL: What in the Hell has come over you, Augustus?
> GUS: ... When was you the happiest, Call?
> CALL: ... Well, I don't know....
> GUS: I was the happiest right here by this little creek [crying]. Me and Clara discovered it, one day when we was out for a buggy ride.
> CALL: I might have knowed it had something to do with Clara.
> GUS: That was a long time ago now. God, she was beautiful. I expect it was the mistake of my life, letting her slip away like I did.

Later in the narrative, we learn that Gus let Clara slip away because he was too devoted to being a partner to Call in the Texas Rangers. Clara (Anjelica Huston) confirms this later in the series, when she confronts Call and says, "I loved Augustus McCrae, but I wasn't willing to share him with you every time you decided to ride off on some adventure. I despised you for what you were then, Captain Call."

Gus's tragic flaw was that he was not able to commit to the woman he truly loved, and who loved him. In the same conversation, Gus reveals that Call's flaw is similar—and, in fact, worse—as they continue to reminisce beside the creek:

> CALL: Well, you've always got your whores.
> GUS: ... I don't know why you're so down on whores, Woodrow. You've had yours, as I recall.
> CALL: Yeah, and that was the worst mistake I ever made.
> GUS: It ain't a mistake to be a human being once in your life, Woodrow. Poor little old Maggie left you a fine son before she quit this world.
> CALL: You don't know that. That boy could be yours or Jake's, or some damn gambler's.

> Gus: But he ain't, he's yours. Now, anybody with a good eye can see it. Besides Maggie told me.... You know what hurt her most? You wouldn't call her by name. You never would say "Maggie"—that's what hurt her most.
> Call: I don't know what it amounts to if I had.... She was a whore!
> Gus: Well, whores got hearts, Woodrow. And Maggie's was the most tender I ever saw.
> Call: Well, why didn't you marry her then?
> Gus: She didn't love me—she loved you.... Maggie needed you and you let her down, and you know it too, don't you? ... And that's why you won't claim that boy as your own, 'cause he's a reminder, see, a living reminder that you failed somebody.

Clearly, Call's failure was fundamental—he failed to acknowledge the humanity of the woman who loved him and failed to acknowledge their son. Here we see the revelation of what the Greeks called *hamartia*—the critical flaw of a character which brings about their tragic Destiny.[30] Gus' and Call's character flaws and hubris—putting their careers and ambition above love—set the stage for their ill-fated expedition to Montana all these years later. Their long-time friend and partner Joshua Deets (an African American man played by Danny Glover) poignantly asks Gus, "What we doin' up here, Captain? This ain't our land." Gus replies, "Woodrow is determined to be the first man to graze cattle in Montana, even if it kills all of us."

Deets becomes the next of their comrades to die because of Call's *hubris*. A group of starving Indians happens upon their horses and steals some for food. Call chases after them, sending the Indians fleeing away from their camp. The Indians were starving as a result of U.S. Indian policy in Montana, which hearkens back to the scene in San Antonio when Gus noted that he and Call as Rangers had killed all the Indians and left it safe for bankers. Native American tribes were signing treaties that were quickly undermined by gold miners and farmers coming into Montana (Phippen). U.S. policy was to renegotiate smaller and smaller treaty lands, which led to starvation. As Deets tries to reclaim the horses, he finds a frightened and blind Native American boy who was left behind in the chaos of the Indian camp. Deets runs down to the boy to gather him up and comfort him, but a returning Indian warrior mistakes his intentions and runs a spear through Deets' heart. The poignancy of the scene rests in Deets' kindness being mistaken for aggression.

For the ancient Greeks, the realm of the dead was a shadowy and distant place, difficult to understand for the living.[31] More real than any afterlife for most ancient Greeks, and for the characters in *Lonesome Dove*, are the memories and deeds of one's companions. George Fain, in his book *Ancient Greek Epigrams: Major Poets in Verse Translations* writes that epigrams "[l]ike inscriptions on our own memorials and gravestones … are forthright expressions of patriotism or personal sentiment, sometimes moving but often formulaic and usually short, occasionally consisting of a single line."[32] An example can be found inscribed on the Kroisos figure from Anavyssos, which was used as a grave marker for a young warrior inscribed with the epigram: "Stay and mourn at the monument for dead Kroisos whom violent Ares destroyed, fighting in the front Rank."[33] When Call carves an epigram for Deets on a wooden headstone, he reveals *Lonesome Dove's* relationship with memory and death, which echoes that of the ancient Greeks. Gus finds it remarkable that Call would carve a testament to Deets, when he had not done so for their other companions who have died over the years, and he reads the headstone aloud to Pea (Timothy Scott) and Newt (Ricky Schroeder): "Josh Deets served with me 30 years, fought 21 engagements with the Comanche and Kiowa. Cheerful in all weathers. Never shirked a task."

The next to die is Gus. Not long after saying to Pea that someday all the wild buffalo will be gone, Gus whimsically rides up a hill to scatter a herd of buffalo, almost like Quixote tilting at windmills. Separated from the group, Gus encounters a dozen or so Native American warriors on horseback, and is seriously injured in the ensuing battle. The wounds he sustains eventually lead to the amputation of one of his legs. But when it becomes clear that his other leg must be amputated as well if he is to have any chance of surviving, Gus decides not to go through with it. In his last conversation with Call before his death, Gus extracts some promises from his partner:

> GUS: I want you to bury me down yonder in Clara's orchard.... By the creek we stopped at back in Texas.
> CALL: Back in Texas? You want me to haul you back to Texas? We just got to Montana!
> GUS: ... There is something else. Now, I want you to tell Newt that you're his Daddy. I've already told him myself, but I want him to hear it from you.
> CALL: You ought not to have told him that....
> GUS: Reach in that drawer there and find me something to write on. I want to leave a couple of notes to Lorie and Clara.
> CALL: [Getting the paper and pencil] You want me to do anything about them Indians that shot you?
> GUS: We got no call to be vengeful. They didn't invite us here. [Gus starts to write.] It's a dangerous business writing to two women at the same time. I'm so light-headed I can hardly remember which one's which. Now this one's—this one's for Lorie. Take it. And this one, here—by God.
> CALL: [Seeing that Gus is fading] You want me to help you with that?
> GUS: What would you know to say to a woman? [Gus writes a bit, and then closes his eyes.]
> CALL: Augustus?
> GUS: Aye God, Woodrow. It's been quite a party, ain't it?
> CALL: Yes, sir.

When watching Robert Duvall's performance in this scene, it is difficult to remain unmoved. This cathartic function of drama is described by Aristotle as being similar to the experience of listening to moving music. Aristotle writes, "Those who are influenced by pity and fear," and experience these emotions through drama, "have a like experience" to listening to emotional music, for "all are in a manner purged, and their souls lightened and delighted" by experiencing catharsis.[34] Through catharsis, audience members experience their connection with humanity by feeling what others suffer. This communal purging of emotions—for a moment at least—helps people accept mistakes and mortality as fundamental parts of the human condition.

In Homer's *Odyssey*, Odysseus's son Telemachus grows up without knowing his father, meeting him only when he is on the verge of adulthood. The tension between Newt and Call recalls the distant relationship of father and son in the *Odyssey*. After Gus's death Call makes Newt the top hand at his Montana ranch, over the objections of one of his senior hands. Call also gives Newt his beloved horse, as well as his own father's watch, just before he sets off to rebury Gus in Texas after the long winter:

> CALL: See how your saddle fits this gray.
> NEWT: The Hell Bitch?
> CALL: Put your saddle on her. You're the Range Boss now, Newt. I told them other boys. Pea—you help him. He's gonna need a steady man.
> PEA: Yes, sir, Captain. I will.
> CALL: [Handing to Newt his father's gold pocket watch] That was my father's. Newt I—

Woodrow F. Call (Tommy Lee Jones) regards Gus McCrae's (Robert Duvall) headstone, a plank with the Latin motto from the sign Gus made: "*Uva uvam vivendo varia fit.*" *Lonesome Dove* (Motown Productions, 1989).

NEWT: Yes, sir?
CALL: I—

These are the last words that Call says to Newt in the miniseries. Pea is impressed by the affection Call has demonstrated, but Newt is not. After Call leaves, their exchange illustrates that Newt is the lonesome dove of the title:

PEA: Dern, Newt. He acted like you was his kin.
NEWT: No. I ain't kin to nobody in this world, Pea.

Call goes on to Texas to bury Gus's body in the place where he was happiest, by the stream where Gus had had—and also had lost—the most important love of his life in Clara. By this time the wagon has disintegrated, and all that Call has for a headstone is the plank with the Latin motto from the sign Gus made: "*Uva uvam vivendo varia fit.*" In a letter to Ernestine P. Sewell, an English Professor at East Texas State University, McMurtry wrote:

> I found it [the Latin phrase] in Gurney Benham's "Putnam's Complete Book of Quotations." … There the proverb is translated as "the grape changes its hue (ripens) by looking at another grape…[and] to a Persian proverb, very similar, (one grape gets color by looking at another grape)." Those are the translations I worked from.[35]

For Aristotle, a reversal—*peripetea*—in the plot of a tragedy was part of the experience of *catharsis*. This reversal set up a more complex narrative, which he identified as one of the qualities for a successful tragedy. *Peripetea* can be seen in *Lonesome Dove* when Call finally recognizes that the ambitious ideas that led him to Montana did not make him a visionary, but instead a victim of his own hubris, which also cost the lives of many of his friends. By this time Call, fulfilling the Latin motto at least somewhat, has ripened and now shares some of the wisdom that Gus had developed, for Call has a better understanding of the importance of love and the dangers of hubris. When Call finally makes it back to the tiny town of Lonesome Dove, which is even more desolate and lonely than when he left, he runs into a young reporter who says to him: "They say you carried your friend three thousand miles just to bury him. Is that true? They say the both of you were Texas Rangers back in the old days—that you cleaned the Comanches out, and the bandits. Is that true? They say you started the first cattle ranch up in Montana. They say you're a man of vision!" We then see Call thinking back to what's happened during the narrative of *Lonesome Dove*, as we see a series of flashbacks featuring the beautiful cinematography by Douglas Milsome. We see the adventures, but even more the deaths of Call's friends, and finally we see Newt still waiting for his father's acknowledgment. After a long pause, Call finally replies, bitterly and ironically, with tears in his eyes, in recognition (*anagnorisis*) of the role that his own hubris has played in the tragedy, "Hell of a vision."

Notes

1. Larry McMurtry, *Lonesome Dove* (New York: Simon and Schuster, 1985), 89.
2. Larry McMurtry, *Comanche Moon* (New York: Simon and Schuster, 1997), 133.
3. Homer, *The Essential Homer*, trans. Stanley Lombardo (Indianapolis, Indiana: Hackett Classics, 2000), 91.
4. Larry McMurtry, *Walter Benjamin at the Dairy Queen* (New York: Simon and Schuster, 1999), 51.
5. McMurtry, *Walter Benjamin at the Dairy Queen*, 15.
6. *Ibid.*, 47.
7. *Ibid.*, 25.
8. *Ibid.*, 44; Larry McMurtry, *Books: A Memoir* (New York: Simon and Schuster, 2008), 10.
9. McMurtry, *Walter Benjamin at the Dairy Queen*, 113.
10. *Ibid.*, 115.
11. McMurtry, *Books*, 10.
12. Howard Mancing, *Don Quixote: A Reference Guide* (Westport, CT: Greenwood, 2006), 88.
13. Larry McMurtry, *Literary Life: A Second Memoir* (New York: Simon and Schuster, 2009), 32.
14. *Ibid.*
15. Tom Milne, *Time Out Film Guide*, 13th Rev Edition (London: Time Out Publishing, 2004), 597.
16. John Spong, *A Book on the Making of* Lonesome Dove (Austin: University Press of Texas, 2012), 37.
17. Spong, 37.
18. Larry McMurtry, *Hollywood: A Third Memoir* (Simon and Schuster, 2010), 15.
19. McMurtry, *Hollywood*, 74.
20. *Ibid.*, 90.
21. McMurtry, *Walter Benjamin at the Dairy Queen*, 55.
22. McMurtry, *Literary Life*, 98.
23. Spong, 47.
24. Aristotle, *Poetics*, ed. Richard Koss, trans. S.H. (Butcher: Dover Press, 1997), 23.
25. Charles H. Reeves, "The Aristotelian Concept of the Tragic Hero," *The American Journal of Philology* Vol. 72, No. 2 (1952): 172–188.
26. Reeves, 172.
27. *Ibid.*, 173.
28. *Ibid.*
29. *Ibid.*
30. J.L. Moles, "Aristotle and Dido's 'Hamartia'," *Greece & Rome* Vol. 31, No. 1 (1984): 49–50.
31. Robert Garland, *The Greek Way of Death*, Second Edition (Ithaca: Cornell University Press, 200), 1–5; 50–54.
32. George L. Fain, *Ancient Greek Epigrams: Major Poets in Verse Translation* (Berkeley: University of California Press, 2010), 1.
33. In I.E. S Edwards, C. J Gadd, N.G. L Hammond, John Boardman, David M Lewis, F.W. Walbank, A. E Astin, et al, eds. *The Cambridge Ancient History*, 3rd Ed.n. (Cambridge England: Cambridge University Press, 1970), 330.
34. Quoted in Reeves, "The Aristotelian Concept of the Tragic Hero," 185.
35. Kent Biffle, "A Spirited 'Dove' Hunt: Viewers Fire Away at anything that moved in the series," *Philadelphia Daily News*, February 23, 1989, 42.

Filmography

Heaven's Gate. Dir. Michael Cimino. United Artists, 1980.
Lonesome Dove. Dir. Simon Wincer. CBS, February 5–February 8, 1989.
Red River. Dir. Howard Hawks. United Artists, 1948.
The Searchers. Dir. John Ford. Warner Bros, 1956.

Works Cited

Alexiou, Margaret, and Dimitrios Yatromanolakis. Παναγιώτης A Ροϊλός, *The Ritual Lament in Greek Tradition*. Lanham, MD: Rowman & Littlefield, 2002.
Aristotle. *Aristotle on the Art of Poetry*, trans. Ingram Bywater. Oxford: Oxford University Press, 1909.
Aristotle. *Poetics*, ed. Richard Koss, trans. S.H. Butcher. Dover Press, 1997.
Biffle, Kent. "A Spirited 'Dove' Hunt: Viewers Fire Away at anything that moved in the series." *Philadelphia Daily News*, February 23, 1989, 42.
Busby, Mark, *Larry McMurtry and the West: An Ambivalent Relationship*. Denton: University of North Texas Press, 1995.
Butler, Samuel, trans. *The Iliad of Homer*. London: Longmans, Green, & Co., 1898; Bartleby.com, 2011.
Caro, Robert A., *The Years of Lyndon Johnson: The Path to Power*. New York: Knopf, 1982.
de Cervantes, Miguel. *The History and Adventures of the Renowned Don Quixote*, trans. Tobias Smollett. Athens: University of Georgia Press, 2003.
Classics Illustrated. *The Iliad*. New York: Gilberton, No. 77, 1950.
Classics Illustrated. *The Odyssey By Homer*. No. 81. New York: Gilberton, 1951.
Day, Kirsten. *Cowboy Classics: The Roots of the American Western in the Epic Tradition*. Edinburgh, AU: University of Edinburgh Press, 2016.
Edwards, I.E. S, C. J Gadd, N.G. L Hammond, John Boardman, David M Lewis, F. W Walbank, A. E Astin, et al (eds). *The Cambridge Ancient History*. 3rd Ed. Cambridge England: Cambridge University Press, 1970.
Fain, George L. *Ancient Greek Epigrams: Major Poets in Verse Translation*. Berkeley: University of California Press, 2010.
Garland, Robert. *The Greek Way of Death*. Second Edition. Ithaca: Cornell University Press, 2001.
Homer. *The Complete Works of Homer*, trans. Andrew Lang, Walter Leaf, Ernest Myers. New York: Modern Library, 1935.
Homer. *The Essential Homer*, trans. Stanley Lombardo. Indianapolis, Indiana: Hackett Classics, 2000.
Kirk, G.S. *Homer and the Oral Tradition*. Cambridge: Cambridge University Press, 1976.
Kitto, H.D.F. *Greek Tragedy: A Literary Study*. New York: Methuen, 1939.
Mancing, Howard. *Don Quixote: A Reference Guide*. Westport, CT: Greenwood, 2006.
McMurtry, Larry. *Books: A Memoir*. New York: Simon & Schuster, 2008.
_____. *Comanche Moon*. New York: Simon & Schuster, 1997.
_____. *Hollywood: A Third Memoir*. Simon & Schuster, 2010.
_____. *Literary Life: A Second Memoir*. New York: Simon & Schuster, 2009.
_____. *Lonesome Dove*. New York: Simon & Schuster, 1985.
_____. *Walter Benjamin at the Dairy Queen*. New York: Simon & Schuster, 1999.
Miller, Olive Beaupré (ed.) *My Bookhouse: Volume Five, From the Tower Window*, 423–35. Chicago: The Bookhouse for Children Publishers, 1921.
Milne, Tom. *Time Out Film Guide*. 13th Rev Edition. London: Time Out Publishing, 2004.
Moles, J.L. "Aristotle and Dido's 'Hamartia.'" *Greece & Rome* Vol. 31, No. 1 (1984): 48–54.
Myrsiades, Kostas. *Reading Homer: Film and Text*. Madison: Fairleigh Dickinson University Press, 2009.
Phippen, J. Weston. "'Kill Every Buffalo You Can! Every Buffalo Dead is an Indian Gone.'" *The Atlantic*, May 13, 2016.
Pollitt, J.J. *Art and Experience in Classical Greece*. New York: Cambridge University Press, 1972.
Reeves, Charles H. "The Aristotelian Concept of the Tragic Hero." *The American Journal of Philology* Vol. 72, No. 2 (1952): 172–188.
Reilly, John M. *Larry McMurtry: A Critical Companion*. Westport, CT: Greenwood Press, 2000.
Spong, John. *A Book on the Making of* Lonesome Dove. Austin: University Press of Texas, 2012.
Thornburn, David. "Interpretation and Judgement: A Reading of *Lonesome Dove*." *Critical Studies in Mass Communication* Vol. 10, No. 2 (1993): 113–127.
Winkler, Martin M. (ed) *Classical Myth and Culture in the Cinema*. Oxford: Oxford University Press, 2001.

Blondie's Odyssey

The Homeric Journey and American Mythmaking in The Good, the Bad, and the Ugly

Christopher J. Olson

> "'Popular culture' thus embraces all levels of our society and culture other than the Elite—the 'popular,' 'mass,' and 'folk.' It includes most of the bewildering aspects of life which hammer us daily."
> —Ray B. Browne, "Popular Culture: Notes Toward a Definition"

Echoing Ray Browne's pioneering discussion regarding the importance of popular culture in society, Darrell William Davis notes that mass art objects such as films can provide insight into the concerns and issues of nations throughout history.[1] Of all the popular culture texts produced throughout the 20th and early 21st centuries, Westerns best exemplify the American national identity, because they portray a mythologized version of the United States' past, people, and purpose. Indeed, the Western has emerged as "the quintessentially American melodrama,"[2] largely because such stories are concerned with and perpetuate the frontier myth that lies at the heart of the American national identity. Rooted in the folkloric tradition and ensconced in popular culture texts, including dime novels, comic books, films, and television shows, the frontier myth often rests on historical facts while creating and reinforcing idealized versions of the U.S. and the American national identity. As Nathalie Massip notes, "the West has had a special place in the nation's self-image, and it has always been considered as central in the construction of American identity."[3] Arguably, over time, notions of the frontier have become more important to the American character than historical reality, and continue to influence everything from individual identity to public policy, impacting how other nations perceive the U.S.

Critics and scholars have observed the similarities between traditional Hollywood Westerns and ancient heroic epics like the *Iliad* and the *Odyssey*. For instance, Kristen Day contends that Western films and Greco-Roman epics both define foundational ideologies for their respective cultures. Martin M. Winkler argues that Westerns function as "a modern descendant of ancient and medieval heroic epic [sic]" because they each "tell stories of conflict, battle, or war, with explicit descriptions of violence and slaughter."[4] Mary Whitlock Blundell and Kirk Ormand contend that Westerns perform "an equivalent cultural role to that of the *Iliad* in Classical Greece" because they also define "the qualities necessary for those heroes who will build civilization out of wilderness."[5] Richard Slotkin and Philip French note that both Westerns and epics "deal with a nation's culture and its past and thus [act] as a paean to the greatness of that nation."[6] Such parallels reveal that Westerns and epics "offer a carefully circumscribed view of human existence, foregrounding certain fundamental issues and values" via an idealized version of the past.[7] Other nations and cultures have produced their own Westerns, or at least put their own cultural spin on traditional Westerns, remixing the signifiers associated with the American West into new contexts that deconstruct and destabilize this frontier myth. Perhaps the most famous were the Italian Westerns (aka Spaghetti Westerns) that emerged in the 1960s and tended to demythologize traditional Hollywood Westerns.

Sergio Leone, the man perhaps most associated with the Spaghetti Western, once remarked, "Probably the greatest writer of westerns himself was Homer. His characters were never all good or all bad. They're half and half, these characters, as all human beings are."[8] Aptly, the narrative structure of Leone's 1966 film *The Good, the Bad, and the Ugly* (*GBU*) recalls that of the *Odyssey*, connecting the frontier myth to classical tales that deal with the foundation of Western civilization. Here, however, it must be noted that *GBU* is a revisionist Western. Borrowing the general "journey" structure from Homer, Leone's masterpiece deconstructs the frontier myth and destabilizes the values and ideologies it perpetuates, while also critiquing notions of the American national identity advanced by traditional Westerns.

Epics, Westerns, and Mythmaking

Since the time of Homer, the difference between history and literary accounts of history "has been almost indissoluble."[9] Heroic epics operate as the foundational myths of Western civilization in part because they offer an idealized view of human existence and consider how values like heroism, honor, glory, exploration, and family contribute to the overall social order. Many of these tales feature heroic figures that embody the values of their civilizations.

The *Odyssey* is no exception to this rule, providing "the myths that have formed the foundation of Western civilization for over two-thousand years."[10] A cunning hero, Odysseus embodies the best qualities of human nature (at least as conceptualized by the Ancient Greeks), and therefore serves as "a moral example, a symbol of man's voyage through life and quest for wisdom."[11] Portraying various sociopolitical structures, the *Odyssey* positions Ithaca as a bastion of "hospitality, faithfulness, narrative, ritual, intelligence," and other beneficial values.[12] Accordingly, Odysseus's journey home to Ithaca becomes a quest to return to correct values and proper social order. Like other ancient heroic epics, the *Odyssey* provides a blueprint for civilization filtered through mythology and folklore which anticipates the Western's idealized portrayals of settling the U.S.

André Bazin observes that Westerns and ancient epics both deal with idealized or mythologized versions of history and feature superhuman heroes performing legendary feats. He writes that the Western "has turned [the Civil War] into the Trojan War of the most modern of epics," and refers to the westward expansion of the U.S. as "our Odyssey."[13] Similarly, Doug Williams argues that "just as John Wayne stands as an icon of the American identity so once stood Odysseus for the Greeks."[14] Spaghetti Westerns, however, frequently deconstruct and demythologize the notion of the idealized frontier myth advanced by traditional Hollywood Westerns.

Deconstructing the Frontier Myth

Spaghetti Westerns first appeared in the early 1960s and persisted until the late 1970s. Aping the stylistic and thematic conventions of traditional Hollywood Westerns,[15] Spaghetti Westerns portray an idealized version of an already mythological interpretation of history, and they frequently subvert this history by highlighting the violent and amoral natures of the people (usually men) who tamed the frontier. In traditional Hollywood Westerns, "the corruption in society is open and visible, exemplified in specific individuals," and the hero works to "remove those individuals to remove the corruption."[16] Spaghetti Westerns frequently present viewers with a murkier type of morality, highlighting the moral ambiguity of both the frontier myth and the idea of manifest destiny. Accordingly, Spaghetti Westerns feature more graphic violence than their Hollywood counterparts[17] and often invert the genre's established tropes and conventions. For example, the good guys tend to wear black rather than white hats.

Critics generally read Spaghetti Westerns as texts that critique and deconstruct traditional Hollywood Westerns. Christopher Frayling, for example, observes that while Hollywood Westerns emphasized the significance of a mythological and symbolic frontier,[18] Spaghetti Westerns tended to ignore the clash between wilderness and civilization and instead foregrounded capitalism as the primary ideological concern of the U.S.[19] According to Frayling, "Leone's odysseys (if that is the appropriate term) are more concerned with vengeance [...], treasure hunting [...], or blood money,"[20] and therefore they subvert the "cherished myths of frontier society."[21] Other scholars have noted the Spaghetti Western's ability to deconstruct the clichés of Hollywood Westerns. Austin Fisher argues that Spaghetti Westerns often approach the genre's tropes with a sly irreverence, even as they treat the historical reality with a sense of reverence.[22] He notes that such films originally occupied the realm of cult cinema, and that critics frequently dismissed them for supposedly glorifying brutality and violence.[23] Because cult films often clash "with hegemonic, dominant systems of culture,"[24] their outsider status enables their critiques of that culture. Situated "outside the Hollywood myth factory," Leone could "exploit the conventions of the Western genre" and debunk its morality.[25]

The most famous of all Spaghetti Westerns, *GBU* transcribes "traditional Western 'codes'—without being subject to the usual ideological constraints."[26] Unlike the morally upstanding heroes in films directed by John Ford and Howard Hawks, *GBU*'s hero, Blondie, is driven by greed.[27] He exists outside of moral law, and his independence results from cynicism regarding civil authority.[28] *GBU* deals with subjects that rarely appeared in traditional Hollywood Westerns, including confrontations between Anglos and Mexicans; bounty hunters and other hired guns; cemeteries and death; and Civil War brutality. The film also positions money as the Western hero's primary concern and exposes the usury, economic terrorism, and neo-feudalism that frequently fueled frontier towns.[29]

In a 1984 interview, Leone explained that he had little interest in furthering "the myth of the West" and the "mythical notions of America,"[30] concentrating instead in *GBU* to challenge and critique the myth of the American West by depicting main protagonist Blondie (Clint Eastwood) as a morally-dubious individual. Homer's *Odyssey* provides another avenue by which to understand Leone's demythologization of the West, America's national identity, and even the idea of mythmaking.

GBU *and the* Odyssey

Many critics and scholars have drawn parallels between Homeric epics and Western films.[31] Functioning as an allegory for the human experience which encourages individuals to strive for happiness and exceed the limits of their individuality, Odysseus's journey operates as a stand-in for life itself. With metaphors representing the act of transforming a barbaric frontier into a civilization, his trials signify those things that tempt people to settle down. Odysseus's story also offers a comforting myth about the founding of Western morality because it "expresses nostalgia for a return to the glories of a bygone age from a degenerate present."[32]

While they differ in terms of specific incidents and outcomes, the *Odyssey* and *GBU* both follow a similar narrative structure. The *Odyssey* is divided into 24 separate "books" that work together to create an overarching narrative about Odysseus's long and difficult journey home. *GBU* is split into several distinct episodes or chapters that combine to relate a journey-like story that builds toward a clear object. Frayling notes the film's "collage" structure, which consists of several "almost self-contained episodes."[33] In his review of *GBU*, critic Roger Ebert describes the film's episodic nature:

> There is the opening shootout, involving unrelated characters. There is the con game in which [Eli] Wallach plays a wanted man, Eastwood turns him in for the reward, and then Eastwood waits until he is about to be hanged and severs the rope with a well-aimed shot. There is the magnificent desert sequence, after Eastwood abandons Wallach in the desert, and then Wallach does the same to Eastwood, and the sun burns down like a scene from "Greed." There is the haunting runaway wagon, filled with dead and dying men.[34]

Both stories also unfold against the backdrop of war (the Trojan War in the *Odyssey*, and the Civil War in *GBU*) and involve characters traveling from one point to another, during which they undergo several trials.

During his journey, Odysseus surmounts many obstacles and displays qualities that mark him as a true hero. His trials include battling the Ciconians on Ismarus; escaping the land of the Lotus-eaters; outwitting the Cyclops, Polyphemus; surviving the wrath of Poseidon; confronting his own disloyal men; encountering giant cannibals in Laestrygonia; outwitting the witch, Circe; traveling to the underworld to speak with the dead prophet, Teiresias; resisting the Sirens' call; encountering Scylla and Charybdis; and finally driving off the suitors occupying his home and courting his wife. Odysseus' challenges serve as "both a moral training and testing-ground for virtue,"[35] and reveal his resilience, cunning, and determination.

Blondie's challenges perform a similar function in *GBU*. He faces four main trials throughout the film, each of which demonstrate his intelligence, guile, and willpower. In the first, Blondie sits alone in a hotel room cleaning his revolver, unaware that three bandits lurk outside his door. Confederate soldiers march through the streets, retreating from a recent defeat. They stop, and silence descends upon the town, allowing Blondie to hear the jangle of one bandit's spurs. The soldiers resume marching, and Blondie quickly reassembles his gun and uses it to kill the bandits. However, his scheming rival, Tuco (Eli Wallach), sneaks in through the window and orders Blondie to hang himself. Just then, a cannonball rips through the room, and Blondie escapes in the confusion.

In the second trial, Tuco forces Blondie to march through the desert until he succumbs to exposure. Before Tuco can kill him, however, a runaway carriage appears. Tuco stops the carriage and discovers a dying Confederate soldier traveling under the name Bill Carson, who confesses that he buried stolen Confederate gold in a grave in Sad Hill Cemetery. Before he can reveal the name on the grave, however, Carson collapses from dehydration, and a frantic Tuco runs to get water. He returns to find Carson dead and Blondie slumped next to his corpse. Blondie discloses that Carson told him the name on the grave, meaning that Tuco now has reason to keep Blondie alive. Tuco brings Blondie to a frontier mission to recuperate, and afterward the two set out together to find the gold, only to land in Batterville Prison.

In the third trial, Blondie must escape from the villainous Angel Eyes (Lee Van Cleef) and his gang. In Batterville, Blondie encounters Angel Eyes posing as a Union Soldier. After learning the location of the gold, Angel Eyes orders Blondie to accompany him and his men to the cemetery so they can dig up the treasure. During a stop at an evacuated inn, Blondie encounters Tuco, who managed to escape from Angel Eyes' cruel henchman, the hulking Union soldier Wallace (Mario Brega). The two men work together to dispatch Angel Eyes' gang before resuming their search for the gold, only to find their way blocked by Union soldiers battling Confederate troops over a strategic bridge. Blondie and Tuco offer to destroy the bridge, and, while wiring it with explosives, Blondie reveals that the gold is buried in a grave marked Arch Stanton.

The fourth and final trial sees Blondie facing both Tuco and Angel Eyes in a tense three-way duel. After blowing up the bridge, Blondie and Tuco arrive at their destination, at which point Tuco ends their tenuous partnership. He finds Stanton's grave and digs it up, but Blondie arrives shortly after. A moment later, Angel Eyes appears and demands the gold. Blondie opens Stanton's coffin to reveal a rotting skeleton. He divulges that he lied about the gold's location and then writes the real name on a rock before challenging his foes to a three-way duel for the information. After several nerve-wracking minutes, Blondie shoots Angel Eyes and kills him. Tuco, meanwhile, discovers his own gun is empty. Blondie explains that he unloaded it the night before and reveals that the gold is buried in the next grave over. Tuco digs up the gold, and Blondie commands him to stand on an unsteady grave marker with a taut hangman's noose around his neck. Blondie leaves with half the treasure, but returns a few moments later to sever the rope with a rifle shot. Tuco falls to the ground and curses as Blondie rides away.

Through these trials, Blondie demonstrates his heroic qualities, but his successes fail to mark him as a hero. Leone presents Blondie as a preternaturally powerful hero akin to Odysseus, but undermines the idea of the archetypal, mythical hero by portraying Blondie as selfish and morally ambiguous. Odysseus "combined self-concern with a just concern for others,"[36] but Blondie repeatedly subverts the notion of the Western hero who is usually portrayed as a chivalrous loner. He demonstrates his moral ambiguity from the moment he steps onscreen by using a gun concealed inside his coat pocket to kill three rival bounty hunters. He then partners with Tuco to run a bounty scam, turning Tuco in for a reward but saving him from hanging, thus driving up the reward in the next town. Tuco risks his life during their con, only for Blondie to betray him when things turn sour, keeping all the money and leaving Tuco stranded in the desert. This turn of events reveals Blondie's selfishness and dishonesty. Additionally, Blondie lies about the location of the stolen gold, demonstrating a willingness to deceive to further his own ends. These tendencies reveal him as morally dubious and dishonorable, the antithesis of the archetypal Western hero as exemplified by Odysseus.

Here it is important to note that directors of Spaghetti Westerns often set out to intentionally deflate "American myths *because* they were myths."[37] Italian films of the 1950s and 1960s sometimes sought to critique Hollywood films, which frequently promoted an "American exceptionalism which Europeans found deeply puzzling."[38] Depicting the American dream as a false construct built on a foundation of nostalgia, Spaghetti Westerns tended to subvert "the values of one of America's most popular and symbolically powerful film genres" and destabilize the "pieties of the genre, especially the myth of the building of a new (Anglo-Saxon) civilization in the savage West."[39] At the time of *GBU*'s release, American critics viewed the "Dollars" trilogy as an "existential threat to the Western genre,"[40] and many of them circled their wagons to "defend the Western genre [...] against Leone's illegitimate revisionism."[41]

GBU, however, is often as nostalgic and mythologized as the Westerns that Leone sought to deconstruct. In part, Leone's Westerns seek to recreate the mythical America that so enamored him as a child.[42] However, he uses classical Western archetypes (for example, the lone hero doomed to solitude) to reveal the "bitter, cynical, and disillusioned view of the world" that lies behind the rose-colored glasses of nostalgia.[43] In many ways, *GBU* challenges the "'America can do no wrong' mentality" that was "imposed on the film industry by the Hays Code" and subverts the notion that "serving in the military and fighting its wars was a sacred duty."[44] Thus, *GBU* follows in the tradition of the *Odyssey*, which presents a similar critique of war as a valorous enterprise. In the *Iliad*, Odysseus is a wily and cunning warrior, but in the *Odyssey*, he wishes only to return home to his wife and his quiet life.

In *GBU*, Leone's critique of war as a valorous enterprise emerges most starkly in his treatment of the Civil War. As Fisher points out, the Civil War is "one of the most potent symbols of the USA's traumatic transition to modernity," but Leone "consumes the conflict's political complexities in a cloud of dust."[45] Leone intended *GBU* as an anti–Vietnam War parable, and the film portrays "the futility of all war" while offering "a sharp contrast to the typical Hollywood war films still being made."[46] He creates "an atmosphere of decay and death," and "deliberately blurs the traditional distinction between North and South [...] to make the war seem more real."[47] Wallace, for instance, delights in torturing Tuco, thereby destabilizing the image of the gallant and honorable Union soldier, illustrating the moral ambiguity of both the Union and the Confederacy. Similarly, the drunken Union captain at the bridge disrupts the idea of the courageous soldier by declaring, "Whoever has the most liquor to get the soldiers drunk and send them to be slaughtered … he's the winner." Soon after, Blondie sums up the film's attitude toward war, saying, "I've never seen so many men wasted so badly" while watching the two armies battle.

The moral ambiguity of the conflict between North and South is also highlighted by the high cost of war, first with a legless Confederate soldier who provides Angel Eyes with vital information in exchange for money to buy alcohol, and later as Blondie and Tuco ride past a field of dead soldiers left to rot in the sun. These depictions reflect the disappointment Leone himself felt when encountering American soldiers in Italy during World War II. He later negatively compared them to the mythical Americans of the Old West, saying "These were no longer the Americans of the West. They were soldiers like any other, and different only in being victorious. Materialist, possessive, eager for pleasure and worldly goods. [...] Not a breath, or hardly a breath, of the great prairies, the demigods of my childhood."[48]

Another similarity between the *Odyssey* and *GBU* lies in their thematic contents, particularly regarding the purpose for the journey. The *Odyssey* deals with the struggle "to remake order after the chaos of war."[49] The poem presents readers with "a moral tale" in which "the unjust man meets with the censure and punishment of the gods, whereas the suppliant, the stranger and the guest-friend are under their protection."[50] At the same time, "Odysseus's shrewd machinations to preserve and promote the self often come at the expense of those around him," and a closer examination of the character reveals "less and less of the noble stalwart of the greater good and more of the capitalist."[51] Rather than a "story of a just and pious man restored to his rightful place with the help of the gods," the *Odyssey* tells of a resourceful individual who fails to achieve wisdom and thereby raises questions about the very concept of justice.[52]

Like Odysseus, Blondie also promotes his own self-interests at the expense of others. Privileging money over morality, Blondie positions greed and self-interest as central aspects of the American identity. As Geoffrey Nowell-Smith points out in "The American Dream in Post-War Italy," *GBU*'s ideological critique reflects Leone's perception of the U.S. as a nation of people preoccupied with earning power.[53] Leone chose to center *GBU* on "a person like the bounty killer [...] because he was the street sweeper of the desert, a man who put his life at risk exclusively for the money."[54] Using the Western to deconstruct the idea of mythmaking, Leone's presentation of Blondie discloses the primacy of capitalism and materialism in the American national identity, and challenges the idea of the moral upstanding hero who lies at the heart of American Character.

Conclusion

Drawing on the *Odyssey* and elements of classical myth, *GBU* critiques the mythologized—and arguably sanitized—version of frontier expansion and settlement found in the Western. While critics Kirsten Day, Mary Whitlock Blundell, Judith Fletcher, Carl A. Rubino, Kostas Myrsiades, and Martin M. Winkler have made important critical inroads into the classical reception of the Hollywood Western, examining how oaters critique and/or reify the mythic Wild West and the process of American mythmaking, Italian Westerns, such as *GBU*, offer interesting case studies, because they present an outsider's perspective on American mythmaking. Traditional Hollywood Westerns often drew on Homeric epics to reflect and explore the frontier's myths about justice, valor, and family, but Leone's work portrays the archetypal Western hero as a violent and amoral grifter, and positions corruption and greed as integral aspects of the American national identity. Leone contends that his Westerns are "borrowed not from the story of the West in America but from the story of cinema,"[55] and he uses these films to express his own ideas about the world. His mythical West is rooted mainly in his experience of visiting the U.S., which he sums up with the following anecdote: "When I went to America, no one asked me how I was. Everyone always asked me, 'How much do you make?'"[56] Here, Leone situates the valorization of wealth as integral to the American identity, and this notion informs his Westerns and the characters that populate them. Leone's use of classical elements to critique American culture calls for further examination of the use of ancient heroic epics in Westerns produced outside of the U.S., such as *Tears of the Black Tiger* (Wisit Sasanatieng, 2000, Thailand), *The Proposition* (John Hillcoat, 2005, Australia), and *The Good, the Bad, the Weird* (Kim Jee-woon, 2008, South Korea), which feature elements of the Homeric narrative found in *GBU*. In final analysis, storytelling media may have changed since Homer's time, but the impulse of mythmaking practiced in the ancient epics continues to thrive—posing contemporary challenges to our dominant narratives and idealized views of a nation's past, present, and future.

Acknowledgment

The author wishes to thank Dr. CarrieLynn D. Reinhard of Dominican University and Sue Matheson for their valuable feedback.

Notes

1. Darrell William Davis, *Picturing Japaneseness: Monumental Style, National Identity, Japanese Film* (New York: University Press, 1996), 8.
2. Michael Coyne, *The Crowded Prairie: American National Identity in the Hollywood Western* (London: I.B. Taurus & Co. Ltd., 1997), 2.
3. See para. 1 in Nathalie Massip, "The Role of the West in the Construction of American Identity: From Frontier to Crossroads."
4. Kristen Day, *Cowboy Classics: The Roots of the American Western in the Epic Tradition* (Edinburgh: Edinburgh University Press, 2016), 593.
5. Mary Whitlock Blundell and Kirk Ormand, "Western Values, or the People's Homer: *Unforgiven* as a Reading of the *Iliad*," *Poetic Today* Vol. 18, No. 4 (1997): 533.
6. Kostas Myrsiades, "Reading *The Gunfighter* as Homeric Epic," *College Literature* Vol. 34, No. 2 (2007): 279–80.
7. Blundell and Ormand, "Western Values, or the People's Homer: *Unforgiven* as a Reading of the *Iliad*," 536.
8. Editorial@ASX, "An Interview with Sergio Leone (1987)," ASX, December 28, 2012, https://americansuburbx.com/2012/12/interview-interview-with-sergio-leone-1987.html.
9. Richard Hunter, "'Where Do I Begin?': An Odyssean Narrative Strategy and its Afterlife," in Douglas Cairns and Ruth Scodel, eds. *Defining Greek Narrative* (Edinburgh: Edinburgh University Press, 2014), 141.
10. Gerald R. Lucas, "Homer's ODYSSEY: Some notes and an introduction to Homer's epic of return," *Medium* December 29, 2013. At https://grlucas.net/grl/Homer%27s_Odyssey.
11. R.B. Rutherford, "The Philosophy of the Odyssey," *The Journal of Hellenic Studies* Vol. 106 (1986): 146.
12. Gerald R. Lucas, "Homer's ODYSSEY."
13. André Bazin, "The Evolution of the Western," in Hugh Gray, trans. *What Is Cinema? Vol. II* (Berkeley, CA: University of California Press, 1971), 143.
14. Quoted in Kostas Myrsiades' "Reading *The Gunfighter* as Homeric Epic," 279.
15. Jenifer Meynell, "Values and Violence: A Study of the Films of Clint Eastwood," *Journal of Moral Education* Vol. 7, No. 2 (1978): 111.
16. Ibid., 111.
17. William McClain, "Western, go home! Sergio Leone and the 'death of the Western' in American film criticism," *Journal of Film and Video* Vol. 62, No. 1–2 (Spring/Summer 2010): 52.
18. Christopher Frayling, *Spaghetti Westerns: Cowboys and Europeans from Karl May to Sergio Leone* (London: I.B. Tauris & Co Ltd., 1998), 41.
19. Ibid., 51.
20. Ibid., 130.
21. Ibid., 132.
22. Austin Fisher, *Radical Frontiers in the Spaghetti Western: Politics, Violence and Popular Italian Cinema* (New York: I.B. Tauris & Co., 2011), 60.
23. Ibid., 175.
24. Ernest Mathijs and Xavier Mendik, "The Concepts of Cult," in Ernest Mathijs and Xavier Mendik, eds. *The Cult Film Reader* (Toronto: McGraw-Hill, 2008), 17.
25. Frayling, 39.
26. Ibid., 160.
27. James R. Couch, "The Smile and the Spit: The Motivational Polarity and Self-Reliance Portrayed in *The Outlaw Josey Wales* and the *Dollars* Trilogy," in Richard T. McClelland and Brian B. Clayton, eds. *The Philosophy of Clint Eastwood* (Lexington, KY: University Press of Kentucky, 2014), 61.

28. Erin E. Flynn, "The Representation of Justice in Eastwood's *High Plains Drifter*," in Richard T. McClelland and Brian B. Clayton, eds. *The Philosophy of Clint Eastwood* (Lexington, KY: University Press of Kentucky, 2014), 86.
29. Frayling, 162.
30. Pete Hamill, "Leone: 'I'm a Hunter by Nature, Not a Prey,'" *American Film* (June 1984): 23.
31. See Bazin, "The Evolution of the Western"; Blundell and Ormand, "Western Values, or the People's Homer: *Unforgiven* as a Reading of the *Iliad*"; Martin M. Winkler, "Homer's *Iliad* and John Ford's *The Searchers*"; Myrsiades, Kostas. "Reading *The Gunfighter* as Homeric Epic."
32. Erwin Cook, "Structure as Interpretation in the Homeric *Odyssey*," in Douglas Cairns and Ruth Scodel, eds. *Defining Greek Narrative* (Edinburgh University Press, 2014), 100.
33. Frayling, 131.
34. See Roger Ebert's "The Good, the Bad, and the Ugly," *RogerEbert.com*, August 3, 2003, https://www.rogerebert.com/reviews/great-movie-the-good-the-bad-and-the-ugly-1968
35. Rutherford, 146.
36. David Bolotin, "The Concerns of Odysseus: An Introduction to the *Odyssey*," *Interpretation* Vol. 17, No. 1 (1989): 41.
37. William McClain, "Western, go home! Sergio Leone and the 'death of the Western' in American film criticism," *Journal of Film and Video* Vol. 62, No. 1–2 (Spring/Summer 2010): 60 (emphasis in original).
38. Geoffrey Nowell-Smith, "The American Dream in Post-War Italy," in Paul Cooke, ed. *World Cinema's "Dialogues" With Hollywood* (New York: Palgrave Macmillan, 2007), 133.
39. *Ibid.*, 134.
40. McClain, 52.
41. *Ibid.*, 53.
42. Robert Donati, "Once upon a time…: Introduction to the Theme of Nostalgia in the Films of Sergio Leone," *Offscreen* Vol. 12, No. 4 (April 2008), http://offscreen.com/view/nostalgia_leone.
43. *Ibid.*
44. David S. Silverman, "(Re-)Visionist History in Sergio Leone's (De-)Mythologized Old West: The Civil War, Vietnam, and *The Good, The Bad, and The Ugly*," n Douglas Brode, Shea T. Brode and Cynthia J. Miller, eds. *The American Civil War on Film and TV: Blue and Gray in Black and White and Color* (Lanham, MD: Lexington Books, 2017), 184.
45. Fisher, *Radical Frontiers in the Spaghetti Western*, 59.
46. Silverman, 183.
47. Frayling, 128.
48. Nowell-Smith, 134–5.
49. See Gerald R. Lucas, "Homer's ODYSSEY."
50. Rutherford, 146.
51. Scott A. Belsky, "The Poet Who Sings Through Us: Homer's Influence in Contemporary Western Culture," *College Literature* Vol. 34, No. 2 (2007): 218.
52. Bolotin, 42.
53. Nowell-Smith, 135.
54. See Editorial@ASX, "An Interview with Sergio Leone (1987)."
55. *Ibid.*
56. *Ibid.*

Filmography

Easy Rider. Dir. Dennis Hopper. Raybert Productions; Pando Company, 1969.
The Good, the Bad, and the Ugly. Dir Sergio Leone. United Artists, 1966.

Works Cited

Bazin, André. "The Evolution of the Western." In Hugh Gray, trans. *What Is Cinema? Vol. II*, 149–57. Berkeley: University of California Press, 1971.
Belsky, Scott A. "The Poet Who Sings Through Us: Homer's Influence in Contemporary Western Culture." *College Literature* Vol. 34, No. 2 (2007): 216–228.
Blundell, Mary Whitlock and Kirk Ormand. "Western Values, or the People's Homer: *Unforgiven* as a Reading of the *Iliad*." *Poetic Today* Vol. 18, No. 4 (1997): 533–569.
Bolotin, David. "The Concerns of Odysseus: An Introduction to the *Odyssey*." *Interpretation* Vol. 17, No. 1 (1989): 41–57.

Browne, Ray B. "Popular Culture: Notes Toward a Definition." In Ray B. Browne and Ronald J. Ambrosetti, eds. *Popular Culture Theory and Curricula*, 3–11. Bowling Green, OH: Bowling Green University Popular Press, 1970.
Cook, Erwin. "Structure as Interpretation in the Homeric *Odyssey*." In Douglas Cairns and Ruth Scodel, eds. *Defining Greek Narrative*, 75–100. 75–100. Edinburgh University Press, 2014.
Couch, James R. "The Smile and the Spit: The Motivational Polarity and Self-Reliance Portrayed in *The Outlaw Josey Wales* and the *Dollars* Trilogy." In Richard T. McClelland and Brian B. Clayton, eds. *The Philosophy of Clint Eastwood*, 61–76. Lexington: University Press of Kentucky, 2014.
Coyne, Michael. *The Crowded Prairie: American National Identity in the Hollywood Western*. London: I.B. Taurus & Co. Ltd., 1997.
Davis, Darrell William. *Picturing Japaneseness: Monumental Style, National Identity, Japanese Film*. New York: University Press, 1996.
Day, Kristen. *Cowboy Classics: The Roots of the American Western in the Epic Tradition*. Edinburgh: Edinburgh University Press, 2016.
Donati, Robert. "Once upon a time…: Introduction to the Theme of Nostalgia in the Films of Sergio Leone." *Offscreen* Vol. 12, No. 4 (April 2008). At http://offscreen.com/view/nostalgia_leone.
Ebert, Roger. "The Good, the Bad, and the Ugly." *RogerEbert.com*. August 3, 2003. At https://www.rogerebert.com/reviews/great-movie-the-good-the-bad-and-the-ugly-1968.
Editorial@ASX. "An Interview with Sergio Leone (1987)." *ASX*. December 28, 2012. At https://americansuburbx.com/2012/12/interview-interview-with-sergio-leone-1987.html.
Fisher, Austin. *Radical Frontiers in the Spaghetti Western: Politics, Violence and Popular Italian Cinema*. New York: I.B. Tauris & Co., 2011.
Flynn, Erin E. "The Representation of Justice in Eastwood's *High Plains Drifter*." In Richard T. McClelland and Brian B. Clayton, eds. *The Philosophy of Clint Eastwood*, 77–94. Lexington: University Press of Kentucky, 2014.
Frayling, Christopher. *Spaghetti Westerns: Cowboys and Europeans from Karl May to Sergio Leone*. London: I.B. Tauris & Co Ltd., 1998.
Hamill, Pete. "Leone: 'I'm a Hunter by Nature, Not a Prey.'" *American Film* (June 1984): 23–25.
Hughes, Howard. *Once Upon a Time in the Italian West: The Filmgoers' Guide to Spaghetti Westerns*. London: I.B. Tauris & Co Ltd., 2004.
Hunter, Richard. "'Where Do I Begin?': An Odyssean Narrative Strategy and its Afterlife." In Douglas Cairns and Ruth Scodel, eds. *Defining Greek Narrative*, 137–155. Edinburgh: Edinburgh University Press, 2014.
Lucas, Gerald R. "Homer's ODYSSEY: Some notes and an introduction to Homer's epic of return." *Medium*, December 29, 2013. At https://grlucas.net/grl/Homer%27s_Odyssey.
Massip, Nathalie. "The Role of the West in the Construction of American Identity: From Frontier to Crossroads." *Caliban: French Journal of English Studies* No. 31 (2012): 239–48. At http://journals.openedition.org/caliban/486.
Mathijs, Ernest, and Xavier Mendik. "The Concepts of Cult." In Ernest Mathijs and Xavier Mendik, eds. *The Cult Film Reader*, 15–24. Toronto: McGraw-Hill, 2008.
McClain, William. "Western, go home! Sergio Leone and the 'death of the Western' in American film criticism." *Journal of Film and Video* Vol. 62, No. 1–2 (Spring/Summer 2010): 52–66.
Meynell, Jenifer. "Values and Violence: A Study of the Films of Clint Eastwood." *Journal of Moral Education* Vol. 7, No. 2 (1978): 109–113.
Myrsiades, Kostas. "Reading *The Gunfighter* as Homeric Epic." *College Literature* Vol. 34, No. 2 (2007): 279–300.
Nowell-Smith, Geoffrey. "The American Dream in Post-War Italy." In Paul Cooke, ed. *World Cinema's "Dialogues" With Hollywood*, 122–37. New York: Palgrave Macmillan, 2007.
Rutherford, R.B. "The Philosophy of the Odyssey." *The Journal of Hellenic Studies* Vol, 106 (1986): 145–162.
Silverman, David S. "(Re-)Visionist History in Sergio Leone's (De-)Mythologized Old West: The Civil War, Vietnam, and *The Good, The Bad, and The Ugly*." In Douglas Brode, Shea T. Brode and Cynthia J. Miller, eds. *The American Civil War on Film and TV: Blue and Gray in Black and White and Color*, 183–94. Lanham, MD: Lexington Books, 2017.
Weisser, Thomas. *Spaghetti Westerns—The Good, the Bad, and the Violent: A Comprehensive, Illustrated Filmography of 558 Eurowesterns and their Personnel, 1961–1977*. Jefferson, NC: McFarland, 1992.
Winkler, Martin M. "Homer's *Iliad* and John Ford's *The Searchers*." *Gaia: revue interdisciplinaire sur la Grèce Archaïque* No. 7 (2003): 593–599.

Writing and Rewriting History
Myth in the Iliad *and* Heaven's Gate

Brian Brems

In the mythic story of the end of the New Hollywood period, Michael Cimino's *Heaven's Gate* (1980) occupies an almost singular space among several films that arguably brought that era of auteur-dominated mainstream studio product to a crashing halt.[1] Cimino's film is a sprawling effort, a sweeping three-and-a-half hour effort for which the term "epic" seems entirely appropriate. One of the film's executive producers, Steven Bach, working at the time for United Artists (UA), chronicled his experience of the film's production in a book called *Final Cut*. In the book, he describes Cimino's efforts to expand the size and scope of the film's grandiosity by cataloguing his obsessive attention to the smallest details:

> Cimino was building sets and rebuilding them, hiring 100 extras, then 200, then 500, adding horses and wagons and hats, shoes, gloves, dresses, top hats, bridles, boots, roller skates, babushkas, aprons, dusters, buckboards, gun belts, rifles, bullets, cows, calves, bulls, trees, thousands of tons of dirt, hundreds of miles of exposed film.[2]

Costs, too, continued to balloon. According to Bach, before the production completed shooting its main action (a prologue and epilogue would be shot a few weeks later), executives at UA estimated "a possible direct production cost of $43.4 million, almost 600 percent of what this director had said the picture would cost."[3] The final actual cost was not far off from those projections, once editing was finally finished and the picture locked.

Critical reception to *Heaven's Gate*, upon its initial release, was almost entirely negative, with much of the reaction settling around critiques of the film's length, its perceived self-indulgence, its sense of its own seriousness. Bach describes the film's premiere, recalling that members of its audience "were stunned into submission by the sheer weight of the thing, the luxuriant wastefulness, the overbearing sound, the relentlessness of its self-importance, its self-love."[4] Since the initial failure of the film with critics and its subsequent, panicked yanking from theaters by UA, and its catastrophic loss of money, chroniclers of not only the New Hollywood period, but also the Western genre, have laid blame at Cimino's feet for killing both. Peter Biskind, in *Easy Riders, Raging Bulls*, does his part by gathering takes from Cimino's contemporaries, Martin Scorsese and Francis Ford Coppola.[5]

In addition, many of the substantial texts written about the Western genre mention *Heaven's Gate*, almost always in the same context. John Cawelti is critical of the film: "Beginning in 1970, the Western began a long decline that was accelerated by the disastrous failure of Michael Cimino's *Heaven's Gate* in 1980."[6] And Jim Kitses notes, "Michael Cimino's blockbuster failure, *Heaven's Gate* (1980)."[7] And the British Film Institute states, "Michael Cimino may go down in history as The Man Who Killed the Western, in that this incredibly expensive box-office disaster effectively dissuaded the studios from investing in Westerns in the '80s."[8] For these critics, the production and subsequent box office failure of the film has itself achieved mythic proportions; in this telling, Cimino is a carpetbagging villain with no business making a Western, who attempted to elevate the genre past its limits, inducing a stress test under which the entire film genre and a new era of mainstream film innovation collapsed.

Among critics in the rough period of the film's release, Robin Wood stands relatively alone in his praise of the film and its director's work on it. Of Cimino himself, Wood argues he "has established himself decisively as one of the American cinema's great architects and as one of its most authentic formal innovators."[9] Wood, in his book *Hollywood from Vietnam to Reagan*, devotes nearly twenty pages to a close reading of the film, making the case that

> each building block, the architectural metaphor being especially apposite to Cimino—constitutes a separate, lucid, and forceful "history lesson": about privilege, about poverty, about compromise, about being unprepared, about power, about community, about collective action, about the betrayal of the poor by a rising bourgeoisie, about the destruction of a possible alternative America by the one that is so much with us.[10]

Here, Wood attempts to counter the preponderance of critiques against the film that dominated the conversation during its brief release: mostly, that its mammoth running time exacerbated its supposed root problem, which was its meandering, shapeless narrative. For Wood, "the film is about loss in national as well as personal terms, its distinction lying in the way it counterpoints and connects the two. It is an elegy for a possible alternative America destroyed before it could properly exist by forces generated within, yet beyond the control of, democratic capitalism."[11]

In short, Wood attempts to read the film as a radical formal experiment, something that was largely lost on audiences and critics at the time of its release: "the film apparently both exasperated and exhausted its audience by its murky complexity and ambiguity. In the drastically cut version released to theaters and shown on cable television, the film was still profoundly puzzling, particularly if one brought to it the traditional expectation of dramatic and symbolic clarity, associated with the Western genre."[12] The association of *Heaven's Gate* with the Western perhaps explains some of the film's controversial reputation, in that it primarily functions as a challenge to that genre's conventions, rather than a reification of them. The rejection of Cimino's film may be due at least in part to its refusal to adhere to the ideological infrastructure of classic Westerns, which carry with them many tenets of the mythology of the United States. In fact, Cimino's film must instead be seen as adopting the formal structure of the epic in order to critique the myth of the American West. In other words, on its surface, *Heaven's Gate* wears the costume of a typical Western, but inside, its heart is bent on exploding the American myths that Westerns have done so much to create.

Heaven's Gate, in Wood's formulation, "is an epic about failure and catastrophe, both personal and national."[13] If seen from this perspective, Cimino's film is best considered in the context of another epic that shares these themes, Homer's *Iliad*. According to Caroline Alexander, "As an epic, the *Iliad*, by definition, narrates 'the deeds of heroic or legendary figures'—in other words, the actions and events of men, and the emotional weight of the poem is borne by its mortal heroes and its few, but potent, heroines."[14] The same might be said of the scope of *Heaven's Gate*, the very title of which aspires to the celestial. Its plot, too, carries the hallmark of historical epic. The main action is set against the backdrop of the real-life Johnson County War, a disagreement over cattle theft in Wyoming circa 1892. The film exaggerates the scope of historical fact in order to tell a larger story about class in the United States, especially as it has been portrayed in Western films.[15] According to John Davis' history of the event, "What constitutes the 'Johnson County War' has never been strictly defined, but the name refers generally to murderous episodes beginning in late 1891 and culminating in the full-scale invasion of the county in April 1892 by twenty-five big cattlemen and their top hands, along with another twenty-five hired guns."[16] At issue was the Wyoming Stock Growers Association's accusation that Johnson County was rife with cattle thieves who were absconding with their livestock; they conspired, possibly with the force of the state, to send a violent message to the citizens of the county. In Cimino's telling of the story, the mercenaries hired by the WSGA are an occupying army with a death list that contains in excess of one hundred names—nearly everyone in Johnson County.

Cimino's cast of characters, many of whom bear names taken from the historical record, become vehicles for this epic story: Marshall James Averill (Kris Kristofferson), the film's Harvard-graduate and reluctant hero; Nate Champion (Christopher Walken), a local hired gun developing a conscience; Ella Watson (Isabelle Huppert), a madam caught between the two men; Frank Canton (Sam Waterston), the agent for the big cattlemen.[17] According to Bach, "Cimino hoped to weld not only a romantic triangle but also a sort of three-tier class cake that represented a rough American social system of the period: the Harvard-educated eastern aristocrat; the American-bred laborer; the immigrant entrepreneur."[18] During pre-production, it was clear to the executives at UA that "Cimino had a sense of his material as 'epic' in scope and importance, even if history regarded it as not much more than a footnote."[19] Bach himself recalls feeling impressed by the screenplay: "Cimino's script seemed more than a western. That its portrait of America was sensationalist, ruthless, and bloodthirsty did not seem excessive or 'political' [...] If anything, the robber baron juggernaut lent a feeling of moral force to the doom encircling the characters marked for slaughter on the association's death list."[20] The film's climax is its most radical departure from history; using the historical siege of the WSGA's invading army by the angry residents of Johnson County as a jumping off point, Cimino stages a bloody battle between the opposing forces that leaves many of the invaders and the townsfolk dead. The melee itself was not historical—no one was killed in the siege at the TA Ranch that Cimino used for inspiration—but it was, unquestionably, cinematic.

Here too, parallels with the *Iliad* may find purchase: the historical veracity of the Trojan War depicted in Homer's poem is unlikely ever to be definitively confirmed. The *Iliad* itself has long been the modern world's access point to a past that is more mythological than historical; the Greek gods of old routinely interfere in the action of the story, and narrative elements related to the story of the fall of Troy (the Trojan Horse, the death of Achilles, the sack of the city) are often assumed to be related in the *Iliad*, despite their absence. The *Iliad* functions not as a matter of historical record, but as mythology of ancient warfare. In this sense, the debate over whether the "real" story of

Troy happened as Homer tells it is irrelevant, just as it is in the context of Cimino's film; the end result of both texts is the use of the epic form to achieve the mythic. They seek to make a grand statement not just about individual human beings, but about humankind and its relationship to the organizing principles of its social systems. In the *Iliad*, the supposed glory of war is undermined by the poem's two dominant subjects: the savagery of the violence, and even darker, the futility of it all.[21] In *Heaven's Gate*, the American mythology of the glory of the West, and its promise of boundless opportunity for all who strived, is attacked through the film's elevation of a minor historical conflict into an apocalyptic struggle for the soul of a burgeoning nation, in which the forces of capital march on the bones of the individual. In this way, *Heaven's Gate* is a kind of American *Iliad*; its use of the epic form situates it in the context of its genre precedents, especially when considered in light of the American Western film, but its primary effort is to rewrite the history it purports to depict by radically departing from its historical basis. In essence, it is ignoring the historical truth as it happened in order to restructure the mythological truth as it is commonly believed.

To properly interrogate the place of *Heaven's Gate* amongst its generic forebears, I wish to return to the panoply of writers who have written on the subject of American westerns and their role in creating the myth of the West. Author Will Wright suggests "myth—together with ritual, art, kinship, and politics—can be seen as a necessary symbolic strategy to reintegrate the experience that language makes detached and problematic. Through their stories and characters, and their unconscious, structural significance, myths organize and model experience. Familiar situations and conflicts are presented and resolved."[22] Essentially, when applied to the Western genre, myths are an organizing system whose primary function is to carry ideological weight; through these myths, the members of a culture gain shared experience though, especially in an age of mass communication, they may never meet. According to Wright, myths are intimately connected to a culture's sense of its own place in historical time. For Wright, myths "use the setting of the past to create and resolve the conflicts of the present. Myths use the past to tell us how to act in the present."[23]

Such a time-focused perspective on myths lends credence to the preponderance of Western literature and films (before Michael Cimino single-handedly killed them, of course) in American culture. The number of Western films produced in Hollywood increased in the aftermath of World War II, since which "the West has become increasingly symbolic of traditional American rugged individualism."[24] Many critics of Western films have seen them as inextricably linked with the American way of life, for good and ill: "it provides a fascinating and never-ending series of diverse spectacles and rituals: the pioneer community's odyssey and putting down of roots, its gunfights and poker games, dances and funerals; journeys of stagecoach and rider, cattle and cavalry; the land and its awesome vistas that incorporate the picturesque and the sublime; scenes of galvanizing action and adventure, as in the robberies and pursuits, cattle drives and buffalo stampedes, Indian wars and cavalry rescues."[25] Others argue that the Western "offers a serious orientation to the problem of violence such as can be found almost nowhere else in our culture. One of the well-known peculiarities of modern civilized opinion is its refusal to acknowledge the value of violence. This refusal is a virtue, but like many virtues it involves a certain willful blindness and it encourages hypocrisy."[26] Nearly all Western critics are cognizant of the disparity between the historical truth of the West and the generic myth of "The West" as depicted in literature and film: "the

Western has so little to do with an actual West that it might better be thought of as its own epitaph, written by an exuberant East encroaching on possibilities already foreclosed because [they are] represented in terms of a West that 'no longer exists,' never did, never could."[27]

To summarize: the Western is about the individual; it is about the community; it is about the ways in which the individual comes into conflict with the community, and vice versa; it depicts a world of the past that never really existed so that we might adhere to its idealized principles in the modern world. The foremost interpreter of myth and its relationship to the American West is Richard Slotkin, whose three-volume exploration of the "Myth of the Frontier" is an expansive, definitive work. Slotkin organizes the principles articulated above in this way: "The terminology of the Myth of the Frontier has become part of our common language, and we do not require an explanatory program to make it comprehensible."[28] For Slotkin, American culture has so effectively internalized the iconography of the mythological West that it governs our unifying metaphors, symbols, and archetypes almost totally. He might as well be describing Cimino's efforts in *Heaven's Gate* in this passage: "myth has a paradoxical way of dealing with historical experience: although the materials of myth are historical, myth organizes these materials ahistorically. When historical memory is carried by mythological metaphors, it is falsified in the most fundamental way. [...] The past is made metaphorically equivalent to the present; and the present appears simply as a repetition of persistently recurring structures identified with the past."[29] In other words, the altering of historical fact is a given if myth is to function according to its ideological purpose.

In this way, Cimino's revision of the comparatively bloodless Johnson County War to frontier bloodbath is an effort to achieve the mythic rather than the historical. *Heaven's Gate* reacts to the Westerns that have preceded it, some of which also took the historical record of the Johnson County War as their basis.[30] According to Slotkin, "It is the nature of mythic symbolism to exaggerate, to read particulars as universals, to treat every conflict as Armageddon in microcosm. The primary social and political function of the *extraordinary* violence of myth is to sanction the *ordinary* violence of oppression and injustice, of brutalities casual or systematic, of the segregation, insult, or humiliation of targeted groups."[31] What is true of Westerns is also true of the Homeric: "The glorification of insignificant incidents is common in heroic poetry."[32] Cimino's film deliberately distorts and inflates history in an attempt to become something more, despite the clear consternation of the UA executives, whose reaction to the director's willful ignorance of fact Bach chronicles in *Final Cut*.

One way that Cimino's film adopts the properties of myth is through its appropriation of the epic mode of storytelling, most strongly illustrated by Homer's *Iliad*. The length of the film in its most widely available version is 216 minutes,[33] long by any mainstream Hollywood standard. The film begins with a prologue set in 1870 on the campus of Harvard, where James Averill and his friend Billy Irvine (John Hurt) are graduating. According to Robin Wood, a strong advocate for the film's structure in particular, "the Harvard prologue establishes the major unifying motifs—the dance, the battle, the circle, and the tree—on whose permutations the structure of the entire film is built."[34] After the conclusion of the graduation festivities, the film jumps to 1892, Johnson County, Wyoming, as James Averill wakes up on a train pulling into the town of Casper. The main action of the film takes place in Johnson County, and takes up over three hours of what remains. It is during this portion of the story that the audience is introduced to Champion and Ella; the love triangle among Champion, Ella, and Averill; the machinations of Canton conspiring with the other cattlemen to take over the town; the assault on Champion's cabin that results in his death; the attack on the cattlemen by the townspeople in which many on both sides are killed; and finally, an ambush of Averill, Ella, and local businessman J.B. Bridges (Jeff Bridges) outside Ella's home by Canton, in which Ella and Bridges are killed. The film then concludes with a brief, elegiac epilogue, which finds Averill having returned to the upper class life he abandoned in Johnson County, in 1903. From opening to closing frame, then, the film has covered thirty-three years of time, and more than three-and-a-half hours of screen time.

These are the major plot points, and yet, to list them in such a perfunctory way is to deny them the power they have when positioned as movements in an epic story like Cimino's. The film achieves the epic designation of its storytelling style in the way it luxuriates in its imagery; Cimino frequently holds edits well past the point of normal Hollywood cutting rhythms, simply to show the expanse of the story he is telling.[35] While he uses this strategy throughout the film, it is most evident early in the main action in Wyoming, as Averill arrives in Casper by train. The sequence begins by making a class distinction between Averill and the immigrants arriving in Wyoming by the hundreds; the travelers ride atop the train, their belongings gathered around them. Averill sleeps relatively comfortably inside the train's car, in the dark, and strikingly, all alone. Empty seats surround him. The darkness of the inside of the train is contrasted with the sweeping shots of Casper as the train pulls in, as the camera depicts the expansiveness of the western landscape,[36] but also the enormity of the sets built for the film. The camera holds on a long shot of the town, as Averill, stepping off the train, nearly disappears against the complexity and enormity of the background.[37] Consistently, Averill is dwarfed by the natural and man-made structures of the environment; right away, Cimino is suggesting the epic nature of the world and the hero's place within it. The lingering camera, which emphasizes the scale of the story on display, is best considered a cinematic equivalent to the formal qualities of epic poetry, which "is at once distinguishable by the constant repetition of phrases, lines, and whole groups of lines."[38] The sweeping shots of Casper, with its cast of hundreds, each of whom is dressed in period-authentic clothing, perform the same function as repetition in epic poetry. The splendor of the images, the contents of which have been staged to achieve the appearance of historical authenticity, suggest the grand world of the past as it must have been. Witness this otherwise innocuous description from the *Iliad*, describing Agamemnon in a similar moment—waking from sleep and stepping into his environment: "Agamemnon awoke from sleep, the divine voice drifting / around him. He sat upright and put on his tunic, / beautiful, fresh woven, and threw the great mantle over it. / Underneath his shining feet he bound the fair sandals / and across his shoulders slung the sword with the nails of silver, / and took up the sceptre of his fathers, immortal forever. / Thus he went beside the ships of the bronze-armoured Achaians."[39] Two mythic characters, Averill in *Heaven's Gate* and Agamemnon in the *Iliad*, stagger forth from sleep and greet the world they intend to conquer, carrying with them the signs of their power—Averill his trenchcoat, trunk, and hat, and Agamemnon his tunic, sword, and the scepter that links him to the past.

The stores and restaurants created for the film are a far cry from the phony-looking flat walls of classic Westerns; these are three-dimensional and seemingly practical, a verisimilitude emphasized greatly when Averill enters a bustling general store that is almost deafening in the noise of men sorting through goods. The measured pace of the film continues as Averill makes his way from Casper to Johnson County, and encounters a woman single-handedly pulling a wagon piled with her possessions. Her two children are riding in the back, and atop the wagon is the body of her husband, apparently beaten to death by WSGA mercenaries. After Averill stops to encourage her to turn back to Casper, and she refuses, he continues on ahead of her, driving his own buggy (soon to be a gift for Ella). Cimino lingers with a wide shot of the woman struggling to pull the wagon, loaded with all she has in the world. The film then cuts to a similarly framed shot of Averill riding away from her, and finally, the camera pans as Averill disappears into the distance. The film is foregrounding its counteracting of the myth of class in the American West; the buggy Averill is driving was described as expensive in Casper by Cully (Richard Masur), the train station man. Averill, who is educated and a representative of the upper class, is a tourist; the real struggle, the real poverty, is with the woman who continues to struggle with her own wagon.

One of the film's central sequences, which occurs in the town of Sweetwater, where much of the townspeople live, is a dance where all the community gathers together, with music supplied by a frontier band; many don roller skates and speed in circles around the tented rink, the J.B. Bridges-owned "Heaven's Gate," which gives the film its title. Wood finds both class-oriented and Biblical resonance in the establishment's name, "through which only the rich cannot enter."[40] The scene, like many in Cimino's film, cannot really be said to advance the plot in any meaningful sense. However, as it plays out, it becomes clear that whatever the film appears to be trying to say, at least some portion of it is contained in this sequence, which harnesses the purity of the community's solidarity. This sequence is Cimino's vision of America: businessmen like Bridges, madams like Ella, local politicians like the town's Mayor Lezak (Paul Koslo), business leaders like Eggleston (Brad Dourif), who is the president of the chamber of commerce, lawmen like Averill, and small-time cattle farmers, their wives, their children—all of them come to a place where they are bound together by their faith in one another, their experience of joy, and their commitment to something greater than any one of them individually.

It is not difficult to see how an ordinary filmgoer, or even a studio executive, would watch the sequence in the dance hall and feel downright confused. In his defense of the film, Robin Wood argues that "the story is not being told in the way to which tradition and repetition have long accustomed to us."[41] The tradition and repetition to which Wood refers here is that of classical Hollywood narrative; instead, the film belongs more to the epic tradition, which is foreign to contemporary audiences, especially within the confines of the relatively mainstream Hollywood studio product. There is a useful analogue to these sequences in *Heaven's Gate* in the *Iliad*, which occurs early in the poem: what is referred to as the Catalogue of Ships, which takes up a substantial portion of Book Two. Essentially, "[i]ts purpose is to introduce a long list of 226 verses naming each of the twenty-nine contingents that make up the Achaean army."[42] Like the dance hall sequence, the narrative action contained in the Catalogue is minimal. Both sequences, however, are included in order to achieve an alternative purpose: "Tedious as it can be to modern audiences, the Catalogue with its grave roll call of long-deserted places was undoubtedly warmly received by audiences who knew these names from folk and family lore, an anticipated feature, perhaps, of performances relating the saga of bygone times."[43] Alexander finds the *Iliad* littered with scenes about which the same thing could be said—narratively, they are irrelevant, and yet, they become crucial to the experience of the whole: "In structural terms, the scene between Hektor and Andromache is wholly irrelevant to the *Iliad*. It does not advance the epic story in any substantive way, and it adds nothing at all to the main narrative arc […] yet it is one of the handful of scenes without which the *Iliad* could not have been the *Iliad*."[44]

It is likewise hard to imagine *Heaven's Gate* without the dance hall sequence, mostly because of its grand thematic resonance. It is a place of peace, happiness, and equality. In the dance hall, crucially, the people of Johnson County are free from the aggression of the big cattlemen; they do not harbor prejudice against people who are different from them; they are not divided by the forces of capital that would pit them against one another, fighting for a tiny sweeping of leftover bread crumbs. The irony of the film's progression to its conclusion is that it is under the "Heaven's Gate" canvas that these same citizens will gather to hear the reading of their names from the WSGA's death list; many of these laughing faces will be contorted into pained grimaces in the film's bloody climactic battle, their community destroyed.

The film consistently covers the territory of myth throughout its expansive running time; there is the landscape, with its imposing mountains looming over the action. The big ideas of national identity carried in scenes like the roller skating dance in "Heaven's Gate" attempt to establish an inclusive vision of America that will ultimately be destroyed by violence. But, where the film increasingly begins to parallel Homer's *Iliad* is in its treatment of its heroes—Averill and Champion. It is important at this juncture to stress that Cimino's film is not a retelling of Homer's epic in any direct way; however, both Homer and Cimino rely upon similar narrative devices that are freighted with mythical resonance. Averill is a reluctant hero in the mode of Homer's Achilles. Both characters spend much of the narrative at the margins of the story, defined by their absence from the central conflict rather than participation in it. In Bach's chronicle of the film's production, he demonstrates that the executives at UA were aware of Averill's scripted passivity: "It was assumed that the contemplative character Kristofferson would play was sufficiently dominant (and on screen for most of the picture anyway) that he would act as moral presence rather than conventional cowboy catalyst, the observer through whose eyes and waning idealism we would see and interpret the action."[45] Averill spends much of the film unsure of what to do next. His motivations remain opaque; on one hand, he is shocked by the brazen intentions of the WSGA to carry out the assassinations of the local farmers, but on the other, he appears unconvinced they will actually go through with it. He is cagey about his own past; the twenty-two year lacuna between prologue and main action in the film means we never know how or why he has come to live in Wyoming. The presence of an aged photo in his bedroom above Bridges' bar suggests he is or once was married, which explains, only visually, never in dialogue, why he always changes the subject when Ella asks if he will marry her. The reappearance of the photo, along with the woman in it, in the brief epilogue aboard a yacht, suggest that he returns to his wife in the aftermath of the violence in Johnson County.

This mystery simultaneously aligns and separates Averill from his Western genre compatriots. Often, the central figure is a man of ambiguous or even morally dubious origins, as Averill is. However, he is most frequently a man of action, who fights for the downtrodden with his gun. Some critics have seen allusions to the Homeric in this character archetype—according to Lee Clark Mitchell, "the figure of the principled drifter compels an insistent fasciation that extends back to *The Odyssey*, in part by defining the freedoms that others have sacrificed for the security of civilized life."[46] Averill enters the fray only just before the second skirmish in the climactic siege of the cattlemen; the charging townspeople launch their initial attack without him. His petulant fit of drunkenness, which sidelines him during the first half of the film's climax, is brought about mostly by Champion's proposal to Ella; herein, Averill resembles a hero of classical epic: "The withdrawal of an angry hero from his people is a standard motif in both folktale and epic—a motif that presupposes, however, the angered hero's eventual appeasement and return."[47] In the *Iliad*, "Achilles remains withdrawn until Book Eighteen; most of the epic's action, then, takes place with its main hero absent."[48] Averill is drawn back into the fight after Ella begs him to return, confessing that the cattlemen have killed Champion. Like Achilles returning to the field to avenge the fallen Patroklos, Averill returns to lend his experience to the townspeople in an effort to save their community by laying siege to the surrounded, isolated cattlemen who remain.

If Averill is Cimino's Achilles figure,[49] then Champion is his Hektor (despite the double resonance with the death of Patroklos that his own demise spurs in Averill—remember, this isn't a retelling of Homer, but one that leans on similar narrative structures). The cattlemen ambush Champion's cabin in a scene that is staged in fairly close alignment with the historical record. In reality, an early morning barrage of rifle fire peppered the cabin of the historical Nate Champion and his companion, Nick Ray; one witness "estimated that a hundred shots had been fired."[50] In Cimino's version, Champion, a wayward fur trapper (Geoffrey Lewis), and Nick Ray (Mickey Rourke), are at the cabin, also in the early morning. Canton's forces descend upon the cabin, first killing the trapper, and then opening fire on the remaining two men inside. Bullets riddle the cabin, splintering its wood frame; Ray is killed, and suddenly, Champion is alone, watching the home he has built be ripped to shreds. The cattlemen attempt to smoke Champion out by crashing a blazing hay-filled wagon into its foundation. The fire catches, and Champion writes a death note as he sees the wallpaper made of newsprint, which he put up to impress Ella, burn around him. Champion bursts from the door and, guns firing wildly, is cut to pieces by Canton's forces. His body falls, twisted and bloody, into the dirt.

Champion's function in the film is to evolve morally. He works as a gunman for the WSGA from the outset of the film; the first act of violence in the film is perpetrated by Champion, when he kills a supposed cattle thief in the act of butchering a stolen heifer. However, later events demonstrate Champion is not the cold-blooded killer that Canton purports to be, when he releases a young man he catches in the act of theft. Champion is on more than one occasion upbraided for his betrayal of the community in working for the WSGA, which weighs on his conscience throughout the film. He is pushed to the breaking point by two sequential events—the first is when the WSGA's henchmen attempt to rape Ella and kill her prostitutes, which leads him to charge into Canton's tent uninvited and shoot the man responsible, who had fled the scene. In retaliation, Canton himself executes the young man whom Champion had earlier released. Canton, still unsatisfied, launches the attack on Champion's cabin in an effort to deprive the townspeople of a potentially useful ally. In the brutal rending of Champion's body by Canton's bullets, the narrative offers the vision of an unjust sacrifice. Hektor is in many ways Homer's most noble character; Achilles, in a fit of pique similar to Canton's, degrades Hektor's body after defeating him on the battlefield by dragging his corpse behind his chariot. In both instances, the mutilation of the body of an erstwhile man of honor serves to create sympathy for the fallen hero.

Heaven's Gate thus reveals not one hero, in Averill, nor another, in Champion, but two men who are heroic in different ways, but find themselves on opposing sides of a conflict (both personal, as both men want Ella, and political, as Averill aligns with the community and Champion with the WSGA, before his eventual opposition to them). This, too, is consistent with the epic form: "*Eris*—strife—between heroes, it will be recalled, was a favorite theme of epic. Looked at coldly, stripped of the dignity of their noble epic contexts, these quarrels are almost always petty."[51] Against the backdrop of the near-destruction of Johnson County and the deaths of many of its citizens, the territorial male posturing over who gets to possess Ella seems petty indeed.

The final battle between the townspeople and the mercenary invaders is likewise reminiscent of the story of Troy, both as told by Homer and in its other iterations. A wild exaggeration (but purposeful) of the historical record, the siege of the mercenaries did not end in bloody violence, as it does in the film. Cimino stages a bloodbath in two parts; the initial frenzied charge by the townspeople to the field where the mercenaries have gathered to camp follows the assassination of Champion. Ella, having driven her buggy through the assault on Champion's cabin, tells the panicked and frenetic townspeople that the invaders have arrived; en masse, they climb into their wagons and astride their horses, heading out to meet their oppressors. On the way, Cimino depicts a moment of random cruelty, when Eggleston's hard-charging wagon hits a loose stone on a bridge over a creek, and capsizes—his wife is killed, and he is injured. There is no way out for the townspeople, united in their poverty; even the land is turning against them.

What follows is a bewildering torrent of dust, gunfire, and confusion as the mercenaries circle their own wagons and horses in an effort to hold off the townspeople, who swirl around them like a tornado. As bullets connect with mercenaries and townspeople alike, it is hard not to see resonance with Homeric descriptions of violent clashes on the battlefields of Troy: "Now as these advancing came to one place and encountered, / they dashed their shields together and their spears, and the strength / of armoured men in bronze, and the shields massive in the middle / clashed against each other, and the sound grew huge of the fighting. / There the screaming and the shouts of triumph rose up together / of men killing and men killed, and the ground ran blood."[52] Throughout the film, Cimino's sound design is chaotic; in Casper, in the dance hall, and certainly on the battlefield, noise is constant. The screams of the cattlemen and the peasants swell with the thunder of hooves and wagon wheels, dotted with loud claps of gunfire of all kinds. The horror of war has come to Cimino's Johnson County in a way the historical Johnson County never could countenance.

After reaching something of a standoff, the townspeople ride off to regroup. Averill, after stopping to commune with Champion's body, joins the exhausted, wounded group of desperate men and women waiting to make their next move against the mercenaries. Averill brings the breadth of his education to bear when he advises them to use timber to create what the historical record refers to as "go-devils." Though the historical Averell was dead by the time of the invasion, using "the running gears from the invaders' supply wagons, [the townspeople] constructed a device referred to as an 'ark of safety' or a 'go-devil.' The idea was that when it was pushed forward, close to the invaders' lines, the sheriff would give the invaders a last chance to surrender, and if they refused, their own dynamite would be hurled against them."[53] In an overt classical allusion, Averill, in conversation, credits a Roman general with the idea to build the go-devils and use them against the invaders. For Averill, the Romans may be the inspiration, but in the context of the *Iliad*, it is hard not to be reminded of the creation of the Trojan Horse. To reiterate, the construction of the Horse does not appear in Homer's epic; one has to look to other stories of the Trojan War to find reference to the Horse, despite its being one of the most iconic, if not the singular story point, that most people associate with the War: "It was Odysseus who made the plan which was to lead to the fall of Troy. Under his orders the Greeks made out of wood the figure of a huge horse. The face and nostrils of the horse, its feet and hooves were beautifully carved. Its body was hollow and was of such a size that twenty armed men could hide within it."[54]

Though it is absent from the *Iliad* itself, the crucial point, which is the communal use of creative labor, is present in both *Heaven's Gate* and in stories of the sack of Troy. In order to change the military equation, each contingent must innovate. The historical Johnson County go-devil "was made of heavy logs about six feet high, and its purpose was to allow some forty men to advance on the fortifications."[55] As is depicted in the film, "At dawn the go-devil began its ponderous progression towards the invaders' lines. It was manned by fourteen men with rifles and a box of dynamite. The go-devil advanced about one hundred yards, slowly closing the short gap to the invaders' fort."[56] In the historical Johnson County War, the U.S. Cavalry rode in to rescue the invaders just before the attack could commence. Cimino's invaders are not so lucky. The film's go-devils, built seemingly with their historical antecedents in mind, advance on the invaders' position; the bullets fly, the townspeople toss live dynamite. The carnage of the previous day's battle is reignited, this time claiming more townspeople and more cattlemen. Most of the film's featured cast is killed in the chaos before the Cavalry rides in to stop it; Averill, Ella, and Bridges survive (the latter two, of course, only temporarily—Canton ambushes them just before the time jump to the 1903 epilogue, and is himself killed by Averill).

It is a slaughter of mythic proportions, in which both sides take heavy casualties. It is here, Cimino's film says, that the history of modern America was forged, not through the individual achievements of one lone heroic Westerner, but in the state-sanctioned murder of poor people by rich titans of industry. In the brutality of its violent clash between the forces of capital and labor, *Heaven's Gate* depicts the struggles of the 20th century by rehistoricizing the past as an epic conflict in which the weak never really had a chance. Ultimately, it is this lesson that Averill learns in Canton's murder of Bridges and, especially, Ella. Thinking he had saved his own life and the life of his beloved, she is snatched away by Canton's bullets. The battle is long over by the time of Canton's seemingly pointless assassination of Ella. She dies in his arms after he had apparently made up his mind to go away with her and he, in the epilogue, has retreated to his life of comfort, back to the wife he never directly mentions. In 1903, he is an older man, surrounded by markers of wealth. Averill has decided to rejoin the class he could not definitively defeat.

It is worth returning to Robin Wood's point that *Heaven's Gate* "is an epic about failure and catastrophe, both personal and national."[57] We must consider the role that failure and catastrophe play both within the film itself, on the level of its characters' ultimate defeat at the hands of the relentless forces of capital, but also outside the film; the failure of *Heaven's Gate* on the commercial and critical level at the time of its release is a major part of this film's story. Steven Bach argues that the film was a failure artistically because it failed to connect emotionally with its audience: "No one cared about Averill or Champion or Ella or the plight of the immigrants, who continued to caterwaul unintelligibly. No one cared about the magnificent photography or the majestic scenery or the authentic costumes with their authentic fabrics or the perfect settings or the meticulously re-created buggies and wagons and pushcarts or the nuances of composition or performance or editing."[58] Presumably, this lack of engagement in the story also was responsible for the film's poor box office performance, which, from the studio's perspective, certainly fit the definition of a catastrophe.

Though the film has somewhat been redeemed in the intervening years, its dominant legacy lies in the blame it accrues for the trends it played a role in arresting: the New Hollywood period and the Western as viable genre. On this level, the film's troubled production, its director, and the film itself have all entered the pantheon of myth; they are part of The History of The Movies. The central irony of the fate of Cimino's film is that for all its aspirations to rewrite the mythology of America and its relationship to the Western genre, it has been unable to transcend its own mythology as an all-consuming, cinematic black hole.

So, why did *Heaven's Gate* fail? Assuredly, from a practical perspective, the running time was an imposing hurdle over which audiences were reluctant to jump. The difficulty of the production itself was much-discussed in both Hollywood circles and in the mainstream press, which may have created enough *schadenfreude* in both critics and audiences that they were rooting for its failure. Some backlash against Cimino's meteoric rise post–*Deer Hunter* may have also played a role, especially because of the divisions that film created in the critical community.

Surely, all of these were factors. But, beyond these likely candidates, it is hard to ignore the ideological project of *Heaven's Gate*, which was entirely in contradiction to the typical expectations that audiences have for Westerns. It is not affirmational in its presentation of the idea of America and the West. It is ultimately a film about defeat, where any triumph, no matter how hard won, and how much has been sacrificed, is fleeting, and will be suddenly and violently ripped away. *Heaven's Gate* is tragic for its central characters (Champion and Ella die, Averill seems to wish he had), but their tragedy is simply a personal iteration of the destruction not of the idea of the hero, but that the American West is a place where heroes lived, fought, and triumphed. One of the most influential critics of the Western genre, Robert Warshow, in his essay "The Westerner," may have diagnosed this issue almost thirty years prior to the release and failure of Cimino's film. He says:

> when the impulse toward realism is extended into a "reinterpretation" of the West as a developed society, drawing our eyes away from the hero if only to the extent of showing him as the one dominant figure in a complex social order, then the pattern is broken and the West itself begins to be uninteresting. If the "social problems" of the frontier are to be the movie's chief concern, there is no longer any point in re-examining these problems twenty times a year; they have been solved, and the people for whom they once were real are dead. Moreover, the hero himself, still the film's central figure, now tends to become its one unassimilable element, since he is the most unreal.[59]

Warshow's diagnosis not of Cimino's film specifically, but of socially-minded Westerns whose subject is the community, and not the "Westerner" of his essay's title, is that they fail to resonate fully because the Western should affirm the strength of the singular man (and it was always a man). While Warshow's critique is predicated on the dismissal of some genre classics like Fred Zinnemann's *High Noon* (1952), it is perhaps salient when applied to a film like *Heaven's Gate*, which is willing to experiment formally in more radical ways than earlier socially-conscious Westerns.

The failure of *Heaven's Gate* may also owe to its attempt to re-mythologize the West as a place where opportunity did not flourish, but was hoarded by the powerful, backed by the bullet. The class myth that Cimino's film attempts to rewrite was not, especially at the dawn of the Reagan era, one that audiences particularly cared to hear challenged. In her 2016 book *White Trash*, Nancy Isenberg explores the absence of class discourse throughout the history of the United States dating back to the Colonial period. In it, she makes the case that

> The compression of history, the winnowing of history, may seem natural and neutral, but it is decidedly not. It is the means by which grade school history becomes our standard adult history. And so the great American saga, as taught, excludes the very pertinent fact that after the 1630s, less than half came to Massachusetts for religious reasons. The tall tales we unthinkingly absorb when young somehow remain within; the result is a narrowly conceived sense of national belonging productive of the most uncompromising of satisfying myths: "American exceptionalism." We are unique and different, and the absence of class is one of our hallmarks.[60]

These myths, including the one that suggests that in America, the class story is one of upward mobility and forever expanding opportunity, are deeply entrenched. In *Heaven's Gate*, the weak are crushed by the strong, just as they often have been in the factual history of the United States; its attempt to create a myth, through exaggerating a real-life incident into an apocalyptic battle for the soul of the country's economic future, was likely just as doomed as the poverty-stricken immigrants, cattle farmers, and small business owners who, together, charge the cattlemen's mercenary army. As in the *Iliad*, the struggle is chaotic, triumphant, brutal, and glorious; however, in both Homer's and Cimino's worlds, the superstructure of the futility of war and capital, respectively, render the individual effort pointless. Those efforts are sound and fury, signifying nothing.

Notes

1. The others would be William Friedkin's *Sorcerer* (1977), Martin Scorsese's *New York, New York* (1978), and Francis Ford Coppola's *Apocalypse Now* (1979), all of which would be troubled, expensive productions that failed to recoup their costs.
2. Steven Bach, *Final Cut: Dreams and Disaster in The Making of* Heaven's Gate (Fort Mill, SC: Quill, 1985), 239.
3. *Ibid.*, 252.
4. *Ibid.*, 361.
5. In the concluding chapters of *Easy Riders, Raging Bulls*, Scorsese says "*Heaven's Gate* undercut all of us. I knew at the time it was the end of something, that something had died." Coppola chimes in: "There was a kind of coup d'etat that happened after *Heaven's Gate*, started by Paramount. It was a time when the studios were outraged that the cost of movies was going up so rapidly, that directors were making such incredible amounts of money, and had all the control. So they took the control back." Biskind himself doesn't dispute these contentions, but says that *Heaven's Gate* itself was an expensive example of a larger trend in the relationship between studios and directors. In his telling, *Heaven's Gate* is more pretext for change than its precipitator (404).
6. John G. Cawelti, *The Six-Gun Mystique Sequel* (Bowling Green: Bowling Green State University Popular Press, 1999), 2.
7. Jim Kitses, *Horizons West: Directing The Western from John Ford to Clint Eastwood, New Edition* (London: British Film Institute, 2004), 5.
8. Quoted in Cawelti's *The Six-Gun Mystique Sequel* on page 99.
9. Robin Wood, *Hollywood From Vietnam To Reagan* (New York: Columbia University Press, 1986), 274.
10. *Ibid.*, 303.
11. *Ibid.*, 314.
12. Cawelti, 100.
13. Wood, 316.

14. Caroline Alexander, *The War That Killed Achilles: The True Story of Homer's* Iliad *and the Trojan War* (New York: Viking Press, 2009), 109.

15. Bach, in *Final Cut*, has this to say about Cimino's departure from the historical record: "there was one free use of history that was to loom more important than all the others put together, and that was the fact that the Johnson County War never happened. It was aborted before it started. History calls it a war, and it is indisputable that the Invaders' intentions were murderous; but only two men were killed (Nate Champion and his sidekick, Nick Ray or Rae) in a digressionary move on the march towards Buffalo, giving the townspeople time to mount a counteroffensive and stop the Invaders dead in their tracks about sixteen miles south of their goal. The Invaders holed up at the TA Ranch, barricaded themselves for three days, and were, as in the screenplay, 'rescued' by the cavalry" (153).

16. John W. Davis, *Wyoming Range War: The Infamous Invasion of Johnson County* (Norman, OK: University of Oklahoma Press, 2010), x.

17. All four of these characters are historical figures, but Cimino has taken liberties with their positions in the film. Kristofferson's character (spelled 'Averell' in the historical record) was not a marshal; Huppert's (actually 'Ellen') was really a madam; Walken's character was not a gunman in the hire of the Association, but Johnson County's most respected citizen; and Waterston's was formerly the local sheriff who had lost reelection and had joined the Association after leaving office. Averell and Watson, in the historical record, were accused of stealing cattle and lynched by parties still unconfirmed; Champion was killed in an assault on his cabin that plays out similarly to an action sequence in the film; Canton was not killed in the aftermath of the invasion, but died years later. All of this background, and more, can be found in John W. Davis' informative study, *Wyoming Range War: The Infamous Invasion of Johnson County*.

18. Bach, 154.

19. *Ibid.*, 142.

20. *Ibid.*, 123–4.

21. In the stark beginning to her study of the *Iliad*, Caroline Alexander establishes useful perspective on the apparent pointlessness of the war depicted in the epic: "The greatest war story ever told commemorates a war that established no boundaries, won no territory, and furthered no cause" (1).

22. Will Wright, *Sixguns & Society: A Structural Study of the Western* (Berkeley: University of California Press, 1975), 12.

23. *Ibid.*, 187.

24. Cawelti, 5.

25. Kitses, 19.

26. Robert, Warshow, "Movie Chronicle: The Westerner," in *The Immediate Experience: Movies, Comics, Theatre and Other Aspects of Popular Culture* (Cambridge, MA: Harvard University Press, 1962), 121.

27. Lee Clark Mitchell, *Westerns: Making the Man in Fiction and Film* (Chicago: University of Chicago Press, 1996), 6.

28. Richard Slotkin, *The Fatal Environment: The Myth of the Frontier in The Age of Industrialization 1800–1890* (New York: Harper Perennial, 1985), 18.

29. *Ibid.*, 24.

30. George Stevens' *Shane* (1953) is one notable example; it would be hard to find a classic Western more committed to the ideological goal of mythmaking than this film.

31. Richard Slotkin, *Gunfighter Nation: The Myth of the Frontier in Twentieth-Century America* (New York: Harper Perennial, 1992), 192–3.

32. M.I. Finley, *The World of Odysseus*, in *The New York Review of Books* (1954), 42.

33. The length of *Heaven's Gate* was a hotly contested issue during production. IMDB, for instance, has the film's running time listed at 5 hours, 25 minutes, despite no such cut ever surfacing, not even on the recent Criterion Collection Blu-ray release of the film. For a more exhaustive look at the back and forth over the film's running time in the aftermath of its disastrous premiere, as well as its reported lengths in various stages of editing, read Bach's *Final Cut*.

34. Wood, 310.

35. I use the possessive 'Cimino's edits' here as a shorthand. The film's opening credits list four(!) editors, owing to the enormity of the task of sorting through the millions of feet of film footage Cimino had accumulated during production.

36. Despite being set in Wyoming, the film was shot in Montana, the site of production for Cimino's first film as director, 1973's *Thunderbolt and Lightfoot*, starring Clint Eastwood and Jeff Bridges. According to Bach, "Cimino had selected his 'cathedral,' Glacier National Park in Montana, as his principal shooting site, an area of spectacular physical splendor, if a little remote. He had declared Wyoming 'overexposed,' not scenic enough to convey the 'poetry of America' he wanted to capture" (176). Bach's retelling makes clear that Cimino's vision of the film was epically-minded from its earliest stages.

37. From an auteurist perspective, one can see Cimino's interest in these types of images in other works—the aforementioned *Thunderbolt and Lightfoot* uses the same Montana mountains essentially to make the same point, as do some of the most iconic images in his 1978 Best Picture-winner, *The Deer Hunter*.

38. Finley, 21.

39. Homer, "Book II," in Richmond Lattimore, ed. *The Iliad* (Chicago: University of Chicago Press, 1951), 40–47.
40. Wood, 311.
41. *Ibid.*, 300.
42. Alexander, 41.
43. *Ibid.*, 42.
44. *Ibid.*, 81.
45. Bach, 179.
46. Mitchell, 26.
47. Alexander, 87.
48. *Ibid.*, 12.
49. A probably trivial, but nevertheless interesting connection with Homer's warrior hero, Averill consistently has trouble putting on and taking off one particular boot—his Achilles heel, perhaps?
50. Davis, 149.
51. Alexander, 199.
52. Homer, "Book IV," 446–51.
53. Davis, 171.
54. Rex Warner, *The Stories of the Greeks* (New York: Farrar, Strauss, and Giroux, 1967), 301.
55. Davis, 172.
56. *Ibid.*, 176.
57. Wood, 316.
58. Bach, 361.
59. Warshow, 117.
60. Nancy Isenberg, *White Trash: The 400-Year Untold History of Class in America* (London: Penguin Books, 2016), 7.

Filmography

Heaven's Gate. Dir. Michael Cimino. United Artists, 1980.
High Noon. Dir. Fred Zinnemann. United Artists, 1952.

Works Cited

Alexander, Caroline. *The War That Killed Achilles: The True Story of Homer's Iliad and the Trojan War*. New York: Viking Press, 2009.
Bach, Steven. *Final Cut: Dreams and Disaster in The Making of* Heaven's Gate. Fort Mill, SC: Quill, 1985.
Biskind, Peter. *Easy Riders, Raging Bulls: How the Sex-Drugs-and-Rock 'n' Roll Generation Saved Hollywood*. New York: Touchstone, 1998.
Cawelti, John G. *The Six-Gun Mystique Sequel*. Bowling Green: Bowling Green State University Popular Press, 1999.
Davis, John W. *Wyoming Range War: The Infamous Invasion of Johnson County*. Norman: University of Oklahoma Press, 2010.
Finley, M.I. *The World of Odysseus*. In *The New York Review of Books*, 1954. At http://www.nybooks.com/media/doc/2010/02/23/world-of-odysseus-introduction.pdf.
Homer. *The Iliad of Homer*, Richmond Lattimore, ed. Chicago: University of Chicago Press, 1951.
Isenberg, Nancy. *White Trash: The 400-Year Untold History of Class in America*. London: Penguin Books, 2016.
Kitses, Jim. *Horizons West: Directing The Western from John Ford to Clint Eastwood, New Edition*. London: British Film Institute, 2004.
Mitchell, Lee Clark. *Westerns: Making the Man in Fiction and Film*. Chicago: University of Chicago Press, 1996.
Slotkin, Richard. *The Fatal Environment: The Myth of the Frontier in The Age of Industrialization 1800–1890*. New York: Harper Perennial, 1985.
_____. *Gunfighter Nation: The Myth of the Frontier in Twentieth-Century America*. New York: Harper Perennial, 1992.
Warner, Rex. *The Stories of the Greeks*. New York: Farrar, Strauss, and Giroux, 1967.
Warshow, Robert. "Movie Chronicle: The Westerner." In *The Immediate Experience: Movies, Comics, Theatre and Other Aspects of Popular Culture*, 105–124. Cambridge, MA: Harvard University Press, 1962.
Wood, Robin. *Hollywood From Vietnam To Reagan*. New York: Columbia University Press, 1986.
Wright, Will. *Sixguns & Society: A Structural Study of the Western*. Berkeley: University of California Press, 1975.

Catastrophe

Jeremiah Johnson: Where you headed?
Del Gue: Same place you are, Jeremiah: hell, in
  the end.

   —*Jeremiah Johnson* (Sydney Pollack, 1972)

Gunsmoke's Boot Hill and the Classical Underworld

Jim Daems

When the television series *Gunsmoke* suddenly came to the end of its twenty-year run in 1975, Cecil Smith wrote in the *Los Angeles Times* that

> *Gunsmoke* was the dramatization of the American epic legend of the west. Our own *Iliad* and *Odyssey*, created from standard elements of the dime novel and the pulp western as romanticized by Buntline, Harte, and Twain. It was ever the stuff of legend.[1]

Confirming Smith's appraisal, the series draws on a number of epic conventions in its portrayal of U.S. Marshall Matt Dillon's (James Arness) quest to bring law to the frontier town of Dodge, and in this way the series represents one of the key aspects of the "legend of the west." In his discussion of Mikael Bakhtin's analysis of the epic genre and how that can be used to read the genre's conventions in the western, Colin Irvine focuses on Bakhtin's three key components of epic: "national epic past," "national tradition," and "epic distance." For Irvine, the Western's "national epic past" is the period of westward expansion, which can be viewed historically in relation to both the notion of Manifest Destiny and Frederick Jackson Turner's Frontier Thesis. The role of "national tradition" in the Western is, for Irvine, a foundational story told by Americans for Americans in which the hero stands as the personification of the emerging values and ideals associated with the "national tradition." And, finally, the "epic distance" Bakhtin describes resembles the "temporal, interpretive situation established at the outset of many Westerns."[2]

Gunsmoke's portrayal of western expansion relies on three components of the epic genre: epic as a martial genre, epic as a foundational narrative of nationhood (*translatio*), and the conventions of epic heroism. In the broadest sense, the epic as a genre portrays the violent struggle, conducted in the "national epic past," to found a nation or empire by establishing and maintaining its "national tradition," often represented as a binary of "civilized" values against "barbarism." This struggle is exclusive in that what is defined as "barbaric" is either destroyed or defeated and incorporated into the national or imperial vision. The vehicle for this struggle is the epic hero, the representative carrier of the "national tradition's" "civilized" social values. In *Gunsmoke*, the martial component of the epic tradition is evident on two important levels. First, the presence of Fort Dodge near the frontier town allows for the portrayal of the larger martial conflict between the U.S. Cavalry and the "Indians." This conflict occasionally impinges on the more significant conflict of the series' plot lines—Marshall Dillon's verbal and physical confrontations with threats to social order in and around Dodge. In this way, Dillon is a carrier of "civilized" values which must be established on the frontier in order to enable further westward expansion of the nation. He displays certain characteristics of epic heroes in these conflicts, particularly in regards to Smith's allusion to Homer's epics, those of Odysseus. Dillon is quick with a gun, but this is generally his last resort. Whether the conflict of an episode results in a shootout, or if Dillon can resolve the conflict by convincing the offender to leave Dodge peacefully, he often employs a cunning comparable to the ever "resourceful" Odysseus. In addition, Dillon shares some characteristics of Virgil's Aeneas, particularly in his devotion to public office as a U.S. Marshall which is most notable in his relationship with Kitty (Amanda Blake). There is also one more significant link between Dillon and Homer's and Virgil's epic heroes. Both Odysseus and Aeneas make journeys to the underworld (*katabases*) in order to learn information of importance to their individual quests. Dillon figuratively journeys to the underworld in the Boot Hill opening sequence of the first few seasons of *Gunsmoke*.

In both *The Odyssey* and *The Aeneid*, the journey to the underworld is a key to the quest that Odysseus and Aeneas pursue: Odysseus seeks Tiresias and Aeneas seeks his father. Both are provided with information to complete their quests. For Odysseus, the journey to the underworld to speak with the prophet Tiresias provides important information for him to find his "way home" for Aeneas, passing through the darker underworld "[t]o places of delight, to green park land, / Where souls take ease amid the Blessed Grove" to meet his father, Anchises, realigns him with his founding destiny.[3] Both search for a place to settle—Odysseus seeks to return to a place that already exists, while Aeneas seeks a place that must be created. Peter Jones notes that Odysseus' underworld journey "emphasises [sic] the bravery and daring of Odysseus in making the descent [...]: the descent elevates him above ordinary humanity."[4] Odysseus' descent demonstrates the prevalent theme of justice in Homer's epic, while depicting "a world of failure and success, of excellence and of error, of good and bad judgement, which has had unalterable consequences for the lives of the dead."[5] This is also evident in Virgil's *Aeneid*—those that Aeneas meets in the underworld are there "not without a judge, or jurymen."[6] Matt Dillon's journeys to Boot Hill provide similar insights. They are key reminders of his quest for justice in Dodge, regenerative moments to continue doing his "job" amongst the "useless killing."[7]

Boot Hill closely parallels the development of Dodge—as Dodge grows, so too does Boot Hill, where there are "always new graves, new names" ("Professor Lute Bone"). Dillon's role in this expansion prompts him to ponder, "[w]ho'll be here tomorrow?" ("Reunion '78"). In contrast to Dodge, where life goes on "full blast" ("Helping Hand"), Boot Hill is a city of the dead, populated by those that westward expansion leaves behind, excluded from "civilization" either because of their behavior, their mistakes, or a combination of both. These people are too "bad," as Dillon often refers to them in his Boot Hill monologues, to exist even in the "Gomorrah of the Plains" ("Matt Gets It"). The separation of these two sites, Boot Hill and Dodge (occasionally shown visually during Dillon's monologues), is significant. Discussing the Western genre in general, John G. Cawelti argues,

> The open prairie around the town serves not only as a haven of lawlessness and savagery, but as a backdrop of epic magnitude and even, at times, a source of regenerating power. This characteristic setting reflects and helps dramatize the tripartite division of characters that dominates the Western pattern of action. The townspeople hover defensively in their settlement, threatened by the outlaws or Indians who are associated with the inhospitable and

uncontrollable elements of the surrounding landscape. The townspeople are static and largely incapable of movement beyond their little settlement. The outlaws or savages can move freely across the landscape. The hero, though a friend of the townspeople, has the lawless power of movement in that he, like the savages, is a horseman and possesses skills of wilderness existence.[8]

While Dodge is at a stage of development where some limited movement is afforded the townspeople, Cawelti's tripartite division in spatial terms is important when critically examining the narrative and ideological function of Dillon's Boot Hill monologues in *Gunsmoke*. This is particularly significant when considering Cawelti's point about the hero's intermediary position between townspeople and outlaws / "savages" in relation to his ability to successfully traverse a dangerous transgressive space and return to the settlement. In *Gunsmoke*, Dillon is figuratively an intermediary between the living and the dead by crossing that space to Boot Hill. As in Homer and Virgil, these epic journeys to the land of the dead regenerate and reaffirm the "national tradition" while elevating Dillon "above ordinary humanity."[9]

The first season of the series (1955–6) ably demonstrates the epic components noted above. Whereas the Boot Hill opening scene gradually drops off in subsequent seasons, twenty-eight of the first season's thirty-nine episodes begin with Dillon on Boot Hill (this in contrast, for example, to the fourth season's eight monologues in thirty-nine episodes). The Boot Hill setting of Dillon's opening monologues is important on a number of levels. First, Boot Hill is, of course, where strangers who have transgressed the law are buried outside of the town. It is a place of exclusion from the community—from Dodge, but more largely from the "national tradition's" values and ideals of westward expansion. These men usually "died with their boots on"—violently. As Dillon states,

> Out here I remind myself how violence ends. Buried on the rim of a nation, the edge of a wild frontier. Some of these Boot Hill men are the victims of aimless slaughter. The rest I killed myself. [...] The law comes hard to the frontier ["Hack Prine"].

Being buried on Boot Hill, then, deprives gunfighters of the "glory" and reputation which drives them to eventually confront Dillon in any given episode—a sort of inversion of the central ideals of the classical notion of heroism—as many of the grave markers in the cemetery are inscribed only with the year of the individual's death.

Reputation only exists through memory, and memory is a key element of Dillon's Boot Hill monologues. These interior monologues are not only Dillon's recollections of his role as Marshall; they can also be seen as a sort of collective memory of "taming the West." He demonstrates Cawelti's point that the hero of a western "has internalized the conflict between savagery and civilization."[10] Boot Hill, Dillon tells us, affords a place of "quiet thinking" amongst his "customers" ("Reunion '78"), who, paradoxically, "drew their last breath while life was going full blast in Dodge" ("Helping Hand"). Dillon's quiet time on Boot Hill allows him to reflect on his role in Dodge and the larger frontier narrative of "progress." On Boot Hill, he "remind[s] himself" ("Hack Prine"): "a reason I walk out here to Boot Hill [...is to] remind me it's a day-to-day job to keep people alive" ("The Pest Hole"). Contrasting also with the debased "glory" and reputation sought by the gunfighters that Dillon has put in Boot Hill, Dillon's interior monologues remove any similar pursuit on his part—for him, there is no glory in killing. Killing for Dillon is a last resort, part of his "job" "to keep them from a useless, violent end" ("Reed Survives"). It is a "chancy," "lonely" occupation, "But somebody has to do it"

("Hack Prine"). There is no hubris here on Dillon's part, only a reluctance: "no man's life is worthless, yet the killing goes on […] as the frontier grows west" ("Yorky"). Dillon's personal reluctance and humility in regards to the violence his "job" forces him to commit has larger implications. First, it prompts the viewer to identify with the series' hero by recognizing that, although it "never bother[s] me killing a man whose very presence is an offense to decent people" ("The Killer"), it is just part of the "job" in the service of "civilizing" Dodge and ultimately the expanding western frontier. This identification is one of empathy.

The series furthers this empathetic identification in Dillon's relationship with Kitty. The portrayal of Dillon and his occupation can be fruitfully examined through Kimberly K. Bell's comment on how Virgil portrays Aeneas in *The Aeneid*. Bell states that Virgil "emphasizes his hero's duty in carrying on the tradition of his *patria*, placing greater emphasis on his hero's fulfilment of his public destiny and downplaying his personal glory."[11] Most straightforwardly, one might argue that Dillon's reticence to pursue a relationship with Kitty follows from the daily dangers of his job. On one level, his Boot Hill monologues are reflections on his own mortality: "the process of putting bodies into the ground reminds us of what it is the hero risks and the in the process reveals a key distinction between his sometimes deathlike mask and the actual fact of death itself."[12] But, read through an epic lens, Dillon's "public destiny" is the prime motive for his selfless pursuit of justice—as cited earlier, Dillon calls it a "chancy," "lonely" job and one in which a man has "few friends" ("Word of Honor") in his Boot Hill monologues. This is the epic genre's *translatio studii et imperii*. In the *Aeneid*,

> *translatio* functions through his [Virgil's] hero Aeneas, who serves as the vehicle for transmitting the culture of Troy to Rome. In using the *translatio* topos, Virgil draws certain parallels between his fictional hero and the *princeps* Augustus, transforming his Greek sources to achieve one of his many political aims—constructing a national identity for Rome as glorious and ancient as that of Greece.[13]

In *Gunsmoke*, Matt is the "vehicle for transmitting the culture" of the more "civilized eastern United States, itself a *translatio* of Old World, European concepts" such as classical Greek democracy, into the "wild" frontier. Like Aeneas, Dillon cannot be distracted from this—Aeneas remaining with Dido and Dillon marrying Kitty would be to place the personal over the public / political destiny of the individual and the nation. For the American western legend, the consequences of this are played out in Fred Zinnemann's *High Noon* (1952). In terms of 1950s American politics, it is worth recalling that John Wayne, who detested *High Noon* as "un-American," was offered the role of Matt Dillon, and introduced the first episode of *Gunsmoke* in 1955. Wayne, of course, would go on to star in Howard Hawkes' deliberate rebuttal of Zinnemann's film, *Rio Bravo* (1959).[14] The hero of the American Western cannot be distracted from his public destiny and the values he embodies.

The emotional self-restraint demonstrated in Dillon's relationship with Kitty is a key component of his personality, even in his public role. This is evident in the Boot Hill monologue of the series' first episode, "Matt Gets It":

> I try to remember that if they'd argued a little, they might not be here [Boot Hill]. Arguing doesn't fill any graves. Take me, I'm a U.S. Marshall. How many times I'd rather have argued than gone for guns. Take Dodge City over there—the Gomorrah of the Plains they call it. A jump off spot, people coming and going all the time: good, bad, and worse. Tempers high. A man will draw his gun quicker to prove a point than he'll draw on his logic. That's where I

come in, whether they like it or not. When they draw their gun, somebody's got to be around. Somebody on the law side. Lord knows they hate that.

The monologue recalls points that I have already made, but are worth reviewing in relation to Dillon's self-restraint and the series' premiere. That Dodge is the "Gomorrah of the Plains" highlights the lawless nature of the frontier and the necessity of Dillon's job as a U.S. Marshall to combat lawlessness. It also marks out Dodge, figuratively, as a "jump[ing] off spot" for westward expansion (a point we will return to shortly). The series, then, portrays a sort of "Genesis" of the West—a foundational narrative in the nation's "epic past." We learn of Dillon's reluctance to resort to his gun to keep the law in Dodge, and his preference for a logical, and ultimately peaceful resolution of conflict. In addition, Dillon's preference to "draw" on his logic rather than to draw his gun makes him a cunning opponent like Odysseus. The plot of the first episode closely illustrates the "moral" of the monologue. Dan, a gunslinger, comes to Dodge and kills a couple of men before confronting Dillon. Dillon loses their first gunfight, but once he recovers from his wound, he "draws" on his logic to reflect on and observe Dan's behavior. This allows Dillon to kill Dan in their next confrontation because he knows that the man is fast, but inaccurate, and must, therefore, be in close proximity when he draws his gun in order to hit his target. The impetuousness of those buried on Boot Hill, such as Dan, is a frequent point in Dillon's monologues and stands in sharp contrast to this personality trait. Dillon's emotional self-restraint, then, in his personal relationship with Kitty and in his job are commensurate with his "public destiny."

But the consequences of the viewers' empathic identification with Dillon is ideologically problematic. If we recall Berthold Brecht's critique of "classic" theater, empathy draws viewers into seeing the events portrayed through a specific worldview. More specifically for Brecht, empathy forces proletarians to see their oppression as necessary or "natural" by enforcing the bourgeoisie's worldview on them. Thus, within the "temporal, interpretive situation" that the opening Boot Hill monologues provide,[15] thereby establishing "epic distance," the destruction of both "outlaws" and "savages" is justified as necessary for the larger goal to establish the nation from coast-to-coast. It is, essentially, a justification of the national, imperial, providential, and civilizing mission of Manifest Destiny. That vision is evident in the title sequence of the series' early seasons. With the opening suspenseful notes of *Gunsmoke*'s theme song, our focus is on Dillon's holstered gun. The camera angle looks up at him, making him somewhat larger. As he proceeds down the street, the cross on top of a church emerges and finally his black-clad opponent, before Dillon draws and shoots. Symbolically, the title sequence reaffirms the values and ideals of the "national tradition"—"justice" triumphs and is divinely sanctioned. Although religion plays a very negligible part, at least explicitly, in the series, that Dillon faces the church and the bad guy has his back to it marks the Marshall as on God's side, serving a transcendent notion of "justice" and other values that we can loosely associate with Manifest Destiny.

While Dillon is aligned with those values, this is not to deny that he is sympathetic to those who suffered the most from westward expansion: the Indigenous peoples. For example, he recognizes the consequences for Indigenous peoples of the slaughter of the buffalo herds by white hunters and infringements into "Indian territory." Boot Hill is, in itself, significant in this regard. Andrew Howe notes of cemeteries in the genre that, "The Western's obsession with this narrative trope reminds its viewers of the price of Manifest Destiny."[16] Boot Hill, and cemeteries in general in Westerns, are, as I have argued earlier, not only exclusive in terms of separating the "good" and the "bad," but also racially exclusive—white, Christian people are buried there, not the Indigenous. In a sense, the individual death of an Indigenous person is not acknowledged within the confines of "civilized," white society, and, analogously, neither is the death of entire Indigenous nations and their cultures.

In light of this, it is important here to examine two episodes from *Gunsmoke*'s first season that focus on Indigenous people. In his Boot Hill monologue in "The Hunter," Dillon states,

> Law comes hard to a young country, and especially out here on the frontier. I know just how hard. I'm Matt Dillon, U.S. Marshall, out of Dodge City. It's a roaring town filled to overflowing with cowmen, gamblers, buffalo hunters, killers. This is Boot Hill. There aren't many tears lost for these men lying here, not back there in Dodge. Most men can look at the result of their job and say, "I did that pretty well. Best I knew how." And they'd be proud of their handiwork. But not me, because part of this is my handiwork. I put some of these men here. I take no pride in killing. It's just that sometimes it's a part of my job. A job that has to be done.

The familiar reluctance towards violence of the monologues is here, as is the notion of westward expansion. In the episode, Dillon attempts to prevent Murdoch, a buffalo hunter whom he has had a violent run-in with in the past, from entering "Indian territory," which would be a breach of treaty and exacerbate "Indian trouble." Dillon tells Murdoch at one point that, with the expansion of the frontier, "times have changed" and that there have been "no buffalo around Dodge for three years." Similarly, when Dillon attempts to persuade Murdoch's skinner, Golden Calf, who we later learn is Murdoch's son from a relationship with an Indigenous woman, he comments on the devastating consequences of the buffalo hunt—"meat left to rot on the prairie," resulting in starvation for the Indigenous peoples. Golden Calf's complicity in Murdoch's hunt, Dillon tells him, is "robbing" from his "brothers." But, Dillon's and Murdoch's diametrically opposed attitudes are illustrative of one of the significant ideological functions of the Boot Hill monologues. First, Dillon's reluctance to kill unless he absolutely has to is contrasted with Murdoch's role as a buffalo hunter. Murdoch, Dillon states, "likes to kill." Echoing the monologue, Murdoch takes "pride" in his "handiwork." The episode, then, juxtaposes Dillon's sympathetic statements and, as always, his vision of "justice," with Murdoch's egotistic and materialistic drive. Again, as the viewer is meant to identify empathetically with the Marshall, all of the nation's genocidal complicity is forced onto Murdoch.

"Prairie Happy," however, is more complex in how it accomplishes this ideological move. Dillon's Boot Hill monologue reads,

> When a man gets so scared he stops thinking and goes into a panic, the chances are he'll get himself killed fast. That's a bad thing to watch. But when a whole town full of people take fright and start milling around ready to stampede, that really scares you. What can one lawman do against a couple hundred armed citizens about to cut lose and start blasting anything that moves? It's no easy job, and I sure wish it wasn't mine. Matt Dillon, U.S. Marshall.

Once again, the familiar reluctance is expressed about his "job." The contrast between logic and emotion in the "Matt Gets It" Boot Hill monologue is also repeated—Dillon will have to rely on logic and resourcefulness to persuade the panicked citizens of Dodge in order to allow "justice" to triumph. This episode turns on rumors of an imminent Pawnee attack on the town. Familiar negative stereotypes of Indigenous peoples are voiced by the townspeople: "blood thirsty," "red devils," "savages," and the recounting of atrocity tales. Mr. Jonas, head of the town's "defense committee," blames the "government's milk and water" policies towards the "savages" that allows them to continue to exist as a threat to Dodge, policies which, in "The Hunter," Dillon had praised for providing food and shelter for the Indigenous peoples. Jonas' attitude is later explicitly challenged by Dillon when the Marshall states that he is unclear whether Jonas' intentions are to defend the town or "exterminate Indians." But the source of the rumor adds an interesting aspect. The Pawnee attack rumor is started, and developed, by an old man named Tewksbury, who, we later learn, has lived for many years with the Pawnee as "Lost Warrior." The old man wishes to die like a "warrior," and after unsuccessfully trying to incite the Pawnee to attack Dodge, attempts to incite the people of Dodge to attack the Pawnee. When Tewksbury's plot is discovered, Jonas incites a lynch mob to hang the old man. This is prevented only by the arrival of Tewksbury's Pawnee daughter who gives him "strong medicine" to permit him to die without shame. Similar, then, to Murdoch's in "The Hunter," Dillon's attitude is contrasted with the racism of the townspeople (but not entirely unproblematically because he comments that Tewksbury / Lost Warrior "doesn't belong to either side"). That contrast is strongest when Dillon tells Jonas that he can, because of Tewksbury's suicide, live without the "shame" of being responsible for a racially motivated lynching. Again, the viewers' empathetic identification with Dillon separates them from the racism and violence of Jonas and the citizens of Dodge, and, in particular, with the notion of "exterminating Indians." This despite the fact that the episode arguably ends up revealing the "savagery" at the heart of the "civilized" in the violence that Jonas represents much more so than the egotistical representation of Murdoch in "The Hunter."

Dillon's Boot Hill monologues, although generally focusing on the outlaws he has had to kill, can also be read as nostalgic recollections of the Indigenous peoples that the expanding frontier has eliminated out of "necessity"—an historical hindsight that a nation's guilty conscience constructs into images of "noble savages," seen in the representation of Indigenous peoples and characters in the series, such as Golden Calf in "The Hunter" and Tewksbury's / Lost Warrior's daughter in "Prairie Happy." Hence, Dillon's visits to the land of the dead take on a nostalgic coloring while reaffirming the social values that must be established on the frontier in order to "civilize" it beyond the destruction of individually "bad" people through to the destruction of Indigenous cultures: "bad" people "exterminate Indians," and then Dillon brings the "bad" people to justice. In this way, the *mise-en-scène* of the Boot Hill opening includes another significant element relating to memory, necessity, and "epic distance." The grave markers that are legible are historically "realistic" (the most recent marker I have noticed is dated "1882") in that they set the series in Dodge's heyday as the "Gomorrah of the Plains," located on the Santa Fe Trail, the Great Western Cattle Trail, and post–"Indian Wars" (Fort Dodge closed in 1882). On a mythic, epic level, the "1882" grave marker sets the series within the "epic past" that Irvine argues develops from Owen Wister's paradigmatic Western text, *The Virginian* (1902)—1874–1890. As Cawelti notes, this is a

> relatively brief stage in the social evolution of the West when outlaws or Indians posed a threat to the community's stability [and] has been erected into a timeless epic moment when heroic individual defenders of law and order stand poised against the threat of lawlessness or savagery.[17]

This is, for America, *the* "epic moment when the frontier passed from the old way of life into the present"[18]—the founding of modern America; both its "useless" and necessary killing done and buried in 1882.

The Boot Hill monologues, then, provide a "temporal, interpretive" lens and a moralizing introduction to the individual episodes in which they occur. They do more than simply justify Dillon's use of violence, as an individual representative of the law. Through the audience's empathetic identification with the Marshall, they critique and justify the violence required for "civilized" values to defeat "barbarism." This is the supposedly "natural" course of westward expansion—and, as Dillon often includes in his Boot Hill monologues, his reluctance to resort to violence ultimately points to the necessity of the larger consequences of America's epic westward expansion.

Notes

1. Cecil Smith, "Legend Goes Down The Tubes," *Los Angeles Times*, September 1, 1975, 39.
2. Colin Irvine, "The Popular Western as Epic: A Bakhtinian Understanding of Time in the American West(ern)," *Journal of the West* Vol. 45, No. 1 (Winter 2006): 79.
3. Virgil, *Aeneid*, trans. Robert Fitzgerald (New York: Vintage Classics, 1990), 10. 484; VI. 854–5.
4. Peter Jones, *Homer's Odyssey: A Commentary Based on the Translation of Richard Lattimore* (London: Bristol Classical Press, 2005. London: Bristol Classical Press, 2005), 100.
5. *Ibid.*
6. Virgil, 6. 581.
7. See "General Parcley Smith."
8. John G. Cawelti, *The Six-Gun Mystique Sequel* (Bowling Green, OH: Bowling Green State University Popular Press, 1999), 24.
9. Jones, 100.
10. Cawelti, 30.
11. Kimberly K. Bell, "*Translatio* and the Constructs of a Roman Nation in Virgil's *Aeneid*," *Rocky Mountain Review* (Spring 2008): 14.
12. Lee Clark Mitchell, "Violence in the Film Western," in J. David Slocum, ed. *Violence and American Cinema* (New York: Routledge, 2001), 185.
13. Bell, 11.
14. Louis Gianetti, "Fred Zinnemann's *High Noon*," *Film Criticism* Vol. 1, No. 3 (Winter 1976–7): 4.
15. Irvine, 79.
16. Andrew Howe, "Burying the Past: Cemeteries, Burials and Remembrance in the Western," in Sue Matheson, ed. *A Fistful of Icons: Essays on Frontier Fixtures of the American Western* (Jefferson, N.C.: McFarland, 2017), 257.
17. Cawelti, 45.
18. *Ibid.*, 49.

Filmography

"General Parcley Smith." *Gunsmoke: First Season*. Original airdate: Dec. 10, 1955. CBS, 2007. DVD.
"Hack Prine." *Gunsmoke: First Season*. Original airdate: May 12, 1956. CBS, 2007. DVD.
"Helping Hand." *Gunsmoke: First Season*. Original airdate: Mar. 17, 1956. CBS, 2007. DVD.
"The Hunter." *Gunsmoke: First Season*. Original airdate: Nov. 26, 1955. CBS, 2007. DVD.
"The Killer." *Gunsmoke: First Season*. Original airdate: May 26, 1956. CBS, 2007. DVD.
"Matt Gets It." *Gunsmoke: First Season*. Original airdate: Sept. 10, 1955. CBS, 2007. DVD.
"Pest Hole, The." *Gunsmoke: First Season*. Original airdate: Apr. 14, 1956. CBS, 2007. DVD.
"Prairie Happy." *Gunsmoke: First Season*. Original airdate: July 7, 1956. CBS, 2007. DVD.
"Professor Lute Bone." *Gunsmoke: First Season*. Original airdate: Jan. 7, 1956. CBS, 2007. DVD.
"Reed Survives." *Gunsmoke: First Season*. Original airdate: Dec. 31, 1955.
"Reunion '78." *Gunsmoke: First Season*. Original airdate: Mar. 3, 1956. CBS, 2007. DVD.
"Word of Honor." *Gunsmoke: First Season*. Original airdate: Oct. 1, 1955. CBS, 2007. DVD.
"Yorky." *Gunsmoke: First Season*. Original airdate: Feb. 18, 1956. CBS, 2007. DVD.

Works Cited

Bell, Kimberly K. "*Translatio* and the Constructs of a Roman Nation in Virgil's *Aeneid*." *Rocky Mountain Review* (Spring 2008): 11–24.
Cawelti, John G. *The Six-Gun Mystique Sequel*. Bowling Green, OH: Bowling Green State University Popular Press, 1999.
Gianetti, Louis. "Fred Zinnemann's *High Noon*." *Film Criticism* Vol. 1, No. 3 (Winter 1976-7): 2–12.
Homer. *The Odyssey of Homer*. Trans. Richard Lattimore. New York: Perennial Classics, 1999.
Howe, Andrew. "Burying the Past: Cemeteries, Burials and Remembrance in the Western." In Sue Matheson, ed. *A Fistful of Icons: Essays on Frontier Fixtures of the American Western*, 257-70. Jefferson, NC: McFarland, 2017.
Irvine, Colin. "The Popular Western as Epic: A Bakhtinian Understanding of Time in the American West(ern)." *Journal of the West* Vol. 45, No. 1 (Winter 2006): 74–81.
Jones, Peter. *Homer's Odyssey: A Commentary Based on the Translation of Richard Lattimore*. London: Bristol Classical Press, 2005.
Mitchell, Lee Clark. "Violence in the Film Western." In J. David Slocum, ed. *Violence and American Cinema*, 176–91. New York: Routledge, 2001.
Smith, Cecil. "Legend Goes Down The Tubes." *Los Angeles Times*. September 1, 1975, 39.
Virgil. *The Aeneid*, trans. Robert Fitzgerald. New York: Vintage Classics, 1990.

Orpheus on the Frontier
Slow West

Cynthia J. Miller

For purists, John McClean's *Slow West* (2015) is a flawed Western. The New Zealand landscape is somehow "off," the characters are unsatisfying, and the ties that bind them absurd. Yet for all its flaws, the film very successfully presents a merging of the frontier tale and the classic quest narrative. The two combine to create a visually stunning, surrealist Western that contorts, comments on, and ultimately conforms to the essence of the genre. McClean's film is a vision of the West—a particular, perhaps "outsider," vision—that speaks to the romance and tragedy for which both the frontier and the quest are known, yet it does so in such a way that the nature of both must be continually reconsidered. Set in 1870, the film tells the story of Jay Cavendish (Kodi Smit-McPhee), a Scottish boy, no more than sixteen, who has traveled to America in search of his lost love, Rose Ross (Caren Pistorius). Rose and her father (Rory McCann) fled Scotland after a confrontation over her relationship with Jay resulted in a tragic accident that left Jay's uncle—a Lord—dead. Early in the story, the foolhardiness of his quest is easily apparent, as Jay—pale, naïve, and armed only with a six-shooter and the strength of his convictions—is accosted by Indian hunters. He is rescued from the unsavory characters by Silas Selleck (Michael Fassbender), a bounty hunter who quickly establishes himself as equally dangerous, though more palatable. The young Jay employs Silas to escort him safely through the wilderness, and the pair sets off. It is a tale for the ages: a hero embarks on a perilous journey to strange lands in order to be reunited with his one true love.

But McClean complicates the trajectory of the characters' quest with a larger struggle—by overlaying Joseph Campbell's heroic monomyth with the myth of the frontier—calling into question both the nature of the hero and the idealism of their journey. As the characters' fates become intertwined, the magical and the real collide with tragic results. We witness the death of the hero—and with him, the death of the glory of adventure, the idealism of innocence, and the hopefulness of the frontier—or do we? In this essay, I argue that perhaps we do not; that we simply need to adjust our gaze to look for a deeper, more complex rendering of the monomyth. As we explore the confluence of the myth of the frontier and the classic myths of antiquity through Jay and Silas's quest, we will examine the ways in which the elements of their journey disrupt the typical frontier narrative, illustrating that the reality of the West is, indeed, a contested thing, while at the same time, fulfilling an ages old tradition begun by Orpheus, Odysseus, and others.

Mythic frontiers and underworlds find their parallels and legacies in *Slow West* as we follow Jay and Silas through trials, surreal encounters with men and monsters, ecstasy, and tragedy that rivals any saga of the ancient world as they "descend" into the depths of the wilderness.

Jay Cavendish (Kodi Smit-McPhee, left) sets out on his quest as an icon of Civilization; Silas (Michael Fassbender) embodies the frontier Wilderness. *Slow West* (Lionsgate, 2015).

The Hero's Journey

> Whosoever desires to explore The Way—
> Let them set out—for what more is there to say?[1]

These tales, along with many others of the world's most enduring myths and legends, converge on heroes and their exploits. Epic tales of battles with men and monsters, timeless romance, and the perils and wonders of far-off places have given poetic expression to human existence in narratives ranging from classics such as Theseus battling the fearsome Minotaur to the more contemporary Luke Skywalker saving the imperiled Princess Leia and, of course, here in McClean's West, through Jay's attempt to reunite with his one true love. The key elements and patterns of these myths have been extensively studied across disciplines, by scholars such as anthropologist Lord Raglan, psychoanalyst Otto Rank, philologist David Adams Leeming, and of course, mythologist Joseph Campbell. Campbell's seminal *The Hero with a Thousand Faces*, published in the mid–20th century, still serves as touchstone for scholars, authors, and filmmakers alike, mapping the trajectory of the hero's journey and establishing the monomyth as a template for analyzing heroic tales.[2] Campbell's analysis describes the hero's journey as a succession of eight stages punctuated by trials and transformations that occurred in both the known and unknown worlds. In short:

> A hero ventures forth from the world of common day into a region of supernatural wonder: fabulous forces are there encountered and a decisive victory is won: the hero comes back from this mysterious adventure with the power to bestow boons on his fellow man.[3]

This sequence is echoed in countless Western narratives, as well, where, in accordance with genre conventions, the hero is taken out of society, acquires valuable knowledge through undergoing trials, and returns to bring the benefits of that knowledge back to society.[4]

The elements of Campbell's template are in flux from one tale to the next, and vary with culture, historical moment, and the saga's message, but at its core, it illustrates the trajectory of the ordinary individual who struggles to move beyond his (or her) personal, local, and historical limitations and through that struggle, is transformed into a figure that is universal. Such transformation teaches both personal and wider moral lessons and fills listeners and readers with inspiration and the hope that they, too, may transcend and transform.

Thus, the hero's journey, as elaborated by Campbell and others, may be read as a process of becoming, and Jay's journey in *Slow West* is no exception. Early in the tale, he meets Silas, who takes on the role of his protector and mentor (in Campbell's mythical worlds, his magical guide). Jay is, and for the whole of the film continues to be, what Silas terms "a jackrabbit in a den of wolves." As the two make their way across the frontier landscape, Jay continually learns the ways of men, nature, and the American West—lessons of caution, discernment, acceptance; how good it feels to innovate, how bad it feels to be hungover—and he learns firsthand about the violence that has come to characterize (particularly) masculinity in the West. In flashback, as well as during his journey, Jay clings to his idealized imaginings of Rose, life in the new world, and human nature, but circumstances—and Silas—force him to change and grow. At the film's opening, Jay lies on his bedroll in the woods, gazing at the night sky and tracing the constellations: "Pegasus … the Great Bear … the Dragon…. Andromeda…." Childlike, he pretends to shoot at the stars of Orion's belt. Before long, though, he would use that same gun to shoot a stranger in the back.

This shift echoes classic considerations of the Western genre, elaborated in various ways by scholars such as John Cawelti, Jim Kitses, Elise Marubbio, Noël Carroll, and others, in which the frontier wilderness carries a particular symbolic and cultural meaning. As a fairly "stable" genre, the Western seems to lend itself to the defining of narrative codes and conventions, even in the midst of its diversity of form.[5] Here, Kitses outlines an extensive set of binary oppositions the contrast the Wilderness with Civilization. The former is characterized through tropes of freedom, self-knowledge, experience, pragmatism, savagery and a clinging to the past, while the latter stands in opposition, expressed by tropes of restriction, illusion, textual knowledge, idealism, refinement, and an orientation toward the future.[6] This scaffolding of symbolism is central to American national identity and frontier mythology, and can clearly be seen playing out in the characters of Jay and Silas, both individually and in relation. Jay Cavendish, "son of Lady Cavendish," sets out on his quest as an icon of Civilization, while Silas is the embodiment of frontier Wilderness—plainspoken, independent, dangerous.

Along their journey, Jay posits that Silas needs his help, observing that he is a "lonely, lonely man." When Silas brushes off his comments, Jay continues to press him, and the philosophical and practical collide:

SILAS: No need to concern over me.
JAY: All I'm saying is that there's more to life than just surviving.
SILAS: Yeah, there's dyin.'

While Silas grounds his existence in the practicalities of "knowing when to take a beating and when to strike," the idealistic young Jay aims his six-shooter, literally and figuratively, at the stars, elevating the realities of his day-to-day life to an existential level seen by Silas as both foolhardy and perilous. The fates of both these characters at the film's end complicates their argument in this scene, along with the tension between East and West and also the quest itself, and warrants significant discussion later in this essay. Undeniably, however, the iconic figure of the hero is both an exceptional and critical part of the survival of society; their "boon," of which Campbell writes, is not comprised of material riches, but of the symbolic, psychological, and philosophical tools to persist and thrive.

Jay Cavendish (Kodi Smit-McPhee) finds himself in a surreal setting as he descends into the depths of the wilderness. *Slow West* (Lionsgate, 2015).

Returning to our exploration of the quest itself, however, it is important to note that the hero's transformation happens gradually along the way. During the course of his journey, he must meet and overcome challenges and trials that test (and build) his physical and intellectual abilities and moral character. Through these, he crosses a series of thresholds, each of which adds an embodied dimension to the quest. Widely recognized for their association with liminality or a change in statuses or states, these thresholds act as metaphorical doorways or passages, through which the hero enters in one state, but departs in another.[7] Anthropologist Victor Turner observed that such transitions are key to shaping temporal and social experience, moments "in and out of time" that add a surreal quality to the hero's odyssey.[8] Thus it is for Jay, as we examine his journey through the frontier. On the surface, it is a romantic quest for the ages, like that of Orpheus and Eurydice, full of promise and peril, and destined to fail....

The Road of Trials

> For over all there hung a cloud of fear;
> A sense of mystery the spirit daunted,
> And said, as plain as whisper in the ear,
> The place is haunted![9]

Orpheus, you may recall, is a dreamer—a poet and a musician—who marries his true love, Eurydice, only to watch her die on their wedding day after being bitten by a viper. Distraught, Orpheus descends into the underworld. As his mystical journey takes him deeper, he faces ghostly souls, calms Cerberus, the three-headed dog, and finally wins over Hades with his music. Hades grants his boon, telling him that Eurydice may follow him back to the world of the living, but that if he turns back to look at her, he will lose her forever. Grateful, Orpheus sets off, but just as he has nearly achieved his quest, he loses faith. He turns around to look for Eurydice, and she is swept back to the land of the dead forever. Orpheus thus fails in his quest, and as a romantic hero, because he reaches back instead of heeding the importance of always moving forward. He is, as Helen Sword observes,

> the fallible hero who nonetheless attempts to fuse irreconcilable opposites and to bridge the gap between the possible and the forbidden. His characteristic moment, symbolizing both his success and all his failures, is located in his turn, his enigmatic backward glance at Eurydice: the gesture by which he attempts, and necessarily fails, to embrace the world of light and the world of darkness in a single all-encompassing regard.[10]

Jay is, in many respects, Orpheus on the frontier, attempting to move forward on his quest through the wilderness while always reaching back to a past of his own imagining.

At the film's opening, Jay has already traveled to America, and is journeying through the wilderness, a literal babe in the woods. His heart has answered the "call to adventure" to find Rose and her father and fulfill his destiny at her side; his only guide, a tattered copy of *Ho! For the West!: The Traveler and Emigrant's Hand-book to Canada and the North-West of the American Union*.[11] His quest through the frontier, both alone and with Silas, is, at times, trance-like, and the characters he encounters seem plucked from other places and times, whether as signposts of the human condition or harbingers of doom. Native Americans on foot pass like traces of another time, silent and ghost-like, as Jay rides into the wilderness and slowly enters what appears to be a mist in the woods—adding a sense of haunting to the scene—and later emerges, covered with ash from their burned-out village, realizing only later that his romanticized journey has led him to glimpse one of the frontier's great atrocities.

It is here that he encounters Silas, who begins the tale as the chronicler of the young Scotsman's frontier quest, but quickly becomes his mentor and mythic aide. Silas is a man shaped by his frontier existence. He is hard, dispassionate—"brutish," according to Jay—a gunslinger who, later in their travels, reflects on being among the last of his kind: "There were few of us left. Men beyond the law. But the most dangerous are the last to fall." He and Jay stand in binary opposition—West and East—one an icon of freedom, individuality, practical wisdom, and savagery; the other a caricature of class, community, refinement, and regulation.[12] Yet Silas is also a man of principle and integrity—the "good bad man" so often portrayed in revisionist Westerns.[13] When he rescues Jay from Indian hunters wearing Union blue, killing their leader, Jay objects: "He was an officer." Silas, well versed in the savage ways of the West, counters: "Wearing a dress don't make her a lady." Jay clearly has much to learn. The two strike a deal for Jay's passage to just beyond a forest called Silver Ghost and, with Silas's solemn "Let's drift," the quest continues.

Along the way, the pair encounters a series of surreal figures, trials, and challenges characteristic of the classic hero's journey. In the midst of the desolate landscape, three Congolese men appear beside the trail, singing. Jay pauses in their trek to listen, and trades a surreal line or two with them, in French, about the universal natures of love and death, before Silas urges him on. A trading post—one of the few outposts of civilization—reveals a Wanted poster, offering $2000 for Rose and her father, dead or alive. Silas hides the poster from the boy, offering no clue whether the act is to shield Jay from this new, harsh reality or to buy time to decide his own intentions. As if to reinforce the mounting danger signaled by the poster, a gunslinger in preacher's garb (Edwin Wright) emerges from the post, measures Silas a moment with his gaze, and goes on his way—their way. The respite they seek at the post becomes even more perilous when they meet a family of Polish immigrants whose desperate poverty leads to a shoot-out and their death. Their frantic cries demanding "Money! Money!!!," as they hold first the owner and then Silas at gunpoint, underscore that violence is not the only brutality to be found in the West, despite its promises of hope and a bright future. When Jay and Silas leave the trading post they find the couple's two young children—now orphans—waiting on the dusty trail, and now left to fend for themselves. Unable to reconcile this act, Jay steals away and in yet another surreal moment, encounters Werner (Andrew Robertt), a German anthropologist who seems to share the boy's sensibilities, but makes off with his horse and belongings, leaving him, also, alone.

Once again, Jay is rescued by Silas, and their quest continues. Later, in an absinthe-induced slumber, Jay and Silas share a dream of the future: Silas's future, with Rose. They awaken in a torrential downpour; their belongings, including their guns, washed away in the floods.

Their single greatest challenge on the trail, however, is Payne (Ben Mendelsohn), the leader of Silas's former gang—a gang he joined when he was no older than Jay. Unfettered by morals or sentimentality, Payne and his riders are also tracking Rose and her father, intending to kill them both and collect the bounty. When subterfuge and coercion fail to uncover the Rosses' whereabouts, Payne's gang simply trails Silas and Jay.

> JAY: What do they want?
> SILAS: They're bounty hunters. You know what that means?
> JAY: They hunt bounty?
> SILAS: They hunt Rose. Daddy. Blood. Money.

But the pair has little choice but to lead them right to Rose, if they are to complete their quest.

JAY: We'll lead them south.
SILAS: There'll be others.
JAY: Others?
SILAS: Two thousand dollars entices a certain breed of undesirable.

When Jay finally reaches his goal—the Ross homestead—an epic battle between good and evil ensues. He and Silas, along with the gunslinger from the trading post and Payne's gang, all converge in what both the Western and quest narratives signal as the brutal climax of their story. With a cry of "Kill that house!" violence rains down on the small cabin. When the dust settles, a mortally wounded Jay, shot in error by Rose, gasps his final breaths as she realizes his identity. His tale, though not the film, ends in tragedy.

A Thousand Ways to Die

> These violent delights have violent ends
> And in their triumph die like fire and powder[14]

Jay's death disrupts the narrative cycle of both the romantic hero's quest and the Western saga. Like Orpheus, he has failed; and like Orpheus, his failure teaches a lesson for the ages. Following Campbell's template of the hero's journey, the climax of the narrative—no matter how bleak—should be followed by resurrection, mastery of both the known and unknown worlds, and the hero's reincorporation into the life of the community, but not Jay. Slumped against the wall, dying, he watches Kotari kiss Rose fondly before heading out to battle her assailants, and at that moment a stray bullet shatters the salt cellar above Jay's head. In a stunningly literal moment, salt streams down onto the open wound in his chest—the wound she gave him—causing him to gasp in agony.

This is not how he imagined it would be ... though he had imagined his death at Rose's hand so many, many times. Along his journey through the frontier, his mind drifts back to their dark game of pretend—A Thousand Ways to Die—back home in Scotland:

ROSE: Jay! A thousand ways to die. Choose one!
JAY: Bow and arrow.

Rose pretends to draw a bow and release the arrow at Jay, who tumbles down a rise, as if dead. When she sits astride him in conquest, he gently takes her hands; her discomfort is palpable as she chides him: "Silly boy," and moves quickly away.

These moments of creative play where Rose and Jay blur the lines between fantasy and reality—a line Jay further blurs through romantic fantasies about his relationship with Rose (and the American West) that he seeks to transform into being—creating moments of "magic." Magic is an intuitive aspect of human cognition that may make little sense under the scrutiny of rational thought, but lurks in the subconscious, animating our emotional responses, rationalizations, fears, and fascinations.[15] Magic transcends the boundaries of self and other, the mental and physical, the symbolic and material, allowing individuals to believe that their desires may be made manifest.

A child, Freud suggests, believes in "magic"—in the "omnipotence of thoughts"—and has "an over-estimation of the power of their wishes and mental acts."[16] This magical thinking is one of the most prominent features of Jay's character, often highlighted in his flashbacks to life in Scotland, which not only fill in the narrative gaps between past and present, but also allow viewers to glimpse the contrast between lived reality and Jay's re-visioning of it.

Straddling the line between child and man, Jay attempts to will into being a world of his own imagining, much like Orpheus, whose ecstatic songs call forth the mystical power of the imagination for all who hear it. As Jay sings a simple song of Rose, he—like classic heroes of old—invokes an otherworldly power to guide him on his way. Life, death, love, the frontier, and even Rose are recast with a naïve glow of romance, adventure, and optimism. As viewers, we know it is all doomed to fail, but only later does McClean reveal why. Even at first meeting, this is apparent to Silas who, upon hearing Jay's tale of his one true love fleeing to America, quips "Take a hint, kid?" to which Jay replies, "We love each other." Evidence of a contradictory reality—as well as a forecasting of the tragic future—is abundant: In a flashback of their time together in Scotland, Jay asks Rose directly how she feels about him, and she replies that he is the little brother she never had—an answer he refuses to accept. At once definitive and playful, Rose turns to Shakespeare to warn him of his folly: "I'm sorry, my Romeo, but 'these violent delights have violent ends.'"[17] When he persists, she asks him to leave.

This scene has an echo at the end of the film, when his "violent delights" have, indeed, met a violent end. Silas limps into the cabin and, seeing Jay's body, drops to his knees and removes his hat. Needing to say *something* to eulogize him, he affirms to Rose "he loved you with all his heart." She replies, "His heart was in the wrong place." Jay's overestimation of the power of his own wishes—his attempts to force reality to correspond with fantasy and reshape fate—have led to the most violent possible outcome. The camera cuts from body to body, revisiting the deaths that have punctuated his quest, pointing both to the violence that characterizes life on the frontier and, more pointedly, the toll Jay's quest has taken on everyone it has touched. His willfulness, the camera charges, has ended in death and destruction.

Will, however, may be more complicated than Freud's analysis suggests at first glance. It may also serve as one of the more complex aspects of heroism. Otto Rank, a contemporary and close colleague of Freud, argued that while willfulness and magical thinking are undoubtedly characteristics of a lack of development associated with childhood, "will" is, perhaps, also the essence of the hero. Rank observed that, just as the child must overestimate the power of their own wishes (or will) to shape their worlds, the hero must also overestimate and assert his own will in order to reshape the world through the quest.[18] The rational and the magical, according to scholars such as Paul Harris, Carl Johnson, and Karl Rosengren, coexist in the hero in an uneasy tension.[19]

When individuals (or characters, such as Jay) contemplate possibilities that extend beyond the rational—perilous journeys, fearsome battles, eternal love—these scholars demonstrate, their thinking is guided by forces other than observation and causality. The hero, they argue, and by extension, the heroic quest, is shaped and guided by the conflation of inner/subjective and outer/objective worlds in an attempt to gain control over their environment, be it natural or social.[20] From this perspective, the will (expressed directly, or as wishes, imaginings, or magical thinking) dominates empirical, rational thought, leading to acts beyond the realm of what would be anticipated or considered prudent.

And there we have the quest ... the romantic hero's quest.... Jay's epic, mystical journey. Or is it? I suggested earlier that the narrative of *Slow West* might be more complex, in terms of both the quest and the Western, than it first appears—because Jay is simply a means to an end. An end that belongs to Silas.

"My Sole Company's Been a Brute"

From the outset, the narrative focus of *Slow West* is on Jay—his journey, his love, his survival—after all, the story is introduced as his story:

> Once upon a time, 1870 to be exact, a sixteen-year-old kid travelled from the cold shoulder of Scotland, to the baking heart of America to find his love. His name was Jay—her name was Rose.

The screen is black, the voice is that of Silas, who remains off-camera and unseen for the first seven minutes of the film. He is cast, in the structure of Campbell's classic quest, as Jay's mentor, protector, and "magical guide" (magic, in this case, equating with expert knowledge) as he journeys through the unknown wilds of the frontier. Framed as Jay's binary opposite, he is taciturn, world-weary, and solitary; a rough-around-the-edges drifter with deadly skills and a past only hinted at in voice-over. In genre terms, he is the quintessential revisionist Western anti-hero—a figure that also finds its roots in the tales of classical antiquity—existing outside the law, rejecting the conventions of society, yet moved by his own (complex, and sometimes conflicting) moral code. Through the lens of the hero's journey though, it is actually Silas, through his relationship with Jay, who weathers the trials and fulfills the hero's destiny.

In Silas, McClean and Fassbender create a lyrical figure who transforms, almost imperceptibly at times, throughout the trials and tests in the pair's cinematic quest. He begins the tale as an opportunistic loner who, on one hand, protects Jay from Indian-hunting assailants, but on the other, also displays no reluctance over exploiting a sixteen-year-old boy. Jay is simply a ready source of income, made even more valuable by the discovery of the trading post's Wanted poster for Rose and her father. In voice-over, he muses "Everyone knew about the bounty, except Jay. He was leading me right to it." Yet even then, there are cues to greater depth in Silas's character and vulnerabilities apparent in his demeanor. He quickly closes the door to prevent the children from viewing their parents' bodies. As the pair ride on from the trading post, leaving the orphaned children standing on the trail, he softly whistles to choke back emotion, and the camera zooms in on his left hand, which usually sits motionless on his thigh, but now clenches into a fist that he rubs abrasively on his pant leg as he struggles to avoid the "tell" of sorrow, frustration, and regret.

Silas's inner life surfaces in more complex ways as the journey continues and he reflects on his checkered past. He was once like Jay, a boy of sixteen, making his way in the wilderness; he was once like Payne, an outlaw, surviving by his wits and a gun. Now, he is betwixt and between, a "good bad man" whose inner world is home to both. Along the way, his stance relative to both is continually changing, but the turning point is when those two collide. When Payne arrives at their camp, Silas is wary and protective of Jay. Payne remarks, "It's easy to see how you two crossed paths. One's a falling angel, the other one's a rising devil." In a jarringly intimate scene, Payne embraces the drunk and staggering Silas, and softly questions his motives for helping the boy, suggesting that he'll be done "babysitting" as soon as Jay leads him to the bounty. This proves to be the catalyst for Silas, who breaks the (familial? homoerotic?) tension by raising his gun between them in resistance, affirming "I'm not like you, Payne." In this moment, Silas has crossed the hero's final threshold, and is fully prepared for the narrative climax. He, much like Clint Eastwood's Stranger in *High Plains Drifter* (1973), possesses self-knowledge, and a bleak integrity that he must live with, but that is now tempered by a renewed sense of humanity.[21] He is now visibly committed to protecting Jay and saving Rose, and the two ride into the forest known as Silver Ghost with a transformed sense of their relationship.

When they emerge from the forest, however, this shift has unexpected results. Silas ties Jay to a tree to keep him safe and rides off to save the girl—fully transitioned into the role of a hero—but all that remains is death. John Ross, Victor the Hawk, Payne and his gang, Kotari, and Jay all meet their end amidst a storm of fire and bullets. Only Silas and Rose—the film's two most pragmatic characters—remain, and it is clear that they have each met their match. While Rose's character is unexplored, Silas's has developed in a heroic arc. No longer Jay's image of a "brute," he has (re)incorporated empathy, vulnerability, and humanity into his fierce Western worldview and, with Rose and the orphaned immigrant children, has reconstituted the frontier family. Doug Williams relates that the Western hero has entered the wilderness and gained knowledge of it, without himself degenerating into wilderness.[22] Silas began the narrative moving through the wilderness as if he was made of it, but through his quest with Jay, the wilderness inside him has been, at least to some degree, domesticated. In epilogue, he acknowledges this and delivers the moral message of the quest: "There is more to life than survival. Jay Cavendish taught me that. I owe him my life." Here we have the hero's boon to civilization.

Conclusion: The Importance of Opposites

What Jay Cavendish—and Silas along with him—has taught *us* is a lesson in the importance of opposites. The quest through the Colorado wilderness, while initiated by Jay, belonged to both of them as intertwined symbolic beings. Either might have succeeded alone, but the hero's boon would not have resulted, thus losing the true meaning of the quest. Binary opposites, their fates are linked just as their oppositions are linked in the West—and in human nature writ large. Both are needed if we are to move beyond mere survival.

If we briefly look at their quest through a symbolic lens, it becomes a template with which most viewers are familiar: The educated, creative, naïve, and feminized son of an aristocrat is forced to join forces with a man of lower class. He is a man of practicality—wise in the ways of the world—a man of action who is no stranger to violence and death. Together, using their respective knowledge and talents, they save the female in distress. (In *Slow West*, even Jay gets his moment, when he uses Silas's rope to create a laundry line between their two horses for drying their rain-soaked clothes as they ride.) In other Westerns, or films of other genres, the narrative resolution would turn on which man (rough or refined) was ultimately chosen as the recipient of her love. Here, however, Jay's accidental death at Rose's hand shifts that template. She does not have to remain with Silas, but it seems natural to viewers that she does so. If we view the two men as symbolically intertwined, it is also natural for the resolution of the hero's mystical journey. The epic voyage ends. Jay's death, we see, is a necessary precursor for Silas—the symbol of wilderness—to complete his heroic transformation and be reintegrated into society. As one dies, the other rises to fullness of being, and hope springs from tragedy. Much as in the Classics the hero must die in order for his song to be sung, Jay's idealized love must perish to make way for a love rooted in reality. Only through Jay's demise is Silas able to merge key elements of "civilization" into his personal "wilderness" and become a true hero of the frontier, integrating the opposing worldviews and becoming an embodiment of both. Had Jay survived, the two poles of difference would have continued to be at odds in the two men: intellect versus instinct, knowledge versus experience, community versus independence, idealism versus pragmatism, and all the rest.

In the final scene of the film, as Silas, now at home in Rose's home, considers his fate in voiceover, and acknowledges that he owes Jay his life, he is not referring to his physical existence—Jay had little to do with Silas's survival—but rather, to his existential life as a man able to live in both worlds, wilderness and civilization. Once one of the "last of his kind," he is now able to fully participate in the future of the frontier, and the domestication of the wilderness. Ending the film in a gesture that speaks of both domesticity and optimism, he turns upright a horseshoe hanging over the cabin door—a symbol of good fortune, and a sign of the idealism imparted by Jay.

Notes

1. Farid ad-Din Attar, *The Conference of the Birds* (New York: Penguin Classics,1984), 35.
2. Joseph Campbell, *The Hero with a Thousand Faces,* Commemorative Edition (Princeton, NJ: Princeton University Press, 2004): 21.
3. Ibid., 23.
4. Doug Williams, "Pilgrims and the Promised Land: A Geneology of the Western" in Kitses and Rickman, *The Western Reader* (New York: Limelight, 1998), 93–113.
5. Jim Kitses, *Horizons West: Directing the Western from John Ford to Clint Eastwood.* (London: BFI Publishing, 2004), 13.
6. Ibid., 12.
7. Campbell, 20. On liminality, see Victor Turner, "Liminality and Communitas," in *The Ritual Process: Structure and Anti-Structure* (Chicago: Aldine Publishing, 1969), 94–113.
8. Turner, 94–113.
9. Thomas Hood, "The Haunted House" in *The Poetical Works of Thomas Hood.* (Boston: Crosby, Nichols, Lee, and Company, 1861).
10. Helen Sword, "Orpheus and Eurydice in the Twentieth Century: Lawrence, D.H., and the Poetics of the Turn." *Twentieth Century Literature* , Winter, 1989, Vol. 35, No. 4 (Winter, 1989), 407–428.
11. Edward Hepple Hall, *Ho! For the West!! The Traveller and Emigrant's Hand-Book to Canada and the North-West of the American Union.* (1856. London: Algar and Street, 1858).
12. Kitses, 1969.
13. Kitses, 1969.
14. William Shakespeare, *Romeo and Juliet,* Act 2, scene 6.
15. Carla Nemeroff and Paul Rosen, "The Makings of the Magical Mind" in *Imagining the Impossible: Magical, Scientific, and Religious Thinking in Children* (Cambridge: Cambridge University Press, 2000), 1–34.
16. Sigmund Freud, "On Narcissism: An Introduction," *On Metapsychology: The Theory of Psychoanalysis*, trans. James Strachey, Penguin Freud Library, Volume II (Harmondsworth: Penguin, 1984), 69–106.
17. This quote from Romeo and Juliet also makes its way into the first season of the futuristic *Westworld* television series the following year.
18. For a thorough analysis of Rank and the hero, see Nancy Gordon Seif, "Otto Rank: On the Nature of the Hero" *American Imago* Vol. 41, No. 4 (Winter 1984): 373–384.
19. *Imagining the Impossible: Magical, Scientific, and Religious Thinking in Children* (Cambridge: Cambridge University Press, 2000).
20. For more on this, see Bernard Malinowski, *Magic, Science, and Religion* (New York: Doubleday, 1955) and Stanley J. Tambiah, *Magic, Science, Religion, and the Scope of Rationality* (Cambridge: Cambridge University Press, 1990).

21. For more on Eastwood's heroes, see Fred Erisman's "Clint Eastwood's Western Films and the Evolving Mythic Hero. *Hungarian Journal of English and American Studies,* Vol. 6, No. 2 (Fall, 2000) 129–143.

22. Doug Williams, "Pilgrims and the Promised Land: A Genealogy of the Western" in Kitses and Rickman, *The Western Reader* (New York: Limelight, 1998), 5.

Works Cited

Attar, Farid ad-Din. *The Conference of the Birds.* New York: Penguin Classics, 1984.
Campbell, Joseph. *The Hero with a Thousand Faces.* Commemorative Edition. Princeton, NJ: Princeton University Press, 2004.
Erisman, Fred. "Clint Eastwood's Western Films and the Evolving Mythic Hero." *Hungarian Journal of English and American Studies* Vol. 6, No. 2 (Fall 2006): 129–143.
Freud, Sigmund. "On Narcissism: An Introduction." In *On Metapsychology: The Theory of Psychoanalysis,* trans. James Strachey, Penguin Freud Library, Volume II, 69–106. Harmondsworth: Penguin, 1984.
Hall, Edward Hepple. *Ho! For the West!! The Traveller and Emigrant's Hand-Book to Canada and the North-West of the American Union.* 1856. London: Algar and Street, 1858.
Hood, Thomas. "The Haunted House" in *The Poetical Works of Thomas Hood.* Boston: Crosby, Nichols, Lee, and Company, 1861.
Kitses, Jim. *Horizons West: Directing the Western from John Ford to Clint Eastwood.* London: BFI Publishing, 2004.
Malinowski, Bernard. *Magic, Science, and Religion.* New York: Doubleday, 1955.
Nemeroff, Carla, and Paul Rosen. "The Makings of the Magical Mind" in *Imagining the Impossible: Magical, Scientific, and Religious Thinking in Children,* 1–34. Cambridge: Cambridge University Press, 2000.
Rosengren, Karl, Carl Johnson, and Paul Harris. *Imagining the Impossible: Magical, Scientific, and Religious Thinking in Children.* Cambridge: Cambridge University Press, 2000.
Seif, Nancy Gordon. "Otto Rank: On the Nature of the Hero" *American Imago* Vol. 41, No. 4 (Winter 1984): 373–384.
Shakespeare, William. *Romeo and Juliet,* Act 2, scene 6.
Sword, Helen. "Orpheus and Eurydice in the Twentieth Century: Lawrence, D.H., and the Poetics of the Turn." *Twentieth Century Literature,* Winter, 1989, Vol. 35, No. 4 (Winter, 1989), 407–428.
Tambiah, Stanley J. *Magic, Science, Religion, and the Scope of Rationality.* Cambridge: Cambridge University Press, 1990.
Turner, Victor. "Liminality and Communitas," In *The Ritual Process: Structure and Anti-Structure,* 94–113. Chicago: Aldine Publishing, 1969.
Williams, Doug. "Pilgrims and the Promised Land: A Geneology of the Western." In Kitses and Rickman, eds. *The Western Reader,* 93–113. New York: Limelight, 1998.

Influence of Classical Literature in Western Film
A Selective Bibliography
Camille McCutcheon

Below is a selective bibliography of books, book chapters, and journal articles on the influence of classical literature in western film. Among the books listed below range from texts devoted to classical subjects to others which examine classical allusions in Western films.

Books

Bazin, André. *What Is Cinema?* Translated by Hugh Gray, vol. 2, University of California Press, 2005.
Cawelti, John G. *The Six-Gun Mystique.* Bowling Green University Popular Press, 1971.
Day, Kirsten. *Cowboy Classics: The Roots of the American Western in the Epic Tradition.* Edinburgh University Press, 2016.
Fenin, George N., and William K. Everson. *The Western, From Silents to the Seventies.* New and Expanded ed., Grossman, 1973.
Ferrell, William K. *Literature and Film as Modern Mythology.* Praeger, 2000.
Frankel, Glenn. The Searchers: *The Making of an American Legend.* Bloomsbury, 2013.
French, Peter A. *Cowboy Metaphysics: Ethics and Death in Westerns.* Rowman & Littlefield, 1997.
Günsberg, Maggie. *Italian Cinema: Gender and Genre.* Palgrave Macmillan, 2005.
Indick, William. *The Psychology of the Western: How the American Psyche Plays Out on Screen.* McFarland, 2008.
Kitses, Jim. *Horizons West: Directing the Western from John Ford to Clint Eastwood.* New ed., BFI Publishing, 2004.
Kitses, Jim, and Gregg Rickman, editors. *The Western Reader.* Limelight Editions, 1998.
Kopff, E. Christian. *The Devil Knows Latin: Why America Needs the Classical Tradition.* ISI Books, 1999.
Mast, Gerald. *Howard Hawks, Storyteller.* Oxford University Press, 1982.
Matheson, Sue. *The Westerns and War Films of John Ford.* Rowman & Littlefield, 2016.
McMahon, Jennifer L., and B. Steve Csaki, editors. *The Philosophy of the Western.* University Press of Kentucky, 2010.
Meuel, David. *The Noir Western: Darkness on the Range, 1943–1962.* McFarland, 2015.
Parks, Rita. *The Western Hero in Film and Television: Mass Media Mythology.* UMI Research Press, 1982.
Paul, Joanna. *Film and the Classical Epic Tradition.* Oxford University Press, 2013.
Rhodes, Gary Don, and Robert Singer, editors. *ReFocus: The Films of Budd Boetticher.* Edinburgh University Press, 2017.
Simons, John L., and Robert Merrill. *Peckinpah's Tragic Westerns: A Critical Study.* McFarland, 2011.
Voytilla, Stuart. *Myth and the Movies: Discovering the Mythic Structure of 50 Unforgettable Films.* Michael Wiese Productions, 1999.
Wildermuth, Mark E. *Feminism and the Western in Film and Television.* Palgrave Macmillan, 2018.
Winkler, Martin M. *Cinema and Classical Texts: Apollo's New Light.* Cambridge University Press, 2009.
_____. *Classical Literature on Screen: Affinities of Imagination.* Cambridge University Press, 2017.
Winkler, Martin M., editor. *The Fall of the Roman Empire: Film and History.* Wiley-Blackwell, 2009.

Book Chapters

Coelho, Maria Cecilia De Miranda N. "Horses for Ladies, High-Ridin' Women and Whores." *A Fistful of Icons: Essays on Frontier Fixtures of the American Western*, edited by Sue Matheson, McFarland, 2017, pp. 113–23.

Day, Kirsten. "'All that Glitters': Problematizing Golden-Age Narratives in Vergil's *Aeneid* and the Western Film Genre." *Screening the Golden Ages of the Classical Tradition*, edited by Meredith E. Safran, Edinburgh University Press, 2019, pp. 157–74.

Holtsmark, Erling B. "The Katabasis Theme in Modern Cinema." *Classical Myth and Culture in the Cinema*, edited by Martin M. Winkler, Oxford University Press, 2001, pp. 23–50.

Matheson, Sue. "'When You Side with a Man, You Stay with Him!'—Philia and the Military Mind in Sam Peckinpah's *The Wild Bunch* (1969)." *Love in Western Film and Television: Lonely Hearts and Happy Trails*, edited by Sue Matheson, Palgrave Macmillan, 2013, pp. 225–37.

McDonough, Christopher M. "Ancient Allusions and Modern Anxieties in *Seven Brides for Seven Brothers* (1954)." *Screening Love and Sex in the Ancient World*, edited by Monica Silveira Cyrino, Palgrave Macmillan, 2013, pp. 99–110.

Seydor, Paul. "*The Wild Bunch* as Epic." *Doing It Right: The Best Criticism on Sam Peckinpah's* The Wild Bunch, edited by Michael Bliss, Southern Illinois University Press, 1994, pp. 113–57.

Walker, Janet. "Captive Images in the Traumatic Western: *The Searchers*, *Pursued*, *Once Upon a Time in the West*, and *Lone Star*." *Westerns: Films through History*, edited by Janet Walker, Routledge, 2001, pp. 219–51.

Winkler, Martin M. "Homer's *Iliad* and John Ford's *The Searchers*." *The Searchers: Essays and Reflections on John Ford's Classic Western*, edited by Arthur M. Eckstein and Peter Lehman, Wayne State University Press, 2004, pp. 145–70.

———. "Tragic Features in John Ford's *The Searchers*." *Classical Myth and Culture in the Cinema*, edited by Martin M. Winkler, Oxford University Press, 2001, pp. 118–47.

Journal Articles

Bakewell, Geoffrey W. "Oedipus Tex: *Lone Star*, Tragedy, and Postmodernism." *Classical and Modern Literature*, vol. 22, no. 1, Spring 2002, pp. 35–48.

Blundell, Mary Whitlock, and Kirk Ormand. "Western Values, or the Peoples Homer: *Unforgiven* as a Reading of the *Iliad*." *Poetics Today*, vol. 18, no. 4, Winter 1997, pp. 533–69.

Clauss, James J. "Descent into Hell: Mythic Paradigms in *The Searchers*." *Journal of Popular Film and Television*, vol. 27, no. 3, Fall 1999, pp. 2–17.

Day, Kirsten. "'What Makes a Man to Wander?': *The Searchers* as a Western *Odyssey*." *Arethusa*, vol. 41, no. 1, Winter 2008, pp. 11–49.

Eckstein, Arthur M. "Darkening Ethan: John Ford's *The Searchers* (1956) from Novel to Screenplay to Screen." *Cinema Journal*, vol. 38, no. 1, Autumn 1998, pp. 3–24.

Fletcher, Judith. "The *Catabasis* of Mattie Ross in the Coens' *True Grit*." *The Classical World*, vol. 107, no. 2, Winter 2014, pp. 237–54.

Grant, Barry Keith. "Anti-Oedipus: Feminism, the Western, and *The Ballad of Little Jo*." *Cineaction*, no. 96, 2015, pp. 60–9.

Harris, John R. "Narrative Technique in Vergil's *Aeneid* and Modern Cinema: From Reiteration to Slow Motion." *The Comparatist*, vol. 17, May 1993, pp. 59–80.

Marston, Vincent. "Epics and Westerns." *The Classical Outlook*, vol. 54, no. 7, Mar. 1977, pp. 76–9.

Matheson, Sue. "'Let's Go Home, Debbie': The Matter of Blood Pollution, Combat Culture, and Cold War Hysteria in *The Searchers*." *Journal of Popular Film and Television*, vol. 39, no. 2, 2011, pp. 50–8.

Myrsiades, Kostas. "Reading *The Gunfighter* as Homeric Epic." *College Literature*, vol. 34, no. 2, Spring 2007, pp. 279–300.

Noh, Kwang Woo, and Jae-Woong Kwon. "Deconstruction of Western Genre in the 1950's and 1960's: Budd Boetticher, Sam Peckinpah, and Sergio Leone." *Cineforum*, no. 24, 2016, pp. 443–64.

Redmon, Allen. "Mechanisms of Violence in Clint Eastwood's *Unforgiven* and *Mystic River*." *The Journal of American Culture*, vol. 27, no. 3, Sept. 2004, pp. 315–28.

Rubino, Carl. A. "Wounds That Will Not Heal: Heroism and Innocence in *Shane* and the *Iliad*." *Dialogue: The Interdisciplinary Journal of Popular Culture and Pedagogy*, vol. 1, no. 1, 2014, journaldialogue.org/.

Warshow, Robert S. "Movie Chronicle: The Westerner." *Partisan Review*, vol. 21, Mar. 1954, pp. 190–203.

Winkler, Martin M. "Classical Mythology and the Western Film." *Comparative Literature Studies*, vol. 22, no. 4, Winter 1985, pp. 516–40.

———. "Homeric *kleos* and the Western Film." *Syllecta Classica*, vol. 7, 1996, pp. 43–54.

———. "Oedipus in the Cinema." *Arethusa*, vol. 41, no. 1, Winter 2008, pp. 67–94.

About the Contributors

Brian **Brems** is an associate professor of English at the College of DuPage where he teaches film courses. His academic work has focused on genre, with numerous pieces on horror. He is the coeditor of *Refocus: The Films of Paul Schrader* (2020). In addition, he publishes regularly in online film magazines and websites, including *Bright Wall/Dark Room*, *Vague Visages*, and *Film Inquiry*.

Maria Cecília de Miranda N. **Coelho** is an associate professor of philosophy at the Universidade Federal de Minas Gerais in Brazil. She holds a Ph.D. in classics from the Universidade de São Paulo. She also holds degrees in mathematics and philosophy from the Universidade de Brasília. She has published papers on Greek tragedy, Gorgias, and Plato. She is the editor of *Retórica, Persuasão e Emoções* (2018) and coedited *Cinema: Lanterna Mágica da História e da Mitologia* (2009) and *Ensaios sobre Literatura, Teatro e Cinema* (2013), among others.

Jim **Daems** has published articles and books on topics ranging from 16th- and 17th-century English literature to contemporary popular culture. He is the author of *Seventeenth-Century Literature and Culture* (2007) and *"A Warr So Desperate": John Milton and Some Contemporaries on the Irish Rebellion* (2012). He has edited *Eikon Basilike* (2005) and *Games and War in Early Modern Literature* (2019, with Holly Faith Nelson), and *The Makeup of* RuPaul's Drag Race (2014).

Kirsten **Day** is an associate professor and Chair of the Classics Department at Augustana College in Rock Island, Illinois. She is the author of *Cowboy Classics: The Roots of the American Western in the Epic Tradition* (2016), as well as a number of articles on classical receptions and women in antiquity. She also served as editor of a special issue of *Arethusa* entitled *Celluloid Classics: New Perspectives on Classical Antiquity in Modern Cinema* (*Arethusa* 41.1: Winter 2008).

Andrew **Howe** is a professor of history at La Sierra University where he teaches courses in film studies, popular culture, and American history. His scholarship includes book chapters on the postmodern and the classical in *The Three Burials of Melquiades Estrada*, villain typologies in *Star Trek: Voyager*, and religion in *Game of Thrones*. His research projects involve the rhetoric of fear employed during the 1980s killer bee invasions of the American Southwest, as well as the debate over the rediscovery of the ivory-billed woodpecker in Arkansas.

Benjamin **Hufbauer** teaches art history and film studies at the University of Louisville. He earned his B.A. in art history and politics from U.C. Santa Cruz, and his M.A. and Ph.D. in the history of art and architecture from U.C. Santa Barbara. He is the author of *Presidential Temples: How Memorials and Libraries Shape Public Memory* (2005).

Kelly **MacPhail** teaches English, philosophy, and classical mythology as an assistant professor at the University of Minnesota Duluth. His interdisciplinary research focuses on transatlantic literary modernism, environmental criticism, and belief studies. He has published on subjects as diverse as modernist poetry, Puritan sermons, film noir, animal domestication, nautical fiction, and the Western.

Sue **Matheson** is professor of English Literature at the University College of the North, Canada. She teaches American literature, Canadian literature, and film and popular culture. Her work may be found in more than sixty essays published in books and scholarly journals. She is the author of *The Westerns and War Stories of John Ford* (2016) and *The John Ford Encyclopedia* (2019); she is the editor of *Love in Western Film and Television* (2013), *A Fistful of Icons: Frontier Fixtures of the American Western* (2017), and *Women in the Western* (2020).

Camille **McCutcheon** is the Coordinator of Collection Management and Administrative Services at the University of South Carolina Upstate Library. She is a member of the Popular Culture Association (PCA) Governing Board. She has published articles in *CHOICE*, *Against the Grain*, and *Research Strategies* and is the author of the two chapters for the annual reference book, *Magazines for Libraries*. Her research interests include children's literature, film history, and film star biographies.

Cynthia J. **Miller** is a cultural anthropologist specializing in visual media. She teaches in the Institute for Liberal Arts at Emerson College, and is the editor or coeditor of 17 scholarly volumes, including *Dark Forces at Work: Essays on Social Dynamics and Cinematic Horrors* (2019). She serves on the editorial board of the *Journal of Popular Television*, and also edits the Film and History book series for Rowman & Littlefield.

Christopher **Minz** is a Ph.D. candidate at Georgia State University. He has published several essays on the American Western, and especially the films of Budd Boetticher, Jr. His dissertation utilizes psychoanalysis to examine the aesthetic intersection of tragic myth and melodrama in the Western as it pertains to American ideology in the latter half of the 20th century.

Christopher J. **Olson** is a Ph.D. student in the English department at the University of Wisconsin–Milwaukee, with a media, cinema, and digital studies concentration. He is the author, coauthor, or coeditor of *The Greatest Cult Television Series of All Time* (2020); *100 Greatest Cult Films* (2018); *Possessed Women, Haunted States: Cultural Tensions in Exorcism Cinema* (2016); and *Making Sense of Cinema: Empirical Studies into Film Spectators and Spectatorship* (2016).

Fernando Gabriel **Pagnoni Berns** holds a Ph.D. in arts and is a professor at the Universidad de Buenos Aires (UBA)–Facultad de Filosofía y Letras (Argentina). He teaches courses on international horror film and has authored a book about Spanish horror TV series, *Historias para no Dormir* (2020). He has edited a book on the Frankenstein bicentennial and is editing another on the Italian giallo film. He is a coeditor (with Matthew Edwards) of *The Cinema of James Wan* (2022).

Martin M. **Winkler** is a professor of classics at George Mason University in Virginia. His books on classics and cinema are *Cinema and Classical Texts: Apollo's New Light* (2009), *The Roman Salute: Cinema, History, Ideology* (2009), *Classical Literature on Screen: Affinities of Imagination* (2017), and *Ovid on Screen: A Montage of Attractions* (2020). He has also edited essay collections on epic films and published more than a hundred articles, book chapters, reviews, etc. A fistful of these deal with the Western.

Chris **Yogerst** is an associate professor of communication in the Department of Arts & Humanities at the University of Wisconsin–Milwaukee. His latest book, *Hollywood Hates Hitler! Jew-Baiting, Anti-Nazism, and the Investigation into Warmongering in Motion Pictures*, was published in 2020. His work can also be found in the popular press and scholarly journals such as *Los Angeles Review of Books*, *Hollywood Reporter*, *Journal of Popular Film & Television*, and the *Historical Journal of Film, Radio and Television*.

Index

Abilene 141, 144
Achilles 3, 18, 27, 89, 101, 139, 143, 144, 146, 173, 178, 179; Achilles heel 185n
Across the Great Divide (1976) 7
Adventures of Brisco County, Jr. (Fox, 1993-1994) 8
Aeneas 10, 18, 23, 190, 192
The Aeneid 1, 18, 23, 32n, 35n, 112, 124, 190n, 192, 196n
Aeschylus 9, 10, 33n, 60, 69, 70, 79n, 83, 84, 94n, 102, 111, 112, 116, 116n, 124, 124n, 131, 143
Agamemnon 3, 69, 70, 79n, 87, 112, 116, 124n, 176
Agamemnon 69, 70, 116
Ajax 79n, 85
Ajax 57, 70, 93
Alamo 4
The Alamo (1960) 6, 13n, 51
The Alamo (2004) 7
Alexander the Great 29, 33n
All the Pretty Horses (2000) 7, 13n
American Outlaw (2001) 7, 13n
Andreia 3
Andromache 177
Annie Oakley 4, 140
Antigone 10, 68, 128, 129-30, 131-134, 135n
Antigone 10, 93n, 127, 130, 131, 133, 135n
Apache 5, 22, 44, 103, 104, 107
Apache (1954) 6, 12n
Aphrodite 26
Apollonian 71, 129, 133, 134, 135n
Appaloosa (2008) 7, 15n
archetype 3, 166, 175
Ares 156
Aristophanes 92n, 101
Aristotle 2, 3, 9, 10, 11, 12n, 13n, 14n, 33n, 37-48, 62, 66-71, 76, 77, 79n, 80n, 83, 88, 89, 92n, 94n, 131, 151, 152-53, 154, 155, 157, 158
The Art of Rhetoric 37, 39, 41-43, 45, 46, 89
The Assassination of Jesse James by the Coward Robert Ford (2007) 7, 13n
até 9, 10, 93, 128-131, 133-34, 134n
Athena 112-13
Athenian 11, 33n, 54, 113
Athens 23, 33n, 101, 101, 112-13
Augustus 192; in Westerns 17, 19, 26, 32n, 33n, 85, 146, 151, 153, 155, 157

The Bacchae 9, 70-71, 72, 74, 75, 76, 77, 79n, 80n
Bacchus 71, 72, 133; *see also* Dionysus
Bad Girls (1994) 7, 13n
Bandolero (1968) 6, 13n
bank 4, 44, 118, 121, 140; banker 3, 114, 116, 121, 155, 156
Barbary Coast (ABC, 1974-1976) 8
The Beguiled (2017) 7, 13n
Best of the West (ABC, 1981-1982) 8

The Big Country (1956) 6, 13n
Big Jake (1971) 7, 13n
Billy Jack (1970) 7, 13n
Billy the Kid 40, 141
Bite the Bullet (1975) 7, 13n
blacklist 37, 40, 42, 102
Blacksmith Scene (1893) 140
A Bluff from a Tenderfoot (1899) 140
Boom Town (1940) 6
Boot Hill 10, 190-196
Bordertown (CTV, 1989-1991) 8
The Bravados (1956) 6, 13n, 86
Breaking Bad (AMC, 2008-2013) 8
Bret Maverick (NBC, 1981-1982) 8
brother: frontier 4, 5, 20, 29, 38, 75, 76, 87, 88, 89, 106, 107, 108, 114, 115, 117, 123, 194, 205; Greek legend 113, 128, 130, 131, 132, 135n; Roman legend 18
Il buono, il brutto, il cattivo (1967) 6, 13n
Buffalo Bill Cody 4, 40, 140
Butch Cassidy 140
Butch Cassidy and the Sundance Kid (1969) 7, 13n

Cassius 25, 33n
catharsis 62, 66-69, 74, 76, 80n, 101, 128, 151, 153, 155, 157, 158; pity and fear 68, 70, 74, 76, 77, 151, 155, 157; *see also* pity; tragedy
Cato 22
cattle drive 106, 139, 140, 141, 142, 143, 145, 146, 147, 148, 174; cattle drive 10, 139, 142, 143, 148
Cattle Drive (1951) 140
Cattle Fording Stream (1898) 140
cavalry 22, 53, 56, 57, 61, 63n, 140, 145, 174, 181, 184n, 189
cavalryman 3, 22, 45, 53, 56, 59, 60, 61, 62, 103, 104
cemetery 163, 165, 191, 193
chaos 120, 142, 145, 148, 156, 167, 181
Charro! (1969) 9, 102, 106-107, 108
Cheyenne 5, 33n, 53, 54, 55, 56, 57, 58, 59, 60, 62, 63n
Cheyenne (ABC, 1955-1962) 8
Cheyenne Autumn 5, 9, 34n, 44, 46, 53-62, 62
Cheyenne Exodus 9, 53, 63n
Chisolm Trail 141, 143
The Chisholms (CBS, 1979-1980) 8
Chisum (1970) 7, 13n
chorus 9, 53, 54, 56, 57, 63n, 92, 101, 116, 117, 124n, 128, 129, 132, 133
Christian 1, 68, 85, 87, 88, 92, 139, 194; Christ 102
Cicero 1, 2, 32n
Circe 140, 144, 164
citizen 4, 23, 56, 59, 63n, 91, 99, 102, 104-107, 173, 178, 180, 184n, 194, 195; citizenship 100, 102, 103
City Slickers II: The Legend of Curly's Gold (1994) 7, 13n

215

216 Index

civilization 2, 3, 5, 9, 17, 22, 25, 30, 31, 38, 39, 40, 41, 61, 92, 102, 143, 145, 161, 161, 162, 166, 190, 191, 199, 200, 203, 207, 208
cleansing 101, 106, 108; *see also* scapegoat
Clytemnestra 70, 112, 124n
Comanche Moon (CBS, mini-series, 2008) 8, 151
comedy 58, 60, 80n
community 38, 40, 43, 56, 59, 62, 90, 99, 100–105, 108, 128, 133, 172, 174, 175, 177, 178, 179, 182, 191, 195, 203, 204, 208
conquest 2, 7, 29, 103, 119, 204
courage 3, 5, 25, 40, 41, 42–43, 59, 76, 147, 166
cowboy 3, 5, 6, 10, 39, 58 60, 9, 106, 122, 139, 140, 141, 146; cowboy hat 61, 64n
Cowboy (1958) 140
Cowboy Justice (1904) 140
Cowboys (2019) 140
The Cowboys (1972) 140, 148
Crèvecoeur, J. Hector St. John de 1, 2
The Culpepper Cattle Company (1972) 140, 142
Custer 3, 4, 61
Cyclops 139, 164
Cyclops (1957) 139

Damnation (USA, 2017–18) 25
Dances with Wolves (1990) 7, 13n
The Dark Tower (2017) 7, 13n
daughter: frontier 113, 117, 118, 119, 10, 123; Greek legend 20, 85, 112, 124n, 128; indigenous 195
Dead Man's Gun (Showtime, 1997–1999) 8
Dead Man's Walk (ABC, mini-series, 1996) 8
Deadwood (HBO, 2004–2006) 8, 20, 21, 25, 28, 32n, 33n
death: frontier 20, 27, 32n, 41, 45, 85, 87, 90, 91, 108, 118, 123, 142, 146, 148, 156, 157, 159, 163, 166, 173, 176, 177, 178, 179, 180, 191, 192, 203, 204, 205, 207; Greek legend 18, 32n, 69, 71, 73, 75, 83, 89, 101, 113, 130, 131, 132, 133, 146, 173, 179; hero's 198; indigenous 54, 194
The Death of Tragedy 85
Decision at Sundown (1957) 9, 83, 90, 91, 92, 127-31, 134, 135n
deinon 132
democracy 103, 113, 192
Demosthenes 1
desire 4, 18, 40, 42, 84, 86, 108, 112, 114, 116, 118, 129, 130, 131, 132, 133, 134n, 144, 199, 204
Destry Rides Again (1939) 5
Devil's Doorway 5, 115
Dido 192
Dionysian 62, 70- 71, 129, 133, 134, 134–35n

Dionysus 32n, 70, 71, 74, 76, 133, 214n; *see also* Bacchus
Django Unchained (2012) 7, 13n, 38, 45, 46
Doc Holliday 4, 26–27, 39, 40, 58–59, 61
Dr. Faustus 24, n33
Dr. Quinn, Medicine Woman (CBS, 1993–1998) 8
Dodge City 2, 59, 141, 192, 194
Dodge City (1939) 5
drama 2, 7, 9, 32n, 54, 55, 56, 57, 58, 63n, 66, 68, 69, 72, 83, 84, 85, 87, 91, 93n, 101, 102, 103, 105, 114, 139, 152, 153, 154–55, 157; melodrama 53, 134n, 161
dream 166, 167, 202, 203; American Dream 166, 167
Duel in the Sun (1946) 6, 114
duty 23, 57, 112, 131, 166, 192

East 2, 30, 31, 38, 43, 140, 141, 142, 175 192, 201, 203
El Dorado (1967) 6, 13n
Electra 57, 63n, 87
Electra 57, 63n, 87
Electra complex 118, 119, 123, 124n
environment 152, 176, 205
epic 2, 6, 8, 9, 10, 11, 13n, 14n, 17, 27, 28, 32n, 33n, 44, 53, 59, 68, 69, 77, 101, 113, 114, 142, 146, 147
Eteocles (Eteokles) 84, 101, 113
eudaimonia 2; *see also* happiness
Eumenides 111, 112, 113, 124n
Euripides 9, 60, 67, 69, 70, 71, 74, 75, 83–84, 87, 92, 104, 111, 112
Europa 123
Eurydice 202
exodus 62; Northern Cheyenne Exodus 9, 53, 54, 57, 58, 61
expansion 22, 23, 116, 190; westward 2, 11, 17, 20, 162, 167, 189, 190, 191, 193, 194, 196
Eyrines 10, 111; *see also* Furies

family 125n, 128, 149, 162, 167, 203, 207; dysfunction 89, 90, 112, 118; family life 2, 5, 18, 25, 38, 40, 42, 43, 87, 88, 92, 116, 121
fate 10, 23, 26, 27, 29, 44, 71, 73, 76, 85, 90, 91, 99, 105, 122, 130, 131, 133, 134n, 141, 142, 154, 182, 198, 201, 205, 207, 208
father: Founding Fathers 1, 2; frontier 5, 6, 24, 29, 42, 61, 90, 91, 92, 94n, 105, 115, 116, 117, 118, 119, 121, 123, 125n, 143, 157, 159, 198, 202, 203, 206, 222; Greek legend 64n, 85, 112, 113, 124n, 129, 130, 134n, 157, 176, 190
Father Murphy (NBC, 1981–1983) 8
fear 58, 60, 69, 76, 89, 90, 94n, 103, 104, 108, 119, 122, 125, 155, 202, 204; *see also* phobos
force 3–6, 7, 9, 12n, 18, 43, 53, 58, 69, 72, 75, 83, 84, 88, 105, 116, 120, 121, 122, 142, 164, 172, 173, 174, 178, 179, 181, 200, 205, 207
Ford, John 2, 4, 6, 18, 22, 24, 34n, 53–56, 58, 61–62
Fort Apache (1948) 6
Fort Smith 2
freedom 45, 84, 99, 106, 108, 178, 200, 203
Frogs 92n, 101
frontier 1, 2, 3, 6, 10, 11, 18, 37, 38, 39, 40, 41, 42, 43, 45, 46, 61, 62, 64n, 103, 140, 142, 145, 147, 148, 161, 162–63, 167, 175, 182, 189, 190, 192, 193, 194, 195, 198–200, 202, 208; hero 62, 208; justice 6, 10, 41, 42, 45, 115, 167; myth 10, 11, 45, 103, 161, 162–63, 167, 175, 198–200, 202, 208
Furies 10, 87, 111–12, 113–14, 120, 122, 123; see also *Eyrines*
Furies ranch 114, 117–18, 119, 120, 122

gambler 3, 58, 59, 116, 155, 194
Geronimo: An American Legend (1993) 5, 7, 13n
Giant (1956) 6, 13n
god 57, 70–71, 72, 75, 83, 84, 87, 101, 107, 112, 116, 145, 167, 173; God 29, 92, 118, 119, 193; goddess 111, 124n
Godless (Netflix, mini-series, 2017) 8, 25
gold 85, 165
Golden Age: Greece 23; Latin literature 19; Westerns 18
The Golden Bough 101
good badman 5, 11, 58, 59, 62
Gospel of John 1
The Great Cowboy Strike (2017) 141
The Great Train Robbery (1903) 140
Greek culture 1, 2, 3, 14n, 22, 30, 62, 66, 67, 68, 77, 92, 94n, 104, 105, 124n, 153, 156, 162, 192; Maenadism 74–75
Greek theatre 54, 55, 56, 57, 59, 60, 62, 63n, 64n, 69, 70, 73, 101, 114, 110; *choreogoi* 54, 57, 60; dithyramb 54, 56, 59, 60, 62; *dromenon* 55, 63n; ekkyklêma 70; Greek chorus 53, 63n, 64n, 116
grief 5, 108, 113
Gun Shy (CBS 1983) 8
gunfighter 27, 38, 39, 40, 43, 45, 84, 85, 90, 103, 191; gunslinger 84, 86, 143, 193, 203, 204
The Gunfighter (1950) 9, 13n, 85, 86, 87, 92, 139
Gunsmoke (CBS, 1955–1975) 8, 10, 189–96

Hades 85, 113, 140, 202
Haemon 132
Hamlet 128
Hang 'Em High (1968) 6

happiness 2–3, 39–40, 41, 43, 164, 178; see also *eudaimonia*
harmony 4, 5
The Hateful Eight (2015) 13n, 45
Hawkeye (Syndication, 1994–1995) 8
Hawks, Howard 2, 3, 141, 145, 165
Heartland (CBC, 2007–present) 8
Heaven's Gate 3, 153, 171–183, 183n, 184n
Hector (Hektor) 34n, 89, 151, 177, 179
Helen 24
Helen 87
Helios 85, 145
Hell on Wheels (AMC, series, 2011–2016) 8, 20, 26, 28
Hell or High Water (2016) 3, 7, 13n
Henry V 18
Heraclitus 27
Hercules 28
hero 2, 3, 4, 5, 11, 12n, 17, 18, 19, 20, 22, 25, 26, 27, 28, 30, 33n, 34n, 41, 42, 46, 53, 58, 62, 68, 76, 77, 84, 85, 91, 93n, 99, 101, 105, 108, 120, 128–29, 131, 132, 141, 142, 148, 154, 162, 163, 164, 166, 167, 173, 178–79, 180, 182, 185, 191, 192, 195, 198, 199–202, 202, 204, 205, 206, 207; anti-hero 24, 142, 206; Christian 85; epic 189–90; frontier 62, 208; Homeric 3, 34n, 143, 148, 162, 164, 173, 178–79, 180, 185, 190; journey 199–202, 204, 206; Orphic hero 11, 202; psychology 3, 9; romantic 11, 202, 204, 205; tragic 5, 18, 25, 68, 84, 85, 101, 105, 128–29, 131, 154; Western 4, 5, 30, 33n, 41, 42, 58, 99, 108, 132, 134n, 141, 142, 163, 166, 167, 173, 178–79, 182, 189, 191, 192, 195, 207, 208
Herodotus 11
heroine 22, 24, 25, 173
Hesiod 111, 112, 124n
Hidalgo (2004) 7, 13n
High Noon (1952) 5, 6, 23, 37, 42, 43, 182, 192
High Plains Drifter (1973) 7, 13n, 39, 207
Hippolytus 90
Homer 1, 3, 9, 10, 11, 12n, 33n, 34n, 69, 111, 143, 147, 148, 151, 152, 153, 162, 167, 174, 178, 179, 180, 183, 190, 191
Hondo (1953) 6, 12n, 22, 32n
honor 27, 39, 40, 59, 61, 76, 112, 123, 125n, 141, 146, 162, 166, 179, 192; Medal of Honor 115
Horace 19, 27
horror 5, 46, 70, 112, 130, 131, 132, 139, 180
Hostiles (2017) 7, 13n
How the West Was Won (1963) 6
How the West Was Won (ABC, 1976–1979) 8
Huck Finn 145

Hud (1963) 153
humor 18, 59, 73, 139, 151

idealism 31, 178, 198, 200, 208
The Idiot 114, 124n, 125n
The Iliad 3, 8, 10, 11, 12n, 27, 33n, 34n, 69, 111, 139, 143, 144, 145, 151, 152, 161, 166, 171–183, 184n, 189
Indian 22, 38, 42, 45, 53, 56, 57, 59, 88, 143, 154, 155, 157, 189, 190, 195, 198, 203; Indian agent 3; attack 141, 143; culture 44, 50; Indian Territory 2, 54, 193, 194; Indian War 56, 174, 195; stereotype 26, 62, 103, 138; see also Native American
individualism 4, 40, 174
Inferno 25
injustice 4, 30, 41, 42, 43, 44, 45, 104, 116, 175
intellect 2, 3, 11, 23, 37, 43, 69, 135n, 201, 208
Iphigenia 85, 124n
irrationality 70, 84, 104

Jesse James (1939) 5, 13n
Jocasta 130
Joe Kidd (1970) 7, 13n
journey 19, 85, 90, 104, 128, 139, 140, 141, 143, 144, 145, 146, 147, 148, 151, 152, 154, 161, 162–164, 166, 169, 190, 191, 198, 199–200, 201, 202–203, 204–206, 207; epic 146, 191; perilous 139, 198, 205
judgment 41, 145, 155
Julius Caesar 18, 25
justice 2, 5, 27, 33n, 40, 41, 42, 43, 44, 45, 56, 99, 106, 112, 113, 124, 167, 190, 192, 193, 194, 195; frontier 6, 10, 41, 115; natural 57
Justified (FX, series, 2010–2015) 8, 24, 45
Juvenal 19

Keats, John 89, 94n
king 71, 102, 105–107, 109n
King Lear 114
Kroisos 156

land 4, 5, 30, 39, 40, 43, 84, 85, 102, 115, 116, 117, 119, 120, 121, 123, 141, 142, 148, 153, 154, 156, 174, 178, 190, 191, 198, 202; of the dead 195; of freedom 108; homeland 53, 54, 55, 61 landscape 87, 94n, 114, 117, 127, 153, 154, 176, 180, 191, 198, 200, 203; of the Lotus Eaters 139, 142, 147, 164; see also environment
Lassoing Steer (1898) 140
The Last Sunset (1961) 93n, 140
Latin 1, 2, 15, 18, 19, 20, 22, 26, 27, 32n, 33n, 111, 117, 151, 158
law 1, 2, 5, 39, 42, 43, 45, 103, 105, 106, 113, 128, 130, 131, 141, 145, 154, 189, 191, 193, 194, 195; and order 2, 39, 43, 45, 145, 195
lawlessness 5, 42, 43, 44, 147, 190, 193, 195
lawman 4, 27, 41, 44, 58, 105, 148, 194; deputy marshal 2, 27, 58, 64n; marshal 5, 12n, 42, 59, 85, 86, 184n; sheriff 39, 42, 44, 91, 105, 106, 107, 145, 146, 180, 184n; U.S Marshall 45, 189, 190, 191, 192, 193, 194, 195, 196
legend 8, 9, 43, 101, 139, 199; Greek 18, 20, 25, 32n, 69, 70, 71, 72, 73, 75, 83, 85, 87, 89, 101, 112, 113, 124n, 125n, 128, 130, 131, 132, 133, 135n, 143, 157, 159, 166, 198, 202, 203, 206, 222; Roman 24; silver screen 4; Western 39, 46, 58, 59, 62, 34n, 146, 189, 192

The Legend of the Lone Ranger (1984) 7, 13n
Legends of the Fall (1994) 7, 13n
Letters from an American Farmer (1782) 1
The Libation Bearers 70
The Life and Legend of Wyatt Earp (ABC, 1955–1961) 8
The Life and Times of Grizzly Adams (1974) 7, 13n
The Life and Times of Judge Roy Bean (1972) 7, 13n
Life of Romulus 20
Lightning Jack (1994) 7, 13n
Little Big Man (1971) 7, 13n, 44, 53
Little House on the Prairie (NBC, 1974–1983) 8
Livy 1, 32n
The Lone Ranger (2013) 7, 13n
The Lone Ranger (ABC, 1949–1957) 8
The Lonely Man (1957) 9, 83, 90, 91–92
Lonesome Dove (1989) 8, 10, 19, 140, 145–148, 151–159
Lonesome Dove: The Outlaw Years (Syndication, 1995–1996) 8
Longmire (A&E, series, 2012–14; Netflix, series, 2015–2017) 8, 22, 27, 31, 33n
Love Me Tender (1956) 6, 13n
Loving, Frank 2, 12n

Maenad 71, 73, 74, 75
The Magnificent Seven (CBS, 1998–2000) 8
The Magnificent Seven (2015) 7, 13n
The Man Who Shot Liberty Valance (1962) 14n, 25, 31n, 34n, 37, 39, 40, 43
The Mandalorian (Disney, series, 2019–present) 8
Manifest Destiny 23, 31, 40, 53, 58, 163, 193
Mann, Anthony 2, 3, 10, 11, 84, 92, 111–124, 124n, 128
marriage 21, 119, 124, 130

Index

massacre 57, 63n, 74, 76
Maverick (1994) 7, 13n
McCabe and Mrs. Miller (1972) 3, 5, 7, 13n
McLintock! (1963) 6, 13n
McMurtry, Larry 8, 10, 32n, 151, 152–153, 154; father 152
Medea 69, 90, 92, 92n
Megara (Megaera) 89, 112, 113
Menelaus 57, 84, 92n
Metamorphoses 11, 124n
A Million Ways to Die in the West (2014) 7, 13n
Minotaur 103, 123, 199
The Missing (2003) 7, 13n
Missouri Breaks (1976) 3
monomyth 198, 200
morality 37, 56, 63n, 163, 164, 167; amoral 46, 76, 153, 163, 167; moral 1, 31, 41, 43, 57, 59, 77, 86, 92, 99, 102, 112, 127, 128, 133, 142, 162, 163, 164, 165, 166, 167, 173, 178, 179, 193, 196, 200, 201, 203, 206, 213; right action 4, 5, 6, 12, 27, 42, 46, 57, 67, 77, 90, 91, 99; wrong action 4, 5, 6, 15, 30, 40, 43, 44, 46, 57, 59, 67, 77, 91, 99, 102, 112, 121, 147, 154, 166, 205
mother: frontier 6, 90, 94n, 104, 115, 116, 117, 118, 120, 123, 125n, 152; Greek legend 71, 72, 87, 112, 113, 124n, 130, 131, 132, 134n
myth 1, 17, 27, 46, 162, 183, 199–200; American 38, 163, 165, 166, 167, 172, 182, 184; frontier 10, 11, 45, 61, 161, 162, 163, 175, 198, 199; Greco-Roman 9, 17, 19, 20, 24, 25, 69, 71, 111, 112, 114, 123, 129, 134n, 139, 162, 167, 178, 198; Western 40, 46, 58, 59, 99, 103, 111, 141, 152–53, 166, 174, 178

The Naked Spur (1953) 3
nation 10, 17–23, 24–26, 28, 30, 58, 62, 107, 161–62, 167, 168, 174, 190, 191, 192, 193, 194, 195; nation-building 2, 19, 23, 24, 28, 30
national identity 10, 22, 29, 30, 161, 163, 167, 178, 192, 200
Native American 23, 26, 30, 33n, 38, 44, 46, 88, 92, 115, 156, 157, 202; *see also* Indian
nobility 1, 42, 129
North of 36 (1924) 140
Nothing Too Good for a Cowboy (CBC 1998–2000) 8

Odysseus 10, 139, 141, 142, 143, 144, 145, 146, 147, 148, 152, 157, 162, 164, 165, 166, 167, 181, 190, 193, 198
Odyssey 10, 11, 112, 139–140, 141, 142, 143, 145, 146, 147, 148, 149, 152, 157, 162, 163, 164–167, 178, 189, 190
Oedipus 29, 68, 101, 102, 107, 109n, 112, 113, 128, 129, 130, 134n
Oedipus Rex 105, 129, 130, 134n

Once Upon a Time in the West (1969) 7, 13n, 139
Open Range (2003) 7
order 2, 4, 23, 39, 42, 43, 45, 46n, 83, 85, 93n, 94n, 102, 107, 128, 130, 132, 133, 145, 162, 167, 189, 195; social 5, 107, 162, 182, 189; symbolic 128, 132
The Oregon Trail (NBC 1976–1977) 8
Oresteia 102, 112, 124
Orestes 70, 87, 112, 124
Orpheus 198, 202, 204, 205
Orphic 11
outlaw 5, 24, 39, 40, 76, 84, 90, 106, 190, 191, 193, 195
The Outlaw Josey Wales (1976) 7, 13
Outlaws (CBS, 1986–1987) 8
Ovid 11, 32, 111, 124, 152

Pale Rider (1985) 7, 13n
Pandora 25
Paradise (BBC One, 1988–1990) 8
Parker, Isaac C. 2
Pat Garrett and Billy the Kid (1973) 7, 13n
Patroclus (Patroklos) 143, 144, 179
Peacemakers (USA Network, 2003) 8
Peckinpah, Sam 2, 3, 9, 37, 44, 66–68, 69, 70, 71, 72, 73, 74, 76, 77, 78n; death 66
Pegasus 25, 200
Penelope 141, 145, 146, 147, 148
Pentheus 71, 72, 79n, 101
Per qualche dollaro in più (1967) 6, 13n
Per un pugno di dollari (1967) 6, 13n
Phaedra 84, 91
Phaedrus 4
pharmakos 9, 100, 101–108
phobos 88, 89; *see also* fear
Pietas 113
pity 69, 72, 88, 155; see also catharsis
Plato 4, 7, 11, 26, 33, 37, 61, 66, 79n, 143
Plutarch 20, 29, 32n, 33
Poetics 13n–14n, 66, 68–70, 77, 80, 83, 89, 152, 154
pollution 101, 104
Polyneices 113, 129, 130, 131, 132, 135n
Polyphemus 139, 142, 164
Pompey 25, 33n
Ponderosa (PAX TV, 2001–2002) 8
Poseidon 139, 164
pragmatism 200, 208
The Professionals (1966) 6, 13n
progress 12n, 17, 18, 19, 20, 22, 24, 25, 26, 27, 28, 30, 33n, 39, 40, 41, 43, 57, 191
property 24, 87, 66
purification 87, 101

quest 23, 25, 29, 30, 111, 121, 127, 129, 139, 148, 162, 189, 190, 198, 199, 200, 201–203, 204–207
The Quick and the Dead (1995) 7, 13n
The Quiet Man (1952) 6
Quigley Down Under (1990) 7, 13n
Quixote, Don 152, 157

race 30, 38, 62, 91, 104, 107, 109n
rage 5, 113; outrage 73, 183
railroad 5, 20, 28, 74, 141, 142
rape 99, 104, 119, 127, 129, 179
rationality 84, 92, 99; rationalism vs irrationalism 8
realism 182
reason 4, 5, 9, 24, 26, 37, 39, 41, 46, 58, 68, 69, 77, 83, 111, 117, 146, 148, 165, 183, 191
Red River (1948) 3, 10, 21, 140, 141–149, 153
Red Serge (CBC, 1986–1987) 8
republic 1, 2, 23, 25, 51
The Republic 4, 7, 37
restraint 40, 43, 142, 192, 193
Return to Lonesome Dove (CBS, mini-series, 1993) 8
revenge 5, 10, 39, 45, 71, 87, 91, 104, 112, 113, 115, 116, 121, 123, 127, 129, 144
revolution 56, 63n; American Revolution 1, 2
rhetoric 9, 14n, 27, 37–46, 69, 94n
Richardson, Levi 2, 12n
The Rifleman (ABC, 1958–1963) 8
Rio Bravo (1959) 6, 13n, 41, 192
Rio Grande (1950) 4, 6, 22, 141
ritual 9, 31, 54, 61, 63n, 100, 101–30, 104, 108, 122, 162, 174
River of No Return (1955) 6
Roman riding 4, 22
Romans 1, 2, 4, 17, 18, 20–21, 22, 23–24, 25, 28, 30, 31, 32n, 34n, 111, 113, 124n, 152, 161, 180
Rome 17–25
Rome (HBO, 2005–2007) 20
Romulus 18, 20, 24
Rooster Cogburn (1975) 7, 13n
Rubicon 26
Run of the Arrow (1957) 6, 91

Sabine 20
saloon 58, 59, 60, 85, 91, 106, 116, 139; Long Branch Saloon 2, 12n; owner 5, 58; saloon girl 5, 58, 60, 127
Satires: Horace 27; Juvenal 19
satyr 58, 59, 60, 64
satyr drama 9, 58–60, 64n
savagery 31, 41, 76, 92, 174, 190, 191, 195, 200, 203
scapegoat 99–102, 104, 105, 106, 107, 108, 109; *see also* cleansing
Scipio 32n
Scylla and Charybdis 140, 164
The Searchers (1956) 2, 6, 38, 40, 42, 46, 84, 92, 128, 139, 148

Select Orations 1
settlement 2, 11, 113, 116, 167, 190, 191
Seven Brides for Seven Brothers (1954) 20, 29
sexuality 88, 143, 147
Shakespeare 25, 84, 102, 114, 128, 205
Shalako (1968) 6, 13n
Shane (1953) 4, 6, 12n, 40, 184n
Shanghai Knights (2003) 7, 13n
Shanghai Noon (2000) 7, 13n
Shenandoah (1965) 6, 13n
Silverado (1985) 7, 13n
siren 140, 143, 144, 147, 148, 164
sister: frontier 87, 125n; Greek legend 20, 79n, 87, 111, 112, 113, 123, 124n, 131
slavery 45, 116; anti-slavery 145
society 1, 5, 27, 33n, 45, 57, 63n, 102, 104, 161, 163, 182, 200, 201, 206, 208; civil society 99; Greek 101; white 194
Socrates 4, 12n, 26, 27, 83, 84
son: frontier 4, 18, 19, 33, 85, 86, 87, 90, 91, 105, 117, 118, 123, 124, 143, 144, 145, 146, 153, 154, 155, 156, 194, 200, 207; Greek legend 70, 87, 112, 113, 130, 133, 135n, 157; indigenous 104, 105, 107
Sons of Anarchy (2008–2014) 8
The Sons of Katie Elder (1965) 5, 6, 13n
Sophocles 9, 10, 57, 63n, 67, 70, 83, 84, 102, 105, 111, 128, 132, 134n
sorrow 4, 85, 154, 206
soul 3, 4, 12n, 40, 79n, 113, 121, 157, 174, 183, 190, 202; appetite 4, 12n, 43, 58, 60, 141; rational 4, 83, 93, 204, 205; spirited 4, 5, 59
Spaghetti Western 139, 162, 163, 165–66
spirit 24, 46, 88, 139, 148
Stagecoach (1939) 5, 24, 37, 40, 137
Statius 111, 113, 124n
Streets of Laredo (CBS, miniseries, 1995) 8
subconscious 119, 204
sublime 174

Tacitus 1
The Tall Men (1955) 140, 143
Telemachus 142, 143, 145, 146, 157
Tension at Table Rock (1956) 100, 102, 105–108
Thebaid 113
Theogony 112, 124n
Theseus 199
They Died with Their Boots On (1940) 2, 3
3 Godfathers 5
3:10 to Yuma (2007) 7, 13n, 93n, 99, 109
Thucydides 11, 151
thumos 3–8, 12n
Tieresias, 33n, 164
Tisphone 113

Tombstone (1993) 7, 13n, 26, 27, 39
Track of the Cat (1954) 9, 83, 87, 89, 92
tragedy 6, 9, 10, 17, 62, 68, 77, 80n, 84, 85, 89–90, 92, 102, 128, 129, 153, 198–99, 204; *anagnorisis* 76, 77, 151, 154, 159; Aristotle 9, 10, 13n, 14n, 62, 66, 68, 69, 83, 88, 89, 151, 153, 155, 158–59; *Birth of Tragedy* 133–34; *ekplêxis* 69, 70, 76, 77, 79n; Greek tragedy 62, 67, 68, 77, 83, 84, 151; *hamartia*/tragic flaw 68, 122, 123, 151, 155, 156; *hubris* 88, 91, 131, 154, 155, 156, 158, 159, 192; *peripeteia* 76, 77, 79; *see also catharsis*
Trooper Hook (1957) 9, 99, 100, 102, 103–107
Troy 3, 10, 24, 89, 116, 124n, 173, 174, 180, 181, 192
True Grit (1969) 6, 13n, 24, 41
True Grit (2010) 7, 13n, 15, 22, 46
Turner, Frederick Jackson 2, 3, 140, 189
Twain, Mark 145

The Undefeated (1969) 7, 13n
Underworld 10, 111, 116, 124n, 164, 190, 199, 202
Unforgiven (1992) 6, 7, 13n, 38, 39, 43, 44, 46, 93n
Urban Cowboy (1980) 7, 13n

values 2, 10, 17, 27, 31, 58, 83, 84, 102, 153, 162, 166, 189, 190, 191, 192, 193, 195, 196
vengeance 31, 108, 111, 112, 114, 115, 116, 121, 123, 163; personal 10, 111, 114
Vera Cruz (1954) 6, 12n
vice 1, 41, 42, 43, 141, 147
victim 40, 45, 88, 101–102, 111, 112, 122, 131, 147, 158, 199; sacrificial 104, 107; self-willed 131; victimization 100, 121
vigilante
villain 17, 18, 25, 26, 27, 44, 46, 53, 99, 141, 148, 165, 172
violence 9, 26, 27, 28, 30, 37, 39, 40, 43, 44, 45, 61, 66, 67, 69, 70, 74–77, 78n, 79n, 88, 102, 103, 104, 106, 107, 108, 112, 114, 117, 119, 120, 123, 125n, 131, 142, 146, 147, 161, 163, 174, 175, 178, 179, 180, 191, 192, 194, 195, 196, 200, 203, 204, 205, 207; regeneration through 61
Virgil 1, 11, 18, 23, 111, 112, 124n, 152, 190, 191, 192
The Virginian 195
The Virginian (1929) 17, 25, 32n
virtue 2, 4, 5, 24, 39, 40, 41, 42, 43, 61, 148, 164, 174

Wagon Tracks (1919) 140
Wagons East (1993) 7, 13n

Walker, Texas Ranger (CBS 1993–2001) 8
Walsh, Raoul 2, 3, 140
war 3, 4, 5, 6, 7, 19, 20, 22, 31, 40, 54, 56, 59, 60, 61, 62, 102, 105, 113, 116, 124n, 127, 129, 140, 141, 142, 145, 147, 161, 162, 163, 164, 166, 167, 174, 180, 181, 183, 184n; chief 56, 62, 63n; Civil 6, 14n, 105, 115, 129, 140, 141, 142, 145, 148, 162, 163, 164, 166; Cold 103; Dodge City 9, 58, 59, 60, 62n; First Gulf 7; Indian 56, 174, 195; Johnson County 140, 173, 175, 180, 181, 184n; Mexican-American 116; Trojan 124, 145, 147, 162, 164, 173, 181; Vietnam 6, 8; War on Terror 7; warrior 18, 27, 44, 53, 59, 60, 63n, 103, 156, 157, 166, 185n, 195; World War II; 22, 31, 60, 102, 166, 174
The War Wagon (1967) 6, 13n
Westworld (1973) 56n, 37
Westworld (HBO, series, 2016–present) 8, 21, 28, 29, 30, 33–34n, 208n
white hats/black hats 99
white supremacy 26, 31
wife 66; frontier 5, 9n, 20, 25, 29, 30, 41, 85, 86, 87, 91, 117, 125n, 127, 129, 130, 134n, 142, 178, 180, 181; Greek legend 130, 166; indigenous 6, 87
Wild Bill (1995) 7, 13n
The Wild Bunch (1969) 2, 3, 9, 37, 44, 46, 66–77
Wild Side (ABC, 1985) 8
Wild West 4, 30, 37, 38, 39, 40, 41, 44, 45, 46, 58, 140, 167
wilderness 3, 38, 39, 40, 41, 42, 139, 154, 161, 163, 191, 198, 199, 200, 201, 202, 207, 208
Will Penny (1967) 18, 140
Winchester '73 (1950) 2, 115
woman: frontier 11, 20, 25, 45, 58, 91, 93n, 99, 102, 104, 106, 107, 114, 117, 120, 130, 132, 155, 156, 157, 177, 178; Greek legend 25, 71, 130, 132; indigenous 54, 55, 57, 194; *see also* daughter; sister; wife
Wyatt Earp 58, 59, 64n, 140, 141, 145
Wyatt Earp (1994) 7, 13n

Young Guns (1985) 7, 13n
Young Guns II (1990) 7, 13n
Young Maverick (CBS, 1979) 8
The Young Riders (ABC, 1989–1992) 8

Zeus 194n, 123, 133
Zorro (The Family Channel, 1990–1993) 8
Zorro's Black Whip (1944) 18

www.ingramcontent.com/pod-product-compliance
Lightning Source LLC
Chambersburg PA
CBHW060342010526
44117CB00017B/2935